TACTICAL NUCLEAR WEAPON

D1409752

Tom Nichols
Douglas Stuart
Jeffrey D. McCausland

Editors

April 2012

The views expressed in this report are those of the authors and do not necessarily reflect the official policy or position of the Department of the Army, the Department of Defense, or the U.S. Government. Authors of Strategic Studies Institute (SSI) publications enjoy full academic freedom, provided they do not disclose classified information, jeopardize operations security, or misrepresent official U.S. policy. Such academic freedom empowers them to offer new and sometimes controversial perspectives in the interest of furthering debate on key issues. This report is cleared for public release; distribution is unlimited.

*****

*****

Comments pertaining to this report are invited and should be forwarded to: Director, Strategic Studies Institute, U.S. Army War College, 45 Ashburn Dr., Bldg. 47, Carlisle, PA 17013.

*****

All Strategic Studies Institute (SSI) publications may be downloaded free of charge from the SSI website. Hard copies of this report may also be obtained free of charge while supplies last by placing an order on the SSI website. SSI publications may be quoted or reprinted in part or in full with permission and appropriate credit given to the U.S. Army Strategic Studies Institute, U.S. Army War College, Carlisle Barracks, PA. Contact SSI by visiting our website at the following address: *www.StrategicStudiesInstitute.army.mil.*

*****

The Strategic Studies Institute publishes a monthly e-mail newsletter to update the national security community on the research of our analysts, recent and forthcoming publications, and upcoming conferences sponsored by the Institute. Each newsletter also provides a strategic commentary by one of our research analysts. If you are interested in receiving this newsletter, please subscribe on the SSI website at *www.StrategicStudiesInstitute.army.mil/newsletter/.*

CONTENTS

PREFACE

The role and future of *tactical* nuclear weapons in Europe are subjects that sometimes surprise even experts in international security, primarily because it is so often disconcerting to remember that these weapons still exist. Many years ago, an American journalist wryly noted that the future of the North Atlantic Treaty Organization (NATO) was "a subject that drives the dagger of boredom deep, deep into the heart" — a dismissive quip which would have remained true right up until the moment World War III broke out. The same goes for tactical nuclear weapons: compared to the momentous issues that the East and West have tackled since the end of the Cold War, the scattering of hundreds (or in the Russian case, thousands) of battlefield weapons throughout Europe seems to be almost an afterthought, a detail left behind that should be easy to tidy up.

Such complacency is unwise. Tactical nuclear weapons (or NSNWs, "non-strategic nuclear weapons") still exist because NATO and Russia have not fully resolved their fears about how a nuclear war might arise, or how it might be fought. They represent, as Russian analyst Nikolai Sokov once wrote, "the longest deadlock" in the history of arms control. Washington and Moscow, despite the challenges to the "reset" of their relations, point to reductions in strategic arms as a great achievement, but strategic agreements also reveal the deep ambiguity toward nuclear weapons as felt by the former superpower rivals. The numbers in the 2010 New Strategic Arms Reduction Treaty (New START) are lower than at any point in history, but they are based on leaving each side a reliable ability to destroy up to 300 urban targets each. Inflicting this incredible amount of destruction is, on its face, a step no sane national leader would take. But it is here that tactical weapons were meant to play their dangerous role, for they would be the arms that provided the indispensable bridge from peace to nuclear war. Thus, the structures of Cold War nuclear doctrines on both sides remain in place, only on a smaller scale.

How did we get here?

As Major General William Burns notes in his introduction to this volume, the history of the Cold War is a nuclear history, centered around each side's efforts to convince the other of a readiness for a war that neither wanted. Tactical nuclear weapons were crucial to this effort, because they were the link between conventional war in Europe and a central nuclear exchange between the superpowers. The Soviets were unlikely to believe that the President would risk New York and Chicago for the people of Europe, which was the central premise of the short-lived and poorly conceived strategy of "Massive Retaliation." A threat to leap to Armageddon because of a scuffle between the Soviets and the West Germans was on its face incredible, to Moscow as much as to us.

Tactical nuclear weapons provided the solution, such as it was. The West abandoned any hope of matching Warsaw Pact conventional forces man for man or tank for tank, and instead placed nuclear weapons in Europe, many of them directly in front of the assumed axes of Soviet advance where they would assuredly be overrun or employed. This warned the Soviets, in effect, that if Europe were invaded, the choice to use nuclear arms would be forced upon NATO by the successes of the Red Army. Western commanders, faced with imminent defeat, would fire their tactical arms in desperation at advancing Soviet units, commit the whole matter to God, and retreat with as much order and bravery as they could muster while hoping either that the Soviet offensive would collapse or that the United States and its allies could force a cease-fire before things spiraled completely out of control.

This was a terrifying but effective strategy. As we now know, the Soviet High Command wrestled with this dilemma, since taking a Europe in ashes defeated the whole point of invasion in the first place. They worked out their own plans for first-use of tactical nuclear arms, for *massive* use of tactical arms, and for nuclear retaliation. All of the options led to the same dead end of escalation, strategic retaliation, and catastrophe. Combat along the Central Front probably would have decayed into a nuclear war sooner rather than later, with unimaginable consequences.

Today, the Central Front is gone. The inter-German border where NATO and the Warsaw Pact were poised for war has been erased, as has the Warsaw Pact itself. Former Soviet satellites are now free participants in the Atlantic alliance. A Russian dash to invade Europe is no longer physically possible; the suffocation of Berlin, which would have taken only hours by Soviet troops in the city, would now require battle across hundreds of miles of allied Polish and German territory. Even if the Russians, for some unfathomable reason, wanted to invade Poland or Germany once more, they would have to march across 50 million independent Ukrainians to get there, only to find themselves at war with another 26 European nations and two North American powers. Tactical nuclear weapons make no sense in this environment, and yet hundreds of U.S. weapons (and thousands of Russian battlefield arms) still remain in Europe as dangerous souvenirs of Cold War preparation for a showdown in Europe.

This volume is the result of the collaboration of scholars and security experts from many disciplines and nations who have come together to tackle questions that are long overdue for an answer.

- What role is left, if any, for tactical nuclear arms?
- What are the strategic implications of their presence — or their removal?
- How have U.S., Russian, and European views evolved on this issue, and how much opportunity is there to bring them into a coordinated agreement?
- What does it mean for NATO to be a "nuclear alliance?"
- Should arms control processes like the Strategic Arms Reduction Treaties (START) or conventional arms control include NSNWs, or are tactical nuclear arms so outdated that they should be removed from the agenda and reduced unilaterally?

Our authors do not claim to resolve all of these dilemmas, but we are hopeful that this analysis is an important step toward the further reduction of weapons whose role is no longer clear. NATO has never enjoyed such strategic depth and stability so far to its East, but the weapons that were meant to help U.S.,

European, and Russian leaders climb Herman Kahn's famous escalatory ladder from crisis to catastrophe are still deployed across Europe and still ready for battle.

We are not out of the woods yet.

Tom Nichols
Professor, National Security Affairs
Naval War College
Newport, RI

TACTICAL NUCLEAR WEAPONS AND NATO: AN INTRODUCTORY REMINISCENCE

Major General William F. Burns, USA, Retired

Only since World War II has the United States involved itself — contrary to the advice of leaders beginning with George Washington — in foreign alliances in peacetime. This book does not address this question in particular. However, it does consider one of the keystone strategies that serve as the basis for the cohesion of our longest peacetime alliance, the North Atlantic Treaty Organization (NATO). The deployment of tactical nuclear weapons was a major decision not reached lightly by ourselves and our allies and continues to be a point of concern to this day. As a preliminary to the chapters to follow, I want to address the issues surrounding the deployment and potential use of tactical nuclear weapons within NATO from a users' perspective.

My experience coincides roughly with the history of NATO. I took my first oath under the Constitution — as an ROTC cadet — when Harry Truman was President and General Dwight Eisenhower was the first Supreme Allied Commander in Europe. Now in my 80th year, I can look back over the decades and see the evolution of the Alliance and its strategies. Principal among these strategies was the employment of nuclear weapons in defense of Europe. While strategists at high levels debated the "should" and "could" arguments, we at the battery and battalion levels of the U.S. Army and the squadron level of the U.S. Air Force were more interested in "whether" and "how."

As a rather junior first lieutenant of field artillery, I took command of my first battery at Fort Sill, OK, in 1957 with orders to move to NATO-Europe. Our armament was the eight-inch howitzer, a decades-old, multi-ton, towed behemoth newly capable of firing a nuclear projectile almost 10 miles. Following closely on the deployment of the original "atomic cannon" that moved rather clumsily and had been designed specifically to fire a nuclear projectile, the eight-inch howitzer retained its conventional capability. This complicated our work at battery level since we were required to provide conventional fires on call from VII Corps which we supported, and at the same time be prepared to fire our nuclear rounds on very short notice. All this, in the Army's wisdom and during the lean years of the 1950s, was to be achieved without any special personnel augmentation.

A further complication was that the eight-inch nuclear round required careful assembly in the field right before firing. This process of about an hour was critical to accurate detonation and required the unit to undergo numerous inspections over the year from six or seven higher headquarters. Training for these inspections and potential use took up about one third of the battery's time—and there was no augmentation in time, either!

Computation of firing data also took about an hour in the pre-computer era. In order to cause the projectile to detonate in the air over a target, careful measurement of data was necessary. To insure accuracy, two white phosphorous "spotting" rounds were fired to check data and make corrections. Although these were not fired over the actual target, it is safe to say that the Soviet side would see such firing as a warning of imminent nuclear attack. And we in the firing battery wondered about and speculated on the ultimate utility of our nuclear burden.

Security was an additional problem. Long before the McNamara era's permissive action links (PAL) and NATO-centralized nuclear weapons storage sites, each nuclear-capable field artillery battalion stored its atomic weapons more or less as it saw fit. There were few economies to be found under this system, and the security costs to an already overburdened unit were high, but suffice it to say that no weapons were compromised during this period.

I explain all this simply to highlight the complexity of NATO's decision to adopt a strategy of tactical nuclear weapons deployment to offset a perceived conventional forces disadvantage against the Soviet army and its allies. There were recognized costs involved that limited conventional capabilities in the area of fire support. However, NATO's bet on the utility of tactical nuclear weapons as a deterrent apparently paid off.

After returning to the United States in the early 1960s, I found myself undergoing the routine field artillery officer's training and assignments. After the Command and General Staff Course at Fort Leavenworth, KS, we received a "prefix 5" to our military skill identification number, meaning that we were a qualified nuclear weapons fires planner equipped to analyze a target and deliver a nuclear explosive device according to prescription: maximize target damage, minimize collateral damage, and do not make it too difficult for friendly forces — because of tree blowdown or radiation contamination, for example — to traverse the damaged territory in a future advance.

The Army then went to Vietnam, Europe was left with field artillery units stripped of its officers and key noncommissioned officers, and the nuclear mission lost its priority. For those who believed — and perhaps still believe—that the then Soviet Union was simply awaiting the opportunity to strike effectively, the nagging question should arise, why not then?

After returning from Vietnam, I was sent to pursue an advanced degree. During this process, I was assigned for the summer of 1968 on temporary duty to the Office of the Secretary of Defense's Nuclear Planning Group, my only higher staff assignment up to that time. I was immersed in the burning tactical nuclear weapons argument of the day: In the event of hostilities, should we fire our first nuclear round as a warning—as we said, for demonstrative use—and not aim at an enemy target? Various NATO partners had different ideas of a demonstration—the United Kingdom wanted a round fired at sea, West Germany wanted a round fired high in the sky by an air defense missile, etc. Wisely, in my opinion, the United States declined to jump on the demonstrative-use bandwagon, seeing it as a sign of weakness rather than a demonstration of strength.

In the late 1960s and early 1970s, I commanded two nuclear-capable field artillery battalions, both in the United States. Times were lean for nondeployed units at the time, but we continued to maintain our nuclear readiness.

After graduation from the Army's institution of higher learning—you might have read of the U.S. Army War College in Carlisle, PA—I was assigned to the faculty and for a few years had little to do with nuclear issues. Counterinsurgency was the relevant strategy even as the war in Vietnam was winding down. Some, however, raised questions regarding how technical innovation was changing the battlefield and how this in turn would affect tactical nuclear weapons. This re-look grew in importance as the Army embraced lessons learned from the 1973 Arab-Israeli War and developed new tactics to counter a possible Warsaw Pact attack.

In the mid-1970s, I returned to Europe as a field artillery brigade commander. Three of my four battalions were nuclear-capable, and two of those—Lance missile units—were given a conventional capability while I was in command. The third nuclear battalion—an eight-inch howitzer unit—had the same rather cumbersome nuclear projectile that I was cursed with in the 1950s! The Lance battalions were equipped with advanced technology and nuclear explosive devices that required little or no assembly and maintenance. Also, peacetime storage of nuclear weapons was centralized. I had the added responsibility for NATO Nuclear Site 4 in Giessen, Germany, at which were stored several hundred nuclear weapons from a variety of units. In an alert, even in peacetime, these weapons were generally required to be evacuated to delivery units, adding an additional complication to route planning and timing.

In the late 1970s, I was assigned for 2 years to head our liaison office to the Bundeswehr in Cologne. This was an exciting time, during which a number of steps were taken to insure cohesion and interoperability between the West German and U.S. forces. I came to understand the deep-seated wariness of German leaders concerning tactical nuclear weapons and their employment, even though some German units were equipped to deliver U.S.-controlled nuclear devices. Not too many years before this, the U.S. Army had abandoned its Atomic Demolition Munitions when military planners came to appreciate more fully that these devices, intended to be implanted in the path of advancing Soviet forces and detonated at the appropriate time, all had to be buried on West German soil. As this realization sank in, such weapons were quietly retired.

In 1981, after returning to the United States and being selected for promotion to brigadier general, I was heading a Department of the Army task force at Fort Sill, to determine the requirements for a replacement for the Lance battlefield missile. A call from the Army Chief of Staff ended all this, and I found myself just after Thanksgiving across the table from Major General Yuri Lebedev, my Russian opposite number for several years in nuclear arms negotiations.

In 1978, NATO had become alarmed over the beginning of deployment of a new "medium range" missile by the Soviets—the SS-20. This missile delivered three nuclear warheads fairly accurately to a range of some 4,000 kilometers, a vast improvement over its aging predecessors, the SS-4 and SS-5. NATO's response in 1979 was to offer the Soviet side a choice—either abandon the SS-20 deployments or NATO would ask the United States to deploy in Europe a countervailing force. The history of our negotiations is of great interest but not truly relevant to the present discussions except in one aspect: It demonstrated that the Soviet Union was quite competent to play the deterrence game but recognized the advantage that NATO would have if the United States could maintain deployment in Europe of a nuclear delivery system of advanced technology and superior to anything the Soviet side could develop. This insight I gleaned from many hours of discussion with General Lebedev and my own experiences in Europe in earlier decades.

I retired from the Army in 1988 to assume the directorship of the U.S. Arms Control and Disarmament Agency at the invitation of President Ronald Reagan.

I learned here of some of the deep divisions in the political world concerning tactical nuclear weapons. After I left the government in 1989, decisions were made to withdraw most of the U.S. tactical nuclear weapons from Europe and virtually to eliminate U.S. Army participation in nuclear armaments. I was called back in 1992 to initiate negotiations with the new Russian Federation over U.S. help to that fledgling government in eliminating stocks of former Soviet nuclear weapons and the nuclear explosive material they contained. This has been an eminently successful program in which three of the former nuclear states of the Soviet Union have become non-nuclear nations under the Nuclear Non-Proliferation Treaty. Moreover, the Russian Federation has greatly reduced its stocks in a more or less transparent fashion.

Those members of my generation have seen the rise and demise of the Cold War and the ushering in of a new phase of world history that has thus far not been christened with a capital-letter name. Nuclear armaments within NATO played an important role in the Cold War, and NATO owes a debt of gratitude to the soldiers of a number of nations who provided a safe and secure tactical nuclear deterrent over the decades. The question now is the one for political leaders that I broached tentatively at the beginning of my remarks: Can NATO retain a tactical nuclear capability for the foreseeable future? More importantly perhaps is the question, Should it?

PART I

THE HISTORICAL CONTEXT OF
TACTICAL NUCLEAR WEAPONS

CHAPTER 1

THE HISTORICAL CONTEXT

Richard Weitz

The questions to be discussed include: Why and how did we develop tactical nuclear weapons (TNWs) and associated doctrines? How have the weapons developed as well as the associated strategies for deterrence and extended deterrence? What meaning does this have for the future?

Dr. Tom Nichols of the U.S. Naval War College noted in the Preface that the meanings, importance, purposes, and consequences of nuclear weapons can vary with time and context while the weapons themselves remain unchanged. He argued that since nuclear weapons have never been used since 1945, the most important question is what their functions are in peacetime: How do different classes and deployments of TNWs affect the psychology and politics of friends and potential enemies? TNWs are a subclass of military assets intended to reduce adversary military confidence and increase friends' reassurance that they would not be the object of attack.

Nichols described the doctrinal malaise associated with the entire class of TNWs. He argued that the weapons' effects—both military and political— were their most important characteristics, and that the West and the Soviets drew different distinctions between them. Whatever their specific characteristics, Nichols argued, nuclear gravity bombs delivered from a bomber or fighter-bomber platform from thousands of miles away are more of an offensive strategic system than a "tactical" weapon. Many would argue

3

that a nuclear detonation is a strategic event, politically and militarily, regardless of the yield or the delivery means. Nuclear weapons have an inherent potential for rapid and dramatic destruction, shock, and death — regardless of whether they yield one megaton or 20 kilotons. Distinguishing between "strategic" and "tactical" in that sense is more or less academic. As Thomas Schelling once opined, their enormous value is in the pure violence that they signal.

Both the North Atlantic Treaty Organization (NATO) and the Soviets developed doctrines for limited or graduated nuclear war. The intent was to make nuclear war sufficiently costly that local aggression would not be worthwhile, but not automatically so terrible that any threatened countries or allies would shrink from using atomic weapons to defend themselves. NATO saw nuclear weapons simultaneously as tools of deterrence, defense, and denial. NATO planners soon lost enthusiasm for scenarios involving limited nuclear weapons use, but Soviet planners came to see them as just another weapon that could facilitate Soviet military operations. Soviet and, recently, Russian military exercises typically involved the use of some nuclear weapons.

Paul Schulte of Kings College and the Carnegie Endowment has reviewed the history of theater nuclear weapons in Europe, with a focus on the evolution of NATO and Soviet operational policies. He argued that the significance and strategic meaning of TNWs changed over time. From 1953 onwards, the growth of U.S. TNWs in Europe was rapid. In December 1957, the North Atlantic Council agreed to stockpile nuclear warheads in Europe, and a decade later that stockpile peaked at 7,000. There were deliberate attempts to construct a public understanding of nuclear weapons

4

as just another kind of military option for warfighting. But despite much talk of "massive retaliation" in the 1950s, practical policy reflected a much more flexible attitude. Meanwhile, Henry Kissinger, Herman Kahn, and other strategists developed elaborate scenarios for nuclear use short of mutual assured destruction. Forward-based ground TNWs were seen as enhancing deterrence through their "use-it-or-lose-it" quality. But for the most part, TNWs became a substitute for strategy since their low cost made it easy to simply acquire more of them.

During the 1960s, this house of cards began to fold. Government officials and civilian strategists increasingly questioned the credibility of using TNWs and of the entire doctrine of limited nuclear war. By 1957, after exercises like Sagebrush, the U.S. Army had concluded that TNWs did not favor the defense. In addition, NATO exercises made clear that Germany would be devastated through the effects of blast and fallout following even the limited employment of nuclear weapons. NATO governments, experiencing different strategic anxieties from their different geostrategic circumstances, disputed when and how to use — or threaten to use — these TNWs. U.S. officials generally wanted options, firebreaks, and bargaining time; Germany sought to avoid any increase in the possibility of any war occurring on German territory by insisting that NATO threaten the early use of nuclear weapons. TNWs, designed as instruments of reassurance to governments, became symbols of anxiety to large sections of their publics.

By 1960, Kissinger and other analysts had noted the failure of the services to develop a coherent doctrine for TNWs, fundamental disagreements within NATO over them, and the problems for NATO strategy that resulted from the Soviet nuclear buildup. Indeed, the Soviets were beginning to introduce their own TNWs. Soviet leaders believed that TNWs added to the over-all East-West correlation of forces, whose imbalance in their favor could exert pressure, threats, and even blackmail. Most Soviet strategists fell into "nuclear romanticism," a form of delusional thinking, we now see, regarding how nuclear weapons would allow for decisive victory in a war with NATO.

But they still saw them as weapons of mass destruction and likely sources of escalation to all-out exchanges, which could not be used precisely against military targets separated from the civilian population. Rather than reducing the need for manpower, Soviet experts believed that the prospects of further nuclear exchanges required even larger conventional forces for use as replacements and reserves for those killed or incapacitated. They also noted the desirability of preemption but could never be certain that Soviet forces could accomplish this, due partly to the large number of NATO TNW targets.

The doctrine of "Flexible Response" developed in the John Kennedy/Robert McNamara era was a way to reduce reliance on nuclear weapons by fielding credible levels of conventional forces. The corresponding new NATO MC 14/3 plan intended to raise the threshold of nuclear war by deemphasizing nuclear weapons and by increasing reliance on conventional forces and making conventional defense more feasible. Flexible Response essentially confined nuclear weapons to only two roles: deterring a Soviet initiation of nuclear war and serving as weapons of last resort, if conventional defense failed, to persuade the aggressor to terminate the conflict on acceptable terms. But ambiguity was the essence of Flexible Response: without it, the Allies were unlikely to agree in peacetime over the role and timing of TNW use. France's withdrawal from NATO's integrated military structure, the establishment of the Nuclear Planning Group (NPG), and the incorporation of precision-guided munitions into NATO plans also facilitated inter-allied agreement.

Meanwhile, popular opposition cancelled the proposed U.S. Enhanced Radiation Warheads ("neutron bombs"), which might have increased the utility of TNWs against Soviet armored forces. The Soviet-NATO détente of the 1970s enabled mutual reductions in nuclear weapons, and the NATO governments chose to relinquish much of their TNW capacity in order to lubricate the prospects of modernizing their intermediate nuclear forces (INF) in response to a comparable Soviet INF modernization effort, and later to improve relations with a rapidly changing Russia. The December 1979 NATO foreign and defense ministers meeting decided to deploy 572 American ground-launched cruise missiles (GLCMs) and Pershing 2 intermediate-range missiles, while undertaking arms control negotiations with the Union of Soviet Socialist Republics (USSR). They unilaterally withdrew 1,000 U.S. TNWs from Europe. At their October 1983 Montebello meeting, the NPG announced that, without a breakthrough in the INF talks, the deployments of Pershing 2 and the GLCMs would proceed, but announced that another 1,400 American tactical warheads would be withdrawn.

The INF Treaty of December 1987 banned all U.S. and Soviet ground-based ballistic and cruise missiles with ranges of 500 to 5,500 kilometers (km). NATO Supreme Allied Commander Europe (SACEUR) General Bernard Rogers recommended that NATO implement the second half of the 1983 Montebello decision and modernize its remaining short-range nuclear forces (SNF). It never happened, largely due to West German opposition. The Follow On To Lance (FOTL) and the U.S./United Kingdom (UK) Tomahawk anti-ship air-to-surface missile (TASM) were cancelled.

The United States and Russia unilaterally eliminated many TNWs after the Cold War ended, but the NATO cuts were much deeper. Soon after Soviet forces and all nuclear systems were withdrawn to Russia, NATO removed most of its remaining 4,000 U.S. warheads, leaving only "several hundred" gravity bombs of the B-61 Type II. The resultant TNW asymmetry in Moscow's favor is now long established and hard to eliminate. Another asymmetry is in NATO and Russian planners' views of their remaining TNWs. NATO leaders have declared TNWs as weapons of "truly last resort" that should ideally be eliminated through negotiations with Russia, though some analysts, including Nichols, would be willing to relinquish them unilaterally. But Russian policymakers seem to see continuing political and military uses of their own TNWs.

According to Schulte, present-day NATO doctrine and statements offer many possible reasons for retaining TNWs, but the arguments are all contestable:

- Mechanisms for sharing nuclear functions and responsibilities (but with countries that find nuclear weapons increasingly distasteful);
- Signaling devices in crises (but which would be hard to use given present NATO procedures and processes);
- Reaffirming the transatlantic relationship at a time when the United States is shifting its strategic attention to the Pacific (but intra-allied disputes whenever TNW issues become prominent weaken alliance solidarity);

- Assets for future arms control talks (which the Russians resist holding);
- Weapons category (which might undermine NATO investments in more usable capabilities, and that might not be sustainable without renewed commitment to modernize dual-capable aircraft (DCA);
- Reassurance for new East European members of NATO (but the alliance TNWs are not located in these countries, and could not be moved there without provoking a major crisis with Russia);
- Symbols of the continuing U.S. nuclear commitment to its NATO partners (Professor Bunn's Wedding Ring Analogy: it does not matter whether or not you wear a wedding ring, but it does matter a lot if you wear it and then take it off); and,
- Means of deterring Iran (but many more operationally plausible nuclear assets exist for this, and NATO-wide ballistic missile defense (BMD) is becoming the preferred response).

Schulte maintained that, although the nuclear weapons complexes cost the United States and the Soviet Union trillions of dollars, TNWs specifically spared NATO countries the enormous costs of maintaining large standing conventional armies. The compounded economic effects of this have been one factor in higher western European living standards. And, while contributing to the security dilemma throughout the Cold War, TNWs were not in themselves a major cause of instability: they improved the correlation of forces from the NATO perspective and did not lend themselves to "bolt from the blue scenarios" because

9

they were embedded in easy-to-monitor conventional forces.

Elbridge Colby focused on the history of TNWs in U.S. strategy toward Asia. At first, the Pentagon saw TNWs as a cheap and readily available means of enhancing U.S. regional military power in possible wars in Asia. TNWs were integrated as tightly with U.S. forces in Asia as they were in Europe. These forces were not able to fight a conventional war of any duration without the use of TNWs. These weapons were seen as a U.S. advantage over the Soviet bloc and as helping deter or defeat Soviet aggression and avoiding another unhappy experience like the protracted war in Korea. For example, they were seen as essential for countering a People's Republic of China (PRC) attempt to occupy Taiwan. Lacking long-range ballistic missiles, the Pentagon placed TNWs on land as well as on forward-based ships and bombers, establishing a network of U.S. military bases throughout the world.

Even so, the Kennedy and subsequent U.S. administrations refrained from using them in the Vietnam War. In time, the improving accuracy and effectiveness of U.S. conventional weapons, combined with the growing nuclear arsenals of the Soviet Union and China, reduced U.S. reliance on TNWs. Today, unlike in Europe, U.S. nuclear weapons in Asia are no longer relied upon for strictly military purposes. They are designed as means of reassuring key U.S. allies in Asia and for deterring Chinese and North Korean threats while discouraging the further proliferation of nuclear weapons to other Asian countries.

Colby offers several hypotheses as to why the U.S. approaches to TNWs have differed in Europe compared to Asia. First, the regional security environments are dissimilar. Whereas Europe has the unitary multinational NATO alliance, the United States has to manage a diffuse hub-and-spoke alliance system in Asia, which makes it more difficult to pool individual national military forces into an integrated collective asset.

Second, NATO's formal role in shaping U.S. nuclear weapons policy, including its dual-key arrangements for forward-based shared TNWs, and the NPG, considerably constrained Washington's nuclear policies. In contrast, the absence of such an alliance in the Asia Pacific region allowed the United States much more discretion in determining its nuclear weapons policy in the Pacific. The Japanese and other allies benefiting from U.S. nuclear deterrence guarantees declined to probe too deeply into these arrangements to avoid highlighting this nuclear dimension to their nuclear-allergic publics.

Third, the regional geography is dissimilar. The Asia Pacific theater is much larger, and U.S. allies are located on the periphery rather than on the Asian mainland, thus allowing defense by U.S. air and naval forces. In contrast, the United States needed to base an enormous conventional force in central Europe to defend its NATO allies from the feared Warsaw Pact ground attack. The network of U.S. bases in the Pacific also made a forward-based strategy relying on stand-off air and sea power effective in defending them.

Fourth, the United States enjoyed a more advantageous conventional balance in Asia than in Europe. U.S. naval superiority has meant that the United States does not need to rely on nuclear weapons to protect most Asia Pacific countries, with the major exception of South Korea during the Cold War period. In contrast, the United States did not enjoy conventional superiority in Europe during the Cold War, so it lacked credible conventional deterrence options and had to rely on extended nuclear deterrence guarantees.

Fifth, the prospects of further nuclear weapons proliferation is much greater in Asia than in Europe. India, Pakistan, and North Korea have been the most recent states to acquire nuclear weapons, joining Russia, China, and the United States. Japan, South Korea, and Taiwan also have the means to acquire nuclear weapons fairly easily if they want. Even Burma was feared until recently to be considering nuclear weapons options.

Colby notes how changes in the Asian scene are moving it closer to the European pattern. TNWs have recently achieved renewed prominence in the defense debates in South Korea and Japan. Seeking to balance the provocative actions of nuclear-armed North Korea and the growing military power of China, strategists in both South Korea and Japan are openly discussing whether nuclear weapons, either U.S. or possibly indigenous ones, can help them manage both threats. The United States has sought to reassure both countries by affirming that the United States will defend them against external aggression, including the use of nuclear weapons if necessary.

Although U.S. TNWs no longer play the central role in military planning in Asia that they did in the 1950s, Colby argued that they do have an important and possibly growing role in reassuring allies and deterring adversary aggression. He also worried that the United States would be at a disadvantage in local conflicts if its adversaries were prepared to use nuclear weapons while the United States was not.

CHAPTER 2

TACTICAL NUCLEAR WEAPONS IN NATO AND BEYOND: A HISTORICAL AND THEMATIC EXAMINATION

Paul Schulte

INTRODUCTION

Tactical Nuclear Weapons (TNWs) are a U.S. invention deriving from research and development decisions taken around 1947-49, and accelerated by ominous adversarial moves such as the Soviet nuclear test in 1949 and the Korean War in 1950. They became the characteristic, and eventually cheaply mass-produced instrument of U.S. deterrence in Europe and the Korean Peninsula. The Soviet Union also came to deploy large numbers of TNWs with quite different operational concepts. From their peak numbers in the late 1960s to early 1970s, NATO TNWs declined due to doctrinal reevaluation of their utility, the appearance of conventional alternatives, and, in Europe, anti-nuclear political feeling which prevented their modernization or replacement and portrayed them as an obstacle to political change. They remain an important part of the Russian nuclear arsenal.

DEFINITIONS

TNWs pose serious definitional problems. The most cited criteria involve a short range (under the 500 kilometer [km] lower limit established by the Intermediate Nuclear Forces [INF] Treaty of 1987) and a low yield. The first TNWs deployed to Europe in 1953-54 were American gravity bombs, as are the only remaining U.S. TNWs, the variable-yield B-61s. Modern fighter-bombers can potentially deliver them across hundreds of kilometers — distances overlapping with those of weapons previously referred to as Theater Nuclear Forces. The only nuclear weapons ever used in combat, over Hiroshima and Nagasaki, Japan, had TNW-like yields of only about 15 kilotons (kt), but obviously with a decisive strategic effect.[1]

A widely employed alternative term for TNWs is non-strategic nuclear weapons (NSNWs), defined as all nuclear weapons unaddressed by current nuclear arms control arrangements. For example, this definition would exclude U.S. and Russian strategic nuclear weapons (SNWs) covered by the various Strategic Arms Reduction Treaties and U.S. or Russian nuclear and conventional ground-launched ballistic and cruise missiles with intermediate ranges, between 500 and 5,500 km, which are prohibited by the INF Treaty. Additional weapons could fall into this category if, as is frequently called for, TNWs were brought into U.S.-Russian arms control negotiations or perhaps covered by multinational arms control measures. In newly nuclear-capable states such as Pakistan, India, and North Korea, and, perhaps soon, Iran, almost all nuclear weapons, even with a short range and restricted yield, are regarded as "strategic" due to their strategic intent to deter superpower intervention and drive regional security developments and due to their unique status within a country's nuclear arsenal.

Yet another formulation is that TNWs are those nuclear weapons which are incapable of reaching key homeland targets of the Cold War superpowers. However, this would redefine *all* NATO low-yield gravity bombs in Europe as strategic weapons—which is why Moscow often favors this definitional approach.

In view of the lack of consensus on what constitutes TNWs, I propose the following working definition as derived from the military functions expected of their deployment by NATO, the United States, Britain, France, and the Union of Soviet Socialist Republics (USSR)/Russia since the 1950s. TNWs are defined as:

> nuclear devices and delivery systems with relatively short range and low yield by contemporary standards, which are intended for employment against conventional, or nuclear, ground, naval, air targets or transport assets, on the battlefield, or across the theater, to contribute to total conventional and nuclear campaign capability, yet which are not expected to inflict strategically decisive damage to enemy military, economic, or regime targets, but whose use would nevertheless be an unmistakable signal that the stakes in a crisis were regarded as serious enough to transform it into, or continue it, as a nuclear conflict, and so, unavoidably, to risk possible escalation to a strategic level.[2]

CONCLUSIONS AND SCOPE

The main proposition of this chapter is that nuclear weapons experience significant change in their strategic purpose and their political and cultural meanings, depending on time and historical context. This has been true even with little change in the design, production, deployment, maintenance, storage, training routines, and targeting of the weapons themselves. Their purposes, strategic implications, and political meanings have steadily evolved over the decades. TNWs have been subject to changes of international thinking and national feeling about nuclear weapons, and tidal fluctuations in the acceptability and avoidability of early nuclear use.

This chapter concentrates on Europe, with a focus on the evolution of NATO operational policies, but considers some connected developments in the Warsaw Pact and the Russian Federation, and analogous developments on the Korean Peninsula, the other area where TNWs have played a strategic role. The chapter attempts to suggest useful periodicities, but bounding dates should not necessarily be taken as indicating immediate discontinuities, except perhaps for 1989-90. Unsurprisingly, history shows early precursors of current policy disputes and intra-Alliance debates, while providing illustrations for a wide range of contemporary judgments. Let us proceed with our historical and thematic examination of TNWs using the following six periods as our historical frame of reference: I. 1945-1953; II. 1953-1963; III. 1963-1967; IV. 1968-1983; V. 1987-1990; and VI. 1991-2012.

I. 1945-1953. U.S. TNWS TO MEET THE SOVIET EXPANSIONARY THREAT: THE TRUMAN-STALIN YEARS

The Early Strategic and Moral Promise of TNWs.

In the late 1940s and early 1950s, further nuclear research led to smaller and smaller weapons, reducing average warhead weight from 10,000 to 1,000 pounds by 1954.[3] Opponents of the development of a fusion device, such as Robert Oppenheimer, favored small bombs which could be delivered via aircraft, artillery, or missiles for battlefield effect. It took well over 10 years after Hiroshima before the future shape of nuclear strategy began to clarify. There were expectations—perhaps prompted by moral aspirations—that nuclear weapons could develop, in line with previous experiences of war, in a less morally paradoxical direction, which would not favor the attacker and not necessarily involve the destruction of cities.[4] This uncertainty about how exactly TNWs would be employed in war (or, more accurately, how wars involving TNWs would turn out) has meant that development and deployment of TNWs has been marked by various reports and officially endorsed strategies attempting to impose rational order on their use. Such doctrines have over time been forced to accept that control may be impossible in the nuclear spiral which would follow TNW use—and that their deterrent role is probably stronger as a result.[5]

In 1949 General Omar Bradley speculated that "the A Bomb in its tactical aspect may well contribute towards a stable equilibrium of forces since it tends to strengthen the defensive army." Oppenheimer similarly hoped that "battle would be brought back to the battlefield." The U.S. Air Force's Project Vista, conducted in 1951, predicted that synergies between battlefield weapons and small conventional forces would work to defend Europe against overwhelming Soviet forces.

These calculations were later repeatedly disconfirmed by exercise experiments and analytical work, but the efficacy of TNWs was over-estimated owing to a number of factors. Staring into the dawning Cold War, American strategists concluded in the far-reaching National Security Council (NSC) Paper NSC 68 that there was no alternative to achieving a "preponderance of power"[6]—both conventional and nuclear—to back the strategy of containment which would otherwise be simply a bluff. Truman signed NSC 68 into policy in September 1950. Achieving and maintaining this preponderance would require maximum use of the anticipated long-term, though not permanent, U.S. advantage in nuclear weapons of all ranges and yields. Among U.S. allies still slowly recovering from World War II, there was an appetite for reliance upon the marvelous and cost-free guarantee of U.S. nuclear firepower.

The Imperative of the Apparent Soviet Military Threat.

In the years after 1945, the Soviet challenge had seemed essentially political and economic, but by August 1949, just before the North Atlantic Treaty had entered into force, the U.S. Joint Chiefs of Staff (JCS) expressed deep pessimism to British counterparts about whether a Soviet offensive against Western Europe could be defeated, or even whether the planned strategic bombing offensive against Russian cities could force an early end to such war.[7] The need for bolstering Western conventional forces seemed urgent and obvious.[8] In 1949, the first-ever NATO strategy document to receive ministerial endorsement, DC 6/61, included two major propositions fateful for Alliance strategy and the role of TNWs. NATO would plan a forward defense of its territory rather than maneuver to trade space for time in the response to a Soviet attack. Second, NATO would "ensure the ability to carry out strategic bombing promptly by all means possible with all types of weapons without exception." The persisting sense of acute conventional inferiority meant that NATO would be "loud, stubborn, and explicit"[9] in its rejection of any No First Use of Nuclear Weapons (NOFUN) undertaking. Compared with the repeatedly emphasized, if unverifiable, Soviet No First Use pledge, this rejection created a sinister,

Strangelovian image for NATO in the eyes of peace and antinuclear movements, which the USSR was not slow to exploit. It also established a political distaste for TNWs among several European NATO publics which remains today, and is increasingly significant for the weapons' future.

The Imperative of Forward Defense.

Forward defense seemed the indispensable foundation for a large, resilient, and cohesive Alliance, given traumatic recent European memories of Nazi occupation, coupled with the apparently irrevocable consequences of forced assimilation into the Soviet bloc. Moreover, Berlin, Germany, a symbolic outpost of the Cold War, remained indefensible by conventional means.[10] Maintaining the credibility of such an inflexible military strategy against larger Soviet and East European (after 1955, Warsaw Pact) forces, made additional capabilities, such as the nuclear-bolstering which TNWs would provide, seem absolutely essential.

Korea and Rearmament.

The first Soviet nuclear test in 1949, the outbreak of the Korean War in 1950, and a growing perception of armed Soviet expansionist ambitions created anxieties which led to the establishment and rapid growth of NATO. In February 1952, a NATO meeting in Lisbon, Portugal, set 96 divisions as a force goal. This ambitious conventional force level subsequently proved unachievable, due to a combination of cost and inefficiency.[11]

The shock of the Korean War led to plans for the rapid deployment of large numbers of U.S. TNWs into Europe during 1953-54 (although the *first* U.S. nuclear weapons deployed to the European theater seem to have gone to Morocco in 1953, because there they could contribute to the Strategic Air Command [SAC] Emergency War Plan untrammeled by Alliance or theater considerations[12]). But production limitations imposed temporary delays, with the U.S. SAC insisting on first access to fissile materials to build up its stocks of weapons for the all-out strategic attack on Soviet cities which would be the first response to the feared Warsaw Pact invasion.

The Soviet Union lagged in nuclear weapons technology and could not set aside nuclear weapons for tactical purposes during this period. Even so, Soviet leaders could not ignore the nuclear aspects of NATO's growing capability. While Stalin publicly blustered about the relative insignificance of new technology compared to the "Permanently Operating Factors" of war, he was unrelentingly determined to build up the USSR's own nuclear capabilities and acutely aware of the slow growth of the Soviet stockpile. Stalin never in fact ordered a war plan for invasion of Western Europe, despite the West's anxieties about surprise attack which stimulated NATO's expansion and nuclearization.[13] Therefore, the decision to build up nuclear deterrent capabilities may not have helped deter a serious military threat in the early Cold War, although it may still have been psychologically essential to maintain Western European confidence without crippling cost to the postwar recovery.[14]

II. 1953-1963. U.S. STRATEGIC SUPERIORITY: EISENHOWER OPTS FOR "MASSIVE RETALIATION."

After assuming office in early 1953, the administration of former General Dwight Eisenhower raised U.S. and NATO dependence on nuclear weapons to a new level. As a fiscal conservative, Eisenhower saw nuclear weapons as a strategically acceptable and decisively cheaper alternative to conventional forces. He believed in planning for the long competition between liberal democracy and communism by balancing security and solvency. Increasing reliance on the much more cost-effective firepower provided by TNWs was consequently a key aspect of Eisenhower's New Look strategy, which developed out of U.S. NSC Paper NSC 162/2 of October 1953.[15] (The U.S. doctrine was also frequently referred to as "Massive Retaliation," although Eisenhower himself disliked the term.) Eisenhower also judged — probably, it now seems, wrongly — that his threats of nuclear use if the peace talks continued to stall in Korea had been decisive in persuading the Chinese and North Koreas to agree to armistice terms a few months later.

TNWs and the Economics of Massive Retaliation.

When Eisenhower took office, the United States had only about 1,000 nuclear weapons. Massive retaliation needed far more. Orders were placed for the weapons with the Atomic Energy Commission at enormous cost. By the time outlays reached their peak during the Eisenhower era, the Commission was consuming some 10 percent of the total federal budget. By the mid-1950s, a "nuclear production complex" had been created that absorbed 6.7 percent of total U.S. electrical power.[16] Nonetheless, building up such a huge nuclear capability cost only a fraction of what maintaining large conventional forces would have. Since no escape could be negotiated from the huge costs of the global competition between the Soviet and NATO blocs, the defense economics of the New Look seem convincing in retrospect, especially considering the civilian spinoffs from military research and development [17]

The long-term effects of lower military expenditure and smaller conscript armies helped generate the economic and cultural buoyancy which was such a Western competitive advantage in the Cold War.

NATO Takes on the New Look.

Eisenhower's successor as NATO's Supreme Commander Europe (SACEUR), General Matthew Ridgway, commissioned a study of the effects of TNWs on force requirements. The study controversially concluded that NATO would prevail if it had many more TNWs than the Russians and more troops to absorb the higher loss rates, and if SACEUR had pre-delegated authority for immediate nuclear use if war broke out. The study raised all the questions that would dominate NATO TNW debates through the Cold War:

- Could theater nuclear weapons be used on European territory without destroying the societies they were intended to protect?
- Could the military requirements for early release of nuclear weapons be reconciled with the politicians' desire to wait until events made release unavoidable?

- For what political purposes might nuclear weapons be used, and what would determine "victory" in a nuclear exchange?[18]

The incorporation of massive retaliation in NATO doctrine and stockpiling was nevertheless immediate and encountered little resistance. The North Atlantic Council (NAC) agreed in the autumn of 1953 that "special attention should be given to the continuing provision of modern weapons of the latest type [i.e., TNWs]."[19] The following year, Field Marshal Bernard Montgomery, Deputy SACEUR, declared, "We at SHAPE are basing all our planning on using atomic or thermo nuclear weapons in our defence. . . . It is no longer 'they may possibly be used,' it is very definitely: they will be used if we are attacked."[20] There were deliberate attempts to construct a public understanding of nuclear weapons as just another kind of military option for warfighting. Official references to nuclear response, without differentiating between strategic and battlefield use, were designed to increase nuclear deterrence by blurring distinctions. The first U.S. nuclear artillery pieces arrived in Kaiserslautern, Germany, in 1954. The buildup of TNWs accelerated after 1956, so that "before long NATO was looking like a nuclear porcupine,[21] having by 1960 amassed some 3,000 nuclear weapons."[22] Forward-based ground TNWs, despite their short ranges and low yields, were seen as particularly enhancing deterrence through their "use-it-or-lose-it" quality, and because, with the introduction of nuclear shells ("battlefield nuclears"), all dual-capable artillery, especially of the widely available 155-mm class, would have to be regarded as nuclear assets.

The NAC approved MC 14/2 in July 1954 (the MC 14 series set out the overall strategic concept) and MC 48/2 (the MC 48 series addressed the measures to implement that concept) in 1957. Together, they represented a refined version of the Eisenhower/Dulles doctrine of massive retaliation, worded as follows (per MC 14/2):

> A. We must first ensure the ability to carry out an instant and devastating nuclear counteroffensive by all available means and develop the capability to absorb and survive the enemy's onslaught. . . .

> D. Concurrently and closely related . . . we must develop our ability to use our land, sea and air forces for defense of their territories and sea areas of NATO as far forward as possible to maintain the integrity of the NATO area counting on the use of nuclear weapons from the outset.[23]

This was the high point of NATO doctrinal reliance upon TNWs. It seems to have supported a temporary policy of U.S pre-delegation of very short-range battlefield nuclear weapons, including Atomic Demolition Munitions (ADMs), especially on the Central Front in Germany.[24] Under European pressure, MC 14/2, MC 48/2, and MC 70 (which followed in 1958) were soon reinterpreted by the next SACEUR, General Lauris Norstad, to allow for more differentiated reactions than automatic nuclear retaliation. The Hungarian uprising in 1956 showed the need to include a local defense scenario, in which nuclear weapons would not be used, provided no Soviet forces were directly involved in the border clash.[25] These confidential planning moves towards differentiated responses paved the way towards the greater flexibility debated in the early 1960s and publicly adopted in 1967. The widely heralded move to flexible response may have been less of a change in practice than is commonly assumed.[26]

National Attitudes to TNWs.

Quite unlike strategic nuclear forces, TNWs, by their forward-based physical presence and likely use in defensive combat on or over Allied territory, confront members of alliances like NATO with very concrete choices over potential use. Europeans responded in different ways to the deployment of TNWs and the dilemmas posed by timing and conditions of their employment. For most NATO allies, the inescapable choice was between the binary risks of *entanglement*[27] (being caught up, if deterrence failed, in a nuclear war, perhaps starting far from Europe and escalating faster than they would have chosen) or *abandonment* (being left exposed through "decoupling" to the prospect of Soviet intimidation, conquest, or conventionally irreversible seize-and-hold occupation should the Americans fall short on their nuclear guarantees). The recurrent disputes on Alliance nuclear posture involved cycling between these poles of anxiety. For the United States, the concomitant problem of extended nuclear deterrence was, and remains, "simply the international political problem of credibility of retaliation with potentially suicidal consequences against serious, but not inevitably fatal, threats."[28] Reaching agreement on the timing and circumstances of the Alliance's response with TNWs inevitably focused attention on this dilemma, which was logically insoluble, yet had to be—and has been—politically managed, very largely by creating a common *deterrence culture* within which joint planning for nuclear contingencies could be conducted and normalized.

Determinants of national attitudes vary. Geopolitical exposure has been critical, with those states most directly in the front line of the East-West conflict seeing a clear need for nuclear deterrence. Geography interacted, sometimes unstably, with historically determined national strategic cultures and different degrees of determination to preserve national independence.

Britain.

The United Kingdom (UK), facing major financial problems after World War II, but anxious to maintain a leading military role in the Alliance and globally, favored nuclear deterrence with tactical as well as strategic weapons.[29] London constantly sought to preserve a special relationship with the United States, especially its economically rewarding nuclear cooperation. British possession of a national nuclear strategic capability meant the UK was less directly affected by decisions regarding TNWs, but London was prepared to act as a mediator within the Alliance to prevent divisive differences over their employment, and to resist any possibility of strategic decoupling.

France.

France was located well behind the NATO-Warsaw Pact frontline, but Paris prioritized nuclear acquisition because it had a large army in Germany and was determined to regain its status in the world and prevent a repetition of the traumas of 1870, 1914, and 1940. Deploying nuclear weapons to ensure that the French homeland would never be subject to occupation again appealed to all sectors of French political opinion.[30] This hardened into a fixed official national pro-nuclear sentiment for the Alliance and an insistence on achieving and maintaining independent national capability. As a later French nuclear theorist recently encapsulated it: "Every French village displays a memorial to the failure of conventional deterrence."[31] The insistent logic of this position, articulately formulated and largely unchallenged by the political class, was to pursue independent strategic and intermediate-range nuclear capability first, but then to begin working on French TNWs (tactical bombs and a mobile surface-to-surface missile [SSM], Pluton). A few years after its first nuclear test in 1960, France was emphasizing an independent and unconstrained "pre-strategic" use of its national TNWs, using gravity bombs, surface-to-surface missiles, and later air-to-surface missiles, to give a last warning before resorting to the use of France's national strategic forces.

Germany.

West Germany was the fulcrum and decisive prize of the Cold War confrontation, and faced the most politically complex set of choices. Its geopolitical predicament as a narrowly truncated country right up against the East-West fault line of the inner-German border, left it reliant on the threat of early use of U.S. intermediate-range and strategic-range nuclear forces to prevent loss of national territory and widespread devastation, preferably by avoiding *any* war. This idea clashed with German strategic culture which, mindful of the wry observation that "the shorter the (nuclear) range, the deader the Germans," was skeptical and fearful of nuclear provocation or mistakes, yet which also rejected non-nuclear alternatives such as fixed fortifications and barrier defenses because they would present obstacles to eventual German reunification. The Third Reich experience left a strong residue of antimilitarism, which mutated into fears of "a global Auschwitz" or "Atom-Fear."[32] Moreover, it combined with left-wing suspicions of U.S. motives and thereby increased receptiveness to the peace and antinuclear movements. Since both Germanys would be the major battlefield in a third World War and the target for TNWs from both sides, Germany's atomic allergy merged with the conviction that Germany should not be victimized.[33] Yet, Konrad Adenauer's new Federal Republic of Germany resisted Soviet expansion, worked for eventual reunification, and insisted on forward defense of its narrow country at the inner-German border if war came. Adenauer sought a *Politik der Starke* (position of strength) from which to pursue reunification.[34] From this perspective, he considered TNWs as "practically normal weapons."[35]

The resulting controversy led to the signing of the Göttingen Manifesto by leading scientists, which crystallized a lasting aversion to nuclear weapons in German universities. Franz Josef Strauss, the German Defense Minister, determined to force through German nuclear rearmament, told an American audience that these weapons are "the symbol and even the characteristic aspect of the decisive criterion of sovereignty."[36] But due to persistent pressure from the Soviet Union and other countries, Germany was denied a national nuclear weapons option, and even from inclusion in the proposed Multilateral Nuclear Force (MLF), which the State Department proposed to create in the hope of giving European allies shared control over nuclear weapons as an alternative to their creating individual national nuclear forces.

Nevertheless, Germany understandably continued to seek to exercise control over nuclear decisions within the Alliance that could affect how a war was fought on German territory.[37] Germany demanded that it should not be "singularized," that there should be no zones of differential security, that an attack on any member of the Alliance must trigger an automatic and immediate reaction from all others, and that other measures be adopted to avoid any increase in the possibility of war occurring on German territory. To these ends, it insisted that NATO threaten the early use of nuclear weapons. German officials often acted in a "silent but positive partnership" with the British within the Nuclear Planning Group,[38] but TNWs (which due to their short range allowed for the possibility of a nuclear war being fought only on German territory) remained a more anxiety-provoking but inevitable irritant for Germany than for other Alliance members.

Smaller Nations.

Smaller, exposed countries faced their own particular nuclear difficulties and sought to maintain characteristic choices within the Alliance. Norway repeatedly rejected proposals to station nuclear weapons on its soil in peacetime, as well as refusing permanently stationed foreign troops and restricting Allied exercises in the border region, as a *reassurance strategy* to manage its relations with the Soviet Union. However, Norway still participated in preparations and training for *Snowcat*, the TNW-driven, all-out air offensive scenario which dominated NATO air force planning. This was an example of an ally pursuing policies of both *integration* and *screening*: maximizing the Alliance's security guarantee through close cooperation, while limiting the extent of Allied presence or infringement.[39] Similarly, Denmark, while resisting Russian pressures for neutrality, also refused to accept the stationing of TNWs in peacetime.[40]

The USSR.

Like Eisenhower, Nikita Khrushchev emphasized nuclear rather than conventional forces, viewing them as modern, decisive, and cheap. Unlike Joseph Stalin, Khrushchev determined that Soviet forces should develop extremely detailed offensive nuclear war plans.[41] As they began to acquire their own TNWs, Soviet leaders believed that they naturally added to the overall East-West correlation of forces, in which an advantageous overall balance would almost automatically and "scientifically" produce aggregating psychological effects, thus undermining the influence of "warmongering" factions in the West, increasing inducements for them to accept the legitimacy of the Central European Communist states, and generally encouraging them to seek accommodation with Soviet positions.[42] But the Soviets still saw TNWs as weapons of mass destruction and likely incitements to escalation which could not be used precisely against military targets separate from the civilian population, and which could not plausibly be held back in any limited nuclear war. Rather than reducing the need for manpower, Soviet experts judged that the high attrition rates produced by nuclear exchanges would require even larger conventional forces as replacements and reserves. Despite the USSR's ritually repeated NOFUN pledge, "Soviet strategic thought placed considerable emphasis on preemption; if the Soviet Union was sure that the enemy was about to attack, it should strike first in order to break up his forces."[43] The growth of NATO TNWs did not cause the Soviet General Staff to abandon its underlying belief that only a ruthless military offensive could secure victory for the USSR. Revelations after the fall of communism, Warsaw Pact exercises, and doctrine indicate that Soviet Marshals fell into a state of "nuclear romanticism,"[44] consistently planning on the assumptions that early (but never, they insisted, even to themselves, *first*) nuclear strikes of intermediate-range missiles and tactical weapons, combined with mass conventional air attack and armored offensives, would cancel out NATO TNWs, shatter Alliance cohesion, and carry Warsaw Pact forces to the Channel before the Americans could send over sufficient forces to stop them. This seems in retrospect delusional. While the nuclear emphasis later became diluted in favor of paralyzingly rapid conventional advances, not until 1987 did the Warsaw Pact adopt a military doctrine that clearly excluded any nuclear attack option.[45]

The Consequences of Projected Full-Scale Tactical Nuclear Use in Europe during the Cold War.

East German papers from the military archive documenting Command Post Exercise Buria in October 1961 reveal the huge scale, rapidity, and destructiveness of the anticipated nuclear war. It was the first major command post exercise carried out under nuclear conditions and is consistent with the highly influential reference work *Military Strategy* published in 1962 by Marshal V. D. Sokolovski. Warsaw Pact officers were assigned an exercise scenario based on the assumptions that, if the Soviet Union signed Khrushchev's threatened peace treaty with the German Democratic Republic (GDR), ending Berlin's special status, NATO would try to advance to West Berlin and, when blocked, would launch a nuclear first strike. All-out Warsaw Pact reprisal attacks would then follow to establish a favorable balance of forces. Soviet operational calculations of the results of TNW employment were grimly similar to those in previous NATO exercises. The Exercise Buria scenario postulated a Warsaw Pact force numbering over one million men, with more than 350 SCUD and FROG launchers, 1,500 fighter planes, and 1,000 bombers and fighter-bombers. Of these aircraft, 100 were nuclear-capable. The NATO force had 682,000 troops when combat commenced, including 300 nuclear-capable artillery pieces and 334 missile launchers (Honest Johns, Lacrosses, Corporal/ Sergeants, and Redstones); air forces of 1,314 fighters, 1,550 bombers, and fighter-bombers (800 nuclear-capable, with 36 air-launched nuclear cruise missiles). It assumed that more than 2,200 nuclear weapons would be employed, 1,000 by the Soviets, 1,200 by NATO, though total megatonnage would be about the same.[46] Here quoted at length is Matthias Uhl's depiction of the unfolding campaign's horrendous results:

> In their first "strategic" nuclear strike, Warsaw Pact forces would attack a total of 1,200 stationary NATO targets (422 in West Germany) within 30 minutes with approximately 400 nuclear attacks on mobile targets such as troop concentrations or nuclear weapons. The political and military leadership of the Federal Republic would be paralyzed for 8 to 10 days. 70% of TNW and 90% of the radar stations and airfields in West Germany would be immediately destroyed. Nuclear weapons would kill or incapacitate 40% of the troops they were used against. Losses of weapons and equipment would be up to 60%. NATO would detonate 68 surface explosions of nuclear weapons behind War-

saw Pact lines to interdict strategic reserves. Overall, 140,000 km² would suffer radiation of at least 100 Roentgens per hour. Enormous numbers of dead, injured and radiation diseased civilians would confront military and civilian medical services with insoluble problems. Nevertheless, after this decisive initial exchange, Warsaw Pact troops would storm on to Paris and reach Calais on the 10th day.[47]

OPERATION SNOWCAT

Similar operational calculations would likely have been made in NATO, but there are no detailed declassified scenario casualty calculations. An indication of similarly extraordinarily high anticipated loss rates can however be gained from the high-intensity air operations scenario for the opening of nuclear war in Europe, which required coordination of the Alliance's non-nuclear aircraft across the theater. This was designated SNOWCAT: "Support of Nuclear Operations with Conventional Attacks." It would also have taken into account the Alliance's considerable conventional and tactical nuclear naval air capabilities. (The SNOWCAT plan still exists, but its details are classified and it is probably now planned on a much smaller scale.) Winning the initial nuclear exchange in SNOWCAT took priority over air defense of national territory, so that, for example, non-nuclear Norwegian fighter-bombers were expected to be held back to attack enemy air control systems throughout the northern Warsaw Pact so as to assist NATO nuclear strikes, even though SNOWCAT missions in the early 1960s had been privately predicted to be "suicidal" by the Commander in Chief Allied Forces Northern Europe (CINCNORTH).[48]

Nuclear Command and Communication Chaos.

Communications problems would have added to the difficulties on both sides of the nuclear battlefield because of jamming, fears of near instant identification and location by enemy direction finders, and extensive Electromagnetic Pulse (EMP) effects after each nuclear explosion, which would endanger communications over a wide area. All this would interfere with requests for nuclear release and arrangements for secure dispersal and controlled delegation. Even as late as 1987, NATO had "failed to develop a comprehensive system integrating conventional and nuclear C3 . . . that would tie together major headquarters, responsible political officials, and the relevant military commanders down to at least the divisional level."[49] Command and control in the Warsaw Pact is unlikely to have been any more efficient under nuclear conditions (except that communications were more standardized), but since their plans rested on rapid offensive movement, the physical obstacles created by nuclear strikes would have been even more significant.

TNWs in Early Atomic Crises.

The impact of the threat of TNW use, or lack of it, can now be traced in some of the nuclear crises which characterized the early antagonisms of the Cold War. The French, secretly and much too late, requested U.S. TNW strikes to save Dien Bien Phu, Vietnam, in 1954 which were rejected.[50] The Eisenhower administration later openly — and riskily — threatened their use in 1954-55 if the Chinese Nationalist-held islands of Quemoy or Matsu were invaded by Communist China, and again in 1958 to deter any invasion of Taiwan.[51]

The Democratic People's Republic of Korea (DPRK) had no nuclear capability or firm allied nuclear commitment to back any renewed aggression on its part after 1953, but levels of hostility remained high and U.S. TNWs were introduced into the Republic of Korea (ROK) around 1957-58. The buildup which followed, as in Europe, was part of the global forward deployment of nuclear weapons implied by the massive retaliation doctrine. By the end of the 1960s, the number of TNWs in the ROK reached approximately 900, including 100 Lance surface-to-surface missiles, alongside 100,000 U.S. troops. Repeated consideration was given to nuclear use against North Korea, China, and Russia. According to Peter Hayes:

> For most of the Cold War, nuclear deployments in Korea were primarily aimed at the Soviet-Chinese bloc, initially treated as a single set of targets in the sixties; and later, with the deepening Soviet-Chinese antagonism . . . aimed primarily at the former Soviet Union, and only secondarily against North Korea itself.[52]

During the 1961 Berlin crisis, President John Kennedy called on his countrymen to learn what to do to protect their families in case of nuclear attack and announced a major increase in the U.S. defense budget and a call-up of the reserves.[53] Intelligence reports reaching Khrushchev from the Russian secret police (KGB) lent weight to this public signaling. They indicated that if the access routes to Berlin were blocked, the NATO allies intended to respond robustly, using economic and military measures "that could threaten the security of the Soviet Union."[54] A report from East German intelligence was more detailed and alarming. It stated that if conventional forces were unsuccessful in reopening the access routes to West Berlin, NATO would use TNWs.[55] This seems to have been a reflection of discussions between officials from the three occupying powers, which had not yet crystallized into a military plan, but was entirely in line with Kennedy's sentiments.[56] It seems that the disclosure of NATO discussions of TNW use in a territorially circumscribed crisis, involving a highly symbolic location to which a U.S. President had tied his credibility, had a sobering and stabilizing effect. Although Soviet forces had been intermittently blocking the autobahns to Berlin in August 1961[57] when Khrushchev backed Walter Ulbricht, the leader of the GDR, in building the Berlin Wall, he gave up his ultimatum for the Allies to sign a peace treaty with the GDR and end the special status of Berlin. The paradoxically stabilizing effect of the unintended transparency of NATO nuclear plans and deployments to Warsaw Pact espionage networks, however, continued for years.

In September 1962, Khrushchev sent to Cuba 80 F KR1 nuclear cruise missiles, with an anti-ship range up to 150 km, nine warheads for Frog/Lunar battlefield missiles, plus six atomic bombs for short-range *Ilyushin*-28 bombers, to support the 40 intermediate-range ballistic strategic missiles already secretly introduced into Cuba. The military purpose of the TNWs seems to have been to strike possible U.S. invasion forces, or to attack the U.S. naval base at Guantánamo, as the crisis deepened. The TNWs were neither announced nor detected at the time by U.S. intelligence, prompting a shocked response from former Defense Secretary Robert McNamara when told of their deployment decades later, that if the U.S. forces had come under attack from TNWs, the likely result would have been general nuclear war. General Issa Pliyev, the senior Soviet commander in Cuba, was not given release authority by the Soviet General Staff,[58] but it is unknowable whether they or he would have ordered the launch of TNWs had he faced being overrun by the Americans, given the still-enormous Soviet inferiority in overall nuclear capability. Yet keeping these TNWs secret, presumably because of the highly clandestine nature of the whole deployment, also deprived the Soviets of any stabilizing deterrent effect in territorial protection. The TNWs remained in Cuba until early December despite Khrushchev's assurance that all nuclear weapons had been removed from Cuba in November. "Had U.S. intelligence uncovered this fresh deception, the crisis might have restarted amid irresistible pressure for an invasion."[59]

This incident also emphasizes the sheer difficulty of detecting (and therefore verifying) TNWs, even during the most intense local surveillance. Russia has since frequently emphasized its opposition to the deployment of any country's nuclear weapons on the territory of other countries. Potentially the most serious failure of crisis management during the Cuban affair was the unauthorized U.S. depth-charging of Soviet submarines near the U.S. quarantine line. The Americans did not know that those submarines had nuclear-tipped torpedoes aboard and conditional authorization to use them. It was only much later revealed that, but for the intense personal intercession of 2nd Captain Vasily Arkhipov, the commander of B59 might have used a nuclear torpedo against an American destroyer.[60] At the height of the Cuban crisis, on October 27, 1962, a U.S. U-2 reconnaissance aircraft from Alaska accidentally strayed into Soviet airspace over the Chukotski Peninsula and radioed for assistance. A USAF F-102, armed with a nuclear air-to-air missile,[61] was scrambled from Alaska and headed towards the

Bering Sea, while Soviet MiGs took off to intercept the U-2. Fortunately, it managed to exit Soviet airspace without shots being fired.[62] In these three widely separated cases, TNWs came close to unauthorized or unexpected firing in fast-moving, unanticipated, unplanned, and unrehearsed situations. Their use would have surprised the other side and threatened the tight central control that both Washington and Moscow attempted to exercise during the Cuba crisis.

British Tactical Nuclear Out-of-Area Deployments.

Alongside the United States, the UK provided extended nuclear deterrence in behalf of the Central Treaty Organization (CENTO) from 1955 to 1979, covering the Middle East. *Canberra* and later *Vulcan* aircraft of the UK Near East Air Force, equipped with Red Beard and later WE177 bombs, based on the sovereign base areas in Cyprus from about 1961 until 1975, were tasked with missions primarily in the USSR's Central Asian Republics.

Similar arrangements applied in the Far East. *Canberras* with Red Beards (later, WE177s) of the UK Far Eastern Air Force were deployed in Tengah, Singapore, from the early 1960s until the British withdrawal from east of Suez in 1970-71. Their task was to provide support for the Southeast Asia Treaty Organization (SEATO, 1954-77), primarily against possible Chinese aggression. By October 1963, with the intensification of the Second Indochina Conflict, the Americans began asking the British to "take on targets in Burma, adjacent parts of China and in Hainan." Naval aircraft from UK carriers in the Indian Ocean would have been fully integrated into nuclear strike planning.[63] These nuclear deployments were kept secret from the Cypriot and Singaporean government at the time.[64]

III. 1963-1967. EMERGING DOUBTS CONCERNING TNWS — PROMULGATION OF FLEXIBLE RESPONSE

During the late 1950s, doubts about reliance on TNWs began to accumulate. Soldiers, officials, and civilian strategists increasingly questioned the credibility of using TNWs and the feasibility of theories which relied on them for graduated or limited war.[65] By 1957, after exercises like Sagebrush, the U.S. Army had concluded that TNWs did *not* favor the defense. In addition, NATO exercises Carte Blanche in 1955 and Lion Noire in 1957 confirmed that Germany would be devastated through the effects of blast and fallout following even implausibly limited employment of nuclear weapons. Partly because the conclusions reached in these exercises were publicly leaked in the West, NATO TNWs became objects of anxiety to significant sectors of Western public opinion.

During the 1960 U.S. presidential election campaign, Kennedy criticized Eisenhower for the inflexibility and riskiness of massive retaliation. Kennedy evinced a willingness to push for higher conventional Alliance spending in the interests of strategic stability. McNamara made repeated visits to NATO to persuade allies of the desirability of increasing conventional forces to more credible levels so that early recourse to TNWs could be avoided and overall deterrent strengthened. He stressed the need to give the President nuclear options, firebreaks, and bargaining time.[66] His message was not warmly received because it both called for increased expenditures, and could be interpreted as a prelude to U.S. decoupling from the allies. NATO debates in this period were particularly vexing, because the State Department persisted in pushing its cherished MLF proposal in the face of Russian and French opposition until 1965. French President Charles de Gaulle's very different attitude towards nuclear strategy was causing problems for intra-alliance consensus, culminating in France's exit from the integrated military structure and joint nuclear planning in 1966.

The limited pre-delegation of nuclear release for certain forward-deployed and vulnerable U.S. TNWs, which seems to have been allowed at the end of the 1950s, was reversed by McNamara's insistence on centralized control. In a similar vein, the United States also began to apply great efforts to ensure that securely coded Permissive Action Links (PALs) were fitted to all U.S. nuclear weapons throughout the Alliance.[67] (As nearly 50 years of further technical ingenuity have now been devoted to the development of PALs, it must be doubtful whether the B-61s, which have been extensively reworked and redesigned as America's sole remaining TNWs, could be detonated if seized by terrorists or special forces.)

Flexible Response: MC 14/3.

The eventual 1967 compromise adaptation of flexible response was as much an exercise in creative ambiguity as a way to raise the threshold of nuclear war by finally fielding credible levels of conventional forces which would enable the Alliance to respond to any attack at an appropriately calibrated level. NATO would no longer plan to use its nuclear weapons for fighting a war, but for war termination. The aim would be to drive home to the Soviet leadership the seriousness of the situation so they would halt their offensive. Ambiguity had to be the essence of flexible response: without it, the Allies were unlikely to agree in peacetime over the role and timing of TNW use. Here, Sir Michael Quinn describes the tactic of deliberate ambiguity:

> NATO's public declarations were carefully worded for Soviet consumption. . . . We rightly believed Soviet intelligence would obtain accounts of the policy discussions that had taken place behind closed doors, so we tried to ensure that two key messages got through to Moscow—first, NATO had faced up to the tough issues of nuclear use; and second, NATO would not take provocative or hasty action.[68]

General Hans Steyning von Sandrart, Commander of NATO Central Front, elaborated: "We had one great advantage. . . . Despite all its knowledge of NATO, the Soviet General Staff could never be certain of the exact circumstances in which we would 'go nuclear' for the simple reason that the members of NATO themselves did not know."[69] The convenient official formulation was to say that NATO would use TNWs "as late as possible, but as early as necessary."[70] This was deterrence as much by default as design.[71]

Creation of the NATO Nuclear Planning Group.

The Nuclear Planning Group (NPG) grew out of the McNamara Special Committee on Nuclear Consultation in 1965-56.[72] Its major prospective advantage was Soviet acquiescence. The Soviet Union had indicated that, unlike its strenuous objections to Germany's membership in the MLF, Moscow would not object to Germany's accessing nuclear decisionmaking through the NPG, and would therefore not use this issue to block negotiations on the Nuclear Non-

Proliferation Treaty (NPT) then being drafted.[73] The NPG's charter was initially confined to planning, but it was to become the main generator of NATO's common nuclear deterrence culture.

The NPG oversaw the development of NATO nuclear-sharing arrangements, which were initially secret and remained so during the negotiation of the NPT, which was completed in 1968. Under NATO's nuclear-sharing arrangement, the nuclear weapons that the United States provides to allies remain under U.S. ownership, secured in peacetime by U.S. special weapons custodial forces (numbering at their maximum 10,000 to 25,000 troops) until, in war or extreme crisis, a presidential order passes their command to the relevant NATO commanders and the necessary operating codes are given to allies.[74]

Historically, the shared nuclear weapon delivery systems covered most forms of U.S. TNWs, including very large numbers of tactical bombs and U.S. 155 milimeter (mm) nuclear artillery rounds. Surface-to-surface missiles such as Corporal, Sergeant, Honest John, and Lance were widely shared. Greece, Italy, Turkey, Belgian, Dutch, and Greek forces also operated nuclear-tipped Nike-Hercules missiles. Canada had both Bomarc nuclear-armed anti-aircraft missiles and the AIR-2 Genie nuclear-armed air-to-air missile. The UK, although a nuclear power in its own right, used U.S. surface-to-surface missiles and nuclear artillery until 1992. Since all NATO states are NPT members, NATO nuclear-sharing arrangements involve giving conditional access to nuclear weapons to countries that have accepted the official legal status of Non-Nuclear Weapons States (NNWS) under the NPT (i.e., all NATO members except Britain, France, and the United States). The nonaligned movement and various arms control groups argue that this violates Articles I and II of the NPT and have applied diplomatic and legal pressure to terminate these agreements.[75] NATO remains adamant that nuclear-sharing was legally "grandfathered" in the drafting of the NPT. Its position is that control of the nuclear weapons would not be transferred to the NATO NNWS until an actual conflict occurred, at which point the NPT is no longer a constraint, and that nuclear-sharing is a valuable barrier to nuclear weapons proliferation in behalf of which pressures might otherwise build up within the industrially advanced member states of the Alliance.[76]

IV. 1968-1983. TNWS DURING DÉTENTE AND NATO-SOVIET WEAPONS MANEUVERING AS PRELUDE TO THE SOVIET COLLAPSE

Improving political relations between NATO and the Warsaw Pact generally raised European public skepticism about the strategy of nuclear deterrence, of which TNWs were the most concrete, local, and targetable symbols. The peace movement, which had existed since the 1950s, became an increasingly important factor for NATO governments to consider. The activists developed and promulgated a critique claiming that the superpowers had "overdosed" on deterrence, which had in turn "poisoned their relationship. . . . [Yet] they interpreted the tensions and crises that followed as evidence of the need for even more deterrence. . . . The strategy of deterrence was self-defeating; it provoked the kind of behaviour it was designed to prevent."[77] From this perspective, nuclear-dependent flexible response was almost as objectionable as massive retaliation. Another implication of improved East-West relations for TNWs was the new promise and possibility of arms control in Europe. Bloc-to-bloc Mutual and Balanced Force Reductions (MBFR) negotiations to reduce conventional military forces in Central Europe to equal but significantly lower levels began in Vienna in October 1973. Despite being hailed by West Germany leader Willi Brandt as "a proving ground for détente,"[78] the talks were stultified by numerous disagreements, especially over actual numbers. No substantive progress was made, although the process itself, despite its protracted frustrations, was judged by many to have been worthwhile in facilitating strategic dialogue between East and West and laying some of the ground for the subsequent and more successful Conventional Armed Forces in Europe (CFE) Treaty.

To break the deadlock, NATO made an offer, Option 3, in December 1975 as a sweetener to its earlier proposals, offering to withdraw 1,000 nuclear warheads, 54 F-4 nuclear-capable aircraft, and 36 Pershing short-range ballistic missile launchers in exchange for withdrawals of Soviet armored forces. This offer achieved no greater success than any other proposal within the MBFR process, which was formally terminated in 1989. However, it was the first suggestion that NATO could envisage its TNWs becoming counters to be thrown into a reciprocal process intended to reduce military numbers and suspicions on both sides. It also indicated that the NATO stockpile was large enough to accommodate large reductions without significant military risk.

Why Did NATO Keep So Many TNWs For So Long?

The U.S. stockpile size was maintained within the 7,000 to 8,000 range during most of the 1970s.[79] Critics like Richard Rhodes see this as simply a failure of strategic imagination in the long stalemate of the Cold War because, once the massive U.S. nuclear weapons production complex had been built, U.S. nuclear weapons became relatively cheap, eventually dropping in price to $250,000, "less than a fighter bomber, less than a missile, less than a patrol boat, less than a tank."[80] In September 1967, McNamara, soon after his Vietnam-induced retirement as Defense Secretary, also denounced the "mad momentum" of nuclear weaponry: "If something works . . . there are pressures from all directions to acquire those weapons out of all proportion to the prudent level required."[81]

By 1983, studies by the RAND Corporation concluded,

> One thing is certain: the present stockpile is primarily a legacy of the weapon systems and warheads accumulated in the largely haphazard manner in the 1950s and 1960s and while the result may not be incompatible with the requirements of flexible response, it has not been tailored to meet the specific needs of the strategy.[82]

Incremental TNW additions seemed to add to security, if only by dissuading the other side from expecting that it could achieve any decisive advantage through a nuclear buildup. The TNW component of the correlation of forces remained stable, even if at constantly higher levels, but this meant that the numbers grew because NATO and the Warsaw Pact each had to anticipate a huge immediate nuclear counterforce duel, in which nuclear assets and command systems throughout Europe would be targeted by conventional air attack and TNWs. The huge number of nuclear assets, and the unthinkable scale of the consequent destruction if they were ever used, became in itself a source of reassurance. TNWs were also an emblem of U.S. commitment:

> The stockpile size for land-based weapons was pegged at "around 7,000 warheads" by McNamara in 1966 and "was maintained within the 7,000 to 8,000 range by policies of retirement and progressive replacement during most of the 1970s" since the stockpile level itself became a political symbol of American coupling and the political sign of multilateral participation in nuclear use planning and decision-making, the most important of Alliance functions....Regardless of NATO's military requirements, the nuclear weapons stockpile could not be reduced without appearing to diminish political commitment to the Alliance.[83]

Development of a Shared NATO Nuclear Culture.

The NPG with its subordinate committee, the High Level Group (HLG), became an instrument which the United States used to persuade Europeans of the imperatives of nuclear strategy and which Europeans used to persuade the Americans to give them more information regarding the deployment and contemplated use of these weapons on their own territory. NATO's notorious security leakiness made American caution understandable, but it had originally applied even to bilateral contacts at the highest level. When de Gaulle returned to power in 1958, the French President asked the SACEUR whether U.S. forces in

France were equipped with nuclear weapons. When Norstad replied that to his very great regret, he could not answer, de Gaulle responded icily, "That is the last time . . . a responsible French leader will allow such an answer to be made."[84] His humiliation and anger contributed to his 1966 decision to turn all foreign forces out of France.[85] In 1962, the West Germans did not even know how many U.S. nuclear weapons were deployed on their soil, nor at the end of the year, when atomic demolition munitions (ADMs) were furnished to Europe, especially on the Central Front, were the Germans told what the U.S. plans were for these ground-burst weapons with their extremely high fallout and contamination potential.[86]

Thanks to necessary American tolerance of "an impressive degree of anti-hegemonic behavior on the part of its Allies,"[87] this situation changed markedly over the next years. U.S. nuclear deployments in peacetime were by 1987 "governed by a series of closely held bilateral agreements, known as Programs of Co-Operation," between the United States and individual Allied governments:

> At the minimum . . . the agreements cover 3 areas: a general statement on the exchange of classified information about weapons; an agreement specifying the numbers and types of warheads that the US will be earmarking for the Allies forces; and the stockpile agreement covering storage for national use in any other storage on national soil for other NATO forces. All are subject to scrutiny by the US Congress. In 1967, following Flexible Response and French withdrawal, the US agreed to provide an annual deployment report to each host country. The Defense Minister of each country is thus officially aware of the type, quantity, yield, location, and appropriate and projected delivery systems for weapons stored in national territory . . . also general control and security procedures at each site.[88]

Provisional Political Guidelines (PPGs) for the Initial Defensive.

Tactical Use of Nuclear Weapons. Preliminary Anglo-German operational studies presented in the Healey-Schröder Report to the NPG in May 1969 considered draft guidelines for employment of TNWs within the flexible response framework. The report concluded that most existing alliance doctrine on TNWs was politically unacceptable and militarily unsound, that it would not be possible for NATO to gain the military advantage by using them, and that their initial use should therefore be essentially political, that is, to re-create a state of deterrence by convincing the adversary of the risks of continued military action. The report essentially saw NATO TNWs as having a political signaling function rather than being designed to assure a battlefield victory. Compromise formulations accepting this were agreed to at the NPG meeting in Washington in September 1969. But there was no agreement about follow-on use.[89]

Nuclear Softening. Further NATO studies followed, leading to slow amendments of Alliance doctrine as assisted by the further development of conventional alternatives to nuclear weapons use. By about 1973, "due above all to German pleading," NATO gave up the option of inflicting ground bursts on NATO territory, thus contributing to the elimination of ADMs in the early 1980s. The maximum yield of weapons that might be used above NATO territory was limited to 10 kiloton (kt). In 1974 SACEUR Goodpaster was instructed that all NATO nuclear targets should be military, with their selection "based on the twin criteria of achieving essential military objectives while minimizing civilian casualties and collateral damage."[90] This slowly changing deterrence ethos was a politically irreversible move away from the stern nuclear war-fighting assumptions of the 1950s.

Hidden Consequences of Nuclear Disillusion within the Warsaw Pact. There was no equivalent ferment within the Warsaw Pact, where all nuclear weapons were retained under the direct control of KGB detachments, and where the nearest to an alliance debate was a single Czechoslovak request in 1983 for an unprecedented Warsaw Pact training schedule devoted to an actual Warsaw Pact defense—before practicing the inevitable counteroffensive in Exercise Shield 84.[91] But there were slow, intangible, and sometimes covert consequences for planning exchanges of weapons as fateful as TNWs in such an atmosphere. The intensely risky offensive orientation which Russian strategies imposed led to a demotivated and fatalistic view among minor Warsaw Pact allies, aware of the inevitable scale of losses in the scenarios for which they trained. One Polish officer in Warsaw Pact headquarters, Colonel Ryszard Kuklinski, became a defector-in-place (later called "the First Polish Officer in NATO") partly because of his concern over the ruthless and entirely offensive nature of Warsaw Pact plans, which would unhesitatingly sacrifice Polish blood on "a Red Altar." NATO's conventional inferiority would force it to respond to a Warsaw Pact invasion with TNWs, which would leave Poland a wasteland.[92] To avert that future, he became an immensely valuable early western intelligence source on the strategy of deep operations which the Soviets began planning from the late 1970s to mid-1980s. His revelations, along with those provided by the equally disillusioned Russian General Dmitri Polyakov, were crucial to NATO's early recognition of and answer to that strategy.[93]

Mini-Nukes and Enhanced Radiation Weapons: The Strengthening Veto of Public Opinion.

The NATO TNW stockpile had become an established, though largely classified, part of the strategic landscape by 1968. It changed little, except by unilateral reductions, until 1983. Political attention and agitation focused instead on proposed new technical developments. The first such development was the possible introduction of "suppressed radiation weapons," that is, small "clean" warheads which could destroy hard targets while reducing collateral fall-out damage. The largely hypothetical prospect of U.S. development and introduction of "mini-nukes" was discussed at a NATO conference, then leaked and denounced in 1973 as threatening to blur the boundary between conventional and nuclear weapons. This resulted in a mini furor indicating an increased public sensitivity to newly enhanced tactical nuclear warfighting capabilities.[94]

It further complicated President Jimmy Carter's abortive attempt 4 years later to introduce TNW Enhanced Radiation Weapons (ERW). These would have replaced existing nuclear rounds in artillery shells and were designed to offset the Warsaw Pact's armored advantage by eliminating tank crews through instant doses of radiation, while causing less collateral damage than other nuclear devices. The Germans, at great political cost, [95] had given qualified support to their deployment, but the story was prematurely leaked in Washington, and ERW were relabeled as the "Neutron Bomb," and denounced as "the ultimate capitalist weapon" that would kill people but leave buildings standing. The neutron bomb dispute further incited and strengthened Europe's antinuclear movement through widespread protests, openly supported by the Soviet government and clandestinely backed by KGB "active measures," such as the tacit financing of peace movements and the provision of disinformation to the Western news media. President Carter capitulated to multiple pressures and delayed the ERW program indefinitely, though secretly ordering production of components that could be assembled in 48 hours and airlifted to Europe.[96] The conclusion drawn from this affair by one scholar was that determined leadership within NATO (usually the United States) is indispensable for making such decisions since the "modernization of nuclear weapons in Europe cannot be managed by a pluralist approach to decision making."[97]

TNWs and the Euromissile Crisis, 1977-1987. The ERW debacle raised still further the political costs of any NATO nuclear modernization. The Intermediate Nuclear Forces (INF) crisis is a separate and complex subject, but had important interactions with TNWs. The anxieties over the multiple independently targetable reentry vehicled (MIRV) Soviet SS-20s, capable of striking anywhere in Europe from within the Soviet Union, were very much connected with the risk that the immediate escalatory response option represented by SS-20s would negate NATO use of TNWs, then still its main deterrent capability against a Warsaw Pact attack. This prospect would create not only a military weakness but resultant possibilities of intimidation during periods of tension short of war. The crisis that followed focused all of NATO's political attention as the Soviets continued to deploy SS-20s while NATO committed itself to a dual-track decision to deploy new, intermediate-range systems while attempting to negotiate reductions with Moscow, despite intense political opposition.

In general, NATO calculations of the strategic balance in Europe were carried out largely as part of a military "net assessment" process. The judgments of the Soviet leadership involved more complex correlation of forces analysis based on the psychological and political impacts of nuclear deployments. By the 1970s, NATO allies began to realize that the Soviets were not seeking a stable military balance to facilitate further détente, but instead were exploiting East West rapprochement as a means of undermining support among Western Alliance members for its defense policies, especially as to nuclear weapon types, holdings, and doctrine.[98] But while Soviet calculations were more sophisticated and multidimensional, their theories turned out to be inadequate empirical guides to achievable politico-military outcomes.

The politics of this so-called targets crisis brought the first significant change to the TNW stockpile, flowing from the 1979 NATO ministerial decision in Brussels, Belgium, to introduce two INF systems, the Pershing IIs and the Gryphon ground-launched cruise missiles (GLCMs), while simultaneously seeking an arms control agreement that would limit the overall INF category. Equivalent numbers of U.S. Pershing 1As and Nike Hercules were withdrawn, together with 1,000 surplus U.S. Honest John warheads, decreasing the NATO nuclear stockpile to around 6,000, certainly a less politically significant number.[99]

The use of TNWs as symbols of good faith, the lubricating small change of nuclear arms control, was repeated in Montebello in October 1983, when NATO Ministers reaffirmed their determination to persist with the dual-track decision, despite Soviet obduracy in the Geneva talks, which would close in the next month. This time NATO opted to give up 1,400 TNWs, although it decided that the remaining short-range systems, as well as conventional forces, should be modernized. The Soviet Union and the Warsaw Pact would soon collapse, ending the Cold War, so this decision was never carried out.

NATO-Soviet Doctrinal Jousting. The long-term background process which made it militarily acceptable to withdraw so many TNFs was NATO's eventual improvement of its conventional capabilities that, spurred by Warsaw Pact equipment improvements and doctrinal innovations, resulted from Western technical and, especially American, electronic advantages. While continuing to expand their theater nuclear capabilities, the Soviet General Staff, led by Marshal Nikolai Ogarkov, seems to have concluded in the late 1970s that their most effective option against NATO would be conventional but extremely rapid deep operations conducted, after massive aerial surprise attacks, by operational maneuver groups. A tactical nuclear exchange could only slow this offensive down, as well as carrying the obvious risk of total nuclear war. As Catherine Kelleher described the Soviet perspective, "Ogarkov knew that many in NATO doubted that their political leaders would agree quickly to use nuclear weapons."[100] The Soviets would fight and pace "the war in such a way as to delay NATO taking the decision to use nuclear weapons until it was too late for them to be able to influence the outcome of the war."[101] Ogarkov advertised the forces developed for this strategy as part of the military propaganda surrounding Exercise *Zapad* 1981, by which time of course NATO had to take account of the additional inhibitive effect of the SS-20s discussed earlier.

NATO sought to frustrate that Soviet strategic vision, whose operational details had been fully transmitted to the Alliance by Kuklinski and Polyakov by 1981. The subsequent NATO revolution in military affairs, implemented through programs such as the Conventional Defense Improvement Initiative (CDI) and the Conceptual Military Framework (CMF), involved the introduction of widespread precision-guided and "assault breaker" bomblet munitions coordinated in a "reconnaissance strike complex." The U.S. AirLand Battle concept adopted in 1981 involved integrated conventional and nuclear air attacks on second and third echelon targets. High-technology and improved tactical concepts culminated in NATO's non-nuclear Follow-On Forces Attack (FOFA) concept adopted in 1985 – "an intellectual framework in which the latest American technology could be adapted to the realities of European battlefield."[102] FOFA's expected effectiveness very largely negated the Soviet conventional option, thus introducing the necessity for agonizing NATO ministerial decisions on when and whether to employ TNWs. The newly arrived enhancements of NATO forces were deliberately shown off to Warsaw Pact observers in Exercises *Bold Sparrow* and *Certain Strike* in 1987.[103] The case for large TNW numbers also diminished as a result.

TNWs and the Able Archer Scare of 1983.

In notable contrast to the preceding years of détente, President Ronald Reagan's election in 1980, his fierce anti-Communism, and the huge military build-up that he initiated, led to sharply increased tensions with the Soviet Union, which some observers at the time labeled the Second Cold War. At the height of the Euromissile crisis, the Soviet leadership began to fear a surprise U.S. nuclear attack (code-named Ryan) to be concealed by the regular annual NATO November command post exercise, Able Archer. Key Warsaw Pact units went on heightened alert as the exercise approached. NATO was unaware of these fears until informed later by the British spy, Oleg Gordievsky, a senior KGB officer in London. The seriousness of the incident remains unclear, but it caused an unnerving shock within NATO over the unsuspected risk of inadvertent war.

What we have since learned, however, is that Soviet military intelligence was not concerned. Soviet and East German agents regularly drove round Western Europe looking for warning indicators. Consequently, as Ogarkov's deputy explained in later interviews:

> We had confidence in our knowledge of when NATO was preparing to launch nuclear weapons. We would detect mating of warheads to missiles and uploading of nuclear bombs and artillery. We listened to the hourly circuit verification signal and believed we would recognize a release order.[104]

In this case, any crisis based upon fears of surprise attack using aircraft and short-flight-time missiles within Europe would have been ill-founded. The size of the NATO TNW infrastructure (estimated in the later 1980s at around 100 nuclear storage sites in at least seven European countries[105]) and its openness to Warsaw Pact espionage made it impossible to conceal large-scale attack preparations, and so represented in fact an unavoidably stabilizing and confidence-building factor.

Filling in the Blanks: NATO's General Political Guidelines, 1986. During the decade after the PPGs, intra-Alliance differences had made it impossible to achieve consensus on "follow-on use." The Glenneagles meeting of the NPG in October 1986 finally approved the

General Political Guidelines (GPGs), which stated that initial use of nuclear weapons would occur mainly on the territory of the aggressor, viz., the Soviet Union. The principal purpose would be to signal NATO resolve to escalate to the strategic level if necessary. The GPGs shifted the weight of targeting options from the battlefield itself toward deep strikes on Warsaw Pact territory, thus abandoning any notion of demonstrative use as mentioned in the PPGs. It was now accepted that the initial signal had to be militarily effective. But the NATO allies did not resolve the difference between the persistent U.S. preference for battlefield use of TNWs to achieve well-defined military objectives while limiting escalation, on one hand, and the West German insistence on deep strikes precisely to emphasize the risks of escalation. The GPGs were described as shifting further towards signaling and away from warfighting, but they covered every contingency and ruled out none.[106] However, within a very few years these disputes over the development of flexible response would be obsolete.

TNWs in Korea. On the Korean Peninsula, the worldwide reduction of U.S. nuclear weapons was especially complicated. The serious direct threat from reckless DPRK aggression, as well as China's military buildup, promoted interest on the part of U.S. allies in achieving their own independent nuclear weapons capability, which Washington opposed.

TNWs could be used as a signal and a reminder of deterrent realities. In 1975, when DPRK leader Kim Il Sung appeared to be emboldened by the U.S. weakness apparently demonstrated by the fall of Saigon, U.S. Defense Secretary James Schlesinger decided that "we had to stop him in his tracks. I broke a long-established practice and declared we had nuclear weapons in South Korea and would use them if necessary."[107]

However, concerned by the post-Vietnam perception of U.S. unreliability, the rapidly industrializing ROK is understood to have examined the possibility of acquiring its own nuclear weapons in the early 1970s after Richard Nixon withdrew 24,000 U.S. troops from South Korea and recognized the People's Republic of China (PRC). (Discovery of this ROK interest also seems to have strengthened Kim Il Sung's determination to achieve a DPRK nuclear capability.[108]) But ROK President Park Chung Hee was dissuaded by Kissinger's direct threat to withdraw U.S. forces completely and terminate the ROK-U.S. alliance if South Korea pursued its own nuclear weapons. South Korea consequently acceded to the NPT in April 1975 and signed a full-scope safeguards agreement with the International Atomic Energy Agency later that year. Concerns over the terms of the ROK-U.S. alliance were soon revived when President Carter subsequently announced a nearly complete withdrawal of TNWs (and troops) from South Korea in 1977. This announced withdrawal was reversed by 1978, largely because South Korea could plausibly threaten to resume its own nuclear weapons program.

V. 1987-1990. TNWS AND THE WARSAW PACT COLLAPSE: THE AFTERMATH

Mikhail Gorbachev's arrival as General Secretary unfroze the U.S.-Soviet arms control talks, leading to the signing of the INF agreement in December 1987. This treaty banned all U.S. and Soviet ground-based ballistic and cruise missiles globally with ranges of 500-5,500 km. The Federal Republic of Germany (FRG) also gave up its 72 Pershing 1 missiles. The agreement was denounced by retired SACEUR Bernard Rogers as removing NATO's qualitative deterrent edge and so helping the USSR "to intimidate, coerce, blackmail, and neutralize Western Europe without calling troops out of barracks." He therefore called — and in this was representative of wider opinion — for the rapid implementation of the second half of the 1983 Montebello Accords, i.e., the modernization of short-range nuclear forces (SRNF). Those plans envisaged that some older systems like artillery munitions and Lance would be withdrawn, but a number of possible new TNW systems under development would be introduced, including better nuclear artillery shells with increased range, the Follow On To Lance (FOTL), an improved surface-to-surface missile which could be fired from existing NATO Multiple-launch rocket systems, and a supersonic Tomahawk anti-ship air-to-surface missile (TASM) to improve the penetrability of tactical aircraft (some 389 had been planned to be placed in vaults in European airfields).[109]

Political opposition made this proposed modernization impossible. Anti-nuclear campaigners discovered NATO plans more rapidly than at previous TNW decision points and were able to mount effective opposition in the news media, denouncing the proposed package as "like trading in 2 pistols for an assault rifle and calling it arms reductions." The plans needed to be resisted particularly strongly at that historical moment, according to the antinuclear campaigners, because "by keeping alive the traditional NATO doctrine of flexible response, the TASM could slow the process of change in Europe."[110] The Cold War was not yet conclusively over, and after visiting Europe, the new U.S. Secretary of State, James Baker, had concluded that "modernization [of SNF] would indeed show the Alliance's resolve, yet it would simultaneously create a public and, above all, nuclear symbol that the Kremlin could use with Western European people against their governments."[111] German political resistance was also predictably adamant, and the modernization never occurred.

Negotiations in Vienna, Austria, began to move toward signing of the CFE Treaty, aimed at introducing transparency and confidence-building measures, and eliminating many of the most threatening offensive combat assets. The CFE (signed in November 1990) greatly reduced future dangers of surprise conventional attack. In the summer of 1990, the political necessities of securing German reunification involved promises to Mikhail Gorbachev to conduct a comprehensive strategy review, and as the NATO summit approached, a package of measures which would signal reduced nuclear reliance within the Alliance (while still resisting No First Use), and also signal a general move away from early nuclear use. NATO nuclear weapons would "truly become weapons of last resort." This wording was initially challenged by French President Francois Mitterrand and British Prime Minister Margaret Thatcher, but, after intense debate at the NATO heads of government meeting in London on July 5, 1990, the wording was preserved. U.S. proposals to eliminate all nuclear artillery shells from Europe were accepted, and it was agreed that there would be reviews to consider new strategic principles replacing forward defense and flexible response. The London Communiqué, according to Michael Wheeler, represented the end of Cold War nuclear strategy.[112]

VI. 1991- 2012. THE RUSSIAN PREPONDERANCE IN TNWS: POLITICAL STASIS

In 1991 and 1992, Presidents George H. W. Bush and Boris Yeltsin both announced unilateral though unverified TNW reductions. These parallel reductions, which came to be known as the Presidential Nuclear Initiatives, were seen as preludes to negotiations aimed at elimination of TNWs after the Cold War ended. Those negotiations never occurred, and would have posed enormous verification problems even if they had. Soon after Soviet forces withdrew to Russia with all their nuclear weapons, NATO removed most of its remaining TNWs, leaving only "several hundred" B-61 gravity bombs. The United States proceeded to eliminate nuclear artillery and short-range surface-to-surface nuclear missiles from its global stockpile. (It has removed all TNWs from the ROK). The 2010 *Nuclear Posture Review* explicitly sought to reduce the salience of U.S. nuclear weapons, and President Barack Obama is a vigorous supporter of Global Zero.

For various reasons the Russian Federation has not found it expedient to make comparable TNW reductions.[113] The resultant TNW asymmetry in Moscow's favor is now long established and probably impossible to eliminate in the near term, particularly because, in view of its shrunken military capabilities, the Russian Federation has abandoned the Soviet Union's NOFUN posture. Its military doctrine seems to rely significantly upon the deterrent provided, especially at sea, by its remaining TNWs, which may number in the low thousands. In its 1991 *Strategic Concept*, NATO gave up forward defense as a defining principle and flexible response as a nuclear strategy. Alliance leaders have repeatedly reemphasized that NATO regards all nuclear weapons as truly weapons of last resort, though always adding that NATO will remain a nuclear Alliance as long as nuclear weapons exist. NATO has sought to treat Russia as a partner rather than a potential antagonist, but the Russian government has found NATO membership enlargement into former Warsaw Pact countries and the former Soviet republics threatening, and insists on the continuing necessity for deterrence as a basis of the relationship. In such ambiguous political circumstances, the role of NATO TNWs cannot be expected to clarify.

CONCLUSION: THE CONTESTED AND CONTRADICTORY SIGNIFICANCE OF NATO TNWS IN 2012

The foregoing examination of the historical background of TNWs reveals the complexities underlying current disputes over NATO's nuclear posture. Arguments for and against continued deployment of TNWs mostly involve crosscutting themes and disagreements recurrent in the historical record.

The present combination of U.S. B-61 bombs and dual-capable aircraft (DCA) seems to represent:

- Devices to signal commitment during tension, which appear to have been stabilizing in some past crises but which could be hard to use in the future, since "*available evidence does not indicate that consultation will be smooth or timely.*"[114] The difficulties in obtaining consensus within NATO on nuclear weapons can be expected to increase now that the NATO countries in the frontline of potential military threats have become fewer and smaller, while the fear of entanglement is growing stronger than fear of abandonment among the now geopolitically sheltered allies.

- Weapons arrangements that do not lend themselves to permanent territorial occupation by an attacking force and imposition of an alien regime. Thus those arrangements do not pose such a degree of risk that a side would be willing to accept horrendous casualties and destruction in order to avoid that risk.

- Affirmative symbols of moral burden-sharing based on common values—the *schiksalsgemein-schaft*,[115] or shared community of fate—within the transatlantic relationship, this at a time when the United States is announcing its shift of strategic attention to the Pacific (but Alliance solidarity may be further weakened by the predictable intra-allied disputes which have been seen to occur whenever TNW issues become prominent).

- Devices for sharing nuclear functions and responsibilities, but with countries that find the prospect of an injection of what Thomas Schelling called "pure violence,"[116] which is the distinctive, irreducible, strategic function of nuclear weapons, increasingly distasteful within their national strategic cultures. So, at worst, Alliance nuclear-sharing may become less the proudly-displayed wedding ring of a happy couple than the suspiciously indiscernible band of gold of an increasingly ill-matched NATO marriage.

- A class of weapons that was introduced largely because of the extreme cost effectiveness of its firepower, and the powerful deterrence it was judged to generate (but which may now disappear from Europe because the costs of making minor aircraft modifications to make them nuclear-capable will be financially vetoed by parliaments).

- Bargaining chips for future comprehensive arms control talks, which NATO has repeatedly sought (but which the Russians have repeatedly insisted could include TNWs only if all U.S. TNWs were first withdrawn from Europe).

- A strategically high-visibility, but politically high-maintenance weapons category that is internationally and—in many countries domestically—controversial (and which might therefore detract from the urgency of NATO improvements in more usable conventional capabilities). TNWs will not be indefinitely sustainable without governmental willingness to modernize DCAs in the face of parliamentary opposition. The abandonment of these weapons might seem to some a tempting reassurance strategy to improve Alliance or bilateral national relationships with Russia.

- Important emblems of reassurance for new East European members of NATO, which probably fear, but do not publicly speak of, abandonment in crisis from European allies and resent any move which might appear to reduce U.S. defense commitments (yet the history of NATO expansion means that neither American nor U.S.-supplied Alliance TNWs are located in these countries, and could not be moved there without provoking a major dispute with Russia).

- Symbols of the continuing U.S. nuclear commitment to its NATO partners[117] (any changes in nuclear posture theoretically relevant only to those military crises serious enough to make nuclear use imaginable — albeit hypothetical and unlikely — would rapidly feed back into current political atmospherics within the Alliance and the perceptions of neighbors).

- A means of deterring historically novel potential threats from a reckless nuclear Iran and an unstable, proliferation-prone Middle East (but this anxiety has not entered official public discourse; Turkey, which would be most closely affected by it, prefers to avoid any official mention of it; many operationally plausible U.S. strategic nuclear assets exist to offset it; and NATO-wide ballistic missile defense is becoming at least the publicly preferred Alliance response).

ENDNOTES - CHAPTER 2

1. This has been appreciated for a long time: the extract is from the Healy/Schroeder Report presented to the NATO Nuclear Planning Group (NPG) in May 1969 and incorporated into the NATO Provisional Political Guidelines (PPGs) for the Initial Defensive Tactical Use of Nuclear Weapons agreed later that year. Christoph Bluth, *Britain, Germany and Western Nuclear Strategy*, Oxford, UK: Clarendon Press, 1995, p. 188.

2. Author's own definition.

3. "Tactical Nuclear Weapons," *Encyclopedia of the Cold War,* Ruud Van Dijk, ed., London, UK: Routledge, 2008.

4. Lawrence Freedman,*The Evolution of Nuclear Strategy*: Basingstoke, UK, and New York: Palgrave Macmillan, 2003, pp. 62-66.

5. "The position we have reached is one where stability depends on something that is more the antithesis of strategy than its apotheosis on threats that things will get out of hand, that we might act irrationally, that possibly through an inadvertence we could set in motion a process which in its development and conclusion would be beyond human control and comprehension." *Ibid.*, p. 458.

6. Gordon S. Barras, *The Great Cold War: A Journey through a Wilderness of Mirrors*, Stanford, CA: Stanford University Press, 2009, pp. 63-64. Barras was an intelligence insider throughout much of the Cold War. His account is often based on personal knowledge of events and detailed interviews with participants.

7. Michael O. Wheeler, "NATO Nuclear Strategy, 1949-90," Gustave Schmidt, ed., *A History of NATO the First 50 Years*, Vol. 3, Basingstoke, UK, and New York: Palgrave, 2001, p. 122.

8. But the estimates of Russian military power were almost certainly very seriously exaggerated. See the impressive list of references compiled by Vojtech Mastny, "Imagining War in Europe," in Vojtech Mastny, Sven G. Holtsmark, and Andreas Wenger, eds., *War Plans and Alliances in the Cold War: Threat Perceptions in the East and West*, London, UK, and New York: Routledge, 2006, p. 16, n. 1.

9. Stephen E. Miller, "The Utility of Nuclear Weapons and the Strategy of No First Use," Pugwash Conferences on Science and World Affairs, 2002.

10. "It is essential to our policy that we shall have to use nukes in the end; all else fails to save Berlin and it is fundamental that the Russians understand this fact." J. F. Kennedy to General Lucius Clay, October 8, 1961, quoted in Robert J. McMahon, "US National Security Policy, Eisenhower to Kennedy," in Melvin P. Leffler and Odd Arnie Wested, eds., *The Cambridge History of the Cold War*, Vol. 1: *Origins*, Cambridge, UK: Cambridge University Press, 2010, p. 309.

11. Raymond Aron, *On War: Atomic Weapons and Global Diplomacy*, London, UK: Secker and Warburg, 1958, p. 36.

12. And probably unknown to the French colonial authorities. See James J. Heaphey, *Legerdemain: The President's Secret Plan, the Bomb and What the French Never Knew*, New York: History Publishing Company, 2007.

13. "The weight of the fragmentary evidence [about Soviet strategy during the Stalin years] lends support to its defensive rather than offensive character. . . . The 1951 operational plan of the Polish Army [mentioned] only defensive operations. The same was true about contemporary Czechoslovak plans." Vojtech Mastny, "Imagining War in Europe," in Mastny, Holtsmark, and Wenger, eds., 2006, p. 16.

14. Based upon newly available archival documentation from Eastern Europe, "The Western strategy of nuclear deterrence . . . appears . . . irrelevant to deterring a major war that the enemy did not wish to launch in the first place." Mastny, "Introduction," Mastny, Holtsmark, and Wenger, 2006, p. 3.

15. McMahon, pp. 288-297.

16. Richard Rhodes, *Arsenals of Folly: The Making of the Nuclear Arms Race*, New York: Simon and Schuster, 2007, p. 79.

17. Charles S Maier, "The World Economy and the Cold War in the Middle of the 20th Century," in Leffler and Wested, eds., 2010, p. 64.

18. Wheeler, p. 126.

19. *Ibid.*, p. 127.

20. Freedman, p. 203.

21. Gordon S. Barrass, *The Great Cold War: A Journey Through the Hall of Mirrors*, Stanford, CA: Stanford Security Studies, Stanford University Press, 2009, p. 112.

22. *Ibid.*

23. Wheeler, p. 127.

24. Marc Trachtenberg, *A Constructed Peace: The Making of the European Settlement, 1945-1963*, Princeton, NJ: Princeton University Press, 1999, pp. 146-200, quoted in Beatrice Heuser, "Alliance of Democracies and Nuclear Deterrence," in Mastny, Holtsmark, and Wenger, eds., 2006, p. 25.

25. Heuser, 2006, p. 206.

26. Beatrice Heuser, "The Development of NATO's Nuclear Strategy," *Contemporary European History*, Vol. 4, No. 1, 1994, p. 45.

27. This analytical terminology was not used at the time but later developed by Glenn Snyder.

28. Walter Slocombe, "Extended Deterrence," *Washington Quarterly*, Vol. 7, No. 4, Fall 1984, p. 94.

29. In fact, the British Chiefs of Staff produced a paper as early as 1952 to persuade their American counterparts to rebalance Alliance strategy more economically on greater dependence on nuclear retaliation. It was not, initially, welcomed. Freedman, pp. 75-76.

30. Beatrice Heuser, *Nuclear Mentalities? Strategies and Beliefs in Britain and France and the FRG*, Basingstoke, UK: Macmillan Press, 1998, p. 99.

31. Bruno Tertrais, "The Trouble with No First Use," *Survival*, October-November, 2009, p. 23.

32. Heuser, 1998, pp. 180-205.

33. Bluth, p. 38.

34. *Ibid.*, pp. 18, 22.

35. *Ibid.*, p. 38.

36. *Ibid.*, p. 37.

37. *Ibid.*, pp. 301-305.

38. Heuser, 2006, p. 225.

39. Kjell Inge Bjerga and Kjetil Skogrand, "Securing Small State Interests," Mastny, Holtsmark, and Wenger, 2006, p. 233.

40. Jonathan Soborg Agger and Trine Engholm Michelsen, "How Strong Was the Weakest Link?" Mastny, Holtsmark, and Wenger, 2006, pp. 250-251.

41. Mastny, "Imagining War in Europe," Mastny, Holtsmark, and Wenger, 2006, pp. 19-25.

42. For a full discussion of this central concept in Marxist strategic analysis at its intellectual height, see Richard E. Porter "Correlation of Forces: Revolutionary Legacy," *Air University Review*, March-April 1977.

43. David Holloway, *The Soviet Union and the Arms Race*, New Haven, CT: Yale University Press, 1983, p. 57.

44. What former Soviet General Valentin V. Larionov retrospectively dubbed the "romantic" period of naive belief in the nuclear arms' capacity to "achieve any political or military objective, even the most extreme ones." Mastny, "Imagining War in Europe," in Mastny, Holtsmark, and Wenger, eds., 2006, p. 25.

45. Matthias Uhl, "Storming onto Paris," in Mastny, Holtsmark, and Wenger, 2006, p. 65.

46. *Ibid.*, pp. 52-58.

47. "One point is clear, however: at the peak of the second Berlin crisis, the military leadership of the Warsaw Pact believed that nuclear war could be fought, and, in fact, saw nuclear war as the key instrument of destroying the supposed enemy." *Ibid.*

48. General Sir Horatius Murray, Commander in Chief, Allied Forces, Northern Europe (CINCNORTH) 1958-61, quoted by Kjell Inge Bjerga and Kjetil Skogrand, in Mastny, Holtsmark, and Wenger, 2006, pp. 228-229.

49. Catherine McArdle Kelleher, "NATO Nuclear Operations" in Ashton B. Carter, John D. Steinbrenner, and Charles A. Zraket, eds., *Managing Nuclear Operations*, Washington, DC: The Brookings Institution, 1987, p. 460.

50. Martin Windrow, *The Last Valley*, London, UK: Cassell, 2005, pp. 568-569.

51. Robert J. McMahon, "US National Security Policy from Eisenhower to Kennedy," *The Cambridge History of the Cold War, Volume 1: Origins,* Cambridge, UK: Cambridge University Press, 2010, p. 297.

52. Peter Hayes, "Extended Nuclear Deterrence, Global Abolition, and Korea," *The Asia-Pacific Journal: Japan Focus*, December 2009, available at *japanfocus.org/-Peter-Hayes/3268*.

53. Derek Leebaert, *The 50-Year Wound: How America's Cold War Victory Shaped Our World,* Boston, MA: Little Brown Company, 2002, p. 270.

54. Barrass, p. 132.

55. Markus Wolf, *Man without a Face: The Autobiography of Communism's Great Spy Master,* pp. 96-97, quoted in Barrass, p. 133.

56. Barrass, p. 133.

57. Leebaert, p. 270.

58. Barrass, p. 143.

59. James G. Hirschberg, "The Cuban Missile Crisis," in Melvin P. Leffler and Odd Arnie Westad, eds., *The Cambridge History of the Cold War*, Vol. 2, *Crises and Détente,* Cambridge, UK: Cambridge University Press, 2010, p. 83.

60. *Peace Magazine,* January-March, 2003, p. 31; Hirschberg, in Leffler and Wested, eds., 2010, p. 84.

61. Presumably the 1.5 kt AIR-2 Genie, which was in service between 1958 and 1985. Three thousand were produced.

62. Lawrence Chang and Peter Kornbluth, *The Cuban Missile Crisis, 1962: A National Security Archive Documents Reader*, New York: New Press, 1998, p. 388.

63. Kristan Stoddart, *Losing an Empire and Finding a Role: Nuclear Weapons and International Security since 1945*, Vol. 3, *October 1964-June 1970*, Basingstoke, UK, and New York: Palgrave, forthcoming, pp. 107-108.

64. Richard Moore, "British Nuclear Weapons Overseas," *Bulletin of the Atomic Scientists*, January-February, 2001.

65. Freedman, pp. 89-113.

66. Richard Weitz, descriptive summary of the decisionmaking activity within NATO, in McMahon, pp. 303-305; and Wheeler, pp. 129-130.

67. Kelleher, p. 449.

68. As quoted in Barrass, p. 194.

69. General Hans Steyning von Sandrart, Commander of NATO Central Front, quoted in Barrass, p. 195.

70. Barrass, p. 195.

71. *Ibid.*

72. Wheeler, p. 131.

73. *Ibid.*

74. Kelleher, p. 455.

75. Statement by the Honorable Syed Hamid Albar, Minister of Foreign Affairs of Malaysia, on behalf of the group of non-aligned states parties to the treaty on the nonproliferation of nuclear weapons at the general debate of the 2005 review conference of the parties to treaty on the nonproliferation of nuclear weapons, New York, May 2, 2005, available from *www.un.org/en/conf/npt/2005/statements/npt02malaysia.pdf*.

76. Joseph F. Pilat and David S. Yost, "NATO and the Future of the Nuclear Non-Proliferation Treaty," Rome, Italy: NATO Defence College Research Paper, 2007, available from *www.ituassu. com.br/op_21_FULL.pdf.*

77. Richard Ned Lebow and Janice Gross Stein, *We All Lost the Cold War,* Princeton, NJ: Princeton University Press, 1995, p. 360.

78. John N. Hochelson, "MFR: West European and American Perspectives," in Wolfram Hanrieder, ed., *The United States and Western Europe,* Cambridge, MA: Winthrop Publishers, 1974. p. 257.

79. Kelleher, p. 449.

80. Richard Rhodes, *Arsenals of Folly: The Making of the Nuclear Arms Race,* New York: Simon and Schuster, 2007, p. 101.

81. Robert McNamara, speech in San Francisco, CA, September 18, 1967, quoted by Barrass, p. 162.

82. J. Michael Legge, *Theater Nuclear Weapons and the NATO Strategy of Flexible Response,* Santa Monica: RAND, 1983, p. 75.

83. Kelleher, pp. 448-449.

84. Charles de Gaulle, *Memoirs of Hope: Renewal 1958-1962,* 1971, pp. 257-258, quoted in Barrass, p. 158.

85. Heuser, 2006, p. 201.

86. *Ibid.,* p. 202.

87. *Ibid.,* p. 198.

88. Kelleher, pp. 452- 453.

89. Bluth, pp. 185-191; and Heuser, 2006, p. 210.

90. Ivo Daalder, "The Nature and Practice of Flexible Response," quoted in Heuser, 2006, p. 211.

91. Heuser, 2006, p. 212.

92. In November 2005, the Polish Foreign Minister Radek Sikorski displayed a Warsaw Pact exercise plan from 1977, titled "7 Days to the River Rhine" showing very large scale Soviet nuclear strikes against Western Europe (except Britain and France), following a posited NATO nuclear first strike. He emphasized that "the objective [was] to take over most of Western Europe. . . . This is crucial to educating the country on the way Poland was an unwilling ally of the USSR." He called it "a personally shattering experience" to see maps showing Soviet bloc commanders assuming that NATO tactical nuclear weapons would rain down along the Vistula to block reinforcements arriving from Russia. "About two million Polish civilians would have died in such a war, and the country would have been all but wiped off the face of the earth." It was scenarios like this, developed within a one-sidedly Soviet dominated military organization, which seem to have changed Kuklinski's loyalties and presumably had a wider emotional effect, percolating through the millions of conscripts who passed through the Polish Armed Forces and may have contributed to their perceived unreliability towards the end of the Cold War. Nicholas Watt, "Poland Risks Russia's Wrath with Soviet Nuclear Attack Map," *Guardian*, November 26, 2005.

93. Barrass, pp. 213-214.

94. Bluth, pp. 210-211.

95. *Ibid.*, p. 234.

96. Barrass, p. 216.

97. Sheri L. Wasserman, *The Neutron Bomb Controversy: A Study in Alliance Politics*, New York: Praeger, 1983, p. 134, quoted in Jeffrey A. Larsen, *The Future of U.S. Non-Strategic Nuclear Weapons and Implications for NATO: Drifting Toward the Foreseeable Future*, Rome, Italy: NATO Defence College, 2006.

98. Barrass, p. 193.

99. Kelleher, p. 449.

100. Corroborated by Catherine Kelleher: "Available evidence through exercises or historical experience does not suggest that wide political consultation will be smooth or timely. Some simulations have involved 3 days at a minimum to get a clear decision," Kelleher, 1987, p. 464.

101. Philip Petersen, "One of the leading experts on Soviet strategy in the Defense Intelligence Agency," quoted in Barrass, pp. 213-214.

102. Diego Ruiz Palmer, quoted in Barrass, p. 338.

103. *Ibid.*, pp. 339-341.

104. Barrass, pp. 297-301.

105. Kelleher, p. 453.

106. Bluth, pp. 261-262.

107. Barrass, p. 191.

108. "It seems probable that the DPRK's nuclear aspirations were triggered at least in part by the South Korean program," Joshua D. Pollack, *No Exit: North Korea Nuclear Weapons and International Security*, London, UK: International Institute for Strategic Studies, 2011, p. 80.

109. Dan Plesch of the British American Security Information Council, in the *Guardian*, London, UK, May 3, 1990.

110. *Ibid.*

111. Quoted in Wheeler, p. 137.

112. Wheeler, pp. 138-139.

113. Alexander Pikayev, "Tactical Nuclear Weapons," available from *icnnd.org/Documents/Pikayev_Tactical_Nuclear_Weapons. doc.*

114. Kelleher, p. 464.

115. The term "Westintegration" is associated with the Austrian Social Democrat thinker, Otto Bauer, especially in his *National Question and Social Democracy*, Vienna, Austria, 1907. It was applied in the German rhetorical struggles of the earlier Cold War to emphasize the moral and ideological significance of the Federal Republic's integration with the Atlantic Community.

116. Thomas C. Schelling, *Arms and Influence*, New Haven, CT: Yale University Press, 1966, p. 17.

117. See the discussion in George Perkovich: "Wedding Rings or Euros?" available from *carnegieendowment.org/files/nato_ nukes.pdf*.

CHAPTER 3

U.S. NUCLEAR WEAPONS POLICY AND POLICYMAKING: THE ASIAN EXPERIENCE

Elbridge A. Colby

The author would like to thank Brad Glosserman, Michael McDevitt, George Packard, and Richard Weitz for their incisive and helpful comments. Errors and omissions remain the author's own.

While U.S. nuclear weapons in Europe have long been an object of intense study and scrutiny, the role of U.S. nuclear weapons in Asia has received less attention. Yet U.S. nuclear weapons have played an important and at times central part in U.S. strategy and in the history of the East Asian region.[1] Largely driven by the nature of Washington's overarching strategy in the region and its perception of the military balance, the United States has relied on its nuclear forces to extend deterrence on behalf of its allies and partners and to assure those allies of the effectiveness of that deterrence. This has ensured that U.S. nuclear weapons have continued to play a continuing foundational role in Washington's strategic posture in the region since their introduction in the 1940s, even as their relevance has waxed and waned. As the strategic environment in East Asia grows more uncertain and potentially dangerous for the United States and its allies, it is likely that U.S. nuclear weapons will reemerge as a consideration for Washington and its allied capitals.

U.S. NUCLEAR WEAPONS POLICY IN EAST ASIA

The roots of U.S. nuclear weapons policy in East Asia lie in Washington's decisions of the early years of the Cold War to commit to the defense of select nations in maritime and littoral East Asia. Following a period of hesitancy after World War II regarding the extent of its global commitments, a series of perceived Communist aggressions culminating in the Communist victory in the Chinese Civil War and the North Korean invasion of South Korea in June 1950 persuaded the U.S. Government that the Communist bloc was mounting a coordinated global effort to undermine the "free nations," an effort that appeared to Washington to require a vigorous and comparably coordinated response on the part of the anti-Communist world. This shift catalyzed a major militarization of U.S. policy against Communist ambitions around the world, but especially in Europe and Asia. As a consequence, over the course of the late 1940s and 1950s, Washington committed to the defense of Japan, South Korea, Taiwan/Republic of China (ROC), Australia, New Zealand, the Philippines, and Thailand.[2] Other countries, such as South Vietnam and Singapore, received more implicit security guarantees. U.S. defense expenditures turned sharply upward as Washington dispatched hundreds of thousands of U.S. troops to repel the Communist invasion of South Korea, deployed naval forces to protect the Nationalists on Taiwan from invasion by the Chinese People's Liberation Army (PLA), and, more broadly, decided that an assertive, engaged military posture was necessary to protect U.S. interests in the Far East, even as Washington also committed to the defense of Europe through the North Atlantic Treaty Organization (NATO) and to parts of the Middle East through the Baghdad Pact.

The tremendous growth in requirements on U.S. military forces implicit in these new obligations coincided with the early stages of the nuclear revolution, and the combination of these factors led to the thoroughgoing integration of nuclear weapons into the U.S. military posture in Asia and throughout the world. Judging that the Communist bloc possessed a superiority in manpower and a steely willingness to suffer casualties to achieve its objectives, an assessment fortified by the Communists' prolongation of the war in Korea, the United States elected to employ its advantages in the size and technology of its nuclear arsenal to balance the mass and fervor of the Communist bloc. Beginning in 1953, the Dwight Eisenhower administration, in order to ensure the conservation of the United States as a free market society, further accentuated U.S. emphasis on nuclear weapons as it sought to reduce the burden of military expenditure and to avoid enmeshment in costly conventional ground wars like Korea.[3] These decisions were enabled by the fact that, beginning in the early 1950s, nuclear weapons were becoming plentifully available to the U.S. military.[4] In combination, these factors led to a dramatically increased reliance on nuclear forces by the United States, with the result that the United States deployed nuclear weapons on a large scale, integrating them into nearly every facet of U.S. military doctrine and with U.S. forces throughout the world.[5] The U.S. public posture and warfighting doctrine also reflected reliance on nuclear weapons, as throughout the Eisenhower administration the United States held to a policy of "massive retaliation," both threatening and planning to escalate to a massive nuclear strike against the Communist bloc in response to Communist aggression.[6]

In light of this policy, U.S. naval forces deployed with nuclear weapons aboard in the Western Pacific, and U.S. ground and air elements based nuclear weapons onshore in South Korea, the Philippines, and Taiwan, as well as components for nuclear weapons delivery in Japan.[7] U.S. ground, air, and naval forces all planned to employ nuclear weapons as a matter of course in the event of war with the Communist bloc. During the First Taiwan Straits Crisis in 1954 over the Nationalist-held islands off mainland China, U.S. Pacific Command's forces slated to defend Taiwan were prepared for the execution of a war plan involving the use of nuclear weapons. Indeed, to a large extent U.S. forces designated for the defense of Taiwan were incapable of conducting sustained non-nuclear operations. This situation remained true during the Second Taiwan Straits Crisis in 1958, when U.S. forces delayed even preparing a non-nuclear option for defense of Taiwan until several months into the crisis.[8] The same held true in Europe, where, if the Warsaw Pact blockaded or attacked Berlin, Germany, U.S. forces intended to attempt a conventional relief using a relatively small conventional force. If this failed, the United States planned to "resort to general war."[9]

This thoroughgoing reliance on nuclear weapons also played a major role in shaping the nature of the alliances and political relationships into which Washington entered and in determining the footprint of the U.S. military presence abroad. Because in the early Cold War era U.S. military power relied primarily upon nuclear weapons and especially upon the threatened implementation of a general nuclear attack, the requirements of nuclear command and control and delivery exercised a dominant influence on the formation of the U.S. global basing network in Asia and throughout the world.[10] Due to the range and other technical limitations of the U.S. military systems of the era, U.S. bases were constructed around the world as necessary to support the execution of the U.S. nuclear war plan against the Soviet Union and China. U.S. bombers, for instance, required forward bases from which to stage or refuel, or to recover to in the wake of a strike; similar range constraints dictated the need for deployment of U.S. missiles and basing of U.S. vessels nearer to the Soviet Union and China than U.S. territory could provide.[11]

However, in the 1960s, this policy of overweening reliance on nuclear weapons began to change. The "massive retaliation" doctrine's threat to resort to nuclear weapons early and inflexibly in response to a whole range of provocations always seemed somewhat suspect at the lower level of escalation. But the looming advent of an assured Soviet strategic-range nuclear capability and increasing attention to the difficulties of controlling escalation in a nuclear war began to make such heavy reliance on nuclear weapons seem unconscionably dangerous and decreasingly credible during the later 1950s and 1960s, and a resort to massive retaliation seem potentially suicidal. As a result, calls grew louder to focus more on the strengthening of non-nuclear forces, especially in light of the relative neglect such forces had suffered during the 1950s.[12]

With the entry of the John Kennedy administration to office in 1961, this shift away from nuclear weapons became U.S. policy. U.S. strategy in all theaters therefore began a gradual transition from declared reliance on nuclear weapons towards emphasis on non-nuclear forces, though nuclear forces remained central in U.S.

strategy throughout the Cold War, especially in areas where the United States and its allies perceived themselves as weaker than their Communist adversaries. Indeed, due to the nature of the strategic balance in Asia and the character of the threat in the region, the shift away from reliance on nuclear forces progressed more rapidly and completely in Asia than in Europe.

One reason for this swifter and fuller shift was that in Asia, unlike Europe, the United States faced potential conflicts more evidently suitable only for conventional warfare than in Europe, where any conflagration seemed likely to involve nuclear weapons. Asia, rather, presented the challenge of dealing with so-called "brushfire" conflicts, limited struggles for which it was becoming broadly accepted that nuclear use was wholly inappropriate. This principle was amply demonstrated during the war in Vietnam, when it became clear that the United States would almost certainly not use nuclear weapons in situations short of imminent catastrophe, a point proved in particular by the decision not to use nuclear weapons to break the siege of Khe Sanh, Vietnam, in 1968.[13] Short of general war with the Soviet Union or China, by the 1960s it was becoming increasingly apparent to U.S. decision-makers that U.S. military forces needed to fight better conventionally, above all in Asia. This placed substantial downward pressure on the requirements for U.S. nuclear weapons in the region.

The particular geographical nature of the Pacific theater and the strategic balance in the region also enabled the move away from reliance upon nuclear forces. On the European continent, the United States and its allies were consistently outmatched at the conventional level, necessitating an uninterrupted reliance on nuclear weapons to compensate for Warsaw Pact conventional strength.[14] In the Pacific, however, the United States enjoyed the conventional upper hand.[15] This advantage stemmed from the combination of its substantial superiority over its Communist rivals in naval and air power with the geographical situation of U.S. allies, which were mostly island and peninsular nations. As a consequence, throughout the Cold War and after, U.S. naval forces could operate with near impunity throughout the Pacific Basin. Thus, even as U.S. Communist opponents in China, Vietnam, and the Soviet Union generally held the advantage in ground forces in Asia, these forces were of no import against U.S. allies in Japan, Taiwan, the Philippines, and Singapore absent some method of projecting force across large bodies of water, a capability the Communists effectively lacked through most of the Cold War.

The failures of U.S. land forces in successfully projecting sustained power deep into the Eurasian landmass — as with the fate of U.S. aid to the Kuomintang before 1949, the repulsion of United Nations (UN) forces from the Yalu in 1950-51, and the outcome of the war in Vietnam — thus had a limited impact on the security of insular and peninsular U.S. allies because within its main defense perimeter encompassing maritime East Asia, the United States was able to minimize reliance on ground forces. The only significant exception to this rule was the U.S. ground presence in South Korea. Moreover, U.S. air and maritime conventional superiority in Asia became even more secure when China left the Soviet camp just as Soviet naval forces appeared to begin to pose a serious threat to U.S. power in the Pacific. This superiority meant that, once the United States began to seek ways to reduce its reliance on nuclear weapons, conventional military power could responsibly assume a greater role in the Pacific than it could in Europe.[16]

This trend towards greater reliance on non-nuclear forces was accentuated and enabled by the marked qualitative improvements in U.S. conventional forces that began in the early 1970s with the so-called "Revolution in Military Affairs." The exploitation of this sea-change in technology promised to arm U.S. and allied conventional forces with capabilities in: precision delivery of munitions; command and control of forces and weapons; and, intelligence, surveillance, and reconnaissance that would vastly improve the lethality and effectiveness of non-nuclear forces, considerably narrowing the missions for which nuclear weapons would be required.[17] To illustrate, 1950s- and 1960s-era U.S. technology had suffered from delivery accuracies too modest for conventional weapons, and had thus required the destructive radii of nuclear weapons to destroy targets, especially but not exclusively at longer ranges. With advances in technology, however, weapon accuracies greatly improved, allowing military missions previously allocated to nuclear forces to be replaced by highly accurate and therefore much less destructive conventional munitions. These advances allowed the United States to reduce its reliance on nuclear weapons to a degree not widely anticipated in the 1950s.

Thus, beginning only gradually in the 1960s and then progressing more rapidly through the 1970s and into the 1980s, U.S. forces in the Pacific theater outside of Korea sought to dispense with nuclear weapons as a planned warfighting tool in contingencies short of large-scale war with the Soviet Union or the People's Republic of China (PRC). As a result, the arsenal of U.S. nuclear weapons in the Pacific theater decreased by over half, from a peak of 3,200 in the late 1960s to 1,200 by the late 1970s.[18] While U.S. forces maintained the capability to employ such weapons, and continued storing them aboard naval vessels and with air wings and ground formations, the weapons' salience declined significantly in these decades. Even in South Korea, where U.S. strategy dictated continuing reliance on tactical nuclear weapons in the face of the still formidable North Korean threat, the numbers of such weapons declined by approximately 80 percent from their peak in the late 1960s to their mid-1980s level.[19] Combined with the steady advances in technology that enabled U.S. nuclear weapons and their delivery platforms to operate at considerably greater ranges — and thus from U.S. territory — these reductions also enabled the United States to withdraw the great bulk of its nuclear forces from allied territory, with significant implications for the complexion of the U.S. forward military presence in Asia. Thus, from a posture in which nuclear weapons had been stored at bases throughout Asia in the 1950s and 1960s for a great variety of contingencies, by the 1970s these weapons had been withdrawn from storage at bases in the Philippines, Taiwan, and Japan and, with the exception of South Korea, consolidated on U.S. territory.[20]

Thus, by the latter stages of the Cold War, while U.S. forces in Asia retained a substantial nuclear weapons capability, their salience had receded considerably from the peak of their importance in the 1950s. U.S. nuclear weapons had evolved from an integral and invaluable component of U.S. warfighting plans in the 1950s to a means by the late 1980s which the United States could normally use to deter adversaries from exploiting any seams in deterrence created by the unwillingness of the United States to resort to general nuclear war. While U.S. strategic nuclear forces deterred escalation to general war, U.S. forward-deployed tactical nuclear weapons in particular offered U.S. forces the option of at least putatively selective and restrained employment of nuclear weapons in a limited conflict. While U.S. planners struggled in Asia as much as they did in Europe to develop plausible and sensible limited-strike options, the ability to use nuclear weapons in a relatively tailored and militarily effective fashion was seen to add to deterrence because such strikes were viewed as more plausible since they were at least notionally more proportional to the stakes and intensity of a limited conflict.[21]

Even as their military role declined, however, U.S. nuclear weapons grew in importance as methods for assuring allies. This role became increasingly salient in the 1970s as Washington grew more concerned about the problems posed by the proliferation of nuclear weapons even as South Korea and Taiwan, motivated by Washington's insistence that allies shoulder more of their defense, explored acquiring nuclear weapons capabilities of their own.[22] Forward-deployed forces, including nuclear weapons, were seen to help allay allied concerns about abandonment that could drive them to acquire nuclear weapons of their own.

The collapse of the Soviet Union dramatically accelerated the U.S. military's shift away from reliance on nuclear weapons. Already diminished in their salience by the growth of Soviet nuclear forces and the strengthening of U.S. conventional forces, U.S. nuclear weapons were essentially marginalized in U.S. planning for strictly military purposes by the collapse of the only nation that had threatened U.S. pretensions to global military preeminence. In response to these developments, the George H. W. Bush administration sharply cut the arsenal and curtailed the modernization of U.S. nuclear forces, eliminating all ground-launched short-range nuclear weapons, ceasing deployment of nuclear weapons on naval surface vessels and attack submarines, and withdrawing the vast bulk of U.S. weapons from Europe and all U.S. nuclear weapons from South Korea.[23] While U.S. strategic nuclear forces on ballistic missile submarines and at missile and air bases in the United States still covered targets in Asia, these steps had the effect of completely removing U.S. nuclear weapons from visibility in Asia.

In the years following 1991, U.S. nuclear weapons played only the most subdued role in Pacific security dynamics. Other than North Korea, which could threaten the United States and its allies only through asymmetric methods and by exploiting the leverage it enjoyed because it had so much less to lose than its prospering rivals, the United States and its allies faced no serious near-term threat in Asia during the 1990s and 2000s. Especially after the U.S. armed forces' performance in Operation DESERT STORM, U.S. military superiority was so evident in the 1990s and the 2000s that there was no plausible contingency in Asia in which the United States would need to rely on nuclear weapons for strictly military purposes. The overarching deterrent effects of nuclear weapons could be sustained, in the meantime, by the strategic forces of the United States.[24]

In the latter half of the 2000s, these trends began to abate, if not reverse. North Korea's persistent pursuit of a nuclear weapons capability and advanced missile programs, and its aggressive and provocative behavior in sinking the South Korean ship *Cheonan* and shelling Yeongbyeong Island, rattled both Seoul and Tokyo. Meanwhile, capitals throughout the Western Pacific, above all Tokyo, were becoming increasingly unsettled by the rapidity, sophistication, and scale of China's military buildup. These concerns intensified in 2009-10 as China brazenly flexed its muscles, browbeating Japan over the disputed Senkaku Islands and becoming increasingly assertive about its territorial claims in the South China Sea. At the same time, the less stellar outcome of the second war with Iraq and the economic slump that afflicted the United States after the financial crisis of 2008 began to sap confidence in the solidity of the American security guarantee.

Even as the United States pledged under both the Bush and Barack Obama administrations to seek ways to reduce its reliance on nuclear weapons still further by fielding advanced conventional weapons and missile defenses, these anxieties led to a rejuvenation of interest in nuclear deterrence, including tactical nuclear weapons, among key U.S. allies.[25] In South Korea, some credible voices began calling for the reintroduction of U.S. nuclear weapons on the peninsula to menace North Korea and provide a bargaining chip in negotiations on Pyongyang's nuclear program.[26] In Japan, meanwhile, the threat posed by North Korea and, ultimately more importantly, by a rising China strengthened the cohort calling for an independent Japanese nuclear weapons capability, though such voices continued to encounter substantial opposition from the prevailing anti-nuclear sentiment in Japanese public life.[27] While these recommendations were not heeded, Asian allied governments did make clear that they still regarded the nuclear guarantee as central and indispensable and pressed Washington to redouble its nuclear umbrella guarantees.[28]

By the early 2010s, then, while U.S. nuclear weapons had receded to the background of active U.S. security policy in Asia, and U.S. military planning and coercive diplomacy came to rely predominantly on non-nuclear capabilities, these weapons nonetheless continued to play a foundational and elemental role in U.S. and allied strategy in Asia, providing a basic deterrent against significant escalation, assuring allies, and generally backstopping U.S. conventional power, which appeared to be less herculean in its ability to shape strategic outcomes than some had envisioned in the aftermath of the Cold War.

U.S. NUCLEAR WEAPONS POLICYMAKING IN EAST ASIA

The history of U.S. nuclear weapons policy in East Asia did not take place in a political vacuum, however. Rather, the history of U.S. nuclear weapons in the region has also been a history of U.S. nuclear weapons policymaking. Indeed, this latter history is in important respects considerably more distinctive than the actual policy itself, which has generally been of a piece with broader trends in U.S. defense policy. It is particularly illuminating to compare policymaking on these matters with the situation in Europe, the other region in which U.S. nuclear weapons have been brandished, but where nuclear policymaking was markedly different.

As a rule, U.S. nuclear weapons policy in Asia has been substantially more subject to U.S. discretion, within certain bounds, than it has been in Europe. Indeed, until very recently, there has existed no formalized mechanism for allies' participation or input regarding nuclear planning decisions, and U.S. nuclear operations and deployments have been conducted far more opaquely than has been the case in Europe.[29]

During the Cold War, U.S. allies such as Japan and South Korea were effectively excluded from any significant role in U.S. nuclear policy and deployment decisions that directly affected them. Indeed, Japanese and Korean governments were often unaware even of the disposition of U.S. nuclear weapons within or near their territory. In one particularly notorious example, the Ronald Reagan administration authorized U.S. negotiators on the disposition of U.S. and Soviet intermediate nuclear forces in Europe to propose that the Union of Soviet Socialist Republics (USSR) simply shift all their threatening SS-20 intermediate range ballistic missiles (IRBMs) beyond the Urals—right into range of U.S. allies in Northeast Asia. Only after angry protestations at high levels by the Japanese government in particular did Washington revise its negotiating position.[30] In effect, as long as U.S. nuclear forces were not openly visible to Asian populations—an objective that most Asian allies and the United States came to share during the Cold War—there were few constraints on U.S. policy on nuclear weapons in Asia.

This set of relationships differed markedly from U.S. relations on nuclear weapons policy with its allies in Europe, where the United States dealt with its highly advanced and developed allies through NATO, a multilateral alliance operating—often cumbersomely—on the basis of consensus. Though the United States was the primary power in Western Europe, it operated in a highly constrained context, one in which U.S. nuclear weapons policies received significant scrutiny from its allies. Moreover, European allies were progressively integrated into NATO nuclear planning, and serious consideration was even given during the middle of the Cold War to the creation of a Multilateral Force and to deliberate proliferation to NATO allies.[31] At the strategic and political level, mechanisms such as the NATO Nuclear Planning Group (NPG) ensured allied participation in U.S. nuclear policy decisions, and, given NATO's integrated structure, allied military officers participated conjointly in the NATO Supreme Allied Commander's nuclear planning and deliberations. At the operational level, NATO allies were expected to deliver U.S.-owned tactical nuclear weapons as part of NATO's war plans. No such collective decision mechanisms or programs of cooperation existed in Asia.

The primary reason for the far more unilateral nature of U.S. nuclear weapons policymaking in Asia lay in a pair of broader factors relating to the power balance and to Washington's perception of its allies in Asia: to wit, Washington *could* retain discretion over its policy in Asia in a way that was infeasible in Europe; and Washington also thought it *needed* to do so in light of U.S. policymakers' deep concerns about its East Asian partners as "rogue allies." As a result, U.S. alliance relations in Asia as a whole developed in a considerably more hierarchical fashion, arranged in a hub-and-spoke model in which Washington dealt bilaterally and from a position of strength with each allied government rather than collectively through a single multilateral alliance.[32] This decisively shaped the nature of U.S. relations with these allies on nuclear weapons issues.

A basic reality characterizing the development of U.S. relations with its allies was the stark power imbalance between them. In the wake of Japan's total defeat and the collapse of the European Asian colonial empires, not a single strong indigenous government remained in the Far East. Infant or simply weak governments in Seoul, Korea; Taipei, Taiwan; Manila, the Philippines; Singapore; Bangkok, Thailand; and Saigon, Vietnam could not deal with the behemoth United States as anything like equals, and the occupied government in Tokyo had little leverage or desire to pursue a more independent military course.[33] Largely impoverished, struggling for legitimacy, and challenged by internal and external threats, primarily Communist in nature, these governments were in no position to gain insight into or influence over an issue as sensitive as Washington's nuclear weapons policy. Moreover, there was little sense of cohesion among the nations of East Asia, and in some cases outright hostility prevailed, as between South Korea and Japan. Individual allies were also situated in markedly different geographies, sharply distinguishing their perceptions of the nature of the threat.[34] These factors prevented meaningful cooperation among U.S. allies in the region, but even collectively they would have been outweighed by the United States at the zenith of its relative strength. Washington thus enjoyed tremendous leverage over its Asian allies, and could easily ward off attempts to influence matters as sensitive as its nuclear weapons planning.[35]

But the rationale for Washington's policy of preserving discretion did not lie simply in its ability to conduct such a policy. Rather, unlike in Europe (with the exception of Germany), Washington saw many of these putative allies as not only weak and vulnerable, but also as very possibly dangerous and thus requiring restraint if they were to receive potentially emboldening security guarantees. For much of the Cold War, Washington feared that Seoul or Taipei might, for parochial reasons of their own, provoke large conflicts which the United States strenuously wanted to avoid; Washington also feared Tokyo's ambitions in the immediate postwar period. Washington's response was to seek to restrain these allies. With Tokyo, Washington's response was to ensure the substantial demilitarization of the nation, with the United States assuming responsibility for Japan's security interests beyond its immediate territory. Though after the beginning of the Korean War, Washington did encourage the development of the Japanese Self-Defense Forces to aid in the defense of the Home Islands. As Japan enthusiastically embraced its pacification, concerns about a belligerent Japan receded but the model held, convenient for both parties. With often truculent South Korea and Taiwan, the United States sought to retain sufficient control over their military activities to ensure that they did not provoke an unwanted war in Asia. To this end, the United States, in Victor Cha's description, "fashioned a series of deep, tight bilateral alliances with Taiwan, South Korea, and Japan to control their ability to use force and to foster material and political dependency on the United States."[36] Ensuring exclusive U.S. control over nuclear weapons policy was of a piece with this larger approach.

But the approach was not purely a product of Washington's insistence. Rather, Asian allies did not challenge and in some respects even insisted on the maintenance of a hierarchical alliance relationship with Washington. The case of Japan is illustrative, where the "see no evil, hear no evil" posture of the Japanese Government with respect to U.S. nuclear weapons became as much a consequence of Tokyo's preferences as Washington's. In the wake of the devastating war with the United States that had concluded with incendiary and atomic attacks on the Home Islands, Japan elected to pursue the "Yoshida Doctrine" of unitary focus on economic growth and unswerving forbearance of any significant military development. Relying on the protection of the American security umbrella, Japan could pursue growth without any serious investment in military forces, a policy that satisfied both the material ambitions and idealistic impulses in the Japanese body politic. Security was effectively outsourced to the United States, relieving Japan of the economic, political, and moral burdens of providing it for itself.[37] With this background, it is little surprise that successive governments in Tokyo continued to tolerate a highly unequal security arrangement with the United States, one in which they willfully overlooked the entry of U.S. warships carrying nuclear weapons to Japanese ports, a practice Tokyo governments publicly decried but privately tolerated.[38] Indeed, at key junctures Japan appears to have knowingly forsworn deeper involvement and insight into defense and nuclear planning so as to avoid further implication in U.S. security alliance membership.[39] South Korea, meanwhile, remained weak and acutely threatened throughout the Cold War, while Taiwan, of course, had little choice but to cleave to the United States, especially once Washington shifted its diplomatic recognition to Beijing.

The upshot of this environment was that, for the duration of the Cold War, the United States could and was actually expected to maintain a freer hand in Asia, including but not exclusively in the nuclear weapons field, than it was permitted in Europe. Thus, despite the Japanese public's neuralgia over the presence of nuclear weapons in Japan and public commitment by the Japanese government to refuse to allow U.S. nuclear weapons into the country, Tokyo turned a blind eye towards the transit through and docking in Japan of U.S. naval forces carrying nuclear weapons throughout the Cold War and adopted a similar approach towards indications of U.S. nuclear-related activities on Okinawa in the 1960s and early 1970s.[40] In the Republic of Korea (ROK), meanwhile, only the nation's president knew where U.S. nuclear weapons were located in the country, and open discussion of U.S. nuclear weapons on the peninsula was considered potentially seditious.[41] As Army Chief of Staff General Edward Meyer rather impoliticly remarked about planning for limited nuclear operations while in Korea in January 1983, "It's far simpler here than in Europe where consultations have to be made with fifteen different sovereign nations."[42] Consequently, policies such as the U.S. intention to reduce its reliance on nuclear forces could proceed with far less obstruction in Asia than in Europe, where the initiative ran headlong into the Europeans' vocal fear that the Americans were simply seeking to make superpower war safe for the European continent.

In Asia, therefore, governments have historically been far less interested in seriously challenging U.S. nuclear weapons policy, remaining largely unaware of actual U.S. planning and deployments, and until relatively recently, lacking the wherewithal to bring pressure on Washington. Moreover, even despite the narrowing of the power imbalances between Washington and its Asian allies, the fundamentally hierarchical nature of U.S. alliances with its Asian partners has persisted. Indeed, U.S. Asian allies have at times continued to insist in important ways that such a hierarchical relationship endure. The right-leaning Lee Myung Bak administration in Seoul, for instance, in 2010 successfully pressed to delay implementation of the plan to withdraw South Korean forces from wartime U.S. control in a peninsular war, a totemic issue that the left-wing government of Roh Moo-Hyun had trumpeted.[43] Successive governments in Japan, meanwhile, have resisted building up their military forces to take a more equal role in the alliance and have thus far refused to alter the alliance treaty to commit Japan to the defense of the United States, leaving the relationship a unilateral commitment by Washington to defend Japan.

CONTEMPORARY ISSUES FOR U.S. NUCLEAR WEAPONS POLICY IN ASIA

The Asian nuclear landscape is changing, however.[44] Allies such as Japan, South Korea, and Australia are pressing to gain greater insight into and even influence on the U.S. nuclear weapons policymaking process and, ultimately, posture. In recent years, the Japanese government, for instance, has broken from its hands-off tradition on U.S. nuclear weapons policy to importune the United States to reaffirm the nuclear element of its security umbrella both during the Congressional Strategic Posture Commission of 2008-09 and during the Obama administration's *Nuclear Posture Review* of 2009-10, specifically — though unsuccessfully — pushing for the retention of the nuclear variant of the Tomahawk land attack missile (TLAM-N) for attack submarines.[45] The Lee administration in South Korea, meanwhile, insisted that the United States emphasize the nuclear aspect of its security guarantee to the ROK after the resurgence in provocative North Korean behavior that began in 2009.[46] In response the United States has jointly established bilateral committees with Japan and South Korea on nuclear weapons and related strategic issues, and has sought to institutionalize trilateral and quadrilateral forums on these matters, though with less success.[47]

These shifts are the products both of the changing threat perception among Asian allies and of the greater wealth, strength, and stature of the Pacific nations. The failure of efforts to restrain North Korea's nuclear weapons and ballistic missile programs and its aggressive behavior in recent years has resulted in Seoul and Tokyo cleaving closer to Washington and pressing harder for a strong stance against the Kim regime. More significantly, especially for Japan, Australia, and the Philippines, the rise of China, its rapid and barely concealed military buildup, and its more assertive behavior since the financial crisis of 2008 have stoked fears of a domineering behemoth. This more muted but deeper and more substantial anxiety, now more openly discussed, was leading allied governments in Tokyo; Canberra, Australia; Manila; and elsewhere to look to a strengthening of the U.S. strategic position in the region, and to a greater degree of insight into and influence over Washington's decisions in this regard.[48] Greatly adding to this pressure is the fact that East Asia is now acknowledged to be the cockpit of global economic growth. U.S. allies like South Korea that were impoverished agrarian societies in the 1950s are now first-world economies at the forefront of global socio-economic development. Washington thus no longer retains anything like the degree of leverage it enjoyed in the early 1950s, when these alliances were formed.

The confluence of these pressures and the recognition of Asia's central role in the future of the global economy began to tell on U.S. policy particularly in 2010 and 2011, when Washington, responding to aggressive Chinese movements on a variety of territorial disputes in the East and South China Seas, embarked on a policy to reinvigorate its position in the Pacific.[49]

In the conventional military arena, among other efforts this took the form of the joint U.S. Navy-Air Force AirSea Battle effort, designed to develop credible conventional military plans and capabilities to defeat the anti-access/area-denial threat becoming increasingly available to potential U.S. adversaries, and of a very public U.S. commitment to station Marines in Darwin, Australia.[50] At the nuclear level, even as it reaffirmed its nuclear umbrella over its Asian allies and acknowledged the continued foundational role of nuclear weapons in U.S. extended deterrence guarantees, Washington hoped to continue the post-1950s trend towards reducing reliance on nuclear weapons despite facing significant military challenges in the Western Pacific.[51]

Yet the rise of China; the continuing, accumulative proliferation of nuclear weapons, ballistic missiles, and advanced conventional weaponry; and the stern budgetary austerity likely to follow from the economic constraints the United States faced in the early 2010s, make such aspirations to maintain the striking U.S. advantage in non-nuclear arms look, if not hubristic, then at least inordinately ambitious.[52] The U.S. posture in the Pacific, which has traditionally relied on the essentially unchallenged operation of U.S. naval and air forces throughout maritime Asia, seems increasingly under strain as China builds what will be a daunting array of capabilities to target U.S. ships, bases, aircraft, satellites, and other systems, and as North Korea and other rogue countries seek to exploit seams in the U.S. approach to warfare.[53] Of course, the United States and its allies are not helpless — their efforts to shore up their conventional forces can mitigate, if not entirely relieve, this pressure. But the most influential determinants will be the growth of Chinese military power and the proliferation of nuclear and advanced conventional weaponry in the hands of potential U.S. adversaries. Barring the abrupt cessation of China's military buildup, this trend looks certain to make U.S. conventional naval and air operations in the Western Pacific at the very least more contested and perhaps in certain contexts prohibitively difficult.[54]

These dynamics point to the likelihood that U.S. nuclear weapons, while still generally absent from overt policy consciousness and deliberation in East Asia in the early 2010s, will grow in salience in the coming years. U.S. extended deterrence commitments are fundamentally highly ambitious, encompassing most of maritime Asia. In an era of technologically and politically unchallenged U.S. military supremacy, such commitments could safely be wholly entrusted to the purview of U.S. conventional military forces. As U.S. conventional military superiority comes under increasing challenge, however, the United States and, more insistently, its allies will be compelled to choose between appeasing those rising powers that enjoy leverage gained from the diminishment of U.S. conventional superiority, on one hand, and threatening to impose unacceptable costs upon an aggressor that seeks to exploit such leverage, on the other hand. If it is to be the latter, the threat to resort to nuclear escalation is the logical terminus and the most doubtlessly formidable rung on the ladder of such threats.

ENDNOTES - CHAPTER 3

1. This chapter examines the history of U.S. nuclear weapons policy and doctrine in Asia since 1945. It does not focus on the issue of the attempted uses of such weapons for political advantage, an extremely important and well-documented history. For more on this, see, e.g., Richard K. Betts, *Nuclear Blackmail and Nuclear Balance*, Washington, DC: Brookings Institution Press, 1987.

2. A peace treaty with Japan was finalized in 1951, entered into force in 1952, and was revised in 1960. The year 1951 saw the signing of the Australia, New Zealand, United States Security Treaty (ANZUS). The U.S. commitment to South Korea's defense continued after the 1953 armistice, with major U.S. forces remaining on the peninsula. In response to People's Republic of China (PRC) saber-rattling in 1954, Washington signed a mutual defense pact with the Kuomintang (KMT) government in Taipei in 1955 pledging to come to the island's aid (though not necessarily to the defense of the disputed offshore islands). The year 1954 saw the formation of the Southeast Asia Treaty Organization (SEATO), which included the Philippines and Thailand. These alliances, Washington believed, would strengthen the resolve and coherence of the anti-Communist effort while also increasing the effectiveness of U.S. forces, particularly through the ability to use forward bases located on the territory of its allies. For a history of this period, see, for instance, John Lewis Gaddis, *The Cold War: A New History*, New York: Penguin Press, 2005, chaps. 1-2.

3. For Eisenhower's explication of his logic, see Dwight D. Eisenhower, *The White House Years: Mandate for Change, 1953-1956*, New York: Signet, 1965, pp. 543-544. See also Aaron L. Friedberg, *In the Shadow of the Garrison State: America's Anti-Statism and its Cold War Grand Strategy*, Princeton: Princeton University Press, 2000.

4. For an account of this period and the interrelationship of the perception of the Soviets as a clear and present threat and the increasing availability of nuclear weapons, see Ernest R. May *et al.*, *History of the Strategic Arms Competition, 1945-1972*, Washington, DC: U.S. Department of Defense Historical Office, 1981, esp. pp. 104-152.

5. See David Alan Rosenberg, "The Origins of Overkill: Nuclear Weapons and American Strategy, 1945-1960," *International Security*, Vol. 7, No. 4, Spring 1983, esp. pp. 29-31.

6. See David A. Rosenberg, "Nuclear War Planning," in Michael Howard *et al.*, eds., *The Laws of War: Constraints on Warfare in the Western World*, New Haven, CT: Yale University Press, 1994, pp. 171-173.

7. Robert S. Norris *et al.*, "Where They Were," *Bulletin of the Atomic Scientists*, November/December 1999, p. 30, citing the declassified Office of the Assistant to the Secretary of Defense (Atomic Energy), *History of the Custody and Deployment of Nuclear Weapons, July 1945 through September 1977*, February 1978, excerpts of which are available from *www.nukestrat.com/us/1978_Custodyex.pdf.*

8. Peter Hayes *et al.*, *American Lake: Nuclear Peril in the Pacific*, New York: Penguin Books, 1986, pp. 57-59. Hayes and his co-authors cite the reminiscences of then-U.S. Commander-in-Chief, Pacific (CINCPAC) Harry Felt and an Air Force history of the 1958 crisis for this assessment.

9. Marc Trachtenberg, *A Constructed Peace: The Making of the European Settlement, 1945-1963*, Princeton, NJ: Princeton University Press, 1999, p. 257, citing statements of intent by President Eisenhower in closed meetings, and pp. 287-89, citing comparable statements by President Kennedy.

10. See Andrew Krepinevich and Robert O. Work, *A New Global Defense Posture for the Second Transoceanic Era*, Washington, DC: Center for Strategic and Budgetary Assessments, 2007, pp. 97-138. For a contemporary analysis, see Townsend Hoopes, "Overseas Bases in American Strategy," *Foreign Affairs*, October 1958, esp. pp. 69 and 71.

11. For a classic analysis of this point, see Albert Wohlstetter, "The Delicate Balance of Terror," Santa Monica, CA: RAND Corporation, 1958.

12. See Maxwell D. Taylor, *The Uncertain Trumpet*, New York: Harper & Brothers, 1960.

13. For a history of the consideration of nuclear weapons in relation to breaking the siege of Khe Sanh, see William C. Yengst *et al.*, *Nuclear Weapons That Went to War*, Report prepared for the Defense Special Weapons Agency, Washington, DC, October 1996, pp. 204-226.

14. See NATO MC 14/3, "Overall Strategic Concept for the Defence of the North Atlantic Treaty Organisation Area," January

16, 1968, pp. 14-15. See also NATO Information Service, *The North Atlantic Treaty Organisation, 1949-1989*, Brussels, Belgium: NATO Information Service, 1989, p. 218.

15. For a similar view, see Paul Bracken, *Fire in the East: The Rise of Asian Military Power and the Second Nuclear Age*, New York: HarperCollins, 1999, pp. 25-77.

16. Tellingly, U.S. deployment of nuclear weapons to its naval forces in the Pacific was considerably more modest than in the Atlantic, where North Atlantic Treaty Organization (NATO) navies would face the main onslaught of the Soviet Navy. See Norris *et al.*, "Where They Were," p. 32, citing declassified *History*.

17. For an assessment of this phenomenon, originally written in 1991, see Andrew F. Krepinevich, Jr., *The Military-Technical Revolution: A Preliminary Assessment*, Washington, DC: Center for Strategic and Budgetary Assessments, 2002.

18. Norris *et al.*, "Where They Were," pp. 30-31, citing declassified *History*.

19. See Hans M. Kristensen, "A History of U.S. Nuclear Weapons in South Korea," September 28, 2005, available from *www.nukestrat.com/korea/koreahistory.htm*. See also citations in Keith Payne *et al.*, *U.S. Extended Deterrence and Assurance in Northeast Asia*, Fairfax, VA: National Institute of Public Policy Press, 2010, notes 21, 44.

20. Hans M. Kristensen, *Japan Under the Nuclear Umbrella: U.S. Nuclear Weapons and Nuclear War Planning in Japan During the Cold War*, Berkeley, CA: The Nautilus Institute, 1999, pp. 26-29, citing declassified U.S. Government documents. A contemporaneous declassified CINCPAC Command History named only U.S. and South Korean locations for U.S. nuclear weapons as of 1976. See Commander in Chief, U.S. Pacific Command, *CINCPAC Command History 1977*, Vol. II, September 1, 1978, p. 431, available from *oldsite.nautilus.org/archives/library/security/foia/Japan/CINCPAC77IIp431.PDF*; Hayes *et al.*, *American Lake*, pp. 224-225.

21. For more on this topic, see Elbridge A. Colby, "The United States and Discriminate Nuclear Options in the Cold War," in Jef-

frey A. Larsen and Kerry M. Kartchner, eds., *Limited Nuclear War in the 21st Century* (forthcoming).

22. See Jonathan Pollock and Mitchell B. Reiss, "South Korea: The Tyranny of Geography and the Vexations of History," and Derek J. Mitchell, "Taiwan's Hsin Chu Program: Deterrence, Abandonment, and Honor," both in Kurt M. Campbell *et al.*, eds., *The Nuclear Tipping Point: Why States Reconsider Their Nuclear Choices*, Washington, DC: Brookings Institution Press, 2004, pp. 254-313. For discussion of the "Guam Doctrine," see Henry A. Kissinger, *White House Years*, Boston, MA: Little, Brown & Co., 1979, pp. 222-225.

23. See President George H. W. Bush, "Address to the Nation on Reducing U.S. and Soviet Nuclear Weapons," in Jeffrey A. Larsen and Kurt J. Klingenberger, eds., *Controlling Non-Strategic Nuclear Weapons: Obstacles and Opportunities*, Colorado Springs, CO: U.S. Air Force Institute for National Security Studies, 2001, p. 275. For the withdrawal of U.S. tactical nuclear weapons from South Korea, see *USCINCPAC Command History*, Vol. I, 1991, pp. 91-92, available from *www.nukestrat.com/korea/CINCPAC91p90-93. pdf*. The decision to withdraw all nuclear weapons from South Korea due to the collapse of the Soviet Union suggests how limited their role had become by the late 1980s in defense of the Republic of Korea (ROK) from a purely North Korean attack.

24. For a similar view, see Muthiah Alagappa, "Introduction: Investigating Nuclear Weapons in a New Era," in Muthiah Alagappa, ed., *The Long Shadow: Nuclear Weapons and Security in 21st Century Asia*, Stanford, CA: Stanford University Press, 2008, pp. 23-25.

25. U.S. Department of Defense, *Nuclear Posture Review Report*, Washington, DC: U.S. Department of Defense, April 2010, pp. vii-ix.

26. See Monitor 360 Report, "Findings from SME Crowdsourcing in East Asia," Report prepared for the Concepts and Analysis of Nuclear Strategy (CANS) effort, June 1, 2011, p. 41.

27. *Ibid.*, pp. 15-16.

28. See Richard Halloran, "Nuclear Umbrella," *Realclearpolitics.com*, June 21, 2009, available from *www.realclearpolitics.com/articles/2009/06/21/nuclear_umbrella_97104.html*; and Richard Halloran, "Doubts Grow in Japan Over U.S. Nuclear Umbrella," *Taipei Times*, May 27, 2009, p. 9.

29. See David S. Yost, "U.S. Extended Deterrence in NATO and North-East Asia," in B. Tertrais, ed., *Perspectives on Extended Deterrence*, Paris, France: Fondation pour la Recherche Stratégique, 2010, p. 28.

30. Discussions with former Department of Defense official. Even the official U.S. delegation sent to allay Japanese anxieties was relatively junior in rank.

31. For a history of the Allies' role in theater nuclear force planning, see David S. Yost, "The History of NATO Theater Nuclear Force Policy: Key Findings from the Sandia Conference," *Journal of Strategic Studies*, Vol. 15, No. 3, June 1992, pp. 245-248.

32. For analyses of the reasons why U.S. relations with Asian allies developed in this fashion, see Victor Cha, "Powerplay: Origins of the U.S. Alliance System in Asia," *International Security*, Vol. 34, No. 3, Winter 2009/2010, pp. 158-196; and Christopher Hemmer and Peter J. Katzenstein, "Why Is There No NATO in Asia? Collective Identity, Regionalism, and the Origins of Multilateralism," *International Organization*, Vol. 56, No. 3, Summer 2002, pp. 575-607.

33. Australia and New Zealand were different cases but small strategic actors in any case.

34. Peninsular South Korea, for instance, worried primarily about a land attack across the armistice line by North Korean and possibly Chinese forces; archipelagic Japan focused on the threat to the northern islands from Soviet forces in the Russian Far East; and insular Taiwan focused on the peril posed by military coercion or an amphibious attack by the People's Liberation Army (PLA) across the Straits. Once China shifted to the anti-Soviet camp in the 1970s, it saw its main threat as the Soviet forces arrayed across the long Sino-Soviet border. U.S. allies in the region thus lacked the consistency of focus that NATO states possessed, where the majority of the NATO countries were packed into or

near Central Europe and therefore were focused on the peril of a Warsaw Pact land invasion along the Central Front. This gave a coherence and collective quality to the concerns of the European NATO nations.

35. The fact that the U.S. Navy was the only military force among the allies that could range across this vast expanse of territory also added to U.S. autonomy and leverage. In the nuclear weapons arena, these dynamics strengthened U.S. proclivities towards discretionary and opaque decisionmaking, dynamics that were compounded by the U.S. ability to store and operate these weapons from U.S. naval vessels and sovereign U.S. territory. U.S. sovereign territory included Pacific islands such as Guam but also included territorial concessions granted after World War II on the historical territory of allies, such as Subic Bay in the Philippines and Okinawa in Japan.

36. See Cha, pp. 163,168. For a similar point of view, see Jeremy Pressman, *Warring Friends: Alliance Restraint in International Politics*, Ithaca, NY: Cornell University Press, 2008, pp. 29-36.

37. See George R. Packard, "The United States-Japan Security Treaty at 50: Still a Grand Bargain?" *Foreign Affairs*, Vol. 89, No. 2, March/April 2010, pp. 92-103. This reliance was explicitly nuclear. For instance, after the shock of China's first nuclear test in October 1964, a substantial number of powerful Liberal Democratic Party (LDP) leaders approached Prime Minister Sato Eisaku of Japan with a proposal that Japan should create its own nuclear arsenal. Sato let this be known to Ambassador Reischauer who immediately told Secretary of State Dean Rusk, and when Sato arrived for a summit meeting with President Johnson in Washington in January of 1965, he received assurances that the United States would extend its "nuclear umbrella" over Japan, thus obviating Japan's going nuclear itself. This situation continues to this day. The author thanks George Packard for this insight.

38. For the Japanese government's revelation of the existence of so-called "secret agreements" between Tokyo and Washington permitting US transit of nuclear weapons through Japanese ports and waters and the reintroduction of nuclear weapons to Okinawa after the island's reversion to Japanese control, see Jeffrey Lewis, "More on U.S.-Japan 'Secret Agreements,'" *Armscontrolwonk.com*, March 11, 2010, available from

lewis.armscontrolwonk.com/archive/2660/more-on-us-japan-secret-agreements. For documentary evidence of these agreements and how they were practiced, see Robert A. Wampler, "Nuclear Noh Drama: Tokyo, Washington, and the Case of the Missing Nuclear Agreements," National Security Archive Briefing Book, October 13, 2009, available from *www.gwu.edu/~nsarchiv/nukevault/ebb291/index.htm*. The Japanese government continues to deny that it secretly gave the United States permission in 1969 to use bases on Okinawa to store nuclear weapons in the event of war. See George R. Packard, *Edwin O. Reischauer and the American Discovery of Japan*, New York: Columbia University Press, 2010, p. 318, n. 105.

39. See Hans M. Kristensen, *Japan Under the Nuclear Umbrella: U.S. Nuclear Weapons and Nuclear War Planning in Japan During the Cold War*, Berkeley, CA: The Nautilus Institute, 1999, p. 19, citing declassified State Department cables.

40. See the collection of declassified U.S. Government documents contained in Wampler.

41. Don Oberdorfer, *The Two Koreas: A Contemporary History*, U.S.: Basic Books, 1997, p. 259.

42. Quoted in Hayes *et al.*, *American Lake*, p. 231.

43. "U.S., S. Korea Delay OPCON Transfer Until 2015," *Stars and Stripes*, June 27, 2010, available from *www.stripes.com/news/pacific/korea/u-s-s-korea-delay-opcon-transfer-until-2015-1.108947*.

44. For an analysis of the current Asian nuclear landscape, see Christopher P. Twomey, "Asia's Complex Strategic Environment: Nuclear Multipolarity and Other Dangers," *Asia Policy*, No. 11, January 2011, pp. 51-78.

45. "Japan Lobbied for Robust Nuclear Umbrella Before Policy Shift," *Kyodo News*, November 23, 2009, available from *www.breitbart.com/article.php?id=D9C54D680&showarticle=1&catnum=0*.

46. "Obama Pledges Nuclear Umbrella for South Korea," *Korea Times*, June 17, 2009, available from *www.koreatimes.co.kr/www/news/nation/2009/06/116_46976.html*.

47. Available from *armedservices.house.gov/index.cfm/files/serve? File_id=10a50d6f-ece1-475f-bb5e-00ab478aefdb*. For an analysis of some of the issues involved in developing such a committee, see Jeffrey Lewis, "Extended Deterrence Policy Committee," October 19, 2010, available from *lewis.armscontrolwonk.com/archive/3057/ extended-deterrence-policy-committee*.

48. See Thom Shanker, "U.S. Won't Become Isolationist, Gates Tells Worried Asian Leaders," *The New York Times*, June 3, 2011, available from *www.nytimes.com/2011/06/04/world/asia/04gates. html*. For the speech, see Secretary of Defense Robert M. Gates, Remarks at the Shangri-La Dialogue, International Institute of Strategic Studies, Singapore, June 3, 2011, available from *www. defense.gov/transcripts/transcript.aspx?transcriptid=4831*.

49. See Abraham Denmark, "Crowded Waters," *Foreign Policy*, June 7, 2011, available from *www.foreignpolicy.com/articles/ 2011/06/07/crowded_waters*.

50. See, for instance, Richard Halloran, "AirSea Battle," *Air Force Times*, August 2010, available from *www.airforce-magazine. com/MagazineArchive/Pages/2010/August%202010/0810battle.aspx*; and Jackie Calmes, "A U.S. Marine Base for Australia Irritates China," *The New York Times*, November 16, 2011, available from *www.nytimes.com/2011/11/17/world/asia/obama-and-gillard-expand -us-australia-military-ties.html?pagewanted=all*.

51. *Nuclear Posture Review Report*, Washington, DC: U.S. Department of Defense, April 2010, pp. v-ix.

52. See Paul K. Davis and Peter A. Wilson, *Looming Discontinuities in U.S. Military Strategy and Defense Planning*, Santa Monica, CA: RAND Corporation, 2011; and Andrew Krepinevich *et al.*, *The Challenges to U.S. National Security*, Washington, DC: Center for Strategic and Budgetary Assessments, 2008.

53. See *Annual Report to Congress: Military and Security Developments Involving the People's Republic of China*, Washington, DC: U.S. Department of Defense, 2011, esp. pp. 28-32.

54. See Jan van Tol, *AirSea Battle: A Point-of-Departure Operational Concept*, Washington, DC: Center for Strategic and Budgetary Assessments, 2010.

PART II

RUSSIAN PERSPECTIVES ON TACTICAL NUCLEAR WEAPONS

CHAPTER 4

RUSSIAN PERSPECTIVES ON TACTICAL NUCLEAR WEAPONS

George E. Hudson

The principal question the panel was assigned to address concerned the current force structure, doctrine, and strategy for the use of tactical nuclear weapons (TNWs). Discussion, however, ranged beyond this topic to others that concerned the historical, political, and geographical contexts of the Russian perspective on TNWs. A matter of concern became the definition of what constitutes TNWs, since there is no commonly accepted definition.

As became clear from the presentations on the Russian perspective, even the term "tactical nuclear weapons" is not the one that the Russians prefer. Rather, the term "non-strategic nuclear weapons" (NSNWs) far better fits the Russian conception of this category of weapons, reflecting a difference in how the Russians view them compared especially to an American perspective. But as one participant put it during the discussion, *all* NSNWs are "strategic" in the sense that they will wreak destruction and radiation damage on a wide scale among populations and urban centers just as a larger weapon would. Some have yields much larger than the bombs dropped on Hiroshima and Nagasaki, Japan. Generally, Russians believe that NSNWs are those nuclear weapons not covered in the New Strategic Arms Reduction Treaty (New START) and those that are dismantled or on the verge of being dismantled. Given the power of these devices, participants wondered whether it would make sense for Russians to consider using them at all in a future conflict, since they might have to be used on Russian soil, particularly in a possible conflict with China, or could have effects on the Russian populations living near "tactical" nuclear strikes in Eastern Europe.

THE RUSSIAN MILITARY-STRATEGIC PERSPECTIVE

Perceived weakness in the conventional military balance in Europe conditions Russian thinking about NSNWs in part. Russia is faced with a panoply of conventional assets from the North Atlantic Treaty Organization (NATO) side, including conventional precision-guided munitions (PGMs). The result is that Russia wishes to keep its huge superiority of NSNWs—there is a ratio of about 3,000-6,000 Russian NSNWs, a portion of which are deliverable now, to about 180 NATO NSNWs that could be employed in the European theater—to counterbalance NATO's conventional superiority. In other words, the Russian perspective on NSNWs stresses the deterrent utility they possess and, therefore, the existing threat, however remote, that they could actually be used in a conflict.

The objective military balance in Europe may place Russia in one of two positions, according to participants. The first is stasis. Some Russians believe that the situation as it exists currently is acceptable for the time being. During an undetermined period, Russia will be able to hold off any real military threat from nations of the West just by possessing NSNWs and using them as deterrents until such time as Russia is able to develop its own alternatives to them, particularly the construction of PGMs and drone aircraft. The

Russian Navy would be particularly happy with this situation—especially in the Northern theater—since it relies so much on NSNWs as part of its weapons cache. Moreover, to the extent that the small stockpile of U.S. NSNWs in Europe keeps the United States linked to NATO and therefore ensures a more predictable NATO decision structure and U.S. stake in European affairs, Russia will want to keep its own NSNWs to ensure a stable "balance" of these weapons and to make the United States aware that any military aggression against Russia resulting from a NATO decision would produce a Russian strategic strike on U.S. soil. NSNWs are a kind of "crutch" that the Russians are leaning on until reforms, somewhere in the future, can take place. This *status quo* position, purposely or not, adds a Cold War veneer to their arguments and rhetoric.

The second position appears more active and reformist, involving the pursuit of arms control talks while seeking quicker change in the structure of the Russian armed forces. Like the first view, it desires an eventual transformation to PGMs in the future, but is more willing to accede to negotiations both to buy time for Russian military reform and to link a number of issues to negotiations on the reduction of NSNWs. In other words, there is a greater potential in this position for reducing NSNWs in the near to medium term than in the first.[1] NSNWs become a bargaining chip, used to exact concessions on issues that Russia believes the United States ignores in assessing Russian security concerns. Thus, Russians taking this stance would like to link discussions about the reduction of NSNWs to other outstanding issues, such as the reduction of conventional forces in Europe, particularly a renegotiation of the Conventional Forces in

Europe (CFE) agreement; ballistic missile defense; and the inclusion of all states possessing nuclear weapons in the negotiation forum, instead of just a U.S.-Russia bilateral format. Moreover, the resumption of talks could lead to confidence-building measures (CBMs) in the short term to reduce the military threat and to reduce political tensions in Europe. CBMs could include greater transparency, among other matters, resulting in a final resolution of just how many NSNWs NATO and Russia possess.

THE RUSSIAN POLITICAL PERSPECTIVE

Arms control talks are, of course, as political as they are military. Merely pursuing arms control talks with the United States can have political payoffs internationally and domestically by reaffirming the importance of Russia as a key player in the international system. President Vladimir Putin, for instance, pursued strategic arms reduction with the United States, resulting in the Treaty of Moscow (also known as the Strategic Offensive Reduction Treaty or SORT) in May 2002, in part as a way to score a foreign policy victory early in his term.

There are also a number of important political-economic-demographic issues that influence the Russian perspective on NSNWs. These include key domestic elements, such as the elimination of corruption in the military modernization process, which stymies rapid progress toward reform; the efficient allocation of resources to develop PGMs; the production of sufficient oil and gas to generate income in the face of declining oil and gas prices and projected declining production of oil and gas; and the numerical decline of the Russian population, which simultaneously means fewer workers to produce income from Russian foreign trade and to make high-tech weapons for the Russian military.

International factors overlay these domestic ones in helping to determine Russian perspectives on NSNWs. One of the most important factors concerns relations with China, what some might refer to as the "elephant in the room," when it comes to dealing with NSNWs in the European theater. The Russian view may be labeled uniquely "Eurasian," using the term of one colleague, having to take simultaneous account of Russia's security situation in both Europe and Asia. No other nation is so positioned and so potentially vulnerable. With huge population discrepancies across the Russian-Chinese border, the modernization of China's military, and China's possession of long-range nuclear weapons, it makes sense that Russia would rely on NSNWs to deter a Chinese conventional attack. Their use would be limited because of potential damage to Russia and its population. In an actual war, they might use three or four NSNWs before launching strategic weapons on China. This helps to underline the limited utility they have, should they actually be used, and reinforces the notion that Russia needs to develop PGMs as quickly as possible—weapons that could actually be used somewhat more liberally without excessive collateral damage to Russia itself.

Another international factor, which has a significant domestic component to it, is somewhat spectral: Russia's place in the international system and how Russian political elites conceive of it. This element is extremely hard to measure as it relies so much on subjective judgment, but the recognition that other nations give to Russia's power and the prestige that Russian elites feel thereby are in a sense the starting point for Russian willingness to engage in negotiations about what to do with their NSNWs. Thus Russia's self-image can and does have an impact on many other aspects of military thinking.

CONCLUSION

While Russia's perspective on NSNWs deals significantly with military questions, then, it also has to take account of important political factors. Of those, elite perceptions are very important, because it is elites who make foreign and military policies.[2] Although Russia's political system, by design and by culture, is more centralized than most declared democracies, it still matters to Russian leaders what their populace thinks of them — the only explanation for why leaders go so far out of their way to engage the public in discussion or draw the public's attention to their courageous exploits. With approval ratings of between 88 percent and 57 percent since 2008 — at least prior to the recent highly publicized popular protests — both former President Dmitry Medvedev and newly elected President Putin possess significant political capital to spend on Russian foreign and military policies.[3] As the Russian presidential election of March 2012 recedes, it is well to remember that the Russian leader will lead from his domestic strength.

ENDNOTES - CHAPTER 4

1. Most participants agreed that no negotiations could commence until after the U.S. presidential elections, putting off efforts to 2013 at the earliest.

2. In most nations, including in the United States, the audience for foreign and military policies is much smaller than that for domestic policies.

3. These are the results of polls of the Levada Center, the last one of which was taken in October 2011. Since September 2008 — the height of public euphoria over the Georgian-Russian war — the tendency has been downward for both leaders, but no lower than 57 percent for Medvedev and 61 percent for Putin. These are figures most current Western politicians would be envious of. See *www.russiavotes.org/president/presidency_performance_trends.php #190* and *www.levada.ru/08-11-2011/reitingi-odobreniya-pervykh-lits -polozheniya-del-v-strane-elektoralnye-predpochteniya.*

CHAPTER 5

RUSSIAN DOCTRINE ON TACTICAL NUCLEAR WEAPONS: CONTEXTS, PRISMS, AND CONNECTIONS[1]

Jacob W. Kipp

The attention given to tactical or non-strategic nuclear weapons (NSNWs) has undergone a rather rapid metamorphosis since November 2011. Up to that time discussions of reductions in tactical nuclear weapons (TNWs) were tied to progress towards Global Zero and seen as a logical follow-on to the U.S.-Russian strategic arms reduction treaty (START III) agreement reducing strategic nuclear offensive systems.[2] Russia was demanding the withdrawal of U.S. TNWs—the B-61 bombs—from Europe as part of a campaign to bring all TNWs back within the states that own them. At the same time, Russia was demanding that the United States provide "legally-binding statements" that the European missile defense system being developed by the North Atlantic Treaty Organization (NATO) to deal with the ballistic missile threat from certain rogue states would not evolve into a system threatening Russian offensive ballistic missiles and undermine deterrence. Rose Gottemoeller, Assistant Secretary Bureau of Arms Control, Verification, and Compliance, had laid out the U.S. position on negotiations on TNWs, calling for Russia to provide an inventory of its arsenal prior to the start of such negotiations, a position rejected by the Russian Foreign Ministry.[3]

TACTICAL NUCLEAR WEAPONS AND THE
FEAR OF A NEW NUCLEAR ARMS RACE

What has changed is, first, the collapse of U.S./ NATO and Russian conversations on missile defense. On October 21, 2011, Foreign Minister Sergei Lavrov, speaking on the radio station *Golos Rossii* (Voice of Russia) said that Russia saw no evidence of progress on NATO-Russia cooperation on European missile defense because the United States had declined to provide any legally binding statement on the European missile defense system disavowing deployment against Russia.[4] For the next 10 days, the Russian government in one forum or another repeated its warnings about lack of progress on a Russia-NATO agreement on European missile defense. On October 25, Robert Bridge reported that President Dmitri Medvedev had warned that failure to make a deal on missile defense would lead to a new arms race: "In the coming decade we face the following alternatives. . . . Either we reach agreement on missile defense and create a full-fledged joint mechanism of cooperation, or . . . a new round of the arms race will begin."[5] A week later Lavrov repeated his statement that no progress had been made on Russia-NATO cooperation in missile defense. Within the next few days, the Russian press was full of accounts of the beginning of that very arms race. Lavrov declared: "The situation is serious and we will certainly raise this question during the coming contacts on the level of presidents of Russia and the U.S. and the leaders of the leading NATO member states."[6]

Medvedev's arms race view became common knowledge just a day before Lavrov's statement. It began with a story out of the United Kingdom (UK) carried by *The Guardian*, which proclaimed that a new nuclear arms race was already underway. The British government as part of its austerity program has been cutting defense spending while trying to find the means to maintain its nuclear submarine launched ballistic missile (SLBM) forces. As an essential element of the assessment process, the British American Security Information Council (BASIC) had created the Trident Commission to provide input on the debate about UK nuclear weapons policy, specifically, Trident renewal. The BASIC Trident Commission enjoyed the support of former senior defense experts from all major British parties. Its first working paper by Ian Kearns called attention to the accelerated expenditures of other nuclear powers. The United States and Russia plan to spend $700 billion and $70 billion, respectively, on nuclear weapons and delivery systems over the next decade. The report also made the key point that some powers, notably Russia and Pakistan, were shifting their nuclear posture and strategy toward weapons and delivery systems that went beyond strategic deterrence and into warfighting. Others, especially the United States, were pursuing conventional deep-strike strategic systems.[7] Kearns declared that a new nuclear arms race was already underway: "If anything, the evidence points to new nuclear arms races and a huge amount of money (hundreds of billions of U.S.$) being spent over the coming decade."[8]

The Russian news media picked up the report immediately after its release. One day after the appearance of press coverage of the BASIC report, the Russian press was already analyzing the report's message to conclude that the world had embarked upon a new round of the nuclear arms race, with the United States leading the race because of its planned investment in such armaments over the next decade. Looking at

Russia's anticipated spending of $70 billion over the next decade, the author pointed to investments in new mobile, solid-fueled missiles of the Lars class and in naval strategic nuclear systems, especially development of the Bulava solid-fueled missile and the Lainer liquid-fueled, heavy missile, and construction of eight *Borei* class ship submersible ballistic nuclear submarines (SSBNs). The author further noted the long-range development of the Russian *PAK DA* nuclear-capable bomber, and a major investment in nuclear-capable, short-range Iskander missiles, which will number 10 brigades by 2020.[9]

Recent articles have explored other aspects of this new nuclear arms race. On November 1, 2011, *Lenta. Ru* addressed the reasons for the British report, placing it in the context of defense austerity and the rising costs of maintaining Britain's own triad of nuclear forces. The article examined the six major conclusions contained in Kearn's paper: first, the trend toward reduction in nuclear arsenals, which began in the 1980s, has stopped and members of the nuclear club are now increasing their arsenals; second, long-term modernization programs are leading to a new nuclear arms race; third, all the states that have strategic nuclear arms see these as the necessary and vital means to achieve national security; fourth, the programs of other nuclear powers are driving the modernization programs of others such as Russia, with U.S. ballistic missile defense and conventional global strike systems pushing Russian nuclear modernization; fifth, the greater attention given to non-strategic nuclear forces by states with weaker conventional forces is a means of compensation for such weakness; and sixth, START III was a significant diplomatic achievement by the United States and Russia, but it did not resolve a host of issues and will not serve as a brake on the developing nuclear arms race. The author concluded that Kearn's report contained no surprises, but it did address the main trend lines in force development among the nuclear powers.[10]

Victor Litovkin reported on the BASIC Trident Commission paper but then added comments from Aleksei Arbatov, which put a very different interpretation on the nuclear arms race. Arbatov characterized both U.S. and Russian policy as modernization of arsenals of reduced size and stated that China was the only state with the economic and technological means to radically recast and expand its nuclear arsenal. Litovkin did note that the British debate was about extending the life of the U.S. Trident D5 missiles on Britain's four SSBNS, which was a form of international cooperation on ballistic missile development. Litovkin asserted that Britain and U.S. cooperation put them in violation of the "International Code of Conduct against Ballistic Missile Proliferation."[11] Litovkin followed this article with a second 2 days later. This time Arbatov's observations were nowhere to be seen, and the title emphasized a race in nuclear warheads. Now Litovkin stated that the British specialists had asserted that many members of the nuclear club were engaged in a race to perfect new nuclear weapons and delivery systems. Litovkin did see the United States and Russia as the leaders in nuclear force modernization and outlined what each was doing to extend the life of their existing arsenals and to add new nuclear capabilities. Litovkin called attention to new ballistic missiles in India, China, and Israel. The British report about foreign nuclear developments was supposed to contribute to Britain's own debate over Trident renewal, which depended on U.S. and UK cooperation.[12] The nuclear arms race was on, and TNWs would be an important part of the Russian response.

On November 17, General Nikolai Makarov, the Chief of the Russian General Staff, speaking before Russia's Public Chamber on the condition of the armed forces, warned about "the sharp rise" in the threat of armed conflicts along Russia's borders, which could turn into a real nuclear war:

> The possibility of local conflicts practically along the whole periphery of our borders has increased sharply. . . . Under certain conditions I do not exclude the possibility that local and regional armed conflicts could turn into major wars, including the employment of nuclear weapons.[13]

The response of Moscow's mass media to these remarks was, to a certain degree, hysteria: "The General Staff is preparing for nuclear war." Such reporting took Makarov's remarks out of context and missed his point entirely, which was the progress being made in the modernization of the Russian armed forces and the challenges that remained.[14] The conclusion of this article on Moscow's media response to Makarov's speech was a pledge from the paper's editors: "Our paper has stated many times that without the support of civil society no reform, including those in the area of defense, can avoid failure. On this position we stand now."[15]

Viktor Baranets, the defense correspondent for *Komsomol'skaia Pravda* (*Komsomol Truth*), had exactly that understanding of Makarov's remarks as expressed by the editors of *Nezavisimoevoennoeobozrenie* (*Independent Military Survey*). There was nothing new about the possibility of nuclear war along Russia's borders. That has been a part of Russian military doctrine. But Makarov had given the prospect a different context by referencing the progress made on the modernization of Russia's conventional forces under the "New Look" reforms undertaken after the Russo-Georgian War, which, as George Hudson and Evgeny Buzhinsky explain in their chapter in this volume, had revealed so many deficiencies. At the same time, Makarov called attention to the obsolete or obsolescent Soviet equipment still used by the Russian armed forces and noted the inferiority of new Russian-built equipment in many areas to models produced abroad. He called attention to new structures that would ensure greater coordination in the Russian military-industrial complex. Noting the shortage of conscripts fit for military service, Makarov said that the armed forces would be staffed by contract soldiers. "We will conduct this matter in such a way so that our army will gradually become professional."[16]

On November 23, President Medvedev issued a sharp statement on the lack of progress towards a NATO-Russia agreement on a joint approach to European missile defense, complaining that the hopes stimulated by President Barack Obama's initiatives in 2009, which had prepared the stage for the reset of U.S.-Russian relations and laid the foundation for START III, had come to naught. Medvedev outlined a series of measures that Russia would take in response to the U.S. failure to provide a legally binding declaration that the system was not intended to undermine the combat stability of Russian offensive nuclear forces. These Russian measures included putting the air and missile defense radar complex in Kaliningrad Oblast on alert status; investment in a system of aero-space defense to protect strategic nuclear forces; improvement of Russian land and sea-based ballistic missiles to penetrate missile defenses; improved warheads; and improved capacity to use radio-electronic warfare to disrupt information systems supporting missile defense forces. If these measures are not sufficient, Russia will deploy to the west and south side of the country modern strike systems, including moving Iskander missiles to Kaliningrad. If no progress is made in dealing with the U.S. missile defense system in Europe, Russia will abandon all efforts at arms control and even leave START III.[17] Some commentators treated the statement as mere pre-election posturing and saw little effect on long-term relations.[18] Highly-placed sources in the Kremlin and the Ministry of Foreign Affairs have confirmed that the tough line in relations with the United States will continue if Washington does not make any concessions. The next step would be for Vladimir Putin, as President of Russia, to refuse to attend the NATO Summit in Chicago, IL, on May 20, 2012, although he would attend the parallel G8 Summit, also being held in Chicago.[19] This source did not seem to appreciate the irony of speaking of "President" Putin's actions before he had been elected President.

The combination of the BASIC Trident Commission paper, the hysteria over Makarov's remarks in Russian mass media, and Medvedev's statement about measures to counter the U.S.-NATO missile defense system, created a high degree of anxiety among the policy elite in Russia. In response to this situation, several commentators were quick to applaud Medvedev's moves as measured and intended to exert pressure but not to break off relations. Andrei Kokoshin, the former First Deputy Minister of Defense, judged them "completely adequate" to the current situation, but warned that further developments in the area of missile defense would need close watching and could demand additional actions of a political-military and military-technical nature. At the same time, Kokoshin asserted that Russia is willing, as in the past, to seek a "constructive resolution of problems if the other side will be prepared to do so." He put the current problem over missile defense in the context of many decades earlier when missile defense periodically complicated U.S.-Russian relations.[20] He was clearly saying that this crisis would also pass.

Tactical nuclear weapons figured prominently in Medvedev's rhetoric. Unlike missile defense, they have not, however, been an intense topic of negotiations between the United States and Russia until recently. At the end of the Cold War, both sides made pledges to reduce their tactical nuclear arsenals. In 1987 the United States and the Soviet Union signed the Intermediate Range Nuclear Forces (INF) Treaty that banned each side's intermediate-range nuclear forces and broke the intermediate linkage between battlefield nuclear weapons and strategic ones. Their militarized confrontation in Europe disappeared in 1989 with the Velvet Revolutions. Both the United States and the Soviet Union (and then Russia) had good reasons to reduce their existing tactical nuclear arsenals. Two decades later, attention has returned to U.S. and Russian TNWs in a very different geopolitical and military-technical context.

TACTICAL NUCLEAR WEAPONS

Then and Now.

How one looks at the TNWs of the Russian Federation depends very much on the prism and the connections made between these weapons and Russia's national security strategy. Current Western interest in Russia's residual arsenal after 2 decades of significant reductions in that arsenal reflect an increased attention to such arms in the aftermath of START III, and the increased attention to Global Zero as a long-range objective of U.S. national policy. They also became part of a sharpening political debate in the United States over the success of the reset in U.S.-Russian relations and the assessment of Russia as a challenge to the Euro-Atlantic community, especially NATO. Western policymakers seem united in the desire to induce Russia to reduce its tactical nuclear arsenal that faces west. They might disagree on what concessions the West might offer to get Russian reductions.

The semi-official Russian position on any arms control agreement relating to TNWs was stated several years ago in the context of the increased tensions associated with the deployment of missile defense forces in the Czech Republic and Poland. In that context, TNWs were described as Russia's "trump card." Colonel-General Vladimir Verkhovtsev, then Chief of the 12th Directorate of the Ministry of Defense and charged with the storage of nuclear weapons, stated in 2007 that Russia could begin discussion with the United States on the reduction of TNWs only under the condition that two other powers possessing TNWs, France and Great Britain, took part. Verkhovtsev went on to point out that, in his view, the United States and Russia were in quite different geopolitical situations: along Russia's borders, as distinct from the America's, "There are other nuclear powers and therefore, for Russia, TNWs are a deterrent factor in case of aggression against it."[21]

There is, of course, no common agreement about what TNWs or NSNWs are exactly, except by negation; namely, they are all the other nuclear weapons that are not strategic. Beyond that, there are no limits on their yield—less than a kiloton, or in the range of a few kilotons but not excluding weapons of larger yields with specific tactical or operational targets. Nor are these limits on their means of delivery—short-range ballistic missiles, cruise missiles, gravity bombs, mines, depth charges, torpedoes, air defense weapons, and artillery rounds.

In 1998, *Voprosybezopasnosti* published an extensive article on the quantitative and qualitative characteristics of Russian TNWs. The article addressed the nomenclature of tactical nuclear systems, their general number, the actions taken to execute the unilateral reductions announced in 1991, the distribution of TNWs by type (ballistic missiles, cruise missiles of various types, nuclear mines/explosives, nuclear artillery, nuclear bombs, torpedoes, and warheads for missile defense systems). TNWs are divided into those kept on combat alert and those kept in storage. They can also be classified by the branch of service that controls them. This includes speculation about "nuclear suitcases" under the control of *spetsnaz* units belonging to the Russian secret police (KGB) and/or the Russian special forces (GRU). As to exact numbers of Russian TNWs, the article discussed only external speculations by U.S. Department of Defense and Green Peace, claiming a rough minimum and maximum number of 3,100 to 10,000. No official numbers were released by the Ministry of Defense on the size of its arsenal. The article concluded with a lengthy discussion of command and control of tactical nuclear weapons in terms of preventing unsanctioned launch and positive control to guarantee that warheads and delivery systems could be brought together rapidly for employment in a warning period before the outbreak of conflict.[22]

On April 23, 1999, Viktor Nikolaevich Mikhailov, First Deputy Minister for Nuclear Energy and Chair of the Scientific Council of the Ministry of Atomic Energy, published an article on prospects for the technological development of nuclear weapons, which surveyed existing programs in the United States and called upon the Russian government to invest in the renewal of Russia's nuclear infrastructure. Given the ban on test-firing nuclear weapons, Russia had to invest in the technology that would permit the computer simulation of such tests of new weapons. Mikhailov concluded: "The plans of Russian arms makers are clear and well-founded. Now it is necessary to bring about their realization. History will not forgive us if we do not act."[23]

Sixth Generation Warfare and De-Escalation.

On April 29, 1999, during the NATO bombing campaign against Yugoslavia, the Russian Security Council, under the Chairmanship of President Boris Yeltsin and with its Secretary Vladimir Putin in attendance, reviewed the current status and perspectives for future development of the nuclear weapons complex to 2010. Two sealed decrees were issued regarding the concept for the development and employment of NSNWs.[24] Yeltsin asserted that the renewal of all the links in the Russian nuclear weapons complex was a top priority of the military, scientific elite, political leadership, and defense industry. It was Putin who, after the session, spoke of the two degrees and the adoption of a program, which "authorized the conception of the development and utilization of non-strategic nuclear weapons" as part of the policy of nuclear deterrence.[25] Media sources began to speculate on the role of NSNWs in Russian defense policy. Pavel Felgengauer, citing well-placed sources, wrote on Minatom's plans for a whole new generation of TNWs, but went on to say that the weapons would not be just for battlefield use but would affect both tactical and strategic nuclear weapons with the goal of making limited nuclear war possible.[26]

What this emphasis on the development of NSNWs meant in terms of force development was not immediately apparent. What was immediately apparent was an overt shift in the policy governing nuclear first use. In June 1999, as the conflict over Kosovo was ending, the Russian Ministry of Defense and General Staff conducted the first large-scale military exercise since the end of the Cold War. Zapad 99's scenario involved a defense against an attack on Belarus by western forces and the first use of nuclear weapons to de-escalate that conflict. The bombers employed to deliver the simulated strikes over the Atlantic Ocean and along the coast of Norway carried cruise missiles and were supposed to strike operational targets to bring about the end of a local war before it escalated into a general war with risks of strategic nuclear exchange. The political intent in the aftermath of the NATO air campaign over Yugoslavia was to give the West a warning concerning the risks of local war to strategic stability.[27]

Since 1999, the Russian government has remained mum on the exact size, deployment, and modernization of its tactical nuclear arsenal. In 2004 when the U.S. Government raised the issue of Russia's fulfillment of its "obligations" to reduce this arsenal in Europe, the Foreign Ministry raised objections to the word obligations as used in the question:

First of all, the word "obligations" in this particular context is not correct. We are speaking about one-sided initiatives of 1991-1992, which were "strictly a matter of good will" on Russia's side. These measures looked not only to the reduction of tactical nuclear weapons but to a whole series of measures in the area of disarmament.[28]

The Foreign Ministry statement went on to say that the initiatives have been fulfilled and that one can speak of the liquidation of "more than 50% of the nuclear weapons for the navy's tactical missiles and aviation, air defense missiles, and aerial bombs" from their total quantity, which went unstated. The statement affirmed that Russia was fulfilling its self-imposed responsibilities in this area and then noted that Russia's TNWs were deployed only in Russia proper, unlike U.S. TNWs that were stationed in Europe.[29]

There were very few official comments on the status of TNWs, further reductions, or the development of new delivery systems and more advanced TNWs over the next few years. But the press did carry analytical works relating to these issues. The current role of TNWs, which emerged as an operational concept in the late 1990s in association with increased tensions between Russia and NATO, reflects a clear assumption that Russian conventional forces at that time and even today have limited combat utility in case of general aggression against Russia or one of its allies. This is due to both the reduced size of the force and its technological obsolescence in conjunction with the "informatization of warfare" and the possibilities created by deep, precision-strike conventional systems that have been demonstrated in local wars from Operation DESERT STORM to NATO's air operations against Libya. Russian military theorists, particularly the late General Vladimir Slipchenko, categorized this transformation as a "sixth generation of warfare," which is in the process of superseding the fifth generation, that is, nuclear war, which had become both politically and militarily untenable. Slipchenko even held out the prospect of conducting major wars as "no-contact" conflicts, when the forces and concepts driving this transformation have reached maturity.[30] Current efforts at the reform of the Russian Army under the direction of Minister Dmitri Serdiukov and Chief of the General Staff, General Nikolai Makarov, which began in late 2008 after the Russo-Georgian conflict, are based upon the modernization of Russia's conventional forces and include a shift to a brigade-based combat structure and enhanced command, control, communications, computers, intelligence, surveillance, and reconnaissance (C4ISR), associated with the concept of network-centric warfare.

But U.S. advanced conventional systems were not the only concern for the Russian General Staff. Commenting on U.S. research on using an isomeric form of hafnium to create a nuclear weapon that did not require critical mass, Russian analysts noted the interest in the Pentagon in the development of a new generation of advanced TNWs that could be transformed into precision-strike nuclear weapons of various types. These were described as weapons occupying a place between advanced conventional systems and traditional nuclear weapons.[31] First Deputy Chief of the General Staff of the Russian Armed Forces Yuri Baluevsky was reported to have said: "Shouldn't we review our own nuclear strategy? I think, yes." Baluevsky did not go on to say that Russia should pursue such weapons directly, but remarked only that Russia would not reduce its arsenal of TNWs.[32]

By 2004, a young scholar, Aleksei Fenenko, took on the task of redefining sixth generation warfare, recasting it to include a place for a new generation of TNWs. The concept of "sixth generation warfare," as formulated by Major General Slipchenko, had anticipated the gradual decline of the role of strategic nuclear forces until their only function would be to deter other strategic nuclear forces, leaving the possibility of decisive operations conducted by the new means of warfare, especially deep, precision-strike systems. Aleksei Fenenko, however, brought into sixth generation warfare the possibility of creating a new generation of nuclear weapons with low yields but very high accuracy that could be used for counterforce and counter-elite warfare without the risk of crossing the threshold leading to the use of strategic nuclear weapons. Such weapons would include effects based on new physical principles and delivered with great precision. Fenenko discussed U.S. developments in these areas and then proposed that the Conventional Armed Forces in Europe (CFE) Treaty be recast to incorporate limitations on six new classes of weapons: "cruise missiles, self-guided bombs, weapons using depleted uranium, directed-energy weapons, EMP [electromagnetic pulse] weapons, and hafnium warheads."[33] What in the early 1980s Marshall Nikolai Ogarkov had speculated about as "weapons based on new physical principles" as part of a Revolution in Military Affairs, were now transforming warfare.

Fenenko expanded upon this theme in an article devoted to the contemporary understanding of strategic stability in the West. In his conclusion, he argued that the old definition of strategic stability based upon mutual assured destruction no longer applied. The new weapons were making it much easier to cross the nuclear threshold to achieve more limited objectives, which could bring about the end of enemy resistance:

> The development of military strategy has brought about a new global situation in which a limited strike with "near-nuclear" means will be looked upon as an "ordinary" combat situation not involving a general nuclear collapse but only a serious loss for the enemy's military-economic infrastructure. The nuclear threshold will be broken to the extent that employment of missile defenses, hafnium bombs, as well as the destruction of bunkers and caves by strikes with one-two kiloton weapons become feasible.[34]

Regarding Russia's nuclear arsenal today there is good news and bad news. The good news is the claimed radical reduction of the arsenal that Russia inherited from the Soviet Union, estimated in excess of 25,000 warheads in 1991, to a figure one-quarter of that size, as mentioned by Russian Foreign Minister Sergei Lavrov: "Presently, Russia's non-strategic nuclear capability is not more than 25% of the Soviet capability in 1991."[35] That is, Russia has eliminated a major portion of its tactical nuclear arsenal, which was created to support large-scale theater-strategic operations by conventional forces involving multiple fronts and strategic echelons. This reduction, of course, reflects the reduced tensions of the post-Cold War world and Russia's deliberate decision to reduce its conventional forces as part of an effort to revive its national economy. Preparing for mass industrial war contributed to the economic collapse of the Soviet Union. The bad news is that, as the BASIC Trident Commission report made clear, the Russian government sees TNWs as playing a major role in conflict management and de-escalation under certain circumstances. At the same time, it seems to believe that, in the absence of effective conventional forces, low-yield nuclear weapons with special effects can be used to disrupt precision-strike attacks and de-escalate a local war before it can become a general war leading to the use of strategic nuclear forces. The decision announced in April 1999 to develop new TNWs remains unexplained and opaque because of the lack of transparency in this and other areas of Russian defense policy.

The Russian view of its tactical nuclear arsenal involves a very different geo-strategic context, which can best be described as Eurasian. It takes into account Russia's geo-strategic positions and involves the calculations of a great power in a complex geo-strategic environment with multiple and diverse sources of security challenges and threats. Russia's avowed primary objective is strategic stability, and Russia continues to see strategic nuclear weapons as both the technical and political manifestation of strategic stability. Andrei Kokoshin has made this clear in an article celebrating the detonation of RDS-37, the Soviet Union's first thermonuclear device, in November 1955. It was, according to Kokoshin, the very foundation of nuclear deterrence and strategic stability. Russia is perfectly willing to engage in strategic arms reductions insofar as they do not call into question existing strategic stability. In response to Global Zero, Sergei Karaganov said a polite "no thank you" to any developments that would undermine strategic stability. Nuclear weapons to Karaganov become that force which Goethe used to describe Mephistopheles in *Faustus* and Bulgakov subsequently cited at the beginning of his novel *Master and Margarita*: "I am part of that power which eternally wills evil and eternally works good." The immorality of nuclear weapons is unquestioned, but their power imposes restraint upon the actions of princes by holding out the prospect of Armageddon:

> They are an effective means of preventing large-scale wars and mass destruction of people — something that humanity has engaged in throughout its history with surprising perseverance, destroying peoples, countries, and cultures.[36]

Humanity has not yet created any other means to prevent such general wars, and so Karaganov sees nuclear weapons as the only existing check on such destruction: "The world has survived only thanks to the nuclear sword of Damocles hanging over it."[37] Karaganov makes two related points regarding strategic stability and nuclear weapons that are particularly relevant to our discussion of TNWs. First, strategic nuclear weapons can have useful secondary impacts for other powers. He asserts that China's relative freedom of action in the post-Cold War world was conditioned by the existence of the Russian strategic nuclear arsenal, which served to inhibit actions by other powers against China, making its economic transformation and political recognition as a major global power possible:

> One can hardly conceive China's skyrocketing economic upturn, if there had been no Russian-U.S. nuclear parity in the world, which makes any full-blown war inadmissible due to the possibility of its escalation. I will remind [the reader] that big-time players have been suppressing China's development militarily for about 150 years. At present, this kind of policy appears unthinkable.[38]

Karaganov's interpretation of the international system during the Cold War identifies nuclear deterrence as the chief factor that limited conflict and prevented a general war. The nuclear arsenals of the two superpowers had what he calls a "civilizing effect" because they strengthened the hands of pragmatists set on avoiding nuclear war and who guarded cautiously against allowing local wars to turn into major conflicts with their risks of escalation. He doubts that the new nuclear powers will be willing to give up their arsenals without a fundamental shift in what he refers to as the "moral environment," a shift he sees as forthcoming. But in looking at the decades since the end of the Cold War, Karaganov sees a dangerous transition in NATO from a defensive alliance into an instrument for out-of-area intervention. In the context of Russian weakness, NATO intervened against Yugoslavia in 1999 over Kosovo. But with Russia's recovery, such a course of action is now unlikely: "Now that Russia has restored its capability such a move would be unthinkable."[39] Instead, NATO is now involved in more distant out-of-area operations, which carry their own risks of escalation.

Against what Karaganov labels as "antinuclear mythology," he posits a hard-headed realism. He rejects the idea that nuclear arms reductions by the major powers would entice lesser nuclear powers to give up their nuclear arms or convince other states threatened by outside powers or internal instability to forgo nuclear weapons. Such arrangements might be in the interests of the two powers, but some supposed moral transcendence cannot justify them. States must act in their own interests in the absence of an international regime preventing the intervention of other powers. That Libya gave up nuclear weapons after the U.S.-led coalition's campaign against Iraq did not protect Libya from external intervention in what had become a civil war. The presence of nuclear weapons imposes restraint. Their presence restrained the Soviet Union when it enjoyed conventional superiority in Europe during the Cold War. In the post-Cold War period, it has been the compensation for Russia's weakness in conventional forces in the west and east:

> Were it not for the powerful nuclear (especially tactical) armaments, many in Russia would be alarmed over the growing potential of the Chinese general-purpose armed forces, and the specifics of certain military exercises whose scenarios include offensives stretching to hundreds and even more than one thousand kilometers.[40]

What Karaganov describes here is the geo-strategic concept underlining Russia's current position in Eurasia. Russian strategic nuclear weapons deter the United States and NATO from adventures at Russia's expense and provide China with an element of security that permits it to play the role of economic engine of Asia without the risk of American military intervention against it. But at the same time, Russia's TNWs deter China from intervention in the Russian Far East and Siberia. This view certainly can be seen as providing Russia with some immediate security and even some leverage on its periphery. But it does not deal with a future in which nuclear weapons might lose their deterrent capability in the face of more advanced conventional weapons. This was the prospect that Nikolai Spassky had mentioned in June 2009 in conjunction with the development of strategic, conventional-warhead, precision-strike systems. The further development of missile defense systems and their further modernization raise questions about the long-term value of Russia's strategic forces and call for their modernization as a response. The conventional modernization of Chinese forces has raised questions about Russia's deterrent capabilities in Siberia and the Far East. These issues were the subjects of the Vostok 2010 exercise against a hypothetical enemy, which many observers concluded represented both China and U.S.-Japanese forces in different parts of the theater.[41]

Russia's Eurasian Threat Environment.

The core challenge to strategic stability in Russia's TNWs lies in the military-political relationship between strategic nuclear weapons and TNWs in Russian military doctrine. Karaganov, in defining strategic nuclear forces as the core of strategic stability, was right to invoke the lines from Goethe and Bulgakov, but it is important to note the differences between Mephistopheles in Goethe's *Faustus* and in Wolandin Bulgakov's novel. In *Faustus*, Mephistopheles is the agent of the Devil who tempts Faust in every way. But Divine Grace saves Faust because of his striving for meaning and fulfillment. Mephistopheles' evil actions are, in the larger scheme, a part of God's divine activities. But in Bulgakov's *Master and Margarita*, Woland and his gang of petty demons (*melkiebesy*), including witches, vampires, and Begemot—a gigantic talking cat, black as a raven and with outrageous cavalryman's whiskers—are actors in their own right. These little demons perform their own pranks. Unlike Faust, Bulgakov's Master is not saved by his striving, but liberated by Woland and his gang who tempt and punish the wicked, actively administer justice, and consciously want to act as deliverers. Karaganov's metaphor about strategic stability and nuclear deterrence seems more like Bulgakov's world where the little demons have their own active role in bringing good. Tactical nuclear weapons in the Western view are only cogs in the linkage to nuclear escalation and assured destruction, which ensure deterrence. But in the Russian view, the little demons are the very instruments that would prevent a local war from becoming a general war leading to strategic nuclear engagement. They would do this by forcing a pause to bring about political de-escalation of the conflict. How good triumphs over evil in each case is based on very different assumptions, especially regarding the threats against the state and the role of nuclear weapons in dealing with them. The evolution of TNWs seems to make the equation even more ambiguous.

In this regard, it is worth considering what threats and challenges Russian national security strategy is designed to manage. Certainly, Russian statesmen consider threats and challenges from the West to have been the greatest challenge for most of Russia's modern history. In the last 20 years since the end of the Cold War, Russia has faced a relatively benign security environment, with threats of internal instability and possible external intervention along Russia's western and southwestern periphery as the chief concerns. Because of the nature of the collapse of the Soviet Union, some Russians have put greater emphasis upon ideological threats from the West that would lead to unrest and anti-Russian governments. But most Russians do not see conflict with the United States and NATO as imminent, and they consider the risk of general nuclear war to be remote. The primary concern in this period has arisen from NATO's commitment to and execution of out-of-area operations in local conflicts with the associated risks that such interventions will occur in areas affecting Russian national interests. There could be serious risks that such local conflicts would evolve into local wars and even threaten a general war involving Russia. In the absence of conventional forces capable of dealing with such crises, Russia has seen fit to expand the role of its tactical/non-strategic nuclear forces to include the mission of crisis de-escalation by first use.

Until very recently, Russian military analysts spoke of three distinct threats on three distinct axes. The first, coming from the West, was U.S.-NATO out-of-area intervention with a military built around precision-strike technology and advanced C4ISR capabilities. Russian TNWs/NSNWs were intended here for de-escalation by disrupting the West's capacity to conduct tactical and operational combat in theater warfare. Every Western out-of-area intervention has led to long discussions in Russia on how a force might counter such an opponent. Following the invasion of Iraq, intense debates occurred between those who saw "no-contact" warfare as the dominant trend in future war and those who looked upon the invasion as a reversion to operational art, with the addition of advanced technologies. After a brief romantic tryst with partisan warfare among some, the consensus among analysts shifted back to dealing with no-contact operations designed to achieve rapid and decisive defeat of the enemy. Russian attention focused on conventional force modernization.[42]

The author who most directly addressed the evolution of operational art under conditions of sixth generation warfare was General-Major Viktor Riabchuk, a veteran of the Great Patriotic War and professor of operational art at the former Frunze Combined Arms Academy. General Riabchuk sought to apply military systematology to operational art in the epoch of deep-precision strikes.[43] Riabchuk emphasized the increased role of knowledge management in command and control and spoke of making the command and control of combat the cardinal skill of the commander. It demands of him the capacity to manage information to ensure a systemic understanding of the environment, his own forces, and those of the enemy. In this manner, power can be effectively deployed against critical sub-systems of the enemy and bring about collapse without having to engage in annihilation.[44] His approach would target key sub-systems for disruption and depend on the creation of robust mathematical models of complex systems. It requires that the commander have the necessary skills to appreciate their application and to draw conclusions from them. The objective is not the annihilation of enemy combat forces but the disruption of their C4ISR to bring about operational paralysis. Riabchuk did not, however, discuss the use of TNWs/NSNWs to achieve these effects.[45]

The Russian Navy has also embraced sixth generation war, but its focus has been upon the threat posed by U.S.-NATO forces to Russian strategic nuclear forces. Retired Admiral Ivan Matveyevich Kapitanets has written on this mission, noting that by year 2010, Russia would not possess the conventional means to counter such an attack by U.S. naval forces employing conventionally-armed cruise missiles against the bastion areas of the Barents Sea and Sea of Okhotsk. In the absence of its own advanced conventional precision-strike weapons, Kapitanets stated that in that time frame Russia would have to respond to the threat of such an attack with its own preemptive nuclear strike, with all the associated risks of further escalation.[46] Kapitanets laid out a number of scenarios covering armed struggle at sea for the period 2010-20, in which the U.S. Navy would pose the primary threat to Russia from the sea. The emphasis is upon precision-strike systems, including cruise missiles launched from submarines that could otherwise mount a disarming attack against Russian strategic nuclear systems. Kapitanets argued that the only means that Russia would have to counter this threat in this period would be nuclear weapons, and that such a response would lead to "the complete political isolation of Russia in the world arena." Instead, he called for the creation of a "meta-system of non-nuclear deterrence of aggression."[47]

The Russian Navy was, however, also pursuing a nuclear response to counter the threat Kapitanets outlined. In 2009, Chief of the Main Naval Staff Vice Admiral Oleg Burtsev, asserted that naval strategic nuclear forces in the future will remain a part of the nuclear triad of the Russian armed forces. The role of multi-purpose attack nuclear submarines will expand. Burtsev declared:

> There is a possible future for tactical nuclear weapons. Tactical nuclear weapons are getting greater range and more accuracy, which makes it possible to dispense with more powerful warheads and go to less powerful ones that could be deployed on existing models of cruise missiles.[48]

In early November 2009, Prime Minister Vladimir Putin signed a contract with the Unified Shipbuilding Corporation for follow-on construction of five *Lasen'*-class multiple-purpose nuclear attack submarines after the completion of the first ship of the class, the *Severnodvinsk*.[49] However, as Aleksandr Khramchikhin has made clear, Russia's Arctic naval frontier is quite indefensible now. It is precisely in this area where cruise-missile-armed surface ships and attack submarines can attack Russia's strategic nuclear forces on land and at sea with conventional means, while Aegis-equipped warships can intercept the surviving Russian ballistic missiles launched in retaliation.[50] Khramchikhin has been a persistent critic of Russian reactions to U.S. -NATO plans for missile defense, writing a three-part article for *Voenno-promyshlennyikur'er* (*The Military-Industrial Currier*) in October and November 2011. Khramchikhin asked, "Who Is Against European Missile Defense?"[51] He concluded that the building of the U.S.-NATO missile defense system without Russian cooperation did not pose a threat to Russian strategic nuclear forces in the absence of a Russian attack upon Europe or the United States. Khramchikhin did recommend a prudent investment in maintaining Russia's offensive nuclear forces to keep them at the limits provided by START III and proposed the creation of an aero-space defense system. Khramchikhin concluded: "Finally, A[ero] S[pace] D[efense] will serve us very well in case of war with China, which, in distinction from a war with NATO, is quite likely. But that is another topic entirely."

That other topic relates directly to Russian tactical nuclear forces, as Karaganov made clear. Karaganov and Khramchikhin might argue about the likelihood of a Russo-Chinese war. Russia's political leadership simply does not speak of a military threat from China. But Russian defense analysts are broadly agreed that Chinese defense modernization has turned a mass-industrial army into a force for the information age. Aleksandr Kondrat'ev, one of Russia's leading commentators on the U.S. approach to the informationalization of warfare, in March 2010 provided an in-depth analysis of the Chinese approach to network-centric warfare. Citing both Chinese and U.S. sources, he addressed how the leadership of the People's Liberation Army (PLA) has followed and responded to the development of network-centric warfare in the United States. The leadership understands the importance of information flow for advanced C4ISR and has set out to develop a common picture of the entire battlespace, which includes five dimensions (land, air, sea [surface and sub-surface], cosmic, and electromagnetic. The PLA has emphasized the development of what is called "integrated information-electronic warfare." Kondrat'ev concludes that the United States and China are engaged in a high-tech arms race in information systems and means. In China, that has led the PLA to emphasize the human factor in employing such systems and to promote increased professionalism in the armed forces. What this article poses is the real prospect that Russia will face two technologically sophisticated potential adversaries in Eurasia.[52]

As alluded to earlier, in the summer of 2010 the Russian Ministry of Defense and General Staff conducted a major strategic exercise against a "hypothetical opponent" in Siberia and the Russian Far East under the name "Vostok 2010." The exercise underscored the existing geo-strategic isolation of Russia in that region, even as the Ministry of Defense and the General Staff evaluated Russia's "new look" conventional military. Roger McDermott, a prominent Western commentator on the "new look" reforms of the Russian military, offered an excellent overview of Vostok 2010 as an operational-strategic exercise. McDermott correctly pointed to the role of the exercise in testing concepts associated with the "new look" reforms of the Russian armed forces, calling attention to the exercise's testing of the speed of deployment of brigades, their combat readiness, their capacity to engage in combined arms combat in an air/land battle, and their logistical support for sustained combat actions. He also noted that, while the scenario dealt with a wide range of combat actions, including anti-piracy and counterterrorism, the senior military leadership, including the Chief of the General Staff, General Nikolai Makarov, emphasized that the opponent was hypothetical and the exercise was not aimed against "any one country or bloc." McDermott, however, concluded that the actual objective of the exercise was a test of the defenses of Siberia and the Far East from attack by the PLA. McDermott spoke of the very threat about which the Russian political and military elite could not speak openly.[53] To understand this reticence one needs to understand the political-military context of this exercise.

Anyone who has been involved in the construction of a scenario for a war game or exercise knows that the creation of the documents for conduct of such operational-strategic exercise includes a road to war, which portrays the emergence of a conflict between the contending sides. They are usually labeled "red" and "blue" forces in the case of Russian war games — with "blue" being the color associated with the aggressor forces against which Russian "red" forces defend. In the case of the current Vostok-2010, the Russian forces involved in the exercise are facing a "hypothetical opponent" (*uslovnyiprotivnik*). At a press conference at the start of the exercise, General Makarov stated that this exercise is not directed against any country or military alliance:

> First I would note that this particular exercise, like last year's, is not directed against any concrete nation or military-political bloc. It has a strictly defense orien-

tation to maintain security and defense of the state's national interests along its Far Eastern borders from a hypothetical enemy.[54]

When asked about the opponent that drove these vignettes, General Makarov replied:

> We did not look at any particular country and did not look at any particular enemy. We are talking about what direction we will create our own operational-strategic situation in the course of which somewhere a group of terrorists or large group of separatists are active, which is quite characteristic for low-intensity conflicts. For instance, we selected such scenarios.[55]

Looking at the various episodes that made up the scenario for Vostok 2010, one could conclude that the Eastern strategic direction has its own peculiar risks for Russia. The refugee scenario pointing at North Korea highlights the instability of that regime and the likelihood of conflict developing from its disintegration or from its desperate acts to sustain its position. Fear that a U.S.-Chinese conflict in the wake of the collapse of North Korea would impose difficult strategic choices upon Moscow has been a regular theme of press commentary on Korea. The sharp exchange between Moscow and Tokyo over the exercise in the disputed Kuril Islands highlights the troubled state of Russo-Japanese relations and brings into strategic calculations the U.S.-Japanese Treaty of Mutual Cooperation and Security.[56] Just as President Medvedev was visiting the nuclear cruiser *Petr Velikii* (*Peter the Great*) to observe a mock naval battle and amphibious landing, naval officers there informed the news media that the tactical problem of the exercise was the destruction of "an American squadron" and that the probable enemy would remain unchanged. Commenting on the meteorological conditions at the time of this naval exercise, which involved heavy mist and low visibility, the author described Vostok 2010 as "covered in fog," a characterization which would better fit the confused military and political signals being sent.[57] Finally, the air and ground exercises near Chita and Khabarovsk make no sense except as responses to some force threatening the territorial integrity of Eastern Siberia and the Far East. The only forces with the military potential to carry out air and ground attacks that deep into Russian territory are the PLA in support of the so-called separatists identified in the scenario. Reflecting on the vignettes that made up Vostok 2010, Aleskandr Khramchikhin concluded that the hypothetical opponent in these ground and air operations was, indeed, Russia's probable opponent, the PLA. He stated in his assessment of the exercise that *the probable opponent will defeat us in a serious conflict.*[58] [author's italics]

The one branch of the Russian military not involved in direct combat operations during Vostok 2010 was the Strategic Rocket Forces, which carried out no operational launches. Its only role was defense of its bases from terrorist attacks. However, according to press reports, the exercise did end with a tactical nuclear strike. As Khramchikhin noted, such a strike was hardly in keeping with a fight against separatists and bandits.[59] This seems to suggest that conventional forces could not handle such a challenge to the territorial integrity of the Russian state in so vulnerable a region as the Far East. However, the scenario had left open the intervention of a powerful hypothetical opponent in support of the separatists after their defeat on the Onon River. Tactical nuclear weapons are therefore expected to play the same de-escalating role against China in the case of a local war.

PROSPECTS FOR A U.S.-RUSSIAN TREATY ON TACTICAL NUCLEAR WEAPONS

In May 2011, Vladimir Kozin, Chief of the Section of Analysis and Forecasting of the Department of All-Asian Problems of the Ministry of Foreign Affairs, outlined five obstacles to a U.S.-Russian treaty limiting TNWs. Kozin, a frequent commentator on strategic arms negotiations, European missile defense, and TNWs negotiations, sees limiting TNWs as a complex issue that satisfactory progress in the other areas affects. Kozin declared: "Russia should not, by any means, permit an erosion of its position."[60] This hardline view did not promise much room for negotiations.

The five obstacles mentioned by Kozin included, first, defining what is meant precisely by tactical systems, the absence of any preceding arms control regime for such systems, and the fact that the tactical arsenals of other major nuclear powers (Great Britain, France, and China), and de facto nuclear powers (Israel, India, and Pakistan) will have to be part of the negotiations process on such tactical nuclear systems.[61] Second, Kozin sees the asymmetric deployment postures of U.S. and Russian forces as an inhibiting factor to negotiations. U.S. forces are deployed in allied states in Europe, and the United States maintains a theater infrastructure to support such weapons. As Foreign Minister Lavrov has pointed out, negotiations on TNWs cannot begin until U.S. TNWs and infrastructure are removed from Europe. Russia will not respond positively to pressure from NATO states or others to de-nuclearize Kaliningrad Oblast.[62] The third major obstacle is the issue of prescribed accounting of TNWs. The United States wants this done in advance and by international experts to increase transparency, according to Rose Gottemoeller, Assistant Secretary of State for Verification, Compliance, and Implementation. Russian experts favor a more limited exchange of data on delivery systems and warheads, seeing no reason to agree to exchange data before the start of negotiations. This has not been past practice in arms control negotiations.[63]

The fourth obstacle Kozin describes as the integration of a negotiated tactical nuclear agreement into a complex web of other arms control and security issues.[64] Smaller strategic and tactical nuclear arsenals should have as their goal strengthening strategic stability, but lower strategic and tactical nuclear force levels could create incentives for the development of space-based systems, a direction in which Washington appears to be moving. And this would undermine strategic stability.[65] Fifth, there is the issue of modifying the CFE Treaty. The United States and NATO enjoy both quantitative and qualitative superiority in the five classes of weapons counted in the treaty, even as NATO has improved its position by its expansion, including states that were once part of the Warsaw Treaty Organization. NATO also engages in the deployment of its forces in combat roles outside of the territory of alliance members and conducts sustained, high-intensity combat operations that keep these forces on a wartime footing. U.S. plans for the development of a missile defense shield in Eastern Europe offer one further complication to negotiations on limiting TNWs. Kozin concludes that there is little prospect for successful negotiations on limiting TNWs. The need for parallel decisions on a series of other strategically important problems affecting the regional and global balance of forces, including Washington's plans to build a missile defense system in southern and eastern Europe and maintaining its TNWs in Europe, make successful negotiations unlikely.

The difficulties associated with negotiating these issues foreshadowed the crisis of November 2011. Negotiations on TNWs will have to wait for the current crisis of U.S.-Russian relations to pass, which means sometime after the 2012 presidential elections in Russia and the United States. A successful approach will have to take into account the complexity of the political-military challenges, dangers, and threats as Russia's government sees them in Eurasia. That may create too complex a geopolitical forum for the conduct of actual negotiations because Russia will not join them if it sees them seeking to put Russia in a position where it will have to choose between the Euro-Atlantic world and that of a Far East dominated by China. By every means possible, Russia will seek to avoid the dilemma of choice here. As long as Russia's government considers its own conventional forces insufficient and/or ineffective in the defense of Russia's periphery, TNWs will remain the means of choice to de-escalate such conflicts. It is, of course, not altogether clear here that the Russian Woland can avoid being drawn into an expanding conflict because of the actions of his "little demons."

ENDNOTES - CHAPTER 5

1. This chapter is a continuation of work by this author which began a decade ago after *Zapad*-99 and has continued with greater intensity over the last 2 years. The chapter draws upon that body of work and extends the analysis. The relevant works include: "Asian Drivers of Russia's Nuclear Force Posture," Nonproliferation Policy Education Center, August 2010; "Russia's Nuclear Posture and the Threat That Dare not Speak Its Name," Stephen

Blank, ed., *Russian Nuclear Weapons: Past, Present and Future*, Carlisle, PA: Strategic Studies Institute, U. S. Army War College, 2011, pp. 459-504; Russian Nuclear Posture and Policies at a NATO-Estonian Ministry of Defense Conference on *Adapting NATO's Deterrence Posture: The Alliance's New Strategic Concept and Implications for Nuclear Policy, Non-Proliferation, Arms Control, and Disarmament*, in Tallinn, Estonia; and "Russia's Future Arms Control Agenda and Posture," Paper delivered at Conference on Russia, sponsored by the Strategic Studies Institute, U.S. Army War College, Carlisle, PA, September 26-27, 2011.

2. "Ktokhitree: Mir vstupil verugonkiiadernykhvooruzhenii," *Lenta.Ru*, November 1, 2011.

3. "U.S. wants to step up dialogue with Russia on non-strategic weapons," *Russia Today*, January 20, 2011, available from *rt.com/politics/russia-usa-arms-control/*.

4. "No ABM Cooperation without Guarantees–Lavrov," *RIA Novosti*, October 21, 2011.

5. Robert Bridge, "NATO gives Russia 'nyet' on missile defense," *Russia Today*, October 25, 2011.

6. "Lavrov states no progress in Russia-NATO talks on ABM," *ITAR-TASS*, October 31, 2011.

7. Richard Norton-Taylor, "Nuclear Powers Plan Weapons Spending Spree, Report Finds," *Guardian.co.uk*, October 30, 2011; for the text of the BASIC Trident Commission paper, see Ian Kearns, "Beyond the United Kingdom: Trends in the Other Nuclear Armed States," BASIC Trident Commission, October 30, 2011.

8. Ian Kearns, "Beyond the UK: Trends in the Other Nuclear Armed States," *British-American Security Information Council, Trident Commission*, 2011, available from *www.basicint.org/ publications/dr-ian-kearns-trident-commission-consultant/2011/ beyond-uk-trends-other-nuclear-armed-s*.

9. "Britanskievoennyeekspertyuvereny: Mir uzhevstupil v novuiuiadernuiugonku," *Trud*, October 31, 2011.

10. "Ktokhitree: Mir vstupil v erugonkiiadernykhvooruzhenii," *Lenta.Ru*, November 1, 2011.

11. Viktor Litovkin, "V mire nachalsianovyivitokiadernykhvooruzhenii," *Nezavisimaiagazeta*, November 2, 2011.

12. Viktor Litovkin, "Gonkinaiadernykhboegolovkakh," *Nezavisimoevoennoeobozrenie*, November 4, 2011.

13. "Pressfakt," *Zvezda*, November 18, 2011.

14. "Khotiat li russkievoiny? Posleslovie k osveshcheniiumoskovskimi SMI vystupleniianachal'nikaGeneral'nogoShtaba v Obshchestvennoi palate," *Nezavisimoevoennoeobozrenie*, November 25, 2011.

15. *Ibid.*

16. Viktor Baranets, "Genshtab ne iskliuchaetiadernoivoiny," *Komsomol'skaia Pravda*, November 18, 2011.

17. "Koe-chto PRO iskander" *Rossiiskaiagazeta*, November 24, 2011.

18. "Russia Says U. S. Imposes Missile Shield on Europe," *Reuters*, November 23, 2011.

19. Aleksandr Gabuev, "Strategicheskieiadernyesoobrazheniia," *Kommersant*, November 24, 2011.

20. Vladimir Kuzar', "OtvetnaEvroPro," *Krasnaiazvezda*, November 25, 2011.

21. "Taktischeskiiyadernyikozyr'," *VremiaNovostei*, September 17, 2007.

22. "TIaORossii: kolichestvennyeikachestvennyeparametery-gruppirovki," *Voprosybezopasnosti*, November 1, 1998.

23. Viktor Nikolaevich Mikhailov, "Perspektivynovykhtechnologii v razrabotkeiadernogooruzhiia," *Nevzavisimoevoennoe bozrenie*, April 23, 1999.

24. "Iadernyivekotkryldverinovomuperoduistorii," *Voenno-istorciheskiizhurnal*, No. 1, January 2000.

25. Vitalii Denisov, "V sovetebezopasnosti: Osnovavoennoi-moshchiRossiii," *Krasnaiazvezda*, April 30, 1999.

26. Pavel Fel'gengauer, "Ogranichennaiaiadernaiavoina? Pochemu net!" *Segodnia*, May 6, 1999.

27. Vladimir Grigor'ev, "Koridoryvlasti: Uprezhdaiushchii-iadernyiudar," *Profil'*, July 12, 1999; and Rossiiaplaniruet brat' Zapadnaispug, *Kommersant*, July 10, 1999.

28. Press-Tsentr: Otvetofitsial'nogopredstavitelia MID Rossi-inavoprosRossiiskikh SMI na press-konferentsii v RIA 'Novosti-otnositel'noinitsiativRossiiposokrashcheniiutakticheskogoiadern ogooruzhiia, 7 Oktiabria," *Diplomaticheskiivestnik*, November 30, 2004.

29. *Ibid.*

30. V. I. Slipchenko, *Beskontaktnyevoiny*, Moscow: Izdatel' skiidom: Gran-Press," 2001. On the Russian debate over this concept, see Makhmut Gareev and V. I. Slipchenko, *Budushchaaiavoina*, Moscow: Polit.Ru OGI, 2005.

31. "Izomor," September 22, 2003, *Kompiutera Online*, November 26, 2011, available from *xn--80ajoijhiap3hwa.xn--p1ai/xterra/homo/29344/*.

32. Nikolai Dzis'-Voinarovsky, "Votiadernaiapolia poletela, iaga. . . ," *Lenta.Ru*, March 23, 2003.

33. Aleksei Fenenko, "Voinyshestogopokoleniia," *Mezhdunarodnaiazhizn'*, No. 2, February 29, 2004, pp. 31-43.

34. Aleksei Fenenko, "Problematikaiadernoistabil'nosti v sovremennoizarubezhnoipolitologii," *Mezhdunarodnyeprotsessy*, No. 6, 2004.

35. Sergei Lavrov, "The New Strategic Arms Reduction Treaty in the Global Security Matrix: The Political Dimension," *International Affairs*, No. 4, 2010, p. 18.

36. Sergei Karaganov "Global Zero and Common Sense," *Russia in Global Affairs*, No. 2, 2010, p. 28.

37. *Ibid.*

38. *Ibid.,* p. 28.

39. *Ibid.,* p. 29

40. *Ibid.,* p. 30.

41. Jacob W. Kipp, "Asia Drivers of Russian Nuclear Force Structure," Washington, DC: The Nonproliferation Policy Education Center, 2010.

42. Makhmut A. Gareev and Vladimir Slipchenko. *Budushchaiavoina,* Moscow: OGI, 2005.

43. V. D. Riabchuk *et al.*, *Elementyvoennoisistemologiiprimentel 'no k resheniiu problem operativnogoiskusstvaitaktikiobshchevoiskovyk hob'edinenii, soedineniiichastei: Voenno-teoreticheskikhtrud*, Moscow: Izdatel'stvoVoennoiAkademiiimeni M. V. Frunze, 1995.

44. V. D. Riabchuk, *Teoriiaurpavleniiaboem: Nauchnovedcheskiiimetodicheskiiaspekty,* Moscow: AgenstvoPechatiNauka, 2001, pp. 42-54.

45. V. D. Riabchuk., "Elementyvoennoisistemologiisukhopu tnykhvoisk," in V. D. Riabchuk, *Upravlenie, effektivnost', intellect,* Moscow: Agitiplakat, 2001, pp. 269-278.

46. I. M. Kapitanets, "Flotv voinnakhshestogopokoleniia," Moscow: Veche, 2003, pp. 436-459.

47. *Ibid.,* pp. 426-458.

48. "VMF: Zatakticheskimiadernymoruzhiem - budushchee Rossii," *Rossiiskaiagazeta*, March 23, 2009.

49. Dmitrii Petrov, "Rossiiskiivoennyiflotzhdetmasshtabno-eperevooruzhenie," *Vesti.Ru*, November 14, 2011.

50. AleksandrKhramchikhin, "KholodnaiavoinanakryvaetArktiku," *Nezavisimoevoennoeobozrenie*, No. 44, November 18, 2011.

51. Aleksandr Khramchikhin, "ProtivkogoEvroPRO?" *Voenno-promyshlennyikur'er*, Nos. 41-43, October 19-November 2, 2011.

52. A. Kondrat'ev, "Nekotoryeosobennostirealizatsiikontsept sii'setetsentricheskaiavoina' v vooruzhennykhsilakh KNR," *Zaru-bezhnoevoennoeobozrenie*, No. 3, March 2010, pp. 11-17.

53. Roger McDermott, "'Virtual' Defense of the Russian Far East, Vostok 2010," *Eurasian Daily Monitor*, Vol. VII, No. 129, July 6, 2010.

54. "Vostok-2010 bezkonkretnykhprotivnikov," *Interfax,* June 28, 2010).

55. "Opiat' bezprotivnika?" *Nezavisimoevoennoeobozrenie*, July 2, 2002.

56. "V khodeuchenii 'Vosstok-2010' Rossiiskievoennyeo-bidelilaponiiu s osobymrazmakhom," *NEWSru,* July 7, 2010.

57. Aleksandr Kolesnichenko, "Ucheniia, ukrytyetumanom," *Novyeizvestiia*, July 5, 2010.

58. Aleksandr Khramhikhin. "Neadekvatnyivostok," *Nezavi-simoevoennoeobozrenie*, July 27, 2010.

59. *Ibid.*

60. Vladimir Kozin, "Piat' prepiatstviinaputisokrashcheniia-TIaO," *Nezavismoevoennoeobozrenie*, May 27, 2011.

61. *Ibid.*

62. *Ibid.*

63. *Ibid.*

64. *Ibid*

65. *Ibid.*

CHAPTER 6

ASPECTS OF THE CURRENT RUSSIAN PERSPECTIVE ON TACTICAL NUCLEAR WEAPONS

Leonid Polyakov

After a successful conclusion of the ratification process for the New Strategic Arms Reduction Treaty (START III) in January 2011, further progress in the cooperation of the United States and the North Atlantic Treaty Organization (NATO) with Russia on issues of nuclear weapons control and reduction is very important for the security of all countries of Europe and beyond. Meanwhile, it appears from the outset that the most frequently addressed next step in this process as insisted upon by the U.S. Congress — the start of negotiations over tactical nuclear weapons (TNWs) with Russia — will not be easy at all, and the chances for success so far seem very uncertain.

In the absence of trust and good faith between Russia and NATO, the Russian perspective looks quite logical in its increasing reliance on relatively inexpensive TNWs as a kind of "equalizer," which compensates for many existing or potential security shortfalls of Russia. The prevailing mood at the moment reflects the point that,

> possession of the nuclear forces allows Russia to maintain its military might at the level necessary to deter from launching a massive attack the potential aggressor, who may pursue the most decisive goals, including the possibility of the use of nuclear weapons. This allows providing for the defense of the state under a significantly smaller amount of defense ap-

propriations, which is very important due to the current economic situation in Russia.[1]

Many, if not most, Russian politicians and experts still look at NATO as an aggressive bloc, capable of attacking Russia. In their view, Russia should be on the alert to preclude attempts to make it vulnerable through supposedly benign calls for nuclear disarmament. It may thus be much more difficult for the United States to negotiate TNWs with Russia than it was to conclude the recent START III treaty on strategic nuclear weapons. The greater number and complexity of factors at play have raised the threshold at which mutual agreement becomes likely. Indeed, the sheer number of conditions which Russian politicians and arms experts link to the issue of TNW reduction suggests that TNWs are for Russians the *only* realistic answer to the myriad of security challenges facing them.

RUSSIAN MILITARY SECURITY CONCERNS

First of all, issues related to the role of TNWs in the military context look much more security-sensitive to Russia than to the United States and NATO. Indeed, there may be some good reasons for such a Russian perspective. Thus negotiations on TNWs and, correspondingly, on all related aspects may not start soon. The Russian official position at the moment rests on the very sensitive demand for the withdrawal of all TNWs to national territories of their owners as a precondition for the start of any negotiations related to those weapons. This ultimatum is aimed at the essentially symbolic number (if compared with the nuclear deployments during the Cold War) of U.S. nuclear gravity bombs—about 200 or fewer—located in five

NATO countries. During the last 2 years, this position has been declared on numerous occasions by the Russian Minister of Foreign Relations, Sergey Lavrov, and other officials.[2]

Russian experts insist that Russia, unlike the United States and many NATO countries, is located within the range of nuclear weapons of all nuclear states, which elevates the TNW role in Russia's security calculus to a much higher level than the tactical. In addition, long Russian borders ensure a large number of security-sensitive areas. Such half-encirclement could progress even further to become a full circle around Russia because of the future competition for resources in the Arctic. According to one typical opinion:

> After even a quick glance at the geography of conflicts, it is impossible to avoid the . . . conclusion that Russia is surrounded by a half-circle of conflicts. This half-circle will be closed soon—after the start of the process of competition for the resources of the Arctic Ocean shelf.[3]

This situation, in the view of Russian commentators, increases the importance of TNWs to Russia as a factor in national security and deterrence. Hence, Russians argue, calls for parity in numbers of TNWs between the United States and Russia are irrelevant.

Moreover, since Russia failed to modernize its national economy successfully, it cannot compete with the West in research, development, and production of expensive high-speed, high-precision, long-range conventional systems, which can potentially serve as a counterweight to TNWs. These sub-nuclear conventional weapons systems of NATO constitute just one of the many factors that Russians want to put on the table during negotiations on TNW reduction. There are other security factors that Russians link to the issue of TNWs, such as NATO's overall conventional superiority, European missile defense, and American plans to deploy certain systems in space.

As for NATO's overall conventional superiority, Russians continue to stick to a post-World War II perspective of the defense policies of the United States and NATO. Conventional wisdom tells both Russia and NATO that they are not enemies anymore, that real world threats for both of them will almost certainly come from a third party, and that they have common security interests and should seek to establish a firm basis for cooperation. But the psychology of the Cold War still prevails in most of their estimate: In the Russian view,

> Washington does not take into account the established balance of forces in the European and other strategic regions adjacent to the Russian borders, as well as the comparative capabilities of the sides to provide for national security, including . . . the manifold *de facto* superiority of NATO over Russia in the quantity of conventional weapons and total superiority in their combat potentials.[4]

While the degree of NATO's conventional superiority differs in assessments by Russian experts, they were unanimous in assigning TNWs the key role in providing a counterbalance to NATO's conventional potential. According to Dr. Alexey Arbatov, a respected expert in the field of nuclear arms,

> Russia considers its advantage in TNW as compensation for NATO's superiority in conventional forces — especially under the condition of the Conventional Forces in Europe (CFE) Treaty deadlock, as well as a possible answer to the one-sided creation of NATO

ballistic missile defense (BMD), and to the U.S. superiority in non-nuclear precision-guided weapons.[5]

As for ballistic missile defense (BMD), it has already caused and continues to cause a great deal of suspicion and irritation for Russia. In the middle of the last decade, when the first notion about U.S. plans to deploy BMD sites close to Russian borders in the Czech Republic, Poland, Romania, and Turkey was made public, Russia responded by threatening to deploy additional numbers of tactical missiles capable of delivering TNWs near the Russian-Polish border in Kaliningrad Oblast. Owing to this NATO anti-missile defense plan, which did not presuppose Russian participation, Russian strategic planning was inevitably impacted, with Russians immediately suspecting a major anti-Russian trend in NATO policy. Such thinking remains dominant today, and it is naturally present in the discussion over the possibility of U.S.-Russian TNW negotiations:

> Washington could have cancelled its plans to deploy national BMD systems in Eastern and Southern Europe, which would have unavoidably undermined the Russian potential for nuclear deterrence. . . . Even in the case of a minimal preservation in the numbers of U.S. SNW [strategic nuclear weapons] and TNW, even the possibility of their application by Washington on its own will, during a first strike under the cover of the "anti-missile shield," negatively influence the national security of Russia.[6]

Comments on the issue of BMD at the moment are probably more emotion-laden than other subjects in the context of nuclear arms. Russians tend to see in the relevant U.S. and NATO plans numerous negative consequences for Russia's nuclear deterrence policy, regularly issuing warnings about their likely measures in response. In the logic of Russian experts, TNWs may play a decisive role in Russian plans for countermeasures against BMD in Europe by posing a hypothetical threat to the sites of the BMD system's missiles and radars. A recent comment by Deputy Chief of the Russian General Staff and Head of the Main Operational Directorate General Andrey Tretiak, on the plans for a gradual buildup of U.S. BMD in Europe, once again demonstrates deep dissatisfaction in Russia:

> The possibility for the destruction of Russian intercontinental ballistic missiles and submarine-based ballistic missiles becomes a reality. If the implementation of NATO plans on creating a BMD system, on the basis of a four-stage adaptive approach, continue without taking into account Russian opinion — and more so, without Russian participation — we will not be able to accept this threat to a key element of our national security, the strategic deterrence forces. It will compel us to adopt measures in response that would compensate for the negative influence of the NATO BMD system.[7]

Russian concern over the consequences to the strategic balance present in the linkage among NATO, BMD, and Russian TNWs is understandable, as are the reasons why Russians link the possibility of deployment of U.S. weapons in space and Russian TNWs. They would be very much interested to know to what extent the United States is ready to discuss the space system's deployment in the context of TNWs: "The problem lies in the fact that deployment of weapons in space, even while reducing the levels of [strategic and tactical nuclear weapons] between Russia and the U.S., may fundamentally undermine the global strategic stability."[8]

160

Meanwhile, the factor of China (with its large population and its suspected veiled claim on Russian eastern territories) may appear to be a more important and more realistic security concern than NATO for Russia in the context of TNWs. It is thus quite likely that the latest amendments in Russian military doctrine that allow for the possibility of using nuclear weapons against conventional attacks are not accidental.

In spite of the traditional political rhetoric about a strategic partnership between China and Russia, in both countries there is a common opinion among scholars and both societies that the two countries cannot trust each other. With continuous growth in China's political, economic, and military weight, China has become a leading trading partner for the United States and for the European Union (EU). China consistently projects its economic interests not only to Africa, but also to the regions that border Russia and that have for centuries been considered by Russians to be in their sphere of vital interests. They stretch from the countries of Central Asia to Belarus. The routine publication in recent years of scholarly studies and news media articles about problematic relations between Russia and China may indeed be a reflection of the growing tensions between the two countries.[9]

In addition to the major military security concerns related to the TNW issue as discussed above—Russia's geographical vulnerability, NATO conventional superiority, European BMD deployment, American weapons in space, and the challenge of China—Russian experts also talk about many narrower problems dealing with terminology, effectiveness of control, and other peripheral issues. Russian experts discuss at length the criteria for classifying nuclear weapons as "tactical" and the prospects for establishing and maintaining effective verification mechanisms. They insist on the necessity to take into account during negotiations not just U.S. and Russian TNWs, but the nuclear arsenals of other countries of the region as well:

> Russia's position should be based on the evident fact that TNW is a weapon of regional deterrence, and, consequently, during the process of defining the parameters of the Russian TNW arsenal for the purpose of negotiations, the nuclear weapons of France, Great Britain, Israel and Pakistan should be taken into account.[10]

RUSSIAN LINKAGE BETWEEN POLITICS AND TNWs

As of this writing in 2012, the issue of reducing TNWs is too politically sensitive for both sides, with the Russian presidential election only just completed, and the U.S. presidential election coming up in November. Russia is falling significantly behind its two major competitors—the United States and NATO—in economic and technological areas and behind China in terms of population and industrial potential. It is therefore drawn in foreign policy matters to TNWs as a political weapon, threatening to deploy tactical nuclear-capable missiles in response either to NATO enlargement to the East or to plans for BMD in Europe.

Furthermore, it is important to remember that the nuclear weapon is one of the few or, many argue, the only remaining credential supporting the superpower status of Russia. Moscow almost lost this status after the collapse of the Soviet Union. Psychologically, it is still a very important prop for Russians generally and for the Russian leadership:

Today, in fact, only the nuclear umbrella can provide Russia with a stable peaceful environment allowing it to conduct and successfully finish the process of internal reforms in the state and in the armed forces, in particular. Besides, nuclear weapons provide a high international status for our country, justify its membership in the United Nations (UN) Security Council, and allow us to define the rules of the game in the nuclear sphere.[11]

Indeed, Russia still demands to be treated as a superpower, acting on its own as equal to NATO, declaring zones of special privileged interests, and organizing security alliances. This great power pose is central to modern Russia's national identity and is unlikely to be relinquished any time soon. It works against possible disintegrative processes in the federation and acts as a glue to hold the national ethos intact.

Such perceptions and prejudices make Russian experts very suspicious of American proposals, which they traditionally interpret as attempts to undermine the Russian state. Russians are very much worried by the thought that America wants to be the only military superpower capable of delivering an unpunished strike against Russia or any other opponent. They suspect that the true U.S. and NATO intention behind proposals for nuclear disarmament is to achieve global hegemony for themselves:

On the surface, the first version of the U.S. motivation is its desire to broaden the possibilities for external institutional control over Russia. It means the focused limitation of the range of Russia's possible responses to global processes, including via destabilizing events in the military-political sphere. Such limitation may be realized by entrapping Russia into a system of international agreements that channelize the processes in the

163

military-technical sphere toward the preferential (for the West) channel.[12]

Another hypothesis suggests a more subtle U.S. strategy—the so-called "Chinese gambit," whereby America gains Russia's concurrence on substantial bilateral reductions in nuclear weapons, leading to a weakening of Russia's global position. It would downgrade Russia to sixth or seventh place in the geostrategic hierarchy. As one commentator states, "In this case conditions will appear for channelizing the aspirations of . . . China in a northern direction, thus making it clash with Russia. As a result, two major geopolitical competitors (Russia and China) would supposedly be out of action for the foreseeable future."[13]

According to yet another suspicion, Americans are suggesting the exchange of numerical data and subsequent concentration of TNWs in a few centralized depots as a ruse for gathering data to support U.S. first-strike targeting. This idea is quite prevalent among Russian military commanders. Similarly, in their view, the real purpose of BMD in Europe is to deny Russia a retaliatory capability in the event of a nuclear attack from the West. The more authentic concern of western arms control experts is that, owing to the wide dispersal and lack of guaranteed security of TNW warheads, terrorists may acquire them. Such an eventuality does not worry Russian strategists as much as imagined American "treachery." In the same vein, western reservations concerning the amended Conventional Forces in Europe (CFE) Treaty are allegedly rooted in a barely hidden and one-sided desire to maintain NATO conventional superiority, especially in high-precision weapons.

By the same logic, preventing a potential arms race in space and maintaining strategic stability are not the only reasons for Russia to link the issues of TNWs and space. There is concern in Russia that the United States might have in mind the same "trick" it pulled with the Strategic Defense Initiative of the 1980s — exhausting the Russian economy (as happened with the Soviets in the 1980s) by pushing it to spend huge sums of money on expensive space countermeasures.

On the western side, many experts argue that while American nuclear weapons in Europe have essentially only a symbolic military role, they do possess a significant political role — to demonstrate Euro-Atlantic solidarity and to preserve the U.S. commitment to European security.[14] Those who support maintaining the U.S. TNW presence in Europe suspect that Russia's demands that the remaining American bombs in Europe be withdrawn, constitute a covert attempt to deepen American isolationism and undermine Euro-Atlantic solidarity.

But are U.S. TNWs the only viable symbol of the solidarity of NATO nations? Would the withdrawal of the remaining U.S. nuclear weapons from Europe truly have a damaging effect? Are there any alternative (perhaps non-nuclear) symbols that could potentially substitute for this symbolic role of U.S. TNWs?

The logic of the Cold War, which is probably still driving Russia's linkage between the withdrawal of U.S. bombs and the start of negotiations, is evident in Russia's stated position. What is not clear yet is whether the United States and its NATO partners will find a way to delink this issue and how Russia would react if the bombs were withdrawn.

At the moment, Russians offer a token nod to the western fear that the threat of nuclear terrorism is real, but in contrast to U.S. and NATO concerns, they trust the security of their national stockpiles of TNWs and discount western worries about the possibility of Russian tactical weapons falling into terrorist hands in the near time frame.

GENERAL IMPLICATIONS

The dispute seems to be stalemated, with both sides, especially the Russians, unlikely to take the first big step forward. On both sides, there are too many factors and too many interests linked to TNWs to allow for a bold move any time soon. Some Russian experts describe the situation in stark terms: the start of negotiations on TNWs between the United States and Russia is unlikely in the near future. For instance, one of the most authoritative Russian experts, Anatoliy D'yakov, who is a corresponding member of the Russian Academy of Sciences and Director of the Center for Studies of Problems of Disarmament, Energy, and Ecology at Moscow's Physical-Technical Institute, recently opined that "at the moment negotiations on non-strategic nuclear weapons (NSNWs) have little prospect of starting."[15]

Thus further present attempts to persuade Russia to start negotiations on significant overall reductions of its TNW arsenal and the number/location of their storage sites, without major quid pro quo, have a distinctly low probability of success:

> In light of the continued decrease in NATO TNWs and strong public support for eliminating the remaining [NATO] weapons, some Russian analysts could plausibly anticipate that European governments might at some point request their removal regardless of Moscow's response. This perception naturally

diminishes still further Russian interest in making TNW-related concessions without compensation in other areas.[16]

The chance to achieve progress still exists, however. Despite many evident difficulties, the officially acknowledged Russian concern about at least two common security threats may serve to lay the groundwork for future negotiations: (1) the threat of nuclear weapons proliferation, which could increase the probability of nuclear war, accident, or a related catastrophe; and (2) the threat of nuclear terrorism, which could lead to the same dire consequences for Russia.

At the moment, these are broad background issues both for Russia and for NATO, with future agreement on them more likely than on the present sticky details of TNWs. With TNWs, there are just too many divergent opinions on the specifics of location, terminology, transparency, storage, risk calculations, internal politics, multilateralism, and intertwining of TNW issues with U.S. weapons in space, the CFE Treaty, and European ballistic missile defense, to name just a few.

As a result, both sides are seeking symbolic and confidence-enhancing acts that may permit preliminary consultations on the working level and keep the TNW discussion alive. This will also allow the parties to understand each other's positions better and to consolidate argumentation in the hope that, with time, when the political environment becomes more conducive, Russian, U.S., and NATO experts will have accumulated enough sound proposals to find a militarily and politically acceptable formula to start serious negotiations.

As to official consultations and exchanges of data prior to the start of negotiations, Russian experts have rather divergent opinions. Some argue that these actions can be legitimate as an initial step, but only after an official agreement on the conduct of negotiations. But others, such as the earlier-mentioned academician, Anatoliy D'yakov, go a bit further:

> Russia, the U.S., and NATO could have agreed on co-ordinated transparency measures....In particular, it is possible to exchange information on the numbers and places of storage of operational nuclear warheads and take the obligation to keep these warheads in declared places only, as well as to have no plans of transferring the warheads from reserve to operational status.[17]

The history of nuclear disarmament in Europe tells us that practical measures to reduce TNWs are possible even without formal agreements (see Table 6-1). Twenty years ago, in the late 1980s and early 1990s, the American and Soviet leaderships were able to adopt major unilateral decisions in the interests of common peace and security in Europe. Today the situation is different. In Russia, disappointment over the dissolution of the Soviet Union prevails, a mood of distrust of the West is widespread, and harsh Cold War rhetoric creeps in: "Alas, under Gorbachev the Russians stopped believing in universal human values. Russians became used to seeing dirty tricks and detecting double standards. And in recent years, the Americans have regularly provided reasons [for our suspecting deceit]."[18]

1989 —April 12 SHORT-RANGE NUCLEAR FORCE NEGOTIATIONS	The Soviet Union proposes short-range (less than 500 kilometers) nuclear forces (SNF) negotiations between that country and the United States.
1989 —May 11 SOVIET UNILATERAL SNF REDUCTIONS	General Secretary Gorbachev informs U S. Secretary of State James Baker that the Soviet Union intends to announce a unilateral cut of 500 short-range nuclear weapons.
1991 —September 27 U.S. UNILATERAL WITHDRAWAL OF TACTI-CAL NUCLEAR WEAPONS	President Bush announces a major unilateral withdrawal of U S. tactical nuclear weapons: "I am... directing that the United States eliminate its entire worldwide inventory of ground-launched short-range, that is, theater, nuclear weapons. We will bring home and destroy all of our nuclear artillery shells and short-range ballistic missile warheads. We will, of course, insure that we preserve an effective air-delivered nuclear capability in Europe. "In turn, I have asked the Soviets...to destroy their entire inventory of ground-launched theater nuclear weapons.... "Recognizing further the major changes in the international military landscape, the United States will withdraw all tactical nuclear weapons from its surface ships, attack submarines, as well as those nuclear weapons associated with our land-based naval aircraft. This means removing all nuclear Tomahawk cruise missiles from U.S. ships and submarines, as well as nuclear bombs aboard aircraft carriers."
1991 —October 5 SOVIET RESPONSE	President Gorbachev responds to President Bush's unilateral withdrawal of tactical nuclear weapons by calling for the elimination of air-based weapons and announcing that: • "All nuclear artillery munitions and nuclear warheads for tactical missiles shall be eliminated. • "Nuclear warheads for air defense missiles shall be withdrawn from the troops and concentrated in central bases, and a portion of them shall be eliminated. All nuclear mines shall be eliminated. • "All tactical nuclear weapons shall be removed from surface ships and multipurpose submarines. These weapons, as well as nuclear weapons on land-based naval aviation, shall be stored in central storage sites and a portion shall be eliminated. • "Moreover, we propose that the United States eliminate fully, on the basis of reciprocity, all tactical nuclear weapons of naval forces. In addition, on the basis of reciprocity, it would be possible to withdraw from combat units on frontal (tactical) aviation, all nuclear weapons (gravity bombs and air-launched missiles) and place them in centralized storage bases."
1991 —October 17 NATO REDUCTION OF TACTICAL NUCLEAR WEAPONS	NATO agrees to remove all but 400 to 600 nuclear bombs from Europe.
1992 — February-May TRANSFER OF TACTICAL NUCLEAR WEAPONS TO RUSSIA	On February 1, Russian President Boris Yeltsin announces that the transfer of tactical nuclear weapons from Kazakhstan was completed in January. On April 28, Belorussian Defense Minister Pavel Koszlovsky announces that all tactical nuclear warheads in Belarus have been transferred to Russia/On April 28, Ukrainian President Leonid Kravchuk confirms that all tactical nuclear weapons have been transferred to Russia except for those on the ships and submarines of the Black Sea Fleet.

Source: "Arms Control and Disarmament: The U.S. Commitment," Washington, DC: U.S. Information Agency, 1998, pp. 33-35.

Table 6-1. History of American-Soviet Reductions of TNWs in Europe.

Despite Russian hopes about the effectiveness of pressure on the United States and NATO from European public opinion, time may be running out more quickly for the Russians than for NATO. There is a growing disparity between the Russian ability to maintain its TNW arsenal in safe and ready condition and U.S./NATO overall strategic dominance. However, it would be risky for the United States and NATO to bet on gradually exhausting Russia to force a reduction of its TNWs and agreement to more cooperative security relations and arrangements. Such a reactive approach could increase the risk of nuclear warheads falling in the hands of terrorists. This risk already looks quite real to specialists in the West:

> Arms control experts worry that many Russian TNW are dispersed at remote, hard-to-defend storage facilities and that the weapons appear to lack strong electronic locks that would preclude their unauthorized use by terrorists.[19]

On the other hand, it should be taken into account that despite the dominant anti-Western trend, some sober voices in Russia are heard. Again, Dr. Arbatov states:

> In contrast to the current popular opinion in Russia, under certain conditions Moscow should be more interested in negotiations than the U.S. and NATO....A connection with negotiations on TNW may help to push ahead the problems of the CFE Treaty and to stimulate progress on European BMD and U.S. strategic non-nuclear systems. And vise-versa—a deadlock on TNW will lead neither to the withdrawal of U.S. nuclear weapons from Europe nor to progress on the CFE Treaty, BMD, and precision guided weapons,

where Russian interest is higher than Western....A package of agreements on TNW-CFE-BMD may be promising in order for deep strategic substance to fill the Russian idea about a new architecture of Euro-Atlantic security, which so far remains "the shell without the filling."[20]

Whatever the logic in linking negotiations about TNWs with other issues, in some way Russia may be setting a kind of trap for itself. Ironically, by connecting the TNW issue to so many different problems, Russia could forfeit the leverage they confer. That is, when trying to negotiate these other concerns, Russians could hear in response western insistence on discussing TNWs *as a precondition* for the others.

CONCLUSIONS

Analysis of the current Russian perspective on TNWs suggests that the issue of trust between Russia, on one hand, and the United States and NATO, on the other, is still very much at stake. The Russian demand for a U.S. nuclear withdrawal from Europe may be packaged as an attempt to achieve a more equal position before the start of negotiations and even to squeeze out a greater return for their future concessions. Many Western politicians and commentators, however, see it more as an attempt to further isolate America from Europe by driving a wedge between the United States and leading regional powers like Germany, Italy, and the Netherlands. The West is thus attempting to persuade Russia, if not to formalize the TNW reduction process, at least to increase the transparency of Russian TNW-related issues and the stakes involved. Many Russians, in their turn, see this attempt as one more ploy for undermining Russian positions in Europe and the world.

It is evident that the two sides have divergent positions and interests regarding the problem of TNWs. There should therefore be no illusion that formal negotiations on TNWs will be simple to initiate in the near term. However, Russian concerns over so many issues connected to the TNW problem favor Russia's eventually becoming more cooperative. There is thus still a good chance to find a way out, a good chance that the two sides will ultimately find a middle ground — if not through the traditional negotiation process seeking big splashy solutions, then through modest consultations and low-order, coordinated, unilateral steps. Much patience and courage will be required from the political and military leaderships of all sides. Recent history proves that when political will rises at last to a critical mass, it is then quite possible to achieve real progress.

ENDNOTES - CHAPTER 6

1. Vladimir Kozin, "Five obstacles on the way to reduction of TNW," *Nezavisimoye Voyennoye Obozreniye*, May 27, 2011, available from *nvo.ng.ru/concepts/2011-05-27/1_tjao.html*.

2. Sergey Lavrov, "Tactical nuclear weapons should not be located in the third countries," *Vzgliad*, available from *www.vz.ru/news/2010/3/26/387383.html*.

3. Kozin, "Five obstacles."

4. Varfolomey Korobushin and Viktor Kovalev, "Tactical move with tactical weapons," *Nezavisimoye Voyennoye Obozreniye*, March 18, 2011, available from *nvo.ng.ru/concepts/2011-03-18/1_tactic.html*.

5. Alexey Arbatov, "Non-strategic nuclear weapons: dilemmas and approaches," *Nezavisimoye Voyennoye Obozreniye*, May 20, 2011, available from *nvo.ng.ru/concepts/2011-05-20/1_nuclear.html*.

6. Kozin, "Five obstacles."

7. Sergiy Zgurets, "Patriot Games," *Mirror Weekly, Ukraine,* No. 37, October 14, 2011.

8. Kozin, "Five obstacles."

9. See, e.g., Audrey Piontkovsky, "China's threat to Russia," *Project Syndicate,* September 3, 2007, available from *www.inosmi. ru/world/20070903/236371.html*; Alexandr Khramchikhin, "Millions of soldiers plus modern weapons," *Nezavisimoye Voyennoye Obozreniye,* October 9, 2009; and Vladislav Inozemtsev, "China is a threat to Russia," *Rossiyskaya Gazeta,* October 1, 2010, available from *www.rg.ru/2010/10/01/valday-site.html*.

10. Arbatov, "Non-strategic nuclear weapons."

11. Alexandr Radchuck, "Big Nuclear Game in the XXI Century: Disarmament or War?" *Security Index,* Vol. 1, No. 92, 2010, p. 30.

12. Korobushin and Kovalev, "Tactical move."

13. *Ibid.*

14. Kori Schake, "Tactical Nuclear Weapons: Time to Reaffirm NATO Solidarity," *Central Europe Digest,* August 2, 2010, available from *inosmi.ru/europe/20100803/161824622.html*.

15. Vasiliy Belozerov and Elena Lebedkova, "Tactical nuclear weapons—trump card of Russia," June 10, 2011, available from *nvo.ng.ru/concepts/2011-06-10/1_taktical.html*.

16. Richard Weitz, "NATO's Tactical Nuclear Dilemmas," *Second Line of Defense,* June 13, 2011, available from *www.sldinfo. com/nato%E2%80%99s-tactical-nuclear-dilemmas/*.

17. Belozerov and Lebedkova, "Tactical Nuclear Weapons."

18. Vadim Koziulin, "To take the gun back from dictator," *Security Index,"* Vol.. 3, No. 86, 2008, p. 44.

19. Richard Weitz, "NATO's Tactical Nuclear Dilemmas."

20. Arbatov, "Non-strategic nuclear weapons."

CHAPTER 7

INFLUENCES ON RUSSIAN POLICY AND POSSIBILITIES FOR REDUCTIONS IN NON-STRATEGIC NUCLEAR WEAPONS

George E. Hudson and Evgeny Buzhinsky

Russian perspectives about general military policy as well as the narrower subject of tactical nuclear weapons (TNWs), also called non-strategic nuclear weapons (NSNWs), are conditioned of course by the foreign policy context. Students of international politics and security policy recognize the main foreign policy determinants as: the globalization of international relations, interactions with other countries, the exigencies of domestic politics, and the lasting historical/geographical factors that always come into play in helping to determine national interests. This admixture is given emotional moment as they are filtered through belief systems that often, apparently irrationally, crop up in leaders' foreign and military policy statements. This chapter will attempt in its first section to link some of the context mentioned above (domestic politics is more fully covered in the chapter by Nikolai Sokov) to the more substantive discussion about reducing NSNWs contained in the second section. In the end, it should appear evident why the Russian position on the reduction of their TNWs differs from and often collides with U.S. and other western views.

THE CONTEXT FOR NON-STRATEGIC NUCLEAR WEAPONS

Globalization.

The term "globalization" has several meanings. Probably the most well-known in the United States has been coined by Thomas Friedman, *New York Times* columnist, in his well-known books, *The Lexus and the Olive Tree* and *The World Is Flat*. Basically, Friedman argues that the falling costs of and advances in information technology have created an international system that is fundamentally different from the previous one, since the new communication systems give notice and sometimes power even to small nations and groups that previously could not attain voice, notice, or power. Friedman defines globalization as "the inexorable integration of markets, nation-states, and technologies to a degree never witnessed before . . . the spread of free-market capitalism to virtually every country in the world."[1] One could not be blamed for thinking that globalization in this sense is being equated with Americanization or, at the very least, westernization, since Friedman also notes that the United States, as the "dominant superpower," is the chief proponent of this trend and maybe even its chief enforcer. While some writers like Joseph Stiglitz criticize this view of globalization as "accepting triumphant capitalism, American style," they do tend to view it in the context of U.S. relations with developing nations as almost a kind of neo-imperialism.[2]

The view of globalization as Americanization has not been well received in Russia. It has been challenged in a way that has had a strong impact on how Russia has viewed the context of international relations in general and its own position in the international system, particularly concerning relations with the United States and the North Atlantic Treaty Organization (NATO). It has formed the conceptual framework in which the Russian government has approached the topic of reductions in NSNWs. The concept of globalization has been recast to reflect a different view of what it means.

No Russian whom the present writers know challenges the fact that globalization, in the sense of increasing national interdependencies, has occurred; many note that the catalyst for this fundamental change in the international system began, not with technological change so much, but rather with the fall of the Union of Soviet Socialist Republics (USSR) and the unchallenged rise of the United States as a global hegemon. Fyodor Lukyanov, the editor-in-chief of *Russia in Global Affairs*, notes that:

> throughout history, this territory [Russia] sometimes found itself on the periphery and sometimes at the center of world politics. Its collapse was a momentous event in terms of its impact on the structural stability of the international system, especially in the second half of the 20th century when the Soviet Union was not just an influential regional power, but one of the two pillars on which the entire world order was based. Therefore, its collapse was not just a matter of national self-perception, but also a radical change in the foundation of the world order.[3]

When one pillar of a bipolar international system collapses, the remaining pillar — in this case America — tends to occupy its place, creating a unipolar system. In the face of advances in telecommunications, including the internet and, probably more important, the ability to conduct huge quantities of international monetary transactions at the speed of light and to project military power to any part of the earth, the United States was for a while able to make globalization equate to Americanization. As Lukyanov says, "Moscow was ready to assume a subordinate status," in this U.S.-dominated international system at least for the first half of the 1990s.[4]

Such a status raised the hackles of Russian policymakers, particularly Evegeny Primakov, who briefly became Prime Minister under President Boris Yeltsin and who had a more wary outlook than many others about U.S. intentions. Indeed, promised economic assistance to Russia from the United States did not occur, and instead NATO started — from the Russian perspective — to advance toward and threaten Russia's borders. As Russia continued to suffer economically and to undergo various hyper-capitalistic economic experiments that at first enriched only a few individuals, a counter-reaction inevitably occurred in which traditional Russian fears about a diminished place in the international system surfaced.

These international and domestic conditions took place in the context not only of a globalized (Americanized) system based on the soft power of technology, but also of an assertive NATO and United States utilizing the hard power of the military. A sea change in Russian attitudes occurred in March 1999, when talks on the status of Kosovo broke down and NATO bombed Serbian troops, forcing hundreds of thousands of refugees to flee the area during 78 days of fighting. A final settlement occurred after that, eventuating in Kosovo's independence by February 2008 with a constitution approved in June. Moscow was incensed from the beginning of the operation, with a rare show of unanimity from nearly all Russian quarters condemning NATO's "aggressive" behavior.[5] There is not much doubt that this outcome, combined with NATO's movement eastward, has introduced a serious retrogression in Russian-U.S. relations. This trend was accentuated during the presidencies of Vladimir Putin and George W. Bush, in spite of a new strategic arms control treaty signed in May 2002. The invasions of Afghanistan and Iraq strengthened the Russian view that globalization, as proclaimed by the West, meant American and NATO domination.

New thinking started to be formulated at this time about what globalization meant from the Russian perspective. Not so surprisingly, it rejected American and other western views. "Globalism," one analyst stated, "benefits America at the expense of everyone else."[6] Instead of this version of globalization, Russians began to accept the idea of multipolar globalism, the idea that there is a true interdependence among nations and that there can be no single global hegemon by definition.[7] This notion fits Russian foreign policy proclivities very well in rejecting U.S. dominance. A probable new era of Russian policy began with the address of then President Vladimir Putin at the Munich Security Conference in February 2007. In part, he stated that:

> I consider that the unipolar model is not only unacceptable but also impossible in today's world. And this is not only because if there was individual leadership in today's—and precisely in today's—world, then military, political and economic resources would not suffice. What is even more important is that the model itself is flawed because at its basis there is and can be no moral foundations for modern civilization.[8]

He then continues to condemn the predilection for use of force prevailing at the time (read: Iraq and Afghanistan), notes that trade is expanding the range of interdependencies, and proclaims that "there is no reason to doubt that the economic potential of the new centers of global economic growth [the BRIC nations — Brazil, Russia, India, China] will inevitably be converted into political influence and will strengthen multipolarity."[9]

It seems clear that the Russian shift in thinking to multipolar globalism both reflects new realities and represents the preferred line of Russian foreign policy today. Even the "reset" in Russian-American relations is a symbol of that, recognizing as it does the importance of Russian power to the United States and the consequent need for Russian cooperation in a world that is quickly becoming multipolar. The new line has been ratified most recently in the New Strategic Arms Reduction Treaty (START) document and also in the progress of Russia toward membership in the World Trade Organization (WTO) — which Russia both wants and needs and which the United States strongly supports. The new line also finds Russia arguing strongly for a multilateral approach to agreements on the reduction of NSNWs, as we shall see in the latter part of this chapter. The *relative decline* of American power "in which the power resources of other states grow greater or are used more effectively," has helped to advance the new multipolarity and interdependence. This scenario does not reflect the *absolute decline* of the U.S., but rather, as Joseph Nye reminds us, "the loss of ability to use one's resources effectively."[10] The United States is probably stronger than it used to be just looking at the power resources — both economic and military — that it could bring to bear internationally; it is just that others are accelerating faster. Nor does Russia find itself on a steady power gain relative to other nations. It, too, has to deal with realities and weaknesses that help to inform its stance on NSNWs in addition to globalism.

GEOGRAPHY, POPULATION, AND MILITARY MALADIES

No paper on Russian strategy or geopolitics can ignore a factor that will be only briefly mentioned here: Russia's geographical position. The subject is covered more thoroughly in the contributions by Leonid Polyakov and Jacob Kipp in this section of the book, but it must be noted here that Russia borders on many nations — 14 in all — and has strong historical interests in at least five more in the Southern Caucasus and Central Eurasia. No other nation has such a similar complex and troubling geographic situation. How easy the United States has it from this perspective, with only Mexico and Canada as bordering countries! Russia's geography profoundly affects its strategic and geopolitical views and pushes it naturally to a more multilateral approach to international politics today — especially under the conditions more fully discussed below. This is one factor only, of course, but it profoundly influences Russian foreign policy, making it sensitive to challenges from the south and west.

A second factor, stemming from the domestic side, is the Russian population "bomb," or the matter of the decrease in Russia's population. It links closely to Russia's perception of threats to national security because it has a direct impact on maintaining a one million-man army, discussed below, and on Russian economic production, two factors normally associated with measures of power in international relations. The latest version of Russia's national security strategy was released in May 2009; it points directly to this threat in its section called "Raising the standard of living of Russian citizens." It addresses population in part by stating that:

> Reducing the level of social and property inequality among the population, the stabilization of the population size in the medium term, and, in the long term, the basic improvement of the demographic situation constitute the strategic goals for guaranteeing national security in the realm of raising the quality of life of Russian citizens.[11]

It then continues to list a number of other issues such as housing, the crisis of world and regional banking, the domestic production of high quality pharmaceuticals, and a better system of protecting human rights.

The United Nations (UN) has long published population projections for Russia that do not yield optimism for reversing population decline. According to the UN medium projection, Russia will shrink from 143 million in 2010 to 126 million by 2050—a drop of nearly 12 percent. In comparison, the United States will grow in the same period from 310 million in 2010 to 403 million by 2050, an increase of 30 percent.[12] Moreover, the number of Russian conscripts in 2012 will be only one-half of what it was in 2001, and some of these will not be fit for military service because of medical reasons.[13] This is not a good situation for a nation that needs to meet minimum recruitment numbers for its one million-man force. Certainly, it has a negative long-term impact on Russian strategies for national security and foreign policy. It continues to direct Russian toward multilateral solutions to its security.

The third and most directly related factor underlying the Russian position on NSNWs relates to what we might call the military maladies of the Russian armed forces. As we saw above, new efforts on military reform began following the 2008 war with Georgia. This is probably no accident, and so Russian activities in the so-called 5-day war provide a good example of a number of things related to the Russian military. For instance, even though Russian forces had been stationed in the Northern Caucasus and had engaged in military exercises prior to August 2008, the Russian military still appeared to be caught by surprise when the Georgians attacked on August 7. Russian analyst Fyodor Lukyanov puts the blame squarely on inconsistencies in Russian policy, which, taken together with other factors listed below, served to cause hesitation and to limit what the Russians could actually do once the war began. As Lykyanov noted at the time of the war:

> Ever since the disruption of the status quo that had been maintained in the conflict zones for about 10 years, Russia's policy has been getting increasingly contradictory. The desire to simultaneously play the role of a neutral mediator/peacekeeper and a protector/guarantor of security in South Ossetia and Abkhazia has been detrimental to both the former and the latter status. At some point, Moscow essentially stopped trying to help bring about a political settlement, placing its stakes on expanding cooperation with Tskhinvali and Sukhumi and forestalling any outbreaks of tension. At the same time, Russia tried to formally stay within existing legal bounds, and the longer this went on, the more it came into conflict with reality.[14]

In other words, the pursuit of a military solution (guaranteeing the security of South Ossetia and Abkhazia) subverted Russian diplomacy (the peacekeeping role) and placed Russia in the position of being manipulated by all parties in the conflict, including South Ossetia, Abkhazia, and Georgia. It made war almost inevitable. So, in spite of apparent good military planning, Russia was poorly prepared politically. This resulted in a lack of preparedness overall.

Poor political preparation reflected itself in the questionable state of Russian military equipment. Decisions were not made at the top levels of the political/military structure to ensure that Russian troops could achieve victory in the shortest possible time, using the best equipment. This reflected overconfidence, bad acquisition procedures, and confusion about how far Russia wanted to go to achieve its objectives. Certainly Russia could not simply go in and take over the Georgian territory under these conditions. Nor could it overthrow the government of President Mikheil Saakashvili.

Probably the best military analysis of the 2008 war has been done by a group of Russian academics in a work that first appeared as *Tanki Avgusta* in the original and, as translated into English later as, *The Tanks of August*. This work contains some searing critiques of Russian military failures, mostly dealing with poor equipment and poor battle execution. For instance, while the authors note that the Northern Caucasus 42nd Rifle Division was the "only division in the entire Russian Army fully deployed under a wartime manning chart and staffed only with professional soldiers" and had combat-ready regiments ready to fight in 24 hours, it was poorly equipped, having ancient armor, like T-62 tanks and old BMPs.[15] The result was equipment breakdowns during the war, resulting in a longer conflict.[16]

The Russians also experienced "one of the biggest surprises" of the 2008 war in their loss of aircraft against an enemy who, while not defenseless, could not be expected to sustain combat against the better-equipped Russians. Georgian air defenses accounted for only two of Russia's six downed airplanes, while three suffered from friendly fire and one was shot down by unknown causes.[17] The friendly fire casualties demonstrate significant command-and-control problems in implementing the battle plan, according to one specialist. But the high ratio of those to the Georgian-caused downings also calls into question notions of effective Georgian air defenses.[18] At any rate, the Russians seem to have wrought more havoc upon themselves than did the Georgians.

It should be no surprise that military reform efforts began soon after the conclusion of the 5-day war with Georgia. The process of reform is ongoing. It includes, as mentioned, plans to reduce the military's size to one million soldiers and also to increase the number of noncommissioned officers. Generally, it comprises a three-tier plan, according to Minister of Defense Anatoly Serdyukov, that is to last from 2011 to 2020. The first stage is being conducted now, he claims, with the previously mentioned staff issues. The second stage will include "social issues," possibly hazing and the care of troops, while the final stage will deal with acquiring more modern armaments. As Serdyukov states, the final stage will be the most difficult:

> Armament supplies are quite a long process. We have divided it into two parts. At the first stage, which will

last until 2015, modern armaments in our army must comprise no less than 30% while this figure must increase to 70% by 2020. . . .[19]

Such long-term growth in hardware is very expensive overall and has to be evaluated within the context of expected declines in Russian gross domestic product (GDP), as projected by the Bank of Finland, which sees a growth of 5 percent in 2012, down from 8.1 percent in 2007.[20] Five percent growth is still good, especially in comparison with the anemic growth rates of western nations, and should provide some margin at least for the military to grow more quickly — but it will demand sacrifices in other areas of the budget.

In fact, of all categories in the projected budget that are scheduled to grow between 2011 and 2013, only two, defense and debt servicing, are scheduled to increase their share of gross domestic product (GDP). Debt servicing is scheduled to increase from 1.8 to 1.9 percent of GDP in that period, and defense from 2.9 to 3.3 percent: in other words, defense will increase by nearly 14 percent and debt servicing by 5.6 percent. All other broad budget categories — including health care, social measures, and education — would suffer declines as a percentage of GDP, and most (except social policy) will experience absolute declines in funding. These figures can be interpreted to mean that military spending is scheduled to gain strength in the Russian economy after a lapse and that, if the plan works out, by 2020 Russia will have what it wants in military hardware — possibly the necessary precision-guided munitions to take the place of NSNWs. Such an eventuality will likely affect Russian negotiating positions in any talks directed at the reduction of NSNWs.

Reducing Non-Strategic Nuclear Weapons.

The issue of deep reductions of NSNWs, particularly Russian ones, has been discussed very actively lately. The so-called disparity between western non-strategic nuclear arsenals and the greater Russian stockpiles of short-range nuclear weapons has been reflected, first, in the new *Strategic Concept* of the North Atlantic Treaty Organization adopted in Lisbon, Portugal, in November 2010,[21] and, second, in the Resolution on Advice and Consent regarding the ratification of the New U.S.-Russian START Treaty adopted by the U.S. Senate in December 2010. The latter document calls in part,

> upon the President to pursue, following consultation with allies, an agreement with the Russian Federation that would address the disparity between the tactical weapons stockpiles of the Russian Federation and the United States and would secure and reduce tactical nuclear weapons in a verifiable manner.[22]

Western concerns as regards Russian NSNWs are based on the following factors:
- reductions by the United States and Russia of their strategic nuclear arsenals will increase the Russian advantage in nuclear weapons as a whole;
- in case of a serious military conflict, TNWs belonging to the general purpose forces may be employed at an early stage of the conflict with a high degree of nuclear escalation;
- NSNWs are believed not to be equipped with the same highly reliable systems preventing unauthorized use as are strategic nuclear weapons, which makes the possibility of an unauthorized nuclear strike much higher;

- NSNWs, especially of older types, are believed to be less protected by various blocking devices, have smaller weight and size characteristics, and are tempting objects for terrorists.

Russia does not concur in any of the arguments mentioned above, except perhaps the second one. Taking into account the relative weakness of the Russian general-purpose forces, the Russian high command may be tempted in case of a major conflict to use TNWs to compensate for the numerical or technological superiority of the attacking enemy. As to the third and forth arguments, they may not be considered as well-founded since now all Russian TNWs are kept in safely guarded central storage sites and are equipped with highly reliable blocking devices which prevent their unauthorized use. The fact that there is not a single proven instance of loss or theft of a piece of nuclear ammunition testifies to their security.

Since there is no agreed definition of NSNWs, for the purpose of this chapter we shall consider to be non-strategic all nuclear weapons except for the following: (1) strategic nuclear warheads for intercontinental ballistic missiles (ICBMs) and sea launched ballistic missiles (SLBMs), and nuclear bombs and air-launched cruise missiles for strategic bombers as defined by New START; and (2) nuclear weapons that have been retired from the stockpile, are no longer functional, and are in the queue for dismantlement. Although no official data on Russian stockpiles of tactical nuclear weapons was ever published, Russia is believed to have at its disposal an estimated 3,700-5,400 non-strategic nuclear warheads, of which some 2,000 are deliverable. These include cruise missiles of various ranges, gravity bombs, torpedoes, and depth charges.

The Russian inventory has been reduced by at least 75 percent since 1991, down from an estimated 15,000-21,700 weapons at the time. In the 1990s, all of Russia's remaining non-strategic weapons were placed in central storage, in the sites operated by the 12th Main Directorate of the Russian Ministry of Defense, and are not deployed with delivery vehicles.[23] The chapter by Nikolai Sokov provides a more detailed discussion on the numbers of Russian NSNWs.

The status of NSNWs in Russian military strategy is critical. Under the present circumstances they are practically the only means of guaranteeing Russia's independence and territorial integrity. As Chief of the Russian General Staff Army General Nikolai Makarov said at the annual meeting with foreign military attaches accredited in Moscow, Russia (December 2008), "We consider NSNW as a deterrence factor for the huge amount of conventional and highly precision arms in possession of NATO countries in Europe."[24]

According to Russian military strategy, nuclear forces have two types of missions: traditional strategic deterrence, which relies primarily on strategic weapons, and limited-use nuclear forces in response to a large-scale conventional attack. Both missions are reflected in the Military Doctrine of the Russian Federation which says that nuclear weapons may be used: (1) "in response to the utilization of nuclear and other types of weapons of mass destruction against it and (or) its allies," and (2) "in the event of aggression against the Russian Federation involving the use of conventional weapons when the very existence of the state is placed under threat."[25]

The main reason for Russia's need for longer-range NSNWs is that long-range precision-guided conventional weapons provide a key advantage for the United States and NATO. To counter this, Russia is working hard to acquire similar long-range conventional strike assets and, in the meantime, relies on limited nuclear use, employing nuclear weapons of comparable ranges.

The Russian Navy attaches particular importance to NSNWs since, according to the Naval Doctrine of the Russian Federation for the period up to 2020, the Navy is tasked "to protect the territory of the Russian Federation from the sea [and] guard and secure state naval borders of the Russian Federation and air space above them."[26] Its reliance on NSNWs is understandable, considering that, numerically, the Russian Navy was reduced considerably since the beginning of the 1990s. Moreover, in all the latest military conflicts, the main strikes were delivered by cruise missiles from surface warships and submarines as well as naval aviation.

Russian and U.S./NATO rationales for maintaining NSNWs differ. U.S./NATO see their value largely in political terms; that is, providing a security link between the United States and Europe and serving as an element of NATO's nuclear capability. Russia attaches more military significance to its NSNWs. It sees those weapons as offsetting conventional force disadvantage vis-à-vis its neighbors, serving as a force enhancer should conventional defense fail, and offering possibilities for escalating or to controlling escalation. Moreover, Russia considers its TNWs as a counterbalance to the nuclear forces of third countries, the nuclear capabilities of practically all of which are able to reach the territory of Russia. The reduction of Russian strategic nuclear potential in accordance with the bilateral treaties with the United States relatively increases the role of Russian TNWs for the purpose of containing the nuclear countries of Eurasia.

Under present conditions, the range of options for the West in dealing with Russia's NSNWs may include (1) negotiated force limitations and reductions provided some conditions are met; and (2) confidence-building measures. Both options would have a potentially large impact on Russia, since it maintains a larger number of NSNWs. Reciprocity may be difficult given different interests and stockpile structures.

Concerning the numbers of weapons, the disparity between the United States and Russia, mentioned earlier, is quite problematic. Given the estimate that the United States in the near future will have only about 500 NSNWs compared to Russia's 2,000, any limit around 500 would result in reductions only on the Russian side, which is unacceptable to Moscow. On the other hand, any limit above 500 would leave Russia with a *de facto* numerical advantage, assuming the United States was unlikely to increase the number of its NSNWs. That situation, surely, would be unacceptable to Washington.

THE REDUCTION OF NSNWs AND NON-DEPLOYED STRATEGIC NUCLEAR WARHEADS

Before going into detail about weapons reduction, it should be noted that owing to the reasons mentioned above, Russia's attitude to reductions remains cool. Thus, if western nations want Russia to make some concessions on NSNWs issues, they should be receptive to progress concerning other issues on the Russian-U.S./NATO agenda, including the weaponization of space, non-nuclear strategic offensive weapons, missile defense, and conventional forces in Europe. It is a long-standing and oft-repeated position of the Russian government that progress on those questions could facilitate progress on NSNWs. The last time Minister of Foreign Affairs of Russia Sergey Lavrov reiterated such a position was at the Plenary meeting of the Conference on Disarmament in Geneva, Switzerland, on March 1, 2011. He said that:

> the Russian position on nuclear disarmament . . . is defined by the key principle of indivisibility of security. We insist that there is a clear need to take into account the factors that negatively affect strategic stability, such as plans to place weapons in outer space, to develop non-nuclear armed strategic offensive weapons, as well as unilateral deployment of a global BMD system. Nor could we ignore the considerable imbalances in conventional arms, especially against the background of dangerous conflicts persisting in many regions of the world. These factors [and their interrelationships] must be taken into account in the course of discussion on prospects for cuts of tactical nuclear weapons.[27]

There are at least three conditions for the start of negotiations on NSNWs that are part of Russia's official approach to the issue. First, in Russia's view, all nuclear powers should deploy their TNWs only on their national territories. Overseas storage infrastructures should be destroyed. Justification of this demand from the Russian viewpoint is very simple. In the past, when Warsaw Pact conventional superiority was obvious, NATO's tactical nuclear weapons might be considered a means of deterrence. Now with the alliance's obvious conventional superiority, they may be considered a means of offense. Second, Russia must complete the program of reequipping its armed forces and sharply reduce its lag behind the world's leading powers in high-precision weapons. Third, negotiations on the limitation and reduction of NSN-

Ws should be multilateral, with the participation of at least all *de jure* nuclear states, namely, the Russian Federation, the United States, the United Kingdom (UK), France, and China.

There is one more interesting aspect of the possible negotiations on reductions of TNWs. Back in 2000, the United States introduced the concept of "operationally deployed warheads"[28] into the strategic offensive weapons-reduction negotiations, thus changing the whole context of the NSNW problem. According to the provisions of the New START Treaty, operationally deployed warheads are those deployed on ICBMs and SLBMs. Air launched cruise missiles (ALCMs) and bombs in heavy bombers are not counted, since in peacetime they are kept in storage. Driven by the same logic, all tactical nuclear warheads (at least Russian) are not operationally deployed since they are also kept in storage. In this connection, it is rather difficult to imagine how the idea — discussed by Steven Pifer in Chapter 19 of this book — of a single limit covering all U.S. and Russian nuclear warheads (strategic and non-strategic, where each side is free to choose its own mix of strategic and non-strategic nuclear warheads) may be realized. The main problem for the United States with such an approach is that, if all non-deployed strategic warheads are counted, the overall disparity between Russia and the United States in nuclear weapons may disappear.

As to reductions of nondeployed strategic nuclear weapons (warheads and means of delivery), they will be carried out in a natural way within the framework of implementing the New START Treaty. Since the Treaty limits the number of means of delivery, there is no practical sense in storing an excessive number of nuclear warheads. They would be militarily neutralized and too expensive to maintain.

CONFIDENCE-BUILDING MEASURES REGARDING NON-STRATEGIC NUCLEAR WEAPONS

There are a number of possible confidence-building measures (CBMs) intended to create transparency and build trust between Russia and the West that could be agreed upon in a future agreement on NSNWs:

Greater Transparency. Both Russia and the United States have a good idea of the locations where the other stores its nuclear warheads, but less solid information on numbers. Transparency is desirable by itself and essential for any negotiated limits. As one significant step, Russia and the United States might agree to disclose publicly the total number of their non-strategic nuclear warheads in storage and the number of warheads in the dismantlement queue.

"Demating" Warheads from Delivery Systems. Russia has demated nuclear warheads from other non-strategic delivery systems. The sides might consider as a CBM formal statements affirming that nuclear warheads have been demated from their non-strategic delivery systems, and, as a matter of policy, declare that there is no intention of mating non-strategic nuclear warheads with delivery systems in the future.

Security of Nuclear Warheads. Russia and the United States, drawing in part on their Cooperative Threat Reduction experiences and working through the NATO-Russia Council, could conduct a joint threat assessment of the risk of terrorists penetrating a storage site and gaining access to nuclear weapons; partake in a joint security assessment of how site security might be improved to guard against such risks; and continue the practice of conducting recovery exercises in which Russia and U.S./NATO forces work together to recover stolen nuclear weapons or fissile material.

No Increase Commitment. As a minimal step, Russia and the United States might consider announcing that each will not increase the number of its nonstrategic nuclear warheads.

NATO's *Strategic Concept* pledged to seek the relocation of Russian nuclear weapons away from NATO territory. Such a move on the part of Russia is not practical, however, since it would be too costly and could reduce the operational capabilities of the Russian armed forces, especially of the Russian Northern Fleet. But the previously listed CBMs on NSNWs could by themselves build trust and momentum for broader progress on a much wider range of political and security issues.

There is one sensitive issue that must be resolved if U.S.-Russian agreement on CBMs regarding TNWs is to be reached. Transparency on this issue is very important to some European states. In all the informal discussions concerning the question of transparency of NSNWs, it is presupposed that the United States is going to share information on Russian TNWs with its NATO allies. But such an approach is contrary to the Russian official position based on reciprocity. Thus, as with possible limitations and reductions of NSNWs, with regard to CBMs, Russia will definitely insist on French and UK involvement in the process or even discussion of NATO's nuclear potential as a whole.

ENDNOTES - CHAPTER 7

1. Thomas Friedman, *The Lexus and the Olive Tree*, New York: Ferrar, Straus, Giroux, 1999, p. 8.

2. Joseph Stiglitz, *Globalization and Its Discontents*, New York: W. W. Norton & Company, 2002, p. 5.

3. Fyodor Lukyanov, "Russian Dilemmas in a Multipolar World," *Columbia Journal of International Affairs*, Vol. 63, No. 2, Spring-Summer, 2010, p. 19.

4. *Ibid.*, p. 26.

5. See, for instance, Valentin Romanov's comments in "V stremlenii uiti ot kontrolia OON," *Nezavisimoe voennoe obozrenie*, No. 26, July 9-15, 1999, p. 4.

6. Mikhail Molchanov, "Russia and Globalization," *Perspectives on Global Development and Technology*, Vol. 4, Nos. 3-4, 2005, p. 414.

7. This term is adapted from research done by one of Hudson's students, Lacey Davidson, and is embodied in her unpublished paper, "The Shift in Globalization and Its Impact on Russian-American Relations," 2011, p. 8. She coins the phrase "Multipolarity globalism." Others have dealt with the idea, of course. For instance it is the topic of the Doha Round of World Trade Organization trade talks where it is called "Multipolarity at the Globalization Age." See *saopaulo2011.ipsa.org/paper/doha-round-multipolarity-globalization-age*.

8. Available from *wakeupfromyourslumber.com/node/646*.

9. *Ibid.*

10. Joseph Nye, *The Future of Power*, New York: Public Affairs, 2011, p. 155.

11. *Strategiia natsional'noi bezopasnosti Rossiiskoi Federatsii do 2020 goda*, May 12, 2009, para. 45, available from *www.scrf.gov.ru/documents/99.html*.

12. Available from *esa.un.org/unpd/wpp/unpp/p2k0data.asp*.

13. *The Military Balance, 2010,* London, UK: International Institute for Strategic Studies, 2010, p. 211, cites Russian Chief of

the General Staff Nikolai Makarov on the one-half figure; health issues among recruits are discussed on p. 209.

14. Fyodor Lukyanov, "After Tskhinvali," *Vremya novostei*, August 11, 2008, p. 1, as translated in *Current Digest of the Russian Press*, Vol. 60, No. 32, September 2, 2008, p. 4, available from *dlib. eastview.com/browse/doc/20437948*.

15. Anton Lavrov, "Timeline of Russian-Georgian Hostilities in August 2008," in Ruslan Pukhov, ed., *The Tanks of August*, Foreword by David Glanz, Moscow, Russia: Center for Analysis of Strategies and Technologies, 2010, p. 40.

16. See also *The Military Balance, 2009*, London, UK: International Institute for Strategic Studies, pp. 210-212, for an analysis of Russian military performance.

17. Anton Lavrov, "Russian Air Losses in the Five-Day War Against Georgia," in Pukhov, *The Tanks of August*, pp. 99, 104. Lavrov also notes that supposed "Georgian" aircraft shown as shot down on Russian television were actually Russian ones.

18. *Ibid.*, pp. 99, 105.

19. Sergey Guneev, "Russia to reform its armed forces by 2020—defense minister," as reported in *RIA Novosti*, available from *en.rian.ru/mlitary_news/20101031/161152980.html*.

20. *Russian Analytical Digest, No.* 88, November 29, 2010, p. 4. Bank of Finland data.

21. See *www.nato.int/lisbon2010/strategic-concept-2010-eng.pdf*.

22. See p. 25, *www.senate.gov/general/search/search_cfm.cfm? q=REsolution+on+Advice+and+Consent&x=16&y=9&site=default_ collection&num=10&filter=0*.

23. All figures concerning Russian tactical nuclear stockpiles are expert estimates.

24. "Tovarishchi potentsial'nye protivniki—Nachal'nik rossi- iskogo Genshtaba rasskazal inostrannym voennym attache o re-

forme armii," *Vremia novostei*, No. 230, December 12, 2008, available from *www.vremya.ru/2008/230/4/218862.html*.

25. *Voennaia doktrina Rossiiskoi Federatsii*, February 5, 2010, para. 22, available from *news.kremlin.ru/ref_notes/461*.

26. *Morskaya doktrina Rossiiskoi Federatsii na period do 2020 goda*, July 27, 2001, Section I-1, available from *www.scrf.gov.ru/documents/34.html*.

27. Available from *www.reachingcriticalwill.org/political/cd/cdindex.html*.

28. Statement of the President of the United States of America on November 13, 2001, available from *www.armscontrol.org/factsheets/sort-glance#Note3*.

CHAPTER 8

RUSSIAN PERSPECTIVES ON NON-STRATEGIC NUCLEAR WEAPONS

Nikolai Sokov

Russian non-strategic nuclear weapons (NSNWs) remain a hot issue in U.S.-Russian relations, in North Atlantic Treaty Organization (NATO)-Russian relations, and in transatlantic and intra-European relations. The reason they figure so prominently is simple: Russia has many more NSNWs than the United States. Since the United Kingdom (UK) and France no longer have NSNWs, the European balance in that category of nuclear weapons is massively skewed — an estimated 180 B-61 nuclear bombs the United States still keeps in Europe vis-à-vis several thousand Russian weapons, variously estimated to be between 2,000 and 7,000. A significant — but unknown — share of these is deployed in the Asian part of Russia, but usually estimates of the Western-Russian balance proceed from the totality of the Russian NSNW arsenal.

On top of this imbalance, there are also concerns about the safety and security of NSNWs in Russia. Many believe that these weapons are highly vulnerable to theft or diversion and that some of them lack permissive action links (PALs) and thus could be used by unauthorized persons. These concerns, which were quite valid in the 1990s (the present author has written about them in the past), should probably no longer occupy our attention. Older weapons that lacked PALs, which could have remained part of the arsenal 15 or so years ago, have likely been eliminated or at least refurbished and equipped with protection against unauthorized use. The massive shuffle of weapons, which took place in the first half of 1990s, has long been over, and there is no reason to believe that some are still lying around unaccountable. Security of storage sites has been increased as well, often with U.S. assistance.

Finally, there is concern about possible security threats associated with the large number of Russian NSNWs. These include several rather different problems. First, some states in NATO (the Baltic states, in particular) are troubled that Russia has deployed short-range (tactical) nuclear weapons (TNWs) close to their territories and plans to deploy more in Kaliningrad Oblast, an exclave of Russian territory between Lithuania and Poland. This concern has once again heated up acutely after President Dmitri Medvedev in November 2011 threatened to deploy Iskander tactical missiles in that region in response to American plans to station missile defense assets in Europe[1] (a previous threat, in 2008, was withdrawn after the Barack Obama administration revised earlier plans for missile defense formulated under President George W. Bush).

Other worries are more theoretical and have to do with the nature of TNWs, which militaries generally intend to embed with conventional forces during war. Specifically, there is fear that such weapons could be released to troops in time of crisis and that authority to use them could be delegated to combatant commanders. In this case, any acute crisis could easily result in the early use of nuclear weapons, especially if commanders in the field fear losing such weapons to a first strike by the United States and NATO. This apprehension is understandable, given not only the overwhelming qualitative superiority of U.S. conventional assets, but also the fact that the Russian military appears to ascribe to them almost mystical capabilities.

Yet these concerns are most likely poorly founded. First, there is no reason to believe that Iskander missiles are equipped with nuclear warheads. They certainly could be, but so far there have been no indications that the Russian military assigns them nuclear roles. Instead, they fit well the decade-long effort to develop high-precision conventional capability. There are also no reasons to believe that the ground forces have nuclear weapons. This point will be developed in detail later in this chapter, but it is sufficient to note here that, according to available information, all nuclear weapons that were previously assigned to the ground forces have been withdrawn and either eliminated or are awaiting dismantlement. Hence, worries about early use appear highly exaggerated. As in the previous case, such concerns had certain grounds in the 1990s, but hardly 15 years later.

The majority of these trepidations (except those that pertain to safety and security of the NSNW stock) follow traditional logic, which proceeds from two key assumptions: (1) if weapons with certain capabilities and in certain numbers exist, there is a political and military decision behind that fact, and (2) weapons exist to support one or more missions either in the context of deterrence (suasion through credible threat) or in the context of offensive operations. These assumptions have an important corollary: from known facts (that is, concerning an arsenal with reasonably known parameters) one can derive political decisions and military strategy. This logic was widely used during the Cold War for analysis of Soviet nuclear strategy. It has one, but critical, drawback: the existing arsenal can be the result of many other factors — for example, of unrelated decisions, inertia, and research and development (R&D) failures.

This chapter seeks to demonstrate that the existing stockpile of Russian NSNWs, which is but a remnant of the Soviet stockpile, does not reflect any conscious military and political decisions. Instead, it is a residuum of inertia and lacks a discernible mission. Moreover, Russian resistance to any dialogue on NSNWs is a result of domestic politics rather than a desire to protect a valuable asset.

NUMBERS

The size of the Russian NSNW stockpile is notoriously difficult to assess. This author has previously estimated the active stockpile at around 2,000 warheads with perhaps as many as double that number slated for elimination.[2] That figure closely corresponds with the assessment of Hans Kristensen and Robert Norris.[3] While Russia has not provided any official numbers, it has disclosed that the NSNW force was reduced by 75 percent since the adoption of Presidential Nuclear Initiatives (PNIs) in 1991.[4] If one accepts the high-end estimate of the Soviet NSNW arsenal in 1991 as almost 22,000,[5] the figure for the late 2000s should be 5,000 warheads, which closely matches the Sokov and Kristensen-Norris estimates of the entire stockpile, including weapons waiting to be dismantled. It is also possible that the number of weapons slated for dismantlement might be even higher.

Perhaps more important than sheer numbers is the breakdown of the stockpile into categories, which taken together define the non-strategic nuclear posture. Speaking in 2007, General Vladimir Verkhovtsev disclosed that Russia had completed elimination of warheads assigned to the ground forces, which had been promised in 1991 through PNIs by George H. W.

Bush and Mikhail Gorbachev. It is not clear whether dismantlement had been completed or these weapons were only slated for elimination; the latter is probably the case given the large numbers of weapons in question. Verkhovtsev also indicated that Russia no longer deployed tactical nuclear weapons (TNWs, used as a synonym for NSNWs) on surface ships and submarines, but "if necessary . . . could deploy them [and] no one should doubt that."[6] To the extent that one can tease the current NSNW posture out of the available data, it seems to be as follows:

- Weapons assigned to aircraft. These are the only weapons that belong to the "deployed" category under PNIs, although the precise meaning of that designation is unclear as bombs and short-range missiles are not deployed on aircraft in peacetime anyway. This category consists of two subcategories, the difference being potentially very significant. One is bombs assigned to tactical aircraft—the element that is very much the same as the United States has in Europe. The second subcategory is weapons assigned to the medium bomber Tu-22M3. This is certainly not a tactical force by any definition and should be more properly classified as an intermediate-range force. The future of these assets is unclear since the Tu-22M3 is nearing the end of its service life. Which aircraft might assume its nuclear roles (and whether any will) is still unclear. The most obvious candidate, the Su-24 and Su-34, have a significantly shorter range. There are also plans (quite remote, it seems) to develop a new medium bomber.
- Weapons assigned to ships and submarines. These are in the "nondeployed" category,

but by most accounts are kept at naval bases ready to be loaded aboard on short notice. This group includes a variety of weapons — short- and intermediate-range; anti-ship; and those designed to destroy targets on land. Although they can be employed from surface ships, it is strike submarines, especially the new class of strike submarines now emerging in Russia, that serve as the main platforms of these weapons.

- Weapons assigned to air defense and missile defense. The roles of these weapons are unclear, and it is difficult to fathom why Russia still retains them. Warheads for the Moscow missile defense system in particular do not have a discernible role except for various flavors of psychological manipulation. No one in Russia seems enthralled by the idea of high-altitude nuclear bursts over Moscow for purposes of defense, but the system apparently cannot function without nuclear warheads (work on advanced non-nuclear missile defense assets, the S-500, is still in the early stages), so one could conclude that the retention of nuclear warheads for missile defense is a formality. In any event, all warheads in that category are reportedly kept separate from delivery vehicles, meaning that neither the missile defense nor the remaining nuclear-capable air defense assets are operational on short notice.

- Warheads for the ground forces. They have apparently been removed from the active stockpile, but there is probably a fair number of those that still await dismantlement; whether there are any warheads that remain usable (i.e., were refurbished relatively recently) is anyone's guess. As mentioned above, there has been a strong foreign concern, especially in the Baltic states, that the deployment of short-range Iskander missiles signifies a new nuclear deployment, but so far there has been no indication that these missiles are equipped with nuclear warheads or that a stockpile of nuclear warheads is readily available for them. At least one well-placed independent expert, Igor Korotchenko, raised the prospect that Iskanders might be equipped with nuclear warheads,[7] but the meaning of his statement is unclear: first, it seems to suggest that today Iskanders are not nuclear; second, it might represent just another instance of a scare tactic as Moscow tries to persuade NATO to reach accommodation on missile defense.

- Nuclear mines and portable nuclear mines. All have reportedly been eliminated.

Even the very limited available data about the Russian NSNW stockpile allows us to draw several important conclusions about longer-term trends:

- The arsenal is clearly dwindling. Verkhovtsev noted, in the above-referenced interview, that reductions were deeper than in those prescribed by the PNIs—75 percent compared to the required 64 percent. The 75 percent statement was made in 2005. Since then, Russia has continued to report the 75 percent figure, but that most likely reflects a reluctance to go through a complicated interagency process to ascertain and get approval for updated figures.
- All available data suggest that the arsenal will continue to dwindle, albeit at a slow pace, most

likely determined by the limited capacity of warhead dismantlement processes. It is impossible to determine what the end goal is or whether Russia even has a clear-cut development plan for the ultimate size of the NSNW force. It appears possible that no such determination has yet been made. Reductions proceed in a piecemeal fashion, much as the United States gradually reduced its NSNW force in Europe over the last 2 decades.

- The changes in the composition of the NSNW arsenal hint at the degree of utility assigned to different categories. Clearly, the naval warheads represent the most valuable element of the arsenal while the ground forces no longer need them (at least the military and political leaderships do not see value in nuclear missions for these forces). The same might be true for the missile defense and air defense NSNWs, although information about these categories is very sketchy. Non-strategic missions for the Air Force seem to occupy the middle ground between these two extremes.

Evolutionary trends of the NSNW arsenals will be treated in greater depth in the next section. At the moment, the most important conclusion is that the NSNW arsenal will continue to shrink, and the gap between the American and the Russian NSNW forces will slowly narrow on their own accord without extraordinary action on the part of the United States and NATO.

STRATEGY

Russian NSNWs attracted international attention in the mid-1990s, when Russian government, military, and nongovernmental experts were discussing options for a response to the increased perceived-threat level as a result of NATO enlargement.[8] At that time, some regarded enhanced reliance on short-range assets as an attractive way to balance the perceived new threat. The advantages of that response seemed convincing: the arsenal was ready at hand, the military could use existing manuals and doctrines, and the limited-use option appeared more credible than a response solely with strategic weapons.

Such discussion did not translate into policy, however. The Boris Yeltsin government opted for a political solution (the NATO-Russia Charter), so that NSNWs remained in limbo for a few more years. In 1997 and 1998, the Russian government issued a series of policy documents — "The National Security Concept" (December 1997) and several decrees signed by Yeltsin in July and August 1998[9] — which stipulated a single mission for nuclear weapons, that of strategic deterrence (that is, the use of nuclear weapons was confined to the one mission of global war). The only tangible result of the NSNW discussion preceding the Yeltsin decisions was greater attention paid to NSNWs, including making them a target for early deep reductions.

The game-changer for Russian nuclear strategy was the war in Kosovo in 1999. The war was widely regarded in Russia as evidence that the United States and NATO were prone to use force whenever they could not obtain what they wanted through diplomacy. The fact that the war was launched without authorization by the United Nations (UN) Security Council was particularly troubling, as Russia had regarded its right of veto there as an important tool ensuring its immunity to foreign interference in its sphere of influence. It was obvious to everyone that a new round of the war in Chechnya was not far off (in fact, it had started in the fall of 1999, with the incursion of Chechens into neighboring Dagestan; but even without that, a new Russian campaign to restore control over Chechnya was almost inevitable in the next year or two). Moscow came to be seriously concerned about the possible interference of the United States and NATO in that next war—the situation being almost identical to the conflict in Kosovo.

Little wonder, then, that even before the war in Kosovo ended, the Russian Security Council (Vladimir Putin chaired the first meeting in the capacity of Secretary) commissioned the development of a new military doctrine as the fundamental blueprint of the country's defense policy. From the very beginning nuclear weapons were assigned a prominent place. To deter the numerically and qualitatively superior U.S. and NATO conventional forces, the new *Military Doctrine* of 2000 proposed the concept of "de-escalation" — the threat of a limited nuclear strike in response to a large-scale attack that exceeded the defense capability of Russian conventional forces.[10] Essentially, this meant that nuclear weapons were assigned a second mission in addition to deterring a global war.

Many elements of the new doctrine were not developed in detail until subsequent years. The t's were crossed and i's dotted in 2003, in a document titled "Current Tasks for the Development of the Russian Federation's Armed Forces."[11] While the 2000 document replaced the traditional criterion of "unacceptable damage" to the enemy with a narrower one, "tailored damage" (*zadannyi ushcherb*), the 2003 document for the first time defined "tailored damage" to mean "damage, subjectively unacceptable to the enemy, which exceeds the benefits the aggressor expects to gain as a result of the use of military force." Tailored damage is particularly associated with the mission of de-escalation: a limited response with limited damage in response to a limited attack would, it was hoped, de-escalate the crisis.

The 2003 document also provided vital clues to the role of various elements of the Russian nuclear forces. The section on the nature of contemporary wars and armed conflicts emphasized, in particular, that the United States and its allies demonstrated the pattern of using long-range strike weapons, including airborne delivery systems and submarine-launched cruise missiles (SLCMs), at an early stage of wars in the 1990s. It also noted that victory was assured by the ability of the United States and NATO to achieve domination at the early stage of conflict. Accordingly, the new document postulated:

> the utmost necessity of having the capability to strike military assets of the enemy (long-range high-precision weapons, long-range air forces) outside the immediate area of conflict. To achieve this, [we] need both our own long-range high-precision strike capability and other assets that enable [us] to transfer hostilities directly to enemy territory.[12]

By implication, then, the limited nuclear strike had to be executed at an early stage of the conflict.

These provisions left little role for short-range nuclear weapons. Exercises held since the adoption of the 2000 military doctrine simulated limited nuclear use against airbases and aircraft carriers from which the United States was expected to fly missions against Russia, as well as against command and control centers. Targets featured in these simulations were located throughout Europe, the Pacific, South-East Asia, Indian Ocean, and even the continental United States. Short-range weapons (such as tactical land-based missiles or tactical aircraft) could not reach these targets. Instead, simulations featured medium and heavy bombers carrying gravity bombs, short-range missiles, and air-launched cruise missiles (ALCMs).

Nuclear warheads for submarine launched cruise missiles of various ranges, which are stored in 12th Glavnoye Upravleniye Ministerstvo Oborony (GUMO)[13] facilities at naval bases, appear to be another component of the forces Russia could use in a conflict with NATO. Russian naval commanders admit that they simply cannot confront the U.S. Navy—in the case of a direct clash between Russia and the United States—without reliance on these assets. Accordingly, crews of surface ships and submarines have reportedly trained to mate warheads to SLCMs and launch them.[14] In fact, Vice-Admiral Oleg Burtsev, deputy chief of the Navy's Main Staff, declared that the role of TNWs on attack nuclear submarines would increase. "The range of tactical nuclear weapons is growing, as is their accuracy. They do not need to deliver high-yield warheads; instead it is possible to make a transition to low-yield nuclear warheads that could be installed on the existing types of cruise missiles," he asserted.[15]

The 2010 *Military Doctrine* did not change these provisions. The mission of de-escalation was apparently not even discussed in depth, at least not at the public level; attention was concentrated almost exclusively on the new attempt at military reform. The only intrigue pertaining to nuclear weapons concerned the proposal to expand de-escalation to one more category of conflicts: the 2000 document had assigned nuclear weapons only to "global" and "regional" wars,[16] but in 2009 there was a proposal to also assign them to "local wars."[17] This proposal would have applied nuclear weapons to situations like the war with Georgia in 2008 and was finally rejected. Where non-strategic nuclear assets are concerned, the failure of the proposal to expand the role of nuclear missions to a new type of conflict only confirmed that there were few, if any, targets in the immediate vicinity of Russia.

Thus, the Russian strategy regarding use of nuclear weapons for purposes of deterrence has not changed since 1999 (or 2000, the year of its formal adoption). The place of NSNWs in this strategy is not straightforward. It appears that Russia continues to rely on longer-range air- and sea-based NSNWs as well as on shorter-range anti-ship and anti-submarine naval NSNWs. The other NSNWs do not appear to have a discernible role. In fact, Moscow is clearly not concerned about the traditional Cold War-style large-scale invasion using traditional conventional armies. Hence, it does not need TNWs for roles like NATO assigned to them during the Cold War (deterrence of tank armies). The broad assertion about Russia needing NSNWs to compensate for weakness of its conventional forces misses an important point: it is a different type of conventional forces that Russia is concerned about, forces with technologically enhanced capabilities, hence the assets it needs to confront them are also different.

Short-range weapons are also believed to have another role — that of deterring Chinese conventional forces.[18] The logic is similar to that underlying the common belief about the role of TNWs vis-à-vis NATO: if the opponent has superior conventional forces, Russian needs to rely on nuclear weapons. While Russia faces a conventional force in the European theater that is technologically superior, in the Eastern theater Chinese superiority is numerical, hence the role of NSNWs should be the same as the one NATO assigned to them during the Cold War.

It is difficult to judge whether such reasoning is the real view; rumors about simulated use of a tactical nuclear weapon in the Far East during large-scale maneuvers seem to confirm it. In the Far East, Russia does face somewhat the same situation confronting NATO during the Cold War — nuclear weapons would be used on its own territory and against densely populated and relatively economically developed areas. Yet, Russia does not have the same opportunity that NATO had: while NATO could use TNWs against Soviet/Warsaw Pact troops and military infrastructure on the latter's side of the border, Russia does not have this advantage in the Far East because there are few valuable targets on the Chinese side of the Russian-Chinese border. In the absence of sufficiently reliable information about nuclear planning for the Eastern theater, and given General Verkhovtsev's statement that all land-based TNWs have been removed from the active stockpile, one can rely only on what seems most reasonable. It seems that if NSNWs have a role vis-à-vis China, they should be employing air-based delivery systems that have longer ranges than land-based ones.

Confidential interviews with high-level Russian military officials indicate that the nuclear weapons assigned to deter China are the strategic and inter-mediate-range ones, that is, the weapons capable of reaching political, military, and economic targets deep inside China. The logic here is similar to that applied in the military doctrine for deterrence of the United States and NATO: the emphasis is on long-range assets. This makes sense. The quantitative preponderance of China is extremely high while the qualitative gap now favoring Russia is narrowing quickly (perhaps it has already disappeared); thus any deterrence of China can only be strategic in nature if it is to be effective.

DOMESTIC POLITICS

If NSNWs do not have an authentic role in Russian military strategy, at least where NATO is concerned, an obvious question is why Moscow remains so sensitive to even the mildest proposals dealing with the transparency of its NSNW arsenal, to say nothing about proposals for reductions. The answer to this dilemma seems to lie in the realm of the internal politics of Russia rather than its military policy. It is a complex mix of domestic and bureaucratic politics, (mis)perceptions, and idiosyncrasies.

"No More Unreciprocated Concessions."

Western attempts to convince Russia to reduce its sizable NSNW arsenal emphasize reason and fairness: if Russia does not need these weapons, if it has massive superiority in that category, it should accept reductions. To a large extent, this view hearkens back to the late 1980s, during the Gorbachev-Eduard Shevardnadze time, when the Soviet Union would sometimes make what Shevardnadze once called "concessions to common sense." But this is not how the majority of Russians (even those opposed to Putin/ Medvedev government) think today. Among broad sections of the public and elite, the late 1980s and the 1990s are associated with unreciprocated concessions that actually undermined the interests and security of the Soviet Union and later Russia. Proponents of this view cite the enlargement of NATO and the refusal of the United States to include navies under the Conventional Forces in Europe (CFE) Treaty as examples of Western perfidy. Russians also turn the argument around, saying there is no justification for even a limited number of U.S. TNWs in Europe since NATO is much more powerful than Russia — these weapons should have been withdrawn.

Within this dominant political framework, therefore, any Russian advantage, no matter how illusory, should be either preserved or exchanged for Western concessions in areas of interest to Russia. Furthermore, persistent attempts to persuade Russia to reduce its TNWs or at least disclose their location, numbers, and other information, tend to be regarded with reflexive suspicion, without serious thought about the reasoning behind the proposals. Instead, such attempts are seen as "proof" that these weapons are truly valuable. Hence, the "asking price" rises even higher. The bottom line is simple: Russia will likely turn deaf ears to Western entreaties on its NSNWs under any foreseeable leadership configuration whether Putin-Medvedev, Putin, Medvedev, or any realistically electable member of the opposition.

Inertia.

The longer this position is maintained, the more entrenched it becomes. The key elements of the current Russian position have remained unchanged for over a decade. Changing it without manifestly cogent reasons might seem to the other party to be an unjustified concession. Such a dynamic can be changed only with a radical leadership change (as happened when Gorbachev assumed the highest office in the Soviet Union) or with a sea change in the environment. Neither is present or appears on the horizon today.

"CAPABILITIES-BASED PLANNING"

The Russian elite, including the military leadership, acutely feels the uncertainty of the international environment. The main threat is still associated with the United States and its allies, but other potential threats are emerging (China in particular), and the Russian military is reluctant to part with any assets it has at its disposal. In 2005-07, similar arguments were made in favor of Russia's withdrawal from the Intermediate Range Nuclear Forces (INF) Treaty, rationalized by the possession or impending development of intermediate-range missiles by "other states." Although specific states were never mentioned, the culprits were obvious—China, India, Pakistan, Israel, Iran, and perhaps even North Korea. What emerged was the concept of "capabilities-based planning," which favors maintenance of all available assets as insurance against unforeseen (and unforeseeable) threats.

Moreover, Russian efforts to develop a modern conventional capability have been very slow and should be judged as largely unsuccessful. Strong non-nuclear capability will hardly emerge before the end of this decade and will more likely be well into the next one. Consequently, nuclear weapons retain potentially high value, not only in the eyes of the military but also in the eyes of the public, the latter mostly for psychological reasons. The military will be reluctant to sacrifice even assets that are seemingly unnecessary until such time as the new military posture becomes clearer and the outcome of the ongoing stage of military reform can be reasonably well anticipated.

Parochial Group Politics.

The current Russian position on TNWs can also be attributed to a peculiar alignment of relevant interest groups within the military. As was noted above, NSNWs do not figure prominently in the current nuclear strategy, but this generalization does not apply equally to all parts of the military. The Navy is interested in keeping TNWs as a "just-in-case" option,[19] especially vis-à-vis the U.S. Navy. In contrast, the Air Force appears much less interested in TNWs except for weapons assigned to Tu-22M3 medium bombers. Other groups such as the ground forces, having all but lost them, probably have even less interest in TNWs. While the majority of the forces have limited interest in NSNWs and could, with the right set of inducements, support reductions, they will not take the lead in investing political resources to support such a policy. Thus, outside the Navy, support for NSNWs can be characterized as "a mile wide, but a foot deep." The Navy, however, has a strong and focused interest in maintaining NSNWs. In the absence of a strong opposing constituency, its interest inevitably prevails.

In a similar vein, the Foreign Ministry, another important player in the arms control "game," is also reluctant to push for a change of the Russian position: it has many other more pressing items on its agenda, and apparently seeks to exploit NSNWs as a lever to achieve diplomatic goals. In other words, the present lineup of interest groups within the Russian government strongly favors the continuation of the current position. It can be changed only in response to a strong push from above, from the political leadership. The alternative is some sort of package deal that includes major western concessions. Over the years, however, the "asking price" has become so high that NATO concessions on the scale needed to win the national majority to the side of NSNW reduction, or even serious transparency, appear unlikely.

ARMS CONTROL CHALLENGES

Russian ambivalence with regard to NSNWs might also reflect the challenges of crafting a verifiable treaty. The traditional approach, according to which nuclear weapons are accounted for and neutralized through verifiable reduction of nuclear-capable delivery vehicles, is inapplicable to TNWs. New accounting rules and verification procedures need to be designed for these weapons. This endeavor, in turn, involves much more intrusive verification at military bases and, for the first time, at one of the most sensitive categories of nuclear-related facilities—storage sites for nuclear weapons. While such procedures are not, in principle, unthinkable, it would require a huge investment of political resources to overcome entrenched resistance and political opposition.

Paradoxically, transparency itself does not elicit much opposition, especially among the professional military. Resistance seems rather to reflect embarrassment at publicly announcing very high figures (and possibly confirming that unofficial estimates of the Russian NSNW arsenal are reasonably accurate). This putative embarrassment was probably the main reason why Russia did not divulge official data about its nuclear stockpile following the U.S. example in the spring of 2010 at the Non-Proliferation Treaty (NPT) Review Conference. Unofficially, members of the Russian delegation indicated that Moscow would soon do the same and even expressed irritation that Washington went ahead with its announcement without coordinating it with Moscow. Almost two years later, however, the figures have still not been published.

The third popular Western proposal—the withdrawal of NSNWs away from the border with NATO appears the most broadly acceptable, except to the Navy. As a rule, the Russian military responds with the question, How far from the border? It appears reluctant to withdraw NSNWs to an area beyond the Urals because China could interpret that as a hostile move. On the other hand, the military seems quite relaxed about withdrawal by a shorter distance (beyond the Volga, for example). The Navy is an exception here again—the bulk of its NSNWs are at the bases of the Northern Fleet right across the border from Norway. These weapons cannot be moved because the Navy does not have bases further east, so it also argues against proposals involving withdrawal.

THE RUSSIAN NSNW POSITION: LIMITS AND CONDITIONS OF EVOLUTION

The Russian position on TNWs appears very static and also very stable. The rationale for keeping a relatively large arsenal of such nuclear weapons appears relatively weak: short-range weapons do not have a role while retention of intermediate-range assets enjoys limited support in the Air Force, with only the Navy appearing to be a die-hard advocate of keeping them. Of greater importance is the fact that support for the reduction of sub-strategic weapons does not exist at all. While the reasons for that alignment of interests and positions are political and more often than not psychological, their strength should not be underestimated. Hence, again, it is difficult to expect a major shift in the Russian attitude toward NSNWs in the near future.

The current Russian position, which conditions any dialogue on NSNWs in the context of a proposed withdrawal of U.S. TNWs from Europe, has a certain logic behind it, as discussed earlier (since NATO has conventional superiority over Russia, it does not need nuclear weapons). More important, the Russian position is calculated to avoid discussion of Russian NSNWs. Moscow has calculated — correctly — that NATO would not be able to agree on complete withdrawal. Difficult deliberations within the Alliance during the last several years (in the run-up to the Tallinn, Estonia, ministerial meeting, continuing to the Lisbon, Portugal, summit, and now in the context of NATO's upcoming Defense and Deterrence Posture Review (DDPR) have confirmed the validity of this calculation.

If anything, the Russian position has only toughened. During the New START ratification hearings,

Foreign Minister Sergey Lavrov declared on the subject of NSNWs that negotiations cannot be held on just one element of the strategic balance because that balance includes many other elements, such as conventional strategic weapons, space-based weapons, missile defense, and imbalance in conventional forces (in that order).[20] The piling up of additional conditions reflected perhaps the perceived Russian fear of stronger U.S. pressure on Moscow with regard to NSNW negotiations and of the possibility that the Obama administration might actually offer a complete withdrawal of U.S. TNWs from Europe as part of a proposed package (there was widespread belief in 2009 that withdrawal was on the agenda of the new White House team).

Complete withdrawal of U.S. TNWs from Europe remains perhaps the only option to *force* Russia to start discussion of NSNWs: Russia has promised to do so and, whether it wants to or not, it will not have much choice. This option appears closed for the moment, however, since NATO is unlikely to abandon the Lisbon consensus in the near future. Paradoxically, complete withdrawal of U.S. NSNWs from Europe might be regarded in Moscow as less than a positive development because it would force Russia to do *something*, while the domestic lineup is clearly in favor of doing nothing. It seems that Moscow would be satisfied if the current international debate on NSNWs comes to naught, as have previous discussions of the topic. One is forced to question the very existence of any Russian interest in the issue of U.S. NSNWs in Europe that could be leveraged by the United States and NATO.

Given that situation in Moscow, prospects for control, reduction, and/or transparency of NSNWs appear bleak. Of late, the Russian military has gravitated to what it calls an "integrative" assessment of the Russia-NATO military balance, which includes all elements of the equation and seems to point to a very comprehensive package that would be required to achieve movement on this one element. Other chapters in the present book also point this out as a key Russian approach. The package would include all elements listed by Lavrov in the statement referenced above: conventional forces — probably within the framework of Adapted CFE; space-based weapons (it remains unclear exactly how Russians define them); certainly missile defense; and long-range conventional assets.

Within that list, most items are a no-go for NATO. The Alliance has not been able to agree on the withdrawal of TNWs — owing to a large extent to the position of some East/Central European members. Now, even the erstwhile proponents of that move, the Germans, seem to have accepted the consensus position, which foresees reductions on both sides under the assumption that some number — probably a smaller number — of U.S. TNWs would remain in Europe. Progress on the Adapted CFE is blocked by the continuing controversy about the status of Russian troops in Transdniestria, the would-be break-away region from Moldova (Moscow claims their troops do not constitute a base, but rather a small contingent of peacekeepers), as well as the presence of Russian troops in Abkhazia and South Ossetia, which Moscow now regards as independent states to which the original 1999 Istanbul agreements would be inapplicable.

It should be noted, however, that long-range conventional strike assets probably represent the only truly valid concern for Russia. It was noted above that the key security issue for the Russian military is the repetition of what has come to be regarded as standard American strategy—inflicting severe casualties, even near defeat, on the enemy during the opening stage of any military campaign using precision-guided weapons launched from long distances. It was also noted that Russian "de-escalation" strategy foresees limited use of nuclear weapons against bases, aircraft carriers, and command and control centers involved in such a campaign.

Seen from that perspective, the unfavorable balance of traditional conventional forces in Europe, which are subject to the CFE Treaty (as well as to the Adapted CFE) are not much of a concern for Moscow. They expect that an attack, if it took place, would not involve these forces. Hence, one could, under the right set of circumstances, easily drop CFE issues from the package advocated by Moscow. Missile defense could also be discussed separately, in the context of the strategic balance.

Tackling NSNWs and long-range strike assets within the same agreement would be highly uncomfortable and unconventional. Yet, if we cannot agree on the complete withdrawal of U.S. TNWs from Europe, this approach is something to think about. Ukrainian researcher Polina Sinovets proposed in a recent paper that a ratio of one NSNW per an agreed number of conventional strike assets could be established to achieve at least some reduction of Russian NSNWs and a set of transparency measures covering both classes of assets in Europe.[21] This would not be an easy package to negotiate, but at least it would attempt to meet Russian concerns. At the moment, unfortunately, the U.S./NATO position certainly does not force Moscow to negotiate, nor even tempt it to do so.

ENDNOTES - CHAPTER 8

1. "Zayavlenieprezidenta v svyazi s situatsiei, kotorayaslozhilasvokrugsistemy PRO stran NATO v Evrope" (Statement of the President with Respect to the Situation that has Emerged Around the Missile Defense System of NATO Countries in Europe), November 23, 2011, available from *president.kremlin.ru/news/13637*.

2. Miles Pomper, Willian Potter, and Nikolai Sokov, *Reducing and Regulating Tactical (Non-strategic) Nuclear Weapons in Europe*, CNS Occasional Paper, December 2009.

3. Hans M. Kristensen and Robert S. Norris, "Russian Nuclear Forces, 2011," *Bulletin of the Atomic Scientists*, Vol. 67, No. 67, 2011, available from *bos.sagepub.com/content/67/3/67.full.pdf+html*.

4. "Prakticheskie Shagi Rossiiskoi Federatsii Oblasti Yadernogo Razoruzheniya" ("Practical Actions of the Russian Federation in the Area of Nuclear Disarmament"), Report presented at the 7th NPT Review Conference, 2005, slide 13, available from *www.mid.ru/ns-dvbr.nsf/10aa6ac6e80702fc432569ea003612f0/526da0 88ef7526e3c325700d002f81c7/$FILE/Presentation-Russian.pdf*; "Rossiya Perevypolnila Plany po Sokrashcheniyu Yadernogo Oruzhiya" ("Russia Has Overfulfilled the Plan for Reduction of Nuclear Weapons"), *RIA-Novosti*, June 22, 2005, available from *www.rian. ru/politics/20050622/40566772.html*.

5. Alexei Arbatov, "Deep Cuts and De-Alerting: A Russian Perspective," *The Nuclear Turning Point*, Washington, DC: Brookings Institution Press, 1999, p. 320.

6. Nikolai Poroskov, "Takticheskii Yadernyi Kozyr" ("A Tactical Nuclear Ace"), *Vremya Novostei*, September 7, 2007.

7. Igor Korotchenko is a member of the "Public Council" of the Ministry of Defense (MOD)—a body similar in status and function to an advisory board. It consists of public figures selected by the MOD and advises/consults with the military on a variety of issues. The impact on decisions made by the military leadership is apparently barely discernible, but membership on the council provides some public stature, and Korotchenko in particular seems often to serve as a conduit for announcements that the military does not want attributed to itself.

8. For details of the debates on the TNW role in Russia in the mid-1990s, see Nikolai Sokov, "Tactical Nuclear Weapons Elimination: Next Step for Arms Control," *Nonproliferation Review*, Vol. 4, Winter 1997, pp. 17-27.

9. The text of the 1997 National Security Concept can be found at the Internet site of the Russian Security Council, available from *www.armscontrol.ru/start/rus/docs/snconold.htm*. The 1998 decisions included the decree by Boris Yeltsin titled "On urgent measures toward reforming the Armed Forces of the Russian Federation" (July 1997), and two Security Council documents: "The Concept of Development of Nuclear Forces until 2010" and "The Foundations (Concept) of State Policy in the Area of Defense Development until 2005" (July-August 1998). The texts of these documents are classified, but their general thrust could be gleaned from newspaper publications. See "Sovet Bezopasnosti RF Reshil Sokhranit Trekhkomponentnyi Sostav Strategicheskikh Yadernykh Sil," *Interfax*, No. 4, July 3, 1998; "Russia to be Major Nuclear Power in 3d Millennium—Official," *ITAR-TASS*, July 3, 1998; Ivan Safronov and Ilya Bulavinov, "Boris Yeltsin Podnyal Yadernyi Shchit," *Kommersant-Daily*, July 4, 1998; Yuri Golotuyk, "Yadernoe Razoruzhenie Neizbezhno," *Russkii Telegraph*, July 11, 1998; Yuri Golotuyk, "Moskva Skorrektirovala Svoi Yadernye Argumenty," *Russkii Telegraph*, July 4, 1998; Anatoli Yurkin, "Perspektivy Voennogo Stroitelstva," *Krasnaya Zvezda*, August 5, 1998, pp. 1, 3; Oleg Falichev, "Vpervye So Vremeni Miluykovskikh Reform," *Krasnaya Zvezda*, August 18, 1998, pp. 1-2.

10. For an analysis of nuclear policy-related elements of the 2000 *National Security Concept and Military Doctrine*, see Nikolai Sokov, *Russia's New National Security Concept: The Nuclear Angle*, January 2000; and *An Assessment of the Draft Russian Military Doctrine*, October 1999.

11. "Aktualnye Zadachi Razvitiya Vooruzhennykh Sil RF" ("Current Tasks for the Development of the Russian Federation's Armed Forces"), Report of the Ministry of Defense of the Russian Federation, October 2, 2003.

12. *Ibid.*, p. 32.

13. The 12th Main Department of the Ministry of Defense (GUMO) is in charge of handling nuclear weapons from the moment they are received from a production facility and until they are returned to the nuclear complex for refurbishment or dismantlement. The 12th GUMO has storage facilities where nuclear weapons are normally kept to be released to troops in case of emergency; weapons are serviced only by 12th GUMO personnel. One partial exception is the weapons permanently deployed on strategic delivery vehicles, but even then personnel of Strategic Forces or the Navy do not handle them—deployment, removal, and servicing are performed by 12th GUMO personnel, and spare warheads are kept at 12th GUMO storage facilities attached to military bases. This system, which was created in the early days of the Soviet nuclear program, is supposed to ensure that operational commanders cannot have control of nuclear weapons.

14. Interviews with Russian officials (who requested anonymity).

15. "Rol Takticheskogo Yadernogo Oruzhiya na Mnogotselevykh APL Vozrastet – VMF" ("The Role of Tactical Nuclear Weapons on Multipurpose Submarines Set to Grow — the Navy"), *RIA-Novosti*, August 23, 2009, available from *www.rian.ru/defense_ safety/20090323/165742858.html*.

16. The notion of global war is self-explanatory; the category of regional wars pertains to the situation when Russia faces a coalition of states, some from out of the area and/or some of them nuclear. The example the drafters of the 2000 *Military Doctrine* had in mind was escalation of the war in Chechnya through direct military involvement of the United States and its allies. The doctrine also included two other categories: (1) "local war" (in which Russia faces one or more neighboring states that have limited goals); (2) and "military conflict," which means fighting with nonstate actors (such as the war in Chechnya).

17. "Menyaetsya Rossiya, Menyaetsya i ee Voennaya Doktrina" ("As Russia Changes, its Military Doctrine Changes Too"), *Izvestiya*, October 14, 2009.

18. See, for example, Alexei Arbatov, "Deep Cuts and De-Alerting: A Russian Perspective," p. 321.

19. It is ironic that confidential interviews conducted in 1991-92 among U.S. officials attributed the rejection by George H. W. Bush of the Russian proposal to start negotiations on a legally binding and verifiable treaty on TNWs of the U.S. Navy, which was reluctant to allow on-site inspections of ships and submarines to confirm the absence of nuclear warheads.

20. "Stenogramma Vystupleniya Ministra Inostrannykh Del Rossii S.V. Lavrova na Plenarnom Zasedanii Gosudarstvennoi Dumy Federalnogo Sobraniya Rossiiskoi Federatsii npo Novomy Dogovoru o SNV," Moscow, Russia, January 14, 2011.

21. Polina Sinovets, "Minimal Nuclear Deterrence and Strategic Stability: How Much is Enough?" Paper commissioned by Program on Strategic Stability Evaluation (POSSE) to be published by *POSSE* in the spring of 2012.

PART III

EUROPEAN PERSPECTIVES

CHAPTER 9

INTRODUCTION OF EUROPEAN POLICIES AND OPINIONS RELATING TO TACTICAL NUCLEAR WEAPONS

Douglas Stuart

The four chapters in this section provide readers with excellent surveys of the positions taken by European governments on the question of whether tactical nuclear weapons (TNWs) — or non-strategic nuclear weapons (NSNWs), as they are frequently referred to in the present book — should be retained by the North Atlantic Treaty Organization (NATO). Readers will also come away with a good sense of European public opinion relating to this complex issue. What they are not likely to take away from these chapters is a sense of optimism or a sense of policy direction. The European debate over TNWs is, in the words of one influential report, "at an impasse," for four reasons.[1]

The first factor that confounds debate on TNWs is a lack of consensus on the role that they can and do play. On the one hand, there is widespread agreement that TNWs are of little or no military value. On the other hand, the European allies disagree on the political and psychological value of these weapons. Some governments continue to view TNWs as an important symbol of Washington's Article 5 commitment to the security of its NATO allies, while others are less convinced of, or less concerned about, the contribution that TNWs make to America's extended deterrence guarantee.

The fact that the NATO allies cannot agree on the purpose or value of tactical nuclear weapons in Europe is illustrative of a more fundamental problem of strategic incoherence that plagues both NATO and the European Union (EU). Both institutions have engaged in sophisticated forms of obfuscation in order to reconcile the multiple interests and concerns of their member states and preserve maximum policy flexibility. For example, NATO's 2010 *Strategic Concept* drops the specific commitment of its predecessor (the 1999 *Strategic Concept*) to maintain the dual-capable aircraft (DCA) that serve as the delivery systems for the forward-deployed TNWs. This kind of commitment avoidance makes sense from a diplomatic point of view, but it is at the expense of the Alliance's strategic clarity.

The second factor that contributes to the impasse over the future of TNWs is fundamental disagreement within NATO about the removal or retention of these systems. At the core of this disagreement are the positions taken by the two leading nations of the EU. France, which still celebrates its *force de frappe* as a source of status and security, is opposed to the removal of TNWs from Europe, or any significant change in NATO's strategic doctrine, because such action might make it harder for Paris to maintain its own nuclear posture. This position has placed France in direct conflict with Germany, which has taken on the role of leader of the Alliance's pro-nuclear disarmament wing. All other European NATO members have staked out positions between these two poles, or avoided making commitments. The chapters by Paolo Foradori and Götz Neuneck in this section provide readers with information on where most of the major European NATO allies are located on this continuum.

The third barrier to progress is the role played by Russia in the evolving debate over TNWs. Or perhaps it would be more accurate to refer to the "non-role" played by Moscow. NATO governments continue to hope that the issue of tactical nuclear weapons can be resolved through negotiations with Russia. This has made it easier for all NATO members to defer decisions relating to TNWs. But, as discussed earlier in this volume, there is little reason to expect much cooperation from Moscow unless the issue of tactical nuclear weapons can be folded into some larger negotiation involving conventional forces, missile defense, strategic systems, and perhaps space systems.

The fourth complicating factor is the mixed messages sent by the Alliance leader, the United States. Washington could break the logjam on the issue of TNWs either by unilateral removal of these systems or by taking an assertive position on some other approach in Alliance deliberations. It has chosen not to do so largely out of concern for Alliance cohesion. At the same time, however, the Barack Obama administration has contributed to the growing pressure for nuclear disarmament in Europe by its negotiation of the New Strategic Arms Reduction Treaty (New START) in 2010 and by the President's "Global Zero" speech in Prague, the Czech Republic, in 2009. It would be relatively easy for Washington to press the case for the removal of the remaining TNWs from Europe as the next logical step in this campaign.

A strong argument can be made for doing so, because the risks associated with the current impasse are greater than the risks of unilateral or negotiated removal of these militarily obsolete weapons. The first risk is that the current situation will resolve itself by "disarmament by default." This could occur as, one by one, the European nations that currently host TNWs fail to provide the necessary support for maintaining these weapons or their associated DCA. This scenario would probably lead to a new and acrimonious burden-sharing debate at a time when all allied governments are facing intense economic problems, when public support for the Alliance is soft, and when the United States is becoming increasingly preoccupied with the Asia-Pacific region.[2] A second, and perhaps related, risk is that NATO governments will lose control of the issue of TNWs in Europe as a result of political or extra-political actions by anti-nuclear movements. The chapter by Nick Childs in this section should alert readers to how vulnerable European governments are to this type of scenario.

The issue of TNWs in Europe is one of those rare cases in international politics where the process by which a decision is made is probably more important than the specific decision itself. If the current impasse could be sustained indefinitely, then NATO would have little reason for concern. But a number of factors are converging to undermine this prospect. NATO policymakers, who are currently drafting the *Deterrence and Defense Posture Review* (DDPR) to address (among other things) the future of tactical nuclear weapons in Europe, are very aware of the potential risks associated with political mismanagement of the TNW issue. But as Simon Lunn observes in his insightful analysis of the DDPR in this section, "The key differences over nuclear policy that required the compromise in the first place have already resurfaced, making both progress and the final outcome difficult to foresee."[3] Hopefully the NATO representatives who are drafting this document are approaching their task with the appropriate sense of urgency.

ENDNOTES - CHAPTER 9

1. Susi Snyder and Wilbert van der Zeijden, "Withdrawal Issues: What NATO Countries Say About the Future of Tactical Nuclear Weapons in Europe," Report by IKV Pax Christi, Netherlands, March 2011, p. 2.

2. The German Marshall Fund's 2011 Transatlantic Trends survey finds that 62 percent of the public in 12 European countries still see NATO as "essential," but this figure must be tested against the willingness of European publics to contribute financially to the Alliance, available from *www.gmfus.org/publications_/ TT/TT2011_final.pdf*. Regarding the issue of financial support, see the important speech by former Secretary of Defense Robert Gates in which he noted that only four of 26 European allies were exceeding the agreed-upon NATO defense contribution of 2 percent of gross domestic product. Gates warned of the "real possibility of collective military irrelevance" if this trend were to continue. The Secretary also notified his listeners that there was a "dwindling appetite and patience" within the U.S. Congress and among the American people for a situation in which the United States carried a disproportionate amount of the financial burden for NATO's collective defense, available from *www.defense.gov/ Transcripts/Transcript.aspx?TranscriptID=4839*.

3. Simon Lunn, "The Role and Place of Tactical Nuclear Weapons—A NATO Perspective," Chap. 10, *Tactical Nuclear Weapons and NATO*, Carlisle, PA: Strategic Studies Institute, U.S. Army War College, 2012, p. 1.

CHAPTER 10

THE ROLE AND PLACE OF TACTICAL NUCLEAR WEAPONS – A NATO PERSPECTIVE

Simon Lunn

INTRODUCTION

Nuclear weapons have always occupied a special place in North Atlantic Treaty Organization (NATO) affairs as the ultimate deterrent to aggression and also the symbol of the U.S. commitment to the defense of its NATO allies. Finding the right mix of capabilities to prove this commitment has been a major challenge for U.S. and NATO policymakers; and the question of whether or not to deploy U.S. nuclear warheads in Europe has provided a perennial source of debate. The initial deployment in Europe of short-range tactical nuclear weapons (TNWs)[1] had a clear operational purpose, although their value was rapidly diminished by the evident consequences of their use on the home territory. Despite these problems, they remained in substantial numbers as part of NATO's strategy of flexible response until the end of the Cold War. With the end the Cold War, NATO substantially reduced the number and types of TNWs in Europe, leaving a few hundred warheads for the use of allies on dual-capable aircraft (DCA). The operational application of these systems gradually faded from view, and they assumed a primarily political function in terms of ensuring linkage and the participation of the Allies in NATO's nuclear affairs.

Attention was again drawn to NATO's nuclear posture by the decision to develop a new NATO *Stra-*

tegic Concept and the increasingly pressing question of DCA modernization. Expectations of a change in NATO nuclear policy and posture were reinforced by the demand of the German coalition for the withdrawal of U.S. warheads from German territory and the growth of support for the Global Zero initiative. However, these expectations were to be disappointed. The Lisbon, Portugal, Summit was unable to achieve agreement on key aspects of nuclear policy, including the pressure for a specific review of NATO's nuclear posture. Reconciliation of these differences was effectively deferred to a review of NATO's overall deterrence and defense posture (DDPR) to be undertaken by the NATO Council in permanent session.

The DDPR is now underway, and it is expected that the review of nuclear forces will provide the centerpiece. Not surprisingly, the key differences over nuclear policy that required the compromise in the first place have already resurfaced, making both progress and the final outcome difficult to foresee. This chapter will provide an overview of the debate from a "NATO perspective" and a brief assessment of the national agendas which underpin it.

A NATO PERSPECTIVE

Based on an Alliance of independent and sovereign nations, a "NATO perspective" is literally the collective view of the 28 members that emerges from the policy and decisionmaking process founded on the principle of consensus. While attention is always drawn to the final decision or policy, the real story lies in the process itself and the various twists and turns that are necessary in order to achieve the agreement of all members. Each member brings to the table national positions, preoccupations, and priorities. The following are examples relevant to the current discussions of nuclear policy: French sensitivity to any development that could be seen as weakening the role of nuclear weapons, nuclear deterrence, and its own national deterrent; German insistence that arms control and disarmament should play a greater role in the search for security and stability; and the continuing suspicion of members from Central and Eastern Europe (CEE) towards Russia.

Sometimes these positions are of such importance that they become red lines through which the country concerned can move only with difficulty or as the result of compromises and concessions achieved in other areas. Achieving consensus involves responding to and finding a balance between these different and frequently conflicting national priorities.

The process also has to accommodate the groupings of countries who meet informally from time to time and whose consultation outside the formal 28-nation framework can play a significant role in identifying the route to consensus. These groupings would include the three nuclear powers (the United States, the United Kingdom [UK] and France); the big four (or Quad — the United States, UK, France, and Germany), whose agreement is an essential basis for eventual consensus; and the grouping of countries interested in promoting arms control and disarmament, known in the trade as "the usual suspects," normally comprising Germany, Norway, the Netherlands, Belgium, and Canada, with others associated from time to time. This latter grouping provides what they see as an important balance to the influence of the nuclear members. These and other informal groupings which are frequently created in response to circumstances contribute importantly to the deliberations from which NATO policy is developed

By its very nature, the process of consensus lacks transparency and is frequently impenetrable for those outside of the formal policy process. This lack of transparency explains why the decision that emerges often disappoints the expectations of those who are in favor of change. The weakness of the process is that the final decision often represents the lowest common denominator; its strength is that it represents a position to which all members will adhere. An additional consideration, however, is that the need to find compromises that massage national positions means that the final language is often open to multiple interpretations. The language in the new *Strategic Concept* was hailed by some as the first instance of NATO leaders endorsing the goal of a world without nuclear weapons; others, however, pointed to the qualifying words "create the conditions for" as indicating something rather less than a full endorsement of the goal.[2]

It is also important to note that nuclear affairs are rarely featured very high on NATO's agenda. Because of the sensitivity associated with nuclear weapons, there is frequently a reluctance on the part of officials to discuss nuclear matters and a tendency to leave these discussions to those who, for reasons of technical, operational, or policy expertise, are regarded as experts. These factors and the obvious distraction of other events mean that nuclear issues frequently do not occupy the position of importance many believe they should.

In gaining an understanding of the current debate on NATO's nuclear policy, there are two further considerations: the role of the United States and the significance attached to the maintenance of NATO cohesion and solidarity. As the principal provider of nuclear deterrence, the United States has always played a dominant role in NATO's nuclear affairs. But the United States has also been careful to consult and inform the NATO allies to whom it extends nuclear deterrence and to be responsive to their concerns. This has not always been easy, because the signals from the Allies are frequently mixed. As a result, the United States is called upon from time to time to exercise its leadership role. This was the case at the informal meeting of NATO Foreign Ministers in Tallinn, Estonia, on April 22, 2010. Attempting to head off a potentially divisive situation caused by the growing interest of several members in changing NATO's nuclear policy, U.S. Secretary of State Hillary Clinton introduced five principles which it was agreed would constitute the basis for the further development of NATO nuclear policy:[3]

1. As long as nuclear weapons exist, NATO will remain a nuclear alliance;

2. As a nuclear Alliance, sharing nuclear risks and responsibilities widely is fundamental;

3. A broad aim is to continue to reduce the role and number of nuclear weapons while recognizing that in the years since the Cold War ended, NATO has already dramatically reduced its reliance on nuclear weapons;

4. Allies must broaden deterrence against the range of 21st-century threats, including by pursuing territorial missile defense; and,

5. In any future reductions, our aim should be to seek Russian agreement to increase transparency on non-strategic nuclear weapons (NSNWs) in Europe, relocate these weapons away from the territory of NATO members, and include NSNWs in the next

round of U.S.-Russian arms control discussions along-side strategic and nondeployed nuclear weapons.

It would seem that for the United States during this period, the maintenance of NATO cohesion took precedence over other considerations.[4] This emphasis on cohesion was also reflected in the parallel agreement at Tallinn that members would not take unilateral actions, and that decisions on NATO's nuclear policy would be taken by the Alliance as a whole. This agreement, which was alluded to by most Ministers in their statements, indicates the importance attached by all members to NATO solidarity and cohesion. This agreement to ensure that the relevant decisions on nuclear policy are taken collectively also represents a considerable constraint on the various national policies and one that could run counter to domestic pressures, particularly from parliaments.

THE DETERRENCE AND DEFENSE POSTURE (DDPR)

There were expectations before Lisbon that the adoption of a new *Strategic Concept* provided the opportunity for NATO to reassess its nuclear strategy and demonstrate support for the goal of a world without nuclear weapons. In the event, the Lisbon documents left key aspects of nuclear policy and posture unanswered — including the purpose of nuclear weapons, the nuclear posture, the role of missile defense, and the role of disarmament. When the pressure by several members for a specific review of the nuclear posture was resisted by others, a compromise was found by broadening the review to include all elements of NATO's deterrence and defense posture, referred to by the now familiar term "appropriate mix of capabilities."

As is inevitable with all compromises, the Review did not please everyone, and its implementation is viewed by members with varying degrees of enthusiasm. One national official's comment that the DDPR resembles the blind man's elephant reflects the general uncertainty about the nature and the expected outcome of the Review.[5] Furthermore, and equally inevitably, the very differences that required the compromise have reemerged, making progress difficult and the final outcome hard to predict.

Deterrence and Defense Posture Process.

An initial period of reflection comprising seminars with outside experts is to be followed by inputs from the four primary areas considered most relevant to the appropriate mix of forces: conventional forces, nuclear forces, missile defense, and arms control and disarmament. Guidance on what questions should be addressed in each field was provided by the NATO Council (NAC) in the form of what are termed "taskings." The difficulty in agreeing on the wording of these "taskings" — so that they did not prejudge the outcome — gave an indication of the problems that lie ahead. The NAC has emphasized that it wants options rather than conclusions or recommendations, which are the prerogative of the NAC itself. The final document is to be endorsed at the next NATO Summit in Chicago, IL, on May 20, 2012.

It still being too early to foresee outcomes, what follows is a brief overview of each area, with a specific focus on nuclear affairs because they will be the centerpiece of the Review. It should be noted that one of the aspirations for the DDPR is that in defining the mix the Review will establish the relationships between the various components and knit them together in a coherent package that reflects NATO's political aims and the economic resources available with which to work.

CONVENTIONAL FORCES

It can be expected that the input on conventional forces will reflect the ongoing work of the traditional defense planning cycle and the challenges which defense planners are currently facing—the balance between expeditionary forces and those for territorial defense, the commitment to Article 5, and most significantly the severe decline in defense budgets which has led to yet another search for the most effective ways to spend defense dollars. This search, now marketed under the rubric "smart defense," will inevitably involve familiar recipes based on the self-evident proposition that effectiveness and efficiency lie in doing things together. It remains to be seen whether the new language and the severity of the economic situation will at last persuade countries to give precedence to collective solutions over those dictated by national considerations.

Missile Defense.

Missile defense is proceeding on two tracks. The first is the implementation of the NATO system and its integration with the U.S. Phased Adaptive Approach (PAA). There are expectations that an initial operating capability (IOC) of the NATO project will be announced at the Chicago Summit in May 2012.

The second track is an effort to develop a cooperative partnership with Russia. This track is handled in the NATO-Russia Council (NRC) where it would appear that little progress has been made in agreeing on even the basic parameters of cooperation. This work in the NRC has no input into the DDPR. However, whether there is success or failure in this cooperation is crucial to other areas of the DDPR because Russia has made clear that it regards cooperation in missile defense as a condition for cooperation in other areas.

Arms Control and Disarmament.

The work of the new Weapons of Mass Destruction Control and Disarmament Committee (WCDC) is still in its early stages, and, while its exact terms of reference remain ill defined, the battlelines have already been drawn. Several countries would like NATO to adopt a more positive approach towards arms control and disarmament in support of the Prague agenda and the Nuclear Non-proliferation Treaty (NPT). They are looking for ways to enhance the salience of the Alliance in this field. This goal is problematic, as arms control agreements fall within the competence of national governments. Other countries are opposed to this emphasis on disarmament, which they consider inappropriate for a defense alliance and which in their view risks distracting attention from, and at worst weakening, the primary purpose of the Alliance. France is firmly opposed to a higher profile for disarmament and against extending the duration of the Committee.

There is general agreement, however, that if and when the United States and Russia resume arms control negotiations that include sub-strategic systems, the WCDC Committee would provide a forum for the

United States in consulting with its Allies, thus performing a function similar to that of the Special Consultative Group (SCG) for the negotiations on Intermediate Range Nuclear Forces (INF) in the 1980s.

NUCLEAR FORCES

In considering what language should be chosen to describe the purpose of NATO's nuclear weapons and the range of options for the nuclear posture, the DDPR will have to balance and reconcile very different national interests, concerns, and priorities. It is always difficult to generalize about national views, but interviews with a range of national representatives at NATO during the past 18 months have revealed certain broad trends of thought. These may evolve over time as a result of internal and external developments. Views of NATO's nuclear policy vary widely, depending on the degree of nuclear involvement of the country concerned. In some countries, views differ depending on whether the individuals represent the Ministry of Defense or Foreign Affairs, each with its different priorities.

Assessments also need to take account of the fact that, as previously mentioned, for many members the nuclear issue is not high on their list of priorities. Needless to say, views on nuclear policy vary depending on the degree of involvement. Some countries — principally the more recent members — continue to support the presence in Europe of U.S. warheads; others would not be sorry to see them go; others are ambivalent. Opinions are stronger among those who support the status quo than those who seek to change it. Two factors are common to all members: the relevance of Russian sub-strategic systems and the need to maintain Alliance unity.

The United States.

The traditional leadership role of the United States in NATO's nuclear affairs and the complicated dialogue on the presence of U.S. nuclear weapons in Europe have already been discussed. The situation facing U.S. policymakers today is different in two senses. First, as a result of NATO enlargement, there are now several members who are very clear on what they want—they feel strongly that the warheads are an important symbol of the U.S. commitment and that to remove them at this time would be sending the wrong signal. Second, the endorsement by President Barack Obama in his speech in Prague, Czech Republic, of the goal of a world without nuclear weapons has created uncertainty in the minds of the Allies about U.S. priorities. Since the Prague speech, Allies have been asking what role this endorsement will play in U.S. attitudes to NATO's nuclear posture. On the one hand, the Prague commitment, together with the concerns of many U.S. officials over the security and safety of nuclear storage sites—and the associated costs—suggests the need for change. On the other hand, the possibility that such a change could create divisions within NATO argues for maintenance of the status quo. For the Obama administration, therefore, the wish to make progress on the Prague agenda has to be measured against the priority of maintaining Alliance solidarity and cohesion. The evidence for the moment is that solidarity and cohesion have won the day.

The United Kingdom.

The UK's independent nuclear deterrent has always been committed to NATO, and the UK has been consistently supportive of firm language on NATO's nuclear posture. It is a reasonable assumption that this position will continue. Conservative governments have normally adopted what could be termed a robust approach to the question of defense, including the retention of the nuclear deterrent. The renewal of the Trident system provides an interesting backdrop to NATO's discussions. British officials note that in the DDPR discussions, they may well find themselves as the "honest broker" trying to find middle ground between the conflicting views of France and Germany on the significance of disarmament.[6]

France.

French nuclear forces have always been independent of NATO, and France has stayed outside all discussions of NATO's nuclear weapons. However, French officials do participate in the drafting of language on NATO strategic policy in key documents. Despite its return to NATO's defense planning and military structures and to NATO's defense planning system for conventional forces, France remains outside the High Level Group (HLG) and the Nuclear Planning Group (NPG). This means that French officials are present at the discussion of general strategic guidance in the NAC with all 28 members, but absent from more detailed discussions and consultations on nuclear policy in the HLG and NPG which meet with 27 members. The Declaration accompanying the *Strategic Concept* adopted in Lisbon explicitly states that the nuclear discussions apply only to nuclear weapons assigned to NATO.[7] While there were quibbles over the choice of the term "assigned," it is clear that this excludes French forces and that France will not participate in the discussions of NATO's nuclear arrangements in the HLG and NPG working groups. However, the French Ambassador will participate in the NAC discussions that will produce the final DDPR document. These arrangements imply a separation between the purpose and the operational implementation of nuclear weapons that is not always easy to achieve and could be a source of confusion.

In its general approach, France can be said to be firmly in the camp of those who are opposed to change and will resist any move that could be seen as weakening nuclear deterrence, including any change to declaratory policy. French officials usually refrain from commenting on the specific issue of NATO's sub-strategic systems as being none of their business. However, French officials are known to support the existing arrangements, among other reasons as a way of avoiding their own singularity in terms of having nuclear weapons on continental European territory. Their position on NATO force posture is best described as standing on the sidelines but making encouraging noises to those who participate in the mission.[8]

New NATO Members.

The more recent NATO members are against change, as for them the presence of U.S. nuclear warheads unambiguously couples the U.S. nuclear deterrent to Europe and symbolizes the link with the United States—which were the driving forces behind their desire to join NATO. Some are willing to consider reductions but only if Russia undertakes reciprocal measures. Proposals to provide additional Article 5 reassurance through contingency planning and exercises are welcomed, but with an equal insistence that they cannot substitute for the deterrence provided by the presence of U.S. warheads. One such national representative revealed his scepticism of alternative forms of reassurance when he remarked that the allies would "remove the warheads and [then] not do the exercises."[9]

The development of a NATO missile defense system for the defense of territory has been welcomed by the new members of the Alliance as strengthening the transatlantic link and bolstering deterrence. However, several members insist that missile defense performs a different function in deterrence and should not be seen as a replacement for the existing arrangements. One national representative described missile defense as "a flimsy substitute"[10] for these arrangements, particularly in view of the impending reductions of U.S. ground forces in Europe.

For these members, the general uncertainty in the strategic environment and in relations with Russia means that this is not the moment for NATO to make changes to its strategy and that to do so would in fact be sending the wrong message – in several directions. It is sometimes said that Poland is prepared to be more flexible on this issue than other CEE members; some observers see this merely as part of a less confrontational relationship with the Big Neighbor. Polish concerns have focussed on the need to do something about Russian sub-strategic systems, a concern shared by all members. This has meant an emphasis on the need for a dialogue with Russia and initial steps aimed at creating greater transparency of these systems, again supported by other members. However, whether this focus means that Polish views are more congenial to the eventual withdrawal of NATO's own systems is difficult to say. Moreover, given the conditionality of such reductions, they are hardly relevant to discussions today. Furthermore, NATO officials note that the so-called "warming" in relations with Russia was brief and that Polish statements on the need for Alliance solidarity remain as robust as the others.

However, several Alliance members believe that, on the contrary, this *is* an opportunity for NATO to change its nuclear policy and posture. This is a variable-geometry grouping depending on the types of changes sought. Several members, including the United States and the UK, would support adjusting NATO's declaratory policy, both for consistency and also as a political signal. Others, including the "usual suspects," would go further in diminishing the role for nuclear weapons by reducing and eventually eliminating NATO's sub-strategic systems; they also insist on a higher profile for arms control and disarmament in NATO security policy.

The Dual-Capable Aircraft States.

The DCA arrangements are frequently criticized as being militarily useless and therefore having no deterrent value. This is a complicated argument. The DCA are operationally capable. The more pertinent question is how likely is it that they would be used given the other U.S. assets available and the complexity of NATO decisionmaking. The DCA countries themselves accept the mission, but for the most part without great enthusiasm. Views in these countries on the value of the mission vary—often according to the familiar dichotomy of whether the official asked comes from the Ministry of Defense or Foreign Affairs. Some argue that it provides the host country additional status within NATO and a useful means of demonstrating unity of commitment. Others maintain that the mission represents a waste of scarce resources and a missed opportunity for NATO to demonstrate its seriousness about reducing its reliance on nuclear weapons.

Turkey's role in the Alliance and its regional situation mean that Turkish views carry a particular significance. It is also host to U.S. nuclear warheads, and Turkish aircraft continue to have DCA status at a lower level of readiness. Turkish officials also say that they would prefer a continuation of existing arrangements, but they are quick to refute suggestions that changes to NATO's nuclear policy could lead to their own nuclear aspirations. In this respect, some observers claim that potential instability in the Middle East provides an additional rationale for a continuation of the Turkish DCA role as representing a crisis response tool for NATO. However, critics point out that the same arguments concerning the lack of credibility of DCA operational use—and therefore deterrent utility—apply equally to this situation.

The High Level Group.

The input to the DDPR on NATO's nuclear policy will be provided by the HLG which was created in the 1970s to ensure that nuclear issues received high-level political attention. Chaired by the United States, it comprises senior officials from national capitals. The major task for the HLG and thereafter the NAC will be to reach agreement on what NATO says and does concerning its nuclear posture. On the issue of declaratory policy, several members insist that NATO declaratory policy should be consistent with the language in the U.S. *Nuclear Posture Review* (NPR). As previously discussed, France has been firmly opposed thus far to any change in the existing language on the purpose of nuclear weapons, believing that such a change could suggest a diminution of the role of nuclear deterrence. A senior NATO diplomat noted the irony of the situation in which French nuclear forces are outside of NATO, but France continues to influence what NATO says about NATO's nuclear forces.[11] Bridging the current differences on declaratory policy will require imaginative drafting, and in the view of many NATO officials the sensitivities involved mean that this issue will have to be decided at the highest level.

With regard to NATO's nuclear posture, the HLG completed a review of nuclear requirements in 2009 based on the guidance in the 1999 *Strategic Concept*. Since the *Strategic Concept* called for the presence of U.S. nuclear warheads in Europe, it is not surprising that the review confirmed the continuing relevance of the DCA as the most appropriate means of deploying them. As NATO's new *Strategic Concept* contains no reference to the presence in Europe of U.S. nuclear warheads, it is assumed that the HLG will pose the fundamental questions concerning the requirements for extended deterrence and the continuing need for the deployment of these warheads. According to officials, in responding to the tasking set by the NAC, the HLG has developed a range of options which include the status quo but also the possibility of reducing the number of warheads or adjusting the DCA missions.

Two other factors will be important in the HLG's considerations. First, the new *Strategic Concept* appears to attach high importance to burden-sharing by calling for the broadest possible participation of Allies in collective defense planning on nuclear roles, in peacetime basing of nuclear forces, and in consultative and command and control (C3) arrangements. Even allowing for different interpretations of this formulation and efforts to find new ways to give it content, it would appear nevertheless to hint strongly at a continuation of existing arrangements.

Second, the condition that further reductions must be accompanied by reciprocal actions by Russia also constitutes a substantial obstacle to changing the existing arrangements. Thus far, Russia has shown no interest in such discussions. Among several initiatives to secure progress, a "non-paper" was circulated by Germany, the Netherlands, Norway, and Poland at the NATO Foreign Ministers meeting in Berlin, Germany, on April 14, 2011. This "non-paper" urged a number of steps to increase the transparency of U.S. and Russian non-strategic weapons.[12] The U.S. development of an arms control negotiating position with Russia in which sub-strategic systems are included will take time. It also assumes Russian cooperation. Moreover, a U.S. decision to negotiate these systems will have to be made in consultation with the NATO allies, which makes the work of the HLG in deciding NATO's requirements even more relevant.

The conditionality of further reductions on reciprocity with Russia is a consensus position which, in the absence of sustained political engagement at the highest level, represents a formidable obstacle to progress. In order to overcome this impasse, Senator Sam Nunn, a respected authority on NATO and an influential expert on the dangers of nuclear proliferation, has proposed that as part of a new and deepened dialogue with Russia on the full range of Euro-Atlantic security issues, NATO should decide to withdraw unilaterally its sub-strategic systems within a period of 5 years.[13] While the target for completion is 5 years, the final timing and pace would be determined by broad political and security developments between NATO and Russia. This proposal will certainly encounter objections. However, independent of its intrinsic merits, the proposal is an example of the imaginative initiative required if the current deadlock is to be circumvented.

Prospects.

The task of the DDPR is to ensure that the various components of the mix relate to each other in a coherent package that reflects the political goals of the Alliance and the economic resources available. In today's economic climate, there is every incentive to get the balance right and to ensure that scarce defense resources are being spent in the most efficient and cost-effective way. In the nuclear field, there are major fault lines to be crossed: on the purpose of nuclear weapons, on the nuclear posture required, and on the appropriate role for arms control and disarmament. Ideally, the DDPR process itself should contribute to narrowing the differences and finding common ground. The problem is that progress depends on, and is effectively hostage to, Russian reactions. The proposal by Senator Nunn shows one way to confront this problem, but it is unlikely to win universal support. It nonetheless demonstrates the need for imaginative thinking unfettered by traditional constraints and for high-level political engagement, particularly by the United States.

Expectations for the DDPR are modest, with the final document possibly amounting to no more than keeping the process moving and the door open. Much will depend on the priorities assigned in NATO capitals and the inevitable distraction of other developments, including the prospects of elections in several key countries. In the end, as with all NATO processes, imaginative drafting, and the traditional give and take at the last minute will produce a document that accommodates national differences but leaves their reconciliation for further elaboration. At some stage, NATO will have to come to terms with its nuclear dilemmas, but this can happen only under the leadership of the United States.

ENDNOTES - CHAPTER 10

1. The expression "tactical weapons" is used here to reinforce the fact that they were deployed with the expressed intent of being used to alter the conflict on the battlefield. In today's discussions, the term "tactical" is no longer used, and these weapons are normally referred to as non-strategic nuclear weapons (NSNWs).

2. The new *Strategic Concept* is available from *www.nato.int/lisbon2010/strategic-concept-2010-eng.pdf.*

3. For a more complete discussion of the meeting in Tallinn, see Simon Lunn, "Reducing the Role of NATO's Nuclear Weapons—Where Do We Stand after Tallinn?" RUSI Briefing Note, June 2010.

4. *Ibid.*

5. Interviews conducted by the author, November 2011.

6. *Ibid.*

7. NATO Lisbon Summit Declaration, para. 30, November 20, 2010.

8. This is reminiscent of the position adopted by French President Francois Mitterand during the "Euromissile" crisis of the 1980s when he spoke in favor of the deployments despite the fact that France was not involved.

9. Interviews conducted by the author at NATO during the period 2010-11.

10. *Ibid.*

11. *Ibid.*

12. Six other NATO allies — Belgium, the Czech Republic, Hungary , Iceland, Luxemburg, and Slovenia — also supported the paper, which, among other moves, recommended the use of the NATO-Russia Council as the primary framework for transparency and confidence-building concerning tactical nuclear weapons (TNWs) in Europe.

13. Sam Nunn, "The race between cooperation and catastrophe," in Steve Andreasen and Isabelle Williams, eds., *Reducing Nuclear Risks in Europe*, Report by the Nuclear Threat Initiative, Washington, DC, November 2011.

CHAPTER 11

EUROPEAN AND GERMAN PERSPECTIVES

Götz Neuneck

Non-strategic nuclear weapons (NSNWs) or tactical nuclear weapons (TNWs) are remnants of the Cold War. During the bipolar confrontation, both the United States and the Soviet Union deployed thousands of TNWs in different theaters of war on various platforms such as naval vessels, aircraft, and missiles. Different categories such as tactical nuclear warheads on short- and medium-missiles, mines, and artillery shells were intended to be used in support of troops in the field during actual war. There was a direct link to conventional forces in regions of conflict and assurances given to allies by the possessors of these weapons.

TNWs in Europe, although very high in numbers and locations, had lower visibility in the public eye than long-range strategic nuclear weapons. The reduced number of tactical nuclear warheads on European soil today has not been subject to any arms control treaty at all. An important starting point was in 1987, when the United States and the Soviet Union signed the Intermediate Range Nuclear Forces (INF) Treaty and began eliminating medium and intermediate range ballistic and cruise missiles which were intended for use on the European battlefield. Although the United States and Russia addressed TNWs in some arms control talks, most of their efforts focused on negotiations related to strategic nuclear arms. French and British nuclear forces were not included in any arms control arrangements concerning Europe. From a London or Paris perspective, their nuclear arsenals are seen as "strategic." The issue of TNWs was also discussed during the 2000, 2005, and 2010 Non-proliferation Treaty (NPT) Review Conferences. In the Final Document of the 2010 NPT Review Conference, the nuclear weapon states were called upon to "address the question of all nuclear weapons regardless of their type or their location as an integral part of the general nuclear disarmament process."[1] In the pages to follow, we shall discuss the history of efforts to remove TNWs; the complex distinction between strategic and TNWs, their current numbers, and their deployment; the debate in Europe about reducing or removing the remaining warheads; and the arms control prospects in Europe in the aftermath of the *New Strategic Concept*.

ARMS CONTROL EFFORTS IN THE PAST

In 1991, President George Bush and Soviet President Mikhail Gorbachev announced that they would remove from active service most of their TNWs worldwide and eliminate many of them unilaterally. In the Presidential Nuclear Initiatives (PNIs) of 1991 and 1992, both the United States and the Soviet Union acknowledged that these weapons were no longer useful for warfighting. In particular, the United States withdrew its tactical munitions to its own territory and eliminated all TNWs for ground forces, including those from Europe and South Korea. The Soviet Union eliminated TNWs for ground forces and removed tactical nuclear warheads to central storages. One reason was the growing concern about the safety and security of Soviet nuclear weapons at a time of increasing unrest on its territory. Between 1994 and 1995, the two superpowers set up a Joint Working Group to "consider steps to ensure the transparency and irreversibility of nuclear weapons." In 1997, President Bill Clinton and Russia´s President Boris Yeltsin signed a "Framework Agreement" at the Helsinki, Finland, summit that included the obligation to address measures related to "non-strategic nuclear weapons" in a possible Strategic Arms Reduction Treaty (START) III. U.S. and Russian experts were expected to explore, as a separate issue, possible measures relating to "tactical nuclear systems, to include confidence-building and transparency measures." Unfortunately, the previous treaty version, START II, was never activated due to the controversy over the U.S. withdrawal from the Anti-Ballistic Missile (ABM) treaty in 2002, and subsequently START III itself was never negotiated.

When the New START treaty was signed on April 8, 2010, and entered into force on February 5, 2011, it became clear that the definition of TNWs vis-à-vis strategic weapons would be an important issue for the follow-on agreement which is intended to include TNWs. As will be discussed below, today it is estimated that about 150-200 U.S. B-61 nuclear gravity bombs are still deployed in five European North Atlantic Treaty Organization (NATO) countries: Germany, Belgium, the Netherlands, Italy, and Turkey. Russian numbers of active TNWs are much higher, about 2,000 or more, but they are not deployed. Also, Russia has produced and retained many different types of TNWs. Most of them are likely stored in the European part of Russia with warheads separated from their delivery systems.

The 2009 *Final Report of the Commission on the Strategic Posture of the United States* makes it clear that introducing TNWs in the arms control process might become a complicated matter.[2]

One of the most important factors will be the imbalance of non-strategic nuclear weapons. In support of its arms control interests and interest in strategic stability more generally, the United States should pursue a much broader and more ambitious set of strategic dialogues with not just Russia but also China and U.S. allies in both Europe and Asia.

TACTICAL NUCLEAR WEAPONS IN EUROPE

How Many Tactical Nuclear Weapons Exist Today in Europe?

The distinction between strategic and TNWs is not easy to make because the weapon purposes (such as targets and missions) and the technical characteristics (such as range, yield, and deployment) as between the United States and Russia are different in many cases, reflecting differences in their geographical, strategic, and political postures. Early on, the Soviet Union and the United States came to consider nuclear weapons based on their own territory that could be delivered with long-range missiles or bombers against the enemy's homeland as "strategic." Consequently, one simplifying approach has been to define tactical nuclear weapons as *all* nuclear warheads which are not covered by strategic nuclear arms control treaties. But certainly other operational characteristics (such as deployment status, weapon readiness, proximity to delivery system, etc.) are also important for future reduction talks. Despite the fact that both Russia and the United States have reduced their TNW stockpile more than envisaged under PNIs, neither has disclosed exact data about the numbers, status and location of these weapons.

In its 2010 *Nuclear Posture Review* (NPR), the Barack Obama administration underlined the reduced role of nuclear weapons in regional security architectures and stressed America's increased reliance upon "forward U.S. conventional presence and effective theater ballistic missile defense."[3] The NPR also makes clear that "any changes in NATO´s nuclear posture should be taken only after a thorough review within — and decision by — the Alliance."[4] The document calls for retaining the capability for forward-deployed U.S. nuclear weapons to be delivered by tactical fighter-bombers and heavy bombers.[5] The United States also plans to continue with a life-extension program for the B-61 bomb, which is deployed in Europe for delivery by dual-capable aircraft (DCA). It has been estimated that the United States has reduced its total TNW stockpile from 11,500 to some 500-800 and has retained a smaller capability for forward deployment.

Under NATO sharing arrangements, as mentioned earlier, experts assume that the United States still deploys between 150-200 U.S. TNWs in five NATO member states (see Table 11-1). These weapons remain under U.S. control during peacetime, but in a war situation some of the TNWs can be transferred to allies for delivery by their own dual-capable systems. This nuclear-sharing formula in the event of war was developed during the Cold War to maintain a close coupling between European NATO Allies and the United States and to ensure shared decisionmaking. The 2010 *New Strategic Concept* retains the option of nuclear first use, even against a non-nuclear attack, although with the condition that the circumstances calling for such an event are "extremely remote." Many political and military experts declare that such a nuclear mission has no military value. General James Cartwright, former Vice-Chairman of the Joint Chief of Staffs, went so far as to declare that there is no military mission the TNWs could perform that could not be carried out by conventional or strategic weapons.[6]

Country	Airbase	Dual-Capable Aircraft	Estimated Number of B-61 Warheads
Belgium	Kleine Brogel	Belgian F-16	10–20
Germany	Büchel	German Tornado	10–20
Italy	Aviano	U.S. F-16	50
	Ghedi Torre	Italian Tornado	10–20
Netherlands	Volkel	Dutch F-16	10–20
Turkey	Incirlik	U.S. Fighter Aircraft (rotating)	60–70
Total			150–200

Table 11-1. U.S. Nuclear Weapons in Europe, 2011.[7]

Typical arguments for maintaining TNWs within NATO stress Alliance solidarity, discouraging NATO members such as Turkey from acquiring their own nuclear forces, and using TNWs as bargaining chips in negotiations designed to convince the Russians to reduce or eliminate their own TNW stockpiles. The 2010 New Strategic Concept asserts that for any future reductions NATO´s aim should be "to seek Russia´s agreement to increase transparency on its nuclear weapons and relocate these weapons away from the territory of NATO members."[8]

The existing assessments from different sources of the Russian TNW stockpile are based on different methodologies, with results that are vague and varying.[9] Russia might have reduced its TNW stockpile from an estimated 22,000 to some 2,000 deployable TNWs.[10] Deployed warheads are operationally usable, but separated from their delivery systems. Tactical warheads "in reserve" are stored in depots and are either earmarked for dismantlement or no longer routinely maintained. Andrei Zagorski estimated that the total number of the Russian TNWs is between 5,000 and 6,500, that some 2,000 of them are active but not deployed, and that the rest remain in reserve.[11] Officially, all land-based TNWs have been removed from active service and have been destroyed. The new Iskander short-range ballistic missile nevertheless might have a nuclear capability. The remaining Russian TNWs are assigned to the Russian Navy and Air Force and might be stored in depots at Air Force or Navy bases for quick deployment. The Russian Navy might possess 700 TNWs and the Air Force 650 in storages close to military harbors and airfields (see Table 11-2). It has retained longer-range capabilities, e.g., the TU-22M aircraft capable of carrying nuclear air-to-surface missiles (ASM) and gravity bombs against naval aircraft carrier groups. There are also 700 tactical warheads allocated for missile and air defense weapons such as surface-to-air missiles SA-5B and SA-10 for combating enemy aircraft or cruise missiles. Another category of naval armaments is general purpose naval weapons such as the submarine launched cruise missiles: SS-N-9, SS-N-12, SS-N-21, and SS-N-22, plus nuclear torpedos and depth charges.

Armed Service	Number of warheads	Delivery Systems
Air and missile defense	~700	SA-5B and SA-10 & SH-8/11 ABM interceptors
Air force	650	TU-22M; SU-24
Navy	~700	TU-22M; SU-24; IL-38; SLCM, torpedos, and depth charges
Total	**~2,000**	

Table 11-2. Estimates of Operational Tactical Nuclear Weapons in Russia, 2010.

It is reported that the Russian government has reduced its nuclear storage sites from 500 (in the 1990s) to a total of 48. There exist two main categories of TNW storage sites: The first consists of 13 storage sites solely for TNWs, nine of them located in the European part of Russia and four located beyond the Urals, either in Siberia or the Far East. The second category consists of 18 national-level nuclear weapons storage sites at which both strategic and tactical warheads are stored. Of these sites, 10 of them are in the European part, four in the Urals region, and four in Siberia and the Far East.[12] For future verification arrangements, this complex and distributed pattern makes inspections very difficult.

In the Russian view, TNWs are still regarded as compensating for the weaknesses of Russian conventional forces in the European region. Other justifications for retaining these systems include: insurance against further NATO enlargement; a cushion against a possible shortfall in the Conventional Forces in Europe (CFE) Treaty; added protection in the event of a buildup of forces in China; and a response to a future ballistic missile defense capability in Europe and worldwide.[13] Another factor is the growing U.S. military-technological superiority in long-range ballistic and cruise missiles, some of which are armed with munitions guided from space. Andrei Zagorski in a recent study came to the conclusion that "there are virtually no significant Russian constituencies with a vested interest in reducing or limiting TNW."[14]

France and Great Britain, which are nuclear weapon states under the NPT, have developed their own deterrence arsenals. France has 300 strategic warheads on long-range delivery systems, including airborne standoff weapons which can also be used as tactical ("prestrategic") weapons. The French government has announced a one-third cut in its nuclear arsenal, and has closed its nuclear test site along with its plants for the production of fissile material for weapons. Great Britain has 160 operational strategic warheads. The two Western European nuclear powers each have four nuclear submarines with seaborne missiles, maintaining one submarine always at sea.

The Debate in NATO Countries on the Removal of TNWs from Europe.

In his Prague "Global Zero" speech on April 5, 2009, U.S. President Obama declared that America was committed "to seek the peace and security of a world without nuclear weapons." He then emphasized that "thinking in terms of the Cold War must come to an end." The debate was triggered by two op-ed features written by former U.S. Secretaries of State George Shultz and Henry Kissinger, former Defense Secretary William J. Perry, and former Senator Sam

Nunn in 2007 and 2008.[15] This Gang of Four argued in their 2007 article for the elimination of short-range nuclear weapons designed to be forward-deployed. In their subsequent article a year later, they proposed to:

> start a dialogue, including within NATO and with Russia, on consolidating the nuclear weapons designed for forward deployment to enhance their security, and as a first step toward careful accounting for them and their eventual elimination. These smaller and more portable nuclear weapons are, given their characteristics, inviting acquisition targets for terrorist groups.[16]

Another cross-party quartet from Germany — composed of former chancellor Helmut Schmidt, former Foreign Minister Hans-Dietrich Genscher, former President Richard von Weizsäcker and retired Minister of State Egon Bahr — called for steps toward a nuclear-free world and for drastic nuclear reductions.[17] They wrote that "all short-range nuclear weapons must be destroyed" and asserted that "all remaining American U.S. nuclear warheads should be withdrawn from German territory." They also called for a renunciation of the "first-use" option by NATO and Russia:

> Relics of the period of confrontation are no longer adequate for our new century. . . . Partnership fits badly with the still-active NATO and Russian doctrines of nuclear first use even if neither side is subject to a nuclear strike. A general non-first-use treaty between the nuclear-weapon states would be an urgently-needed step.[18]

The American and German quartets were supported and bolstered by op-eds from high-ranking former politicians from Great Britain, Italy, Norway, the Netherlands, Poland, France, and Belgium.[19]

These contributions reflect the debates in important NATO member states.[20] In Germany, the population and the current government are arguing for the removal of NATOs TNWs from German territory. In October 2009, the new Conservative-Liberal government in Germany formed by the Christian Democratic Union (CDU) and the Free Democratic Party (FDP) released its "coalition treaty," stating that it "will advocate within NATO and towards our U.S. allies a withdrawal of remaining nuclear weapons from Germany."[21] At the Munich Security Conference in February 2010, Foreign Minister Guido Westerwelle declared that "the last remaining nuclear weapons in Germany are a relic of the Cold War. They no longer serve a military purpose."[22] Former Secretary-General of NATO, the former Belgian Foreign Minister Willy Claes, together with other former Belgian politicians, stated that "U.S. NSNW in Europe have lost all military importance."[23] The Dutch and Belgian governments also advocated removal of U.S. TNWs from Europe. Together with Germany, Norway, and Luxembourg, these governments sent a letter in February 2010 to the NATO Secretary-General, asking him to put the withdrawal on the agenda of the informal NATO meeting of the foreign affairs ministers in Tallinn, Estonia, in April 2010. At that meeting, a policy rift opened among NATO members. U.S. Secretary of State Hillary Clinton responded with a statement of five principles, including the declaration that "as long as nuclear weapons exist, NATO will remain a nuclear alliance."[24] But she did not rule out further reductions or the development of confidence-building measures in cooperation with Russia.

France stands alone in Western Europe in its rejection of further nuclear disarmament and is blocking reform of NATO's nuclear weapons policy. Paris fears that the debate on a nuclear-free world could weaken the significance of its own nuclear deterrent. France is the only NATO member that does not participate in the Nuclear Planning Group. This French policy is supposed to demonstrate the independence of the French nuclear deterrent, but it also limits opportunities to influence NATO's nuclear weapons policy.[25]

The Central and Eastern European states, as well as the Baltic states, are also quite reluctant to push for the removal of TNWs from European soil. They feel threatened by Russia's conventional forces and tactical nuclear weapons. The Georgian war, Russian maneuvers in the Baltic region (during which the deployment of nuclear weapons was practiced), and Moscow's threat to counter the stationing of U.S. missile defense components with deployment of short-range missiles in Kaliningrad, have all contributed to concerns about Russia's military policy, particularly in the Baltic states. The Central and Eastern European countries, because of their geographical situation and history, are interested primarily in maintenance of a credible NATO security guarantee.[26] On the other hand, in February 2010, two acting foreign ministers (Radek Sikorski from Poland and Carl Bildt from Sweden) called for the reduction and ultimately elimination of European TNWs unilaterally or by negotiations.[27] In northern Europe, there is a special interest in reducing the Russian TNW stockpile in Kaliningrad and the Kola peninsula.

Turkey's attitude to the Alliance's future deterrence and defense posture is ambivalent. Turkish Prime Minister Recip Tayyip Erdogan's government is performing a difficult balancing act. On the one hand, Turkey has advertised the priority it accords to NATO membership by participating in the Alliance's nuclear-sharing program. This is viewed as a symbol of transatlantic burden-sharing.[28] On the other hand, Turkey is endeavoring to defuse conflicts in the Middle East and establish itself in the region as mediator between Western and Islamic states.

The *New Strategic Concept*, adopted at the Lisbon, Portugal, Summit in November 2010, states that "deterrence, based on an appropriate mix of nuclear and conventional capabilities, remains a core element of [NATO's] overall strategy." The leaders of the 28 NATO members have also agreed to conduct a *Deterrence and Defense Posture Review* (DDPR) covering the right balance between nuclear and conventional forces as well as missile defense in NATO's future defense posture. The consultation phase of the DDPR has already ended, and NATO members are now engaged in drafting a report which will be adopted at the May 20, 2012, summit in Chicago.[29]

The DDPR is necessary because the future role of nuclear weapons in NATO was not specified in the *New Strategic Concept*. The document merely states that "the circumstances in which any use of TNWs might have to be contemplated are extremely remote." Moreover, the U.S. NPR is not in line with the NATO nuclear policy. The U.S. NPR renounces the threat or the use of nuclear weapons against non-nuclear weapon states that are parties to the NPT and are in compliance with their nonproliferation obligations. Furthermore, the procurement of new DCA in Europe and the delivery aircraft life-extension program in the United States are looming on the horizon. In Germany, Belgium, and the Netherlands, there would be no public support for acquiring new delivery systems such as fighter aircraft capable of nuclear missions. While some members (Norway and Germany) want to modify the Alliance's nuclear posture in order to synchronize it with the U.S. NPR, others such as France want to avoid spelling out the conditions under which NATO would use or not use nuclear weapons.

At the same time, a new arms control group, the Weapons of Mass Destruction (WMD) Control and Disarmament Committee (WCDC), has been established within NATO. The WCDC was created at the insistence of Germany and in spite of opposition from France. NATO agreed on the WCDC mandate to examine possible "reciprocal measures aiming to reinforce and increase transparency, mutual trust, and confidence with Russia." There is some disagreement whether the WCDC will continue to exist beyond the 2012 summit. [30] Four countries, with support of six other NATO members, have proposed a set of transparency and confidence-building measures to break the arms control deadlock on TNWs with Russia. But NATO member states are deeply divided on what kind of relations the Alliance should have with Russia. The United States and some western European countries would like to pursue a strategic partnership with Russia, while some Central and East Europeans are unwilling to accommodate Russian security interests. This fundamental difference in approaches has hampered NATO's efforts to develop and pursue a coherent arms control policy towards Russia. NATO also hopes to link any reductions in its TNW holdings to reciprocal Russian cuts. In the conventional arena, NATO insists on implementation of the adapted CFE Treaty, which is built on the assumption of strategic parity between the East and West. Russia and Belarus have signed the adapted CFE Treaty, but the Western bloc has not. Russia suspended the CFE data exchange in 2007, and NATO followed suit at the end of 2011, leaving a trail of confusion as to the way ahead for conventional arms control in Europe.

EUROPEAN SECURITY AND ARMS CONTROL IN EUROPE

A recent report by the German Institut für Friedensforschung und Sicherheitspolitik (IFSH) analyzed the challenges and prospects for arms control in Europe.[31] The study noted that 20 years after the end of the Cold War, the military balance in Europe has been reversed, in favor of NATO. The Alliance now has many more member states than in 1989. NATO's conventional military capabilities are vastly superior to Russia's, both in quantitative and qualitative terms. The number of heavy weapons exceeds that of Russia two- or threefold. Russia's equipment is much older and procurement expenditures over the past decade are only 16 percent of that of the European Union (EU) NATO countries. Military superiority is particularly marked with regard to military research and development (R&D). In dollar outlays for R&D, NATO-Europe has an overall 4:1 superiority, as well as a 7:1 superiority in military spending and a 6:1 advantage in procurement. This imbalance is unlikely to change in the foreseeable future, despite Russian increases in defense spending. Nevertheless, in some regions such as the Baltic states, Russian forces still have a regional superiority. This imbalance is viewed with alarm by the states in this region, and it poses a formidable challenge for future conventional arms control. The only other defense category in which Russia is superior in terms of numbers is TNWs.

Thanks to the Obama administration, there has been a revival of interest in arms control in the last 3 years. Signs of progress include the entry into force of the New START Treaty, the successful 2010 NPT Review Conference, and statements by the Russian and U.S. Presidents in support of a world free of nuclear weapons. In spite of these encouraging signs, however, the prospects for successful arms control in Europe are looking rather dim. The CFE Treaty was suspended by Russia in December 2007 and is likely to lapse completely in the near future. Despite several attempts to resolve the deadlock, a solution has not yet been found. The CFE Review Conference in September 2011 did not bring any progress. Following its negotiation in 1989, the CFE Treaty made a historic contribution to the establishment of a safe and peaceful milieu in Central and Eastern Europe. It helped to frame the unification of Germany, the dissolution of the Warsaw Pact, and the fall of the Soviet Union.[32] A new basic framework has not yet been found. Sufficiency instead of parity, a mechanism for addressing sub-regional disparities, and preservation of rules for verifiable transparency, are vital desiderata for a new treaty that provides important sources of predictability and reliability in Europe.

Russia links further progress in arms control to reductions of the imbalances of conventional forces and other armaments. Moscow is worried about the build-up of ballistic missile defense capabilities in Europe, the U.S. investment in precision-guided long-range carrier-based systems, and the use of outer-space for conventional warfare, which could undermine Russia´s nuclear deterrent in the future. Prompt Global Strike (PGS) is a U.S. program to enable accurate strike options against high-value targets worldwide within 1 hour. Some new U.S. long-range delivery systems with high accuracy for preventive strike are of special concern to Russia and also China. These include:

- Conventional precision munitions onboard bombers (B-1/52, F-15/16/18);
- Refitted *Ohio* class submarines with approximately 600 conventional Tomahawk cruise missiles;
- Modification of two of 24 nuclear-equipped Trident missiles for PGS missions;
- Development of hypersonic missiles and glide vehicles; and,
- Potential development of anti-satellite and space weapons.

For all of these options and developments, there exist no arms control framework or regime.

Any improvement of NATO-Russia relations is likely to be incremental. To the degree possible, NATO and Russia should therefore try to untangle the different linkages between political and military aspects of their relationship. According to the IFSH report, four *parallel strategies* to strengthen arms control could have a positive impact on overall relations:

- Both sides should restrict themselves in areas where they have clear military supremacy, such as conventional combat forces on NATO's side and TNWs on the Russian side;
- Both sides should engage in a process of confidence- and security-building which focuses on those military weapon systems that have a reduced relevance for strategic stability, such as TNWs;
- NATO and Russia should support a continuation of treaty-based arms control by agreeing

on a modified CFE regime and a follow-on accord to the New START treaty; and,

- Both sides should reach an understanding about which areas, for the time being, will not be subject to arms control or restrictions. The list might include conventional strategic weapons such as submarine launched cruise missiles or PGS systems.

In the short term, progress on arms control will hinge on the willingness of NATO and Russia to agree on a joint approach to ballistic missile defenses (BMD). The stakes are high, yet NATO's commitment to develop an Alliance-wide system and Russia's insistence on becoming an equal partner in the undertaking appear to have set both sides on a collision course. NATO would be well-advised to allow more time for consultations with Moscow because there is no urgent military requirement to deploy missile defenses in Europe. Russia, on the other hand, needs to recognize that it will not become NATO's equal partner in missile defense, but that BMD cooperation allows further steps to establish common missile defense early warning and data-sharing. Establishing a data exchange center with NATO could be a decisive confidence-building step forward to enhance cooperation on BMD in Europe.[33]

While they are trying to improve their own bilateral relationship, NATO and Russia also need to reach out to China since agreements between Russia and NATO have a potential impact on security in Asia. Beijing's experience with arms control is extremely limited. To draw China further into the arms control and confidence-building process, NATO could for example propose to intensify discussions among the five permanent members of the United Nations Security Council on nuclear confidence-building and transparency. Involving China—and eventually the other nuclear-armed states India, Israel, and Pakistan—in an arms control dialogue could also go some way towards addressing the long-term problem of preserving the strategic balances under conditions of nuclear disarmament. In the end, the real challenge will be to assure others that regional military imbalances and U.S. conventional supremacy are no threats to international stability and security.

ENDNOTES - CHAPTER 11

1. Final Document of the 2010 Nuclear Non-Proliferation Treaty (NPT) Review Conference of the Parties to the Treaty on the Non-Proliferation of Nuclear Weapons, NPT/CONF.2010/50, Vol. I, New York, 2010.

2. William J. Perry and James R. Schlesinger, *Final Report of the Commission on the Strategic Posture of the United States*, "Executive Summary," Washington, DC: U.S. Institute of Peace, May 2009.

3. *Nuclear Posture Review Report*, Washington, DC: Department of Defense, April 2010, p. xiii.

4. *Ibid.*

5. *Ibid.*

6. James Cartwright, Meeting on Nuclear Posture Review, Council of Foreign Relations, Washington, DC, April 8, 2010.

7. Hans Kristensen and Robert S. Norris, "U.S. Tactical Nuclear Weapons in Europe," *Bulletin of the Atomic Scientists*, Vol. 67, No. 1, 2011, pp. 64ff.

8. *NATO New Strategic Concept: Active Engagement, Modern Defense*, Lisbon, Portugal, November 2010.

9. See Miles A. Pomper, William Potter, and Nikolai Sokov, *Reducing and Regulating Tactical (Non-strategic) Nuclear Weapons in Europe*, Monterey, CA: The James Martin Center for Non-proliferation Studies, 2009; *World Armaments, Disarmament and International Security: SIPRI Yearbook*, Oxford, UK: Oxford University Press, 2008, pp. 373-375; Gunnar Arbman and Charles Thornton, "Part II: Technical Issues and Policy Recommendations,"*Russia´s Tactical Nuclear Weapons*, Stockholm, Sweden: FOI-Swedish Defence Research Agency, February 2005.

10. Alexei Arbatov, "Non-Strategic Nuclear Weapons," in *NATO-Russia Relations: Prospects for New Security Architecture, Nuclear Reductions, CFE-Treaty*, Moscow, Russia: IMEMO RAN, 2010, pp. 28-40.

11. Andrei Zagorski, *Russia's Tactical Nuclear Weapons: Posture, Politics and Arms Control*, Hamburg, Germany: Institut für Friedensforschung und Sicherheitspolitik an der Universität Hamburg, 2011.

12. *Ibid.*, pp. 18-21.

13. See in detail the study by Michael Brzoska, Anne Finger, Oliver Meier, Götz Neuneck, and Wolfgang Zellner, *Prospects for Arms Control in Europe*, Berlin, Germany: Friedrich-Ebert-Stiftung, November 2011.

14. Zagorski, p. 6.

15. George P. Shultz, William J. Perry, Henry A. Kissinger, and Sam Nunn, "A World Free of Nuclear Weapons," *Wall Street Journal*, January 4, 2007, p. A15; and "Toward a Nuclear-Free World," *Wall Street Journal*, January 15, 2008, p. A13.

16. See George P. Shultz, Steven P. Andreasen, Sidney D. Drell, and James E.Goodby, *Reykjavik Revisited. Steps Toward a World Free of Nuclear Weapons*, Stanford, CA: Hoover Institution Press, pp. 482-483.

17. Helmut Schmidt, Richard von Weizsäcker, Egon Bahr, and Hans-Dietrich Genscher, "Für eine atomwaffenfreie Welt," *Frankfurter Allgemeine Zeitung*, January 9, 2009, p. 10.

18. Helmut Schmidt, Richard von Weizsäcker, Egon Bahr and Hans-Dietrich Genscher, "Toward a Nuclear-Free World: A German View," Original Version published on January 9, 2009 in the *Frankfurter Allgemeine Zeitung*, available from *www. nytimes.com/2009/01/09/opinion/09iht-edschmidt.1.19226604. html?pagewanted=all.*

19. See Götz Neuneck, "Is a World without Nuclear Weapons Attainable? Comparative Perspectives on Goals and Prospects," in Catherine M. Kelleher and Judith Reppy, eds., *Getting to Zero – The Path to Nuclear Disarmament*, Stanford, CA: Stanford University Press, 2011, pp. 43-66.

20. See Tom Sauer and Bob van der Zwaan, "U.S. Tactical Nuclear Weapons in Europe after NATO's Lisbon Summit: Why Their Withdrawal is Desirable and Feasible," Cambridge, MA: John F. Kennedy School of Government, Harvard University, May 2011; Johan Bergenäs, Miles A. Pomper, William Potter, and Nikolai Sokov, "Reducing and Regulating Tactical (Non-Strategic) Nuclear Weapons in Europe: Moving Forward?" Monterey, CA: Monterey Institute of International Studies, The James Martin Center for Nonproliferation Studies, April 2010.

21. The Coalition Agreement between the CDU, CSU, and FDP, "Growth, Education, Unity", Berlin, Germany, October 26, 2009, p. 170, available from *www.cdu.de/doc/pdfc/091215-koalitions-vertrag-2009-2013-englisch.pdf.*

22. Speech by Foreign Minister Guido Westerwelle at the 46th Munich Security Conference, February 6, 2010.

23. Willy Claes, Jean-Luc Dehaene, Louis Michel, and Guy Verhofstadt, "Het is Nu of Nooit," *De Standaard*, February 19, 2010. An unofficial Translation is available from *www.pugwash. org/reports/nw/nuclear-weapons-free-statements/NWFW_statements_ Belgium.htm.*

24. Sauer and van der Zwaan, p. 13.

25. See Paul Zajac, "NATO's Defense and Deterrence Posture Review: A French Perspective on Nuclear Issues," Nuclear Policy

Paper, No. 7, Washington, DC: Arms Control Association, British American Security Information Council, Institute for Peace Research and Security Policy at the University of Hamburg (IFSH), 2011.

26. Jacek Durkalec, *Reductions of Tactical Nuclear Weapons in Europe: Unbinding the Gordian Knot*, Warsaw, Poland: The Polish Institute of International Affairs, Strategic File #16, May 2011.

27. Carl Bildt and Radek Sikorski, "Next the Tactical Nukes," *The New York Times*, February 2010.

28. Mustafa Kibaroglu, *Turkey, NATO and Nuclear Sharing: Prospects after NATO's Lisbon Summit*, Washington, DC: Arms Control Association, British American Security Information Council, Institute for Peace Research and Security Policy at the University of Hamburg (IFSH), May 2011.

29. Oliver Meier, "NATO Revises Nuclear Policy," *Arms Control Today*, Vol. 40, No. 10, 2010, pp. 28ff.

30. Oliver Meier, "NATO Sets Up Arms Control Committee," *Arms Control Today*, Vol. 41 No. 3, 2011, pp. 32ff.

31. See Michael Brzoska, Anne Finger, Oliver Meier, Götz Neuneck, and Wolfgang Zellner, *Prospects for Arms Control in Europe*, Berlin, Germany: Friedrich-Ebert-Stiftung, November 2011.

32. See Wolfgang Zellner, Hans-Joachim Schmidt, and Götz Neuneck, eds., *Die Zukunft konventioneller Rüstungskontrolle in Europa (The Future of Conventional Arms Control in Europe)*, Baden-Baden, Germany: Nomos, 2009.

33. See Ivanka Barzashka, Timur Kadyshev, Götz Neuneck, and Ivan Oelrich, "How to Avoid a New Arms Race," *Bulletin of the Atomic Scientists*, July 25, 2011.

CHAPTER 12

EUROPEAN PERSPECTIVES

Paolo Foradori

Any discussion of European perspectives on the presence, role, and future of U.S. tactical nuclear weapons (TNWs) must begin with the caveat that Europe (or North Atlantic Treaty Organization [NATO] Europe) is not a unitary actor. Europe is a heterogeneous ensemble of countries with different histories, capabilities, international statuses, and ambitions and with specific security cultures and threat perceptions. This *structural* differentiation within the Alliance must be considered for a full appreciation of the convoluted dynamics of consensus-building that characterize NATO decisionmaking. The expansion of NATO to include former Warsaw Pact countries has added further elements of complexity to the Alliance's institutional and political architecture. Therefore, this analysis will sometimes refer to NATO Europe as a whole and will sometimes differentiate between specific continental, regional, and national positions.

This chapter is divided into three sections. In the first section, I argue that a widespread consensus exists within Europe that the strictly military value of TNWs is now negligible, and that there are no realistic scenarios in which TNWs could be employed. In the second section, I argue that the European position is largely shaped by and must be contextualized in the increasing international support for nuclear disarmament. With one main exception (France), TNWs have lost their attractiveness as symbols of power, status, and prestige. Moreover, their further reduction and eventual elimination are considered important contributions to the objective of nonproliferation and the longer-term objective of Global Zero. In the third section, I argue that, despite the prevailing post-Cold War thinking in most of NATO Europe, different security threat perceptions exist among the allies, and some of the new members in Central and Eastern Europe (CEE) continue to attribute residual political and symbolic importance to the physical presence of TNWs on European soil. However, the status quo position of these members does not seem entirely intransigent, especially when balanced by a NATO/U.S. commitment to their defense by other (i.e., non-nuclear) means. Indeed, the issue of TNW forward deployment in Europe is, to a great extent, a proxy for lack of confidence in the future of the U.S. commitment and the diminished solidarity within the Alliance that these countries have experienced.

NATO leaders are well aware of this complex dialectic within the Alliance and of the risk that decisions that are not unanimous may weaken the solidarity and indivisibility of Atlantic security. NATO has therefore opted to prioritize the Alliance's cohesion—on which its credibility as a security provider depends—in any decision about the presence, role, and future of TNWs, which are widely regarded as having little intrinsic value for Euro-Atlantic security in the 21st century.

WEAPONS OF LITTLE (OR NO) MILITARY VALUE

There is widespread consensus within Europe that the strictly military value of TNWs is negligible, and there are no realistic scenarios in which they could be employed. Tactical weapons are believed to be poorly suited to countering the main international threats to Euro-Atlantic security, and serious credibility problems are raised by their low operational readiness, their vulnerability to surprise attacks, and the limited range of dual-capable aircraft.[1] The most explicit manifestation of this point of view was proposed by German Foreign Minister Guido Westerwelle, who conditioned his support for Angela Merkel's coalition government after the elections of November 2009 on its definite commitment to eliminating TNWs, which he described as "a relic of the Cold War . . . [that] no longer serves a military purpose."[2]

With the end of the Cold War and the collapse of the archenemy against whom the U.S. bombs in Europe were first deployed, the original purpose of TNWs has vanished, and their current military role appears ill-defined at best.[3] NATO itself declares that its "nuclear forces no longer target any country"[4] because it "does not consider any country to be its adversary."[5] The Alliance's present ability to defuse a crisis through diplomatic and other means or, if needed, to mount a successful conventional defense, has significantly improved. Although an appropriate combination of nuclear and conventional capabilities remains a "core element"[6] of NATO's current deterrence strategy, "the circumstances in which any use of nuclear weapons might have to be contemplated are extremely remote."[7] In the words of the 2010 *NATO Strategic Concept*:

> Since the end of the Cold War, we have dramatically reduced the number of nuclear weapons stationed in Europe and our reliance on nuclear weapons in NATO strategy. We will seek to create the conditions for further reductions in the future.[8]

In the post-bipolar international system, TNWs are of little military value to counter the main threats to the Alliance's security, which include terrorism, low-intensity and asymmetric warfare, transnational crime, piracy, cyber-warfare, migration pressures, energy shortages, contagious diseases, and natural and man-made disasters. In the words of Polish Foreign Minister Radek Sikorski and his Swedish counterpart, Carl Bildt, "We still face security challenges in the Europe of today and tomorrow, but from whichever angle you look, there is no role for the use of nuclear weapons in resolving these challenges."[9]

The admission to NATO of most of the former Warsaw Pact countries has further decreased TNW utility. The "three no's" policy, which commits NATO to not deploying TNWs (or establishing nuclear weapon storage sites) on the territories of the new members, has placed nearly all of the weapons (except possibly those hosted in Turkey)[10] far from Russia and other potential enemies and far from the alliance borders, where they might act as tripwires.[11]

The shift of conventional superiority from the Union of Soviet Socialist Republics (USSR)/Russia to NATO adds an extra element to the reduced credibility of TNWs as an effective means of defense, raising doubts about the need for these politically and morally difficult-to-use weapons at a time when NATO is regarded as the strongest conventional military alliance ever created, with no rivals.

In most, if not all, conceivable present and future scenarios, there are much better alternatives to the use or threat of nuclear gravity bombs dropped by short-range dual-capable aircraft, which are vulnerable to modern air defense systems and require refueling to reach distant targets. Both conventional and noncon-

ventional alternatives are operationally and politically preferable. Modern conventional weapons have
become extremely accurate and powerful, and these
are deemed capable of efficiently responding to most
threats to the security of the Alliance. In the words of a
senior official at the Italian Ministry of Foreign Affairs,
"I cannot think of any mission that cannot be accomplished with other means. The value of these weapons
is today essentially political."[12] It is difficult to envisage a realistic scenario in which all NATO members,
including Germany and the Scandinavian countries,
could reach consensus on employing nuclear weapons against any target. Indeed, even in a worst-case
scenario that requires the actual use of nuclear capabilities, it is difficult to imagine that NATO—and,
especially, its strongest member, the United States—
would resort to TNWs hosted in Europe when faster,
more accurate, longer-range U.S. strategic nuclear
weapons based at sea or on American soil are available and ready to launch.[13]

TNWs thus appear short on credibility as weapons
of any real military value. If this is the case, their deterrent potential is also seriously compromised. Furthermore, adding the French and UK nuclear arsenals
to that of the United States, NATO would remain a
formidable nuclear alliance even if the few hundred
remaining TNWs were withdrawn from Europe.

Supporting Nonproliferation and Disarmament.

The debate about the forward deployment of
U.S. tactical weapons must be seen in the context of
the increasing international support for the program
of nuclear disarmament, which is finding adherents
throughout Europe.[14] Despite caveats and different

levels of enthusiasm, most European countries are genuinely committed to nuclear abolishment, and it can be cogently argued that the current debate about TNWs would not have emerged without the global vision for "a world free of nuclear weapons" endorsed by U.S. President Barack Obama.[15]

With the main exception of France, which continues to attribute great value to its nuclear arsenal and remains explicitly against any change in the Alliance's nuclear posture,[16] in most of Europe, nuclear weapons have not only been drastically devalued as effective military instruments but have also lost their attractiveness as symbols of power, status, and prestige. With the end of the Cold War, a process of *delegitimization* of nuclear weapons began. The utility of these weapons was gradually devalued and disparaged, thereby reducing and eventually annulling any positive evaluation of their efficacy, legitimacy, and authority.[17] Even among the more conservative, status-quo-prone countries of CEE, support for U.S. nuclear forward deployment is not ideological and absolute; rather, it is qualified, pragmatic, and *negotiable*, as will be discussed in the next section.

Within this general context, in many NATO European nations, tactical weapons are increasingly regarded as weapons of little or no intrinsic value *per se* and as negative symbols that weaken the credibility of Western countries' commitment to the nonproliferation objectives of Articles I and II of the Nuclear Non-Proliferation Treaty (NPT) and the disarmament objective of Article VI.[18] The forward deployment of U.S. nuclear weapons on the territories of countries that are signatories of the NPT as non-nuclear-weapon states raises issues of compatibility with the spirit (if not the letter) of the Treaty.[19] This is more than a legal issue, it is a political one: if the strongest military alliance in the history of the world maintains that 200 or so nuclear gravity bombs are necessary to preserve peace and prevent coercion, it is only reasonable that other nations with less powerful military forces will decide that they also need to acquire nuclear arsenals for their security.

But the fact is that the further reduction and eventual elimination of TNWs are considered important contributions to nonproliferation and disarmament. Interestingly, the 2011 *Strategic Concept* expressed, for the first time, NATO's commitment "to create the conditions for a world without nuclear weapons in accordance with the goals of the Nuclear Non-Proliferation Treaty."[20]

Finally, in some European host countries, there is growing concern about the security risks connected with the presence of TNWs and the possible danger of unauthorized use, sabotage, or theft of these weapons.[21] This is especially true after a *Blue Ribbon Review* conducted by the U.S. Air Force in 2008 highlighted deficiencies in the custody of American weapons at European bases. The report disclosed that the majority of the bases did not meet the security standards established by the U.S. Department of Defense, and the reduced military salience of these weapons has led to diminished attention by base personnel and to waning expertise.[22] This issue is particularly relevant in Belgium, where much of the discussion of TNWs is kept alive by *bombspotting* actions by the peace movement that showcase the vulnerability of the Kleine Brogel air base, which is believed to host TNWs.[23]

DIFFERING THREAT ASSESSMENTS AND ALLIANCE COHESION

As observed at the outset of this article, NATO Europe is not a unitary actor but rather a heterogeneous alliance system whose internal differentiation and complexity have increased since the membership accession of several former Warsaw Pact countries beginning in the 1990s. Although the type of post-Cold War thinking described in the previous section is widespread in present-day NATO Europe, this thinking is not shared by all members of the Alliance. In addition to the French nuclear exceptions, a number of new NATO members in CEE perceive security differently and continue to place greater value on the physical and visible presence of U.S. TNWs in Europe.[24]

Historical events, both recent and distant, help to explain these countries' security assessments, which place a much stronger emphasis on prudent, worst-case-scenario-based defense planning. These countries' memories of the dramatic events of the 20th century are still vivid. The new allies joined NATO because of its collective defense value in avoiding possible repetition of past events when their very existence was threatened, first by Nazi Germany and later by the Communist USSR. Even if, after half a century of peace, Western European members of NATO believe that their security is not threatened, the positions of CEE members are much more cautious: they do not feel as secure, and they remain concerned about the threat from Russia.

The new NATO members consider U.S.-led NATO to be the ultimate guarantee of their territorial integrity and political independence. Hence, they share a grave concern about *any* change that may weaken the

U.S. commitment to the defense of Europe and transform the classical Article V hard-security mission of the Alliance into a license for out-of-area interventions or, worse, transform NATO into an organization with a constant identity crisis.[25]

For these CEE countries, tactical nuclear weapons still possess a residual political-symbolic value to enhance the credibility of the security guarantees made by the United States to its allies.[26]

> For reasons rooted in the different strategic cultures and the disparities in military might between Western Europe and the United States, Central Europeans believe that their successful defense requires direct U.S. military involvement. So they tend to associate any weakening of the transatlantic link with erosion of their own security.[27]

TNWs are considered a test of U.S. commitment to Europe's defense and of Europe's interest in keeping the transatlantic link strong.[28]

The issue of TNW forward deployment is entirely political and symbolic for the new NATO members in CEE. At its core, it is a proxy for the lack of confidence felt by these nations in the future of the U.S. commitment and concern about the diminished solidarity within the Alliance.[29] In addition to the historical reasons for the apprehension felt by the new NATO members (highlighted above), their insecurity has grown in recent years with the dismaying realization that the reinforcement of conventional forces and the upgrade of infrastructure for their defense, which NATO had promised these countries when they acceded to NATO, would never materialize. The new NATO Allies were also alarmed by the feeble response of the United States to the invasion of Georgia by Russian troops in 2008 and by the decision of U.S. President Barack Obama in 2009 to modify the plans for the deployment of components of a missile defense system in Poland and the Czech Republic.

The perspective of the new NATO members on TNWs does not seem completely intransigent, however. It is likely to be negotiable, especially if balanced by a credible NATO commitment—essentially, a U.S. commitment—to their defense by other means.[30] Indeed, according to Tomas Valasek, "The [tactical nuclear] weapons are a potent symbol of the transatlantic bond, but not necessarily the only, or irreplaceable, symbol."[31]

As has been rightly argued, it is primarily the non-nuclear dimension of the deterrence policy of NATO that must be improved to increase the importance of the collective defense and deterrence function of the Alliance.[32] NATO, and especially the United States, could consider alternatives to or compensations for the forward deployment of TNWs, such as an increase in conventional forces ("boots on the ground") or the deployment in the region of substantial components of Obama's redesigned "Phased Adaptive Approach" to missile defense, to meet the new NATO members' need for reassurance.

Undoubtedly, the issue must be addressed with great caution because it is difficult to reach agreement on perceptions and symbols, especially in the current period of profound transformation and reorganization of Euro-Atlantic security.[33] Decisions that are not shared risk weakening the cohesion of the Alliance on which the credibility of NATO depends. The priority on both sides of the Atlantic is to avoid casting doubt on the principle of indivisibility in the Alliance's security. Consequently, the debate on TNWs is widely perceived as subordinate to the more relevant objective of maintaining NATO's stability and cohesion. As such, and because intermediate options between maintaining TNWs and withdrawing them completely are not easy to envisage,[34] a final decision on nuclear forward deployment can be temporarily postponed.[35]

In this respect, the position of Italy on the presence, role, and destiny of the U.S. TNWs on its soil is telling and exemplifies the general perspective of NATO Europe on the issue.[36] On the one hand, Italy has dramatically devalued TNWs and considers the transatlantic link strong, regardless of the presence of a few B-61 bombs. On the other, with its deeply rooted strategic culture that prioritizes multilateralism over every form of unilateralism, Italy continues to assign paramount value to the cohesion of NATO, seeking to prevent rifts that could compromise its solidarity. To that end, Rome is willing to slow down or postpone the elimination of tactical weapons from its territory if necessary, although it considers these weapons not only of little intrinsic significance but also a hindrance to the program of nuclear disarmament that it supports.

CONCLUSION

In recent years, the military and political value of U.S. tactical nuclear forward deployment in Europe has dramatically decreased. Most NATO members genuinely support global nuclear disarmament and are amenable, in principle, to further reductions in the number of TNWs, and even to their complete withdrawal. However, some NATO members — particularly the new members in CEE — continue to attribute residual symbolic significance to TNWs, with the result that NATO as a whole is willing to delay or postpone the elimination of these weapons for the sake of the Alliance's cohesion.

NATO remains Europe's primary hard security provider. Because the credibility of an organization like NATO depends on solidarity among its members, a widely shared priority on both sides of the Atlantic is to avoid jeopardizing the principle of indivisibility of the Alliance's security. The prevailing trend of devaluing TNWs, therefore, is offset by a cooperative approach to allied security that considers the perceptions of all partners, including those who feel the need for continuing nuclear reassurance.

At the same time, NATO is called to be coherent with its regard to commitment to reducing reliance on nuclear arsenals and to nuclear disarmament. Engaging in earnest and with greater coherence to fight weapons of mass destruction (WMD) proliferation is in the strategic interest of the Alliance. Eliminating the remaining few scarcely useful TNWs deployed in Europe would serve this purpose well and at very little cost. Sooner or later, the fundamental rationale for the forward deployment of TNWs in Europe must be addressed in unambiguous terms.

The discussion, without taboos of any sort, must be pragmatic, non-ideological, and guided by four propositions. First, in the present and foreseeable future security scenario, TNWs have no clear mission, and alternative means of ensuring security exist; second, NATO is currently a truly conventional hyper-power with no rivals; third, NATO can remain a nuclear alliance even without forward deployment of U.S. TNWs, counting among its members three nuclear-weapon states; and fourth, TNWs today retain a residual (though replaceable), symbolic importance for only a few NATO member states.

If the wider concerns of those countries regarding the allied commitment to their defense can be suitably addressed, progress on further reduction in the numbers of TNWs and on softening NATO's nuclear posture might be possible.[37] In the final analysis, one cannot exclude the possibility that a properly tailored and strengthened "Asian model" of extended deterrence, whereby the U.S. nuclear umbrella can continue to function credibly without forward basing, could, in principle, be applicable to the European context.[38]

ENDNOTES - CHAPTER 12

1. According to NATO, the readiness posture of dual-capable aircraft (DCA) has been greatly reduced since the mid-1990s, from minutes to weeks. In 2002, the readiness requirements for these aircraft were further reduced and are now measured in months. See NATO, "NATO's Nuclear Forces in the New Security Environment," January 24, 2008, available from *www.nato.int/nato_static/assets/pdf/pdf_topics/20091022_Nuclear_Forces_in_the_New_Security_Environment-eng.pdf*.

2. Speech by Guido Westerwelle at the 46th Munich Security Conference, February 6, 2010, available from *www.security conference.de*. Similarly, Willy Claes, former Belgian Foreign Minister and former NATO Secretary General, stated, "The Cold War is over....US tactical nuclear weapons in Europe have lost all military importance." See "Ex-NATO chief joins call for no US nuclear arms in Europe," Agence France Presse, February 19, 2010, available from *www.spacewar.com/afp/100219103611.ezoyfew3.html*.

3. Tactical Nuclear Weapons (TNWs) are designed to perform specific military functions that support operations on the ground. They are intended for use in combat to achieve circumscribed (i.e., tactical) objectives in a limited nuclear war. With regard to NATO, the "flexible response" doctrine that was introduced in the 1960s foresaw the use of TNWs on European battlegrounds to counter Soviet conventional superiority and hamper or halt a Red Army advance on allied territory. The definition of TNWs and the

distinction between tactical and strategic nuclear weapons remain controversial. For a thorough discussion, see Harald Müller and Annette Schaper, "Definitions, Types, Missions, Risks and Options for Control: A European Perspective," in William C. Potter, Nikolai Sokov, Harald Müller, and Annette Schaper, eds., *Tactical Nuclear Weapons Options for Control*, New York: United Nations Institute for Disarmament Research, 2000, pp. 19-51; Andrea Gabbitas, "Non-Strategic Nuclear Weapons: Problems of Definition," in Jeffrey A. Larsen and Kurt J. Klingenberger, eds., *Controlling Non-Strategic Nuclear Weapons: Obstacles and Opportunities*, USAF Institute for National Security Studies, Collingdale, PA: Diane Publishing Co., pp. 39-63.

4. NATO, *Strategic Concept for the Defense and Security of the Members of the North Atlantic Treaty Organization*," November 19, 2010, para. 64, available from *www.nato.int/lisbon2010/strategic-concept-2010-eng.pdf.*

5. NATO, *Strategic Concept 2010*, para. 16.

6. *Ibid.*, para. 17.

7. *Ibid.*

8. *Ibid.*, para. 26.

9. Carl Bildt and Radek Sikorski, "Next, the Tactical Nukes," *New York Times*, February 1, 2010.

10. It is worth recalling that Turkey hosts B-61 TNWs on its territory but has no DCA. Its air forces participate in NATO exercises as non-nuclear air defense escort units, rather than a nuclear strike force (Mustafa Kibaroglu, "Reassessing the Role of US Nuclear Weapons in Turkey," *Arms Control Today*, Vol. 40, No. 5, June 2010, pp. 8-13). Despite its drastically reduced and today minimal role in nuclear matters, Turkey is openly against the withdrawal of TNWs from Europe. In the eyes of Ankara, TNWs are important political weapons to strengthen the link with the United States, which is considered indispensable for the country's defense in an international environment perceived as highly uncertain, also in consideration of the geopolitical co-location of the country next to the volatile Middle Eastern region (where the Iranian nuclear pro-

gram is seen with growing apprehension). In addition, Turkish civilian and military authorities view Turkey's NATO membership as a potent symbol of the country's belonging to the West and the U.S. TNWs as an emblem of the country's privileged status within the Alliance which must be preserved. Mustafa Kibaroglu, "Turkey, NATO & and Nuclear Sharing: Prospects after NATO's Lisbon Summit," Nuclear Policy Paper No. 5, Arms Control Association , British American Security Information Council, Institute for Peace Research and Security Policy at the University of Hamburg (IFSH), April 2011, p. 3. In short, especially after the reluctance and sluggishness of some NATO members to respond to Turkey's concerns in the context of the 1991 and 2003 Gulf Wars, Turkish officials are not confident that the extended deterrence of the Alliance would work effectively without the physical presence of U.S. forward-deployment on its soil (*Ibid.*). As correctly observed by a former British secretary of state for defence, TNWs are not important to Ankara because of the weapons themselves or their military value but because the relationship between Turkey, the United States, and the other NATO members is strained for other reasons, including the perception that Turkey's national security priorities are poorly understood by the allies, the damaging experience of the Bush administration, and the perceived failure of the United States to help Turkey in its struggle with the Kurdish Workers' Party (PKK). If Ankara's wider concerns can be addressed, further reduction in TNW numbers might be possible. See Des Browne, "Current NATO Nuclear Policy," in Paul Ingram and Oliver Meier, eds., *Reducing the Role of Tactical Nuclear Weapons in Europe: Perspectives and Proposals on the NATO Policy Debate*, ACA and BASIC Report, May 2011, p. 7.

11. With the main aim of addressing the Russian concerns about the effects of NATO enlargement on the countries of Central and Eastern Europe (CEE). NATO has declared that it has "no intention, no plan, and no reason to deploy nuclear weapons on the territory of new members, nor any need to change any aspect of NATO's nuclear posture or nuclear policy." See *Founding Act on Mutual Relations, Cooperation and Security between NATO and the Russian Federation*, May 27, 1997, available at *www.nato.int/cps/en/ natolive/official_texts_25468.htm*.

12. Author's interview with a senior official of the Italian Ministry of Foreign Affairs, Rome, Italy, September 10, 2010 (name withheld by request). This argument closely mirrors the position that was recently expressed by James Cartwright, Vice Chairman of the Joint Chiefs of Staff of the United States, according to whom there are no missions calling for TNWs that cannot be carried out with American conventional or strategic nuclear weapons. See James Cartwright, "Meeting on Nuclear Postures Review," Council on Foreign Relations, Washington, DC, April 8, 2010, available from *www.cfr.org/publication/21861/nuclear_posture_review.html*.

13. Indeed, the 2010 *Strategic Concept* admits, "The supreme guarantee of the security of the Allies is provided by the *strategic* [emphasis added] nuclear forces of the Alliance. . . ." The TNWs are not mentioned in this context. See NATO, *Strategic Concept 2010*, para. 18.

14. The current debate on the total abolition of nuclear weapons was prompted by an appeal by U.S. statesmen George Schultz, William Perry, Henry Kissinger and Sam Nunn published in "A World Free of Nuclear Weapons," *Wall Street Journal*, January 4, 2007. Interestingly, one of their recommendations was to eliminate "short-range nuclear weapons designed to be forward-deployed" as a concrete step toward a nuclear-weapons-free world. The appeal of the *Four Horsemen* — as Schultz and his associates are often called — has been followed by similar press initiatives worldwide, including the following NATO Europe countries: Belgium, Germany, Italy, the Netherlands, Norway, and the United Kingdom (UK).

15. See Obama's landmark Prague speech, Office of the Press Secretary, "Remarks by the President Barack Obama," Hradcany Square, Prague, Czech Republic, April 5, 2009, available from *www.whitehouse.gov/the_press_office/Remarks-By-President-Barack-Obama-In-Prague-As-Delivered/*.

16. Indeed, France was the main force opposing any change to NATO nuclear policy during the Lisbon summit that approved the new Strategic Concept. See Oliver Meier, "NATO Revises Nuclear Policy," *Arms Control Association*, December 2010, available from *www.armscontrol.org/print/4590*. France maintains a conservative nuclear policy and continues to consider its nuclear arsenal

as an essential element of its security and defense policy as during the Cold War. For Paris, the potential threats to the country's survival, sovereignty, independence and "vital interests" have not disappeared, and the United States guarantees through NATO are not seen as more credible than in the past. French leaders and strategists emphasize the element of high uncertainty of the present international system, and hence deem it prudent to maintain and modernize a national nuclear deterrent. This latter is also valued as a guarantee for pursuing an active and independent foreign policy, limiting the risk of being subject to blackmail or coercion (Bruno Tertrais, "The Last to Disarm? The Future of France's Nuclear Weapons," *Nonproliferation Review*, Vol. 14, No. 2, 2007). Three main features characterize "French nuclear exception": 1) strong and lasting political and public support for continuing current national nuclear policy; 2) a deeply rooted strategic culture which emphasizes independence and nuclear sufficiency; and, 3) an evolving and ambivalent approach to nuclear disarmament—based on non-ideological security considerations, a fairly restrictive interpretation of NPT disarmament commitments, but also on a policy of nuclear restraint—combined with proactive commitment to nonproliferation (Camille Grand, "France, Nuclear Weapons, and Nonproliferation," in Camille Grand *et al.*, eds., *U.S.-European Nonproliferation Perspectives. A Transatlantic Conversation*, Washington, DC: Center for Strategic and International Studies, April 2009). For interesting remarks on the conservative position of France in relation to the specific issue of U.S. TNWs assigned to NATO, see also Susi Snyder and Wilbert van der Zeijden, *Withdrawal Issues: What NATO countries say about the future of tactical weapons in Europe*, IKV Paz Christi, March 2011, pp. 21-22.

17. On the concept of nuclear weapons delegitimization, see Berry Ken, Lewis Patricia Pélopidas Benoît, Sokov Nikolai, and Wilson Ward, *Delegitimizing Nuclear Weapons: Examining the validity of nuclear deterrence*, Monterey, CA: James Martin Center for Nonproliferation Studies, 2010.

18. The *grand bargaining* underpinning of the Nuclear Non-Proliferation Treaty (NPT) calls for non-nuclear-weapon states not to seek to acquire nuclear weapons (Art. II) on the basis of the solemn promise by the nuclear-weapon states to negotiate in good faith to achieve nuclear disarmament (Art. VI).

19. NATO's argument is that the United States maintains control of the weapons, and there is no transfer of the weapons or their control except in war, in which case the NPT ceases to apply. In addition, it is maintained that the NPT was ratified after the countries of deployment had signed the (classified) agreements to host nuclear weapons on their territory, arrangements that were known to other signatories to the Treaty at the time of signing.

20. NATO, *Strategic Concept 2010*, para. 26. Moreover, it should be noted that, on Germany's initiative, the Lisbon Summit strengthened NATO's role in the fight against the proliferation of Weapons of Mass Destruction (WMD) and agreed to establish a new arms control committee charged with providing advice on WMD control and disarmament in the context of the Alliance's review of its deterrence and defense posture.

21. On this point, former U.S. Senator Sam Nunn recently stated, "To persist in maintaining U.S. tactical nuclear weapons in Europe for another decade—in the absence of any real military or political utility—is more of a security risk than asset to NATO, given the nontrivial risk of a terrorist attack against a NATO base with nuclear weapons." Sam Nunn, "The Race Between Cooperation and Catastrophe," in Steve Andreasen and Isabelle Willams, eds., *Reducing Nuclear Risks in Europe: A Framework for Action*, Nuclear Threat Initiative, 2011, p. 20.

22. See "Air Force Blue Ribbon Review of Nuclear Weapons Policies and Procedures," Polly A. Peyer, chair, February 8, 2008, available from *www.fas.org/nuke/guide/usa/doctrine/usaf/BRR-2008.pdf*. See also the analysis by Hans M. Kristensen, "USAF Report: 'Most' Nuclear Weapons Sites in Europe Do Not Meet U.S. Security Requirements," *Federation of American Scientist*, Strategic Security Blog, June 19, 2008, available from *www.fas.org/blog/ssp/2008/06/usaf-report-"most"-nuclear-weapon-sites-in-europe-do-not-meet-us-security-requirements.php*.

23. See Global Security Newswire, "Peace Activists Trespass at Belgian Base Housing U.S. Nukes," available from *www.globalsecuritynewswire.org/gsn/nw_20100217_5906.php*.

24. It is worth noting that this group of states is not unitary either, and different internal assessments exist. Whereas the small

296

and militarily weak Baltic states feel vulnerable and fear abandonment (and therefore are very much pro-status quo), Poland seems
more self-confident as a medium-sized European power and is
more prepared to discuss the issue and conditions of withdrawal,
especially as a bargaining chip to encourage Russia to reduce its
nuclear weaponry based near Central Europe.

25. Lukasz Kulesa, "Polish and Central European Priorities
for NATO's Future Nuclear Policy," in Ingram and Meier, p. 16.

26. Similar dynamics were at work among the "old" NATO
members at the height of the Cold War, when, in the words of
historian Michael Howard:

> The American military presence was wanted in Western
> Europe, not just in the negative role of a deterrent to Soviet
> aggression, but in the positive role of a reassurance to the
> West Europeans; the kind of reassurance a child needs from
> its parents or an invalid from his doctors against dangers
> which, however remote, cannot be entirely discounted.

See Michael Howard, "Reassurance and deterrence: Western defense in the 1980s," *Foreign Affairs*, Vol. 61, No. 2, 1982-83, p. 309.
If Charles de Gaulle was uncertain about American willingness to
sacrifice Washington or New York to save Paris, today there are
even more reasons to wonder whether the nuclearization of an
American city is an acceptable consequence of defending Vilnius
or Tallinn.

27. Tomas Valasek, "Central Europe and NATO's Nuclear
Deterrent," in Malcolm Chalmers and Andrew Somerville, eds.,
If the Bombs Go: European Perspectives on NATO's Nuclear Debate,
Westminster, UK: RUSI, Whitehall Report, Vol. 1, 2011, p. 21.

28. *Ibid.*

29. As previously seen, similar dynamics are at work in the
case of Turkey.

30. At the same time, the new NATO members believe strongly that TNWs should not be further reduced or withdrawn unilaterally, and they see the need to engage the Russians to reciprocate
with their much larger tactical arsenal.

31. Valasek, p. 24.

32. Lukasz Kulesa, p. 16.

33. On the concept of security perceptions, see Emil Kirchner and James Sperling, eds., *Global Security Governance: Competing Perceptions of Security in the 21st Century*, London, UK: Routledge, 2007.

34. Intermediate options, such as the consolidation of TNWs in one or two countries, would be politically unpalatable for any host country after TNWs are withdrawn from any of the five current host countries.

35. Even Germany, whose Ministry of Foreign Affairs had taken a strong position in favor of change in the months leading to the 2010 *Strategic Concept*, now seems to have adopted a more moderate stance and seeks consensus without breaking ranks with the allies.

36. According to open-source data, Italy hosts approximately 50 B-61 bombs at U.S. Aviano Air Base and 20-40 at Italy's Ghedi Torre Air Base. Italy possesses 69 nuclear-capable Tornado IDS aircraft. See Robert S. Norris and Hans M. Kristensen, "Nuclear Notebook: US Tactical Nuclear Weapons in Europe, 2011," *Bulletin of the Atomic Scientists,* Vol. 67, January/February 2011, pp. 64–73. For a thorough analysis of the Italian case, see Paolo Foradori, "Tactical nuclear weapons in Italy: Striking a Balance between Disarmament Aspirations and Alliance Obligations," *Nonproliferation Review*, Vol. 19, No. 1, March 2012 (forthcoming).

37. The 2010 *Strategic Concept* maintains a conservative stance on the purpose of NATO's conventional and nuclear mix and does not change its first-use policy, even against a non-nuclear attack. Paragraph 19 of the *Strategic Concept* states in unambiguous terms, "We will ensure that NATO has the full range of capabilities necessary to deter and defend against *any* threat to the safety and security of our populations" (emphasis added). It is worth noting that this statement creates an important discrepancy between the NATO position and that elaborated by the 2010 *Nuclear Posture Review of the United States*, which commits Washington

"not to use or threaten to use nuclear weapons against non-nuclear weapons states that are party to the NPT and in compliance with their nuclear non-proliferation obligations." See "Nuclear Posture Review Report," Washington, DC: U.S. Department of Defense, April 2010, page 27, available from *www.defense.gov/npr/docs/2010%20nuclear%20posture%20review%20report.pdf*, p. 15.

38. This possibility is discussed in Karl-Heinz Kamp, "NATO's Nuclear Posture Review: Nuclear Sharing Instead of Nuclear Stationing," *Research Paper*, Rome, Italy: NATO Defence College, May 2011, p. 68.

CHAPTER 13

EUROPE, NATO'S TACTICAL NUCLEAR CONUNDRUM, AND PUBLIC DEBATE: BE CAREFUL WHAT YOU WISH FOR[1]

Nick Childs

There is bad news and good news for the North Atlantic Treaty Organization (NATO) in the current state of affairs over its "tactical" nuclear weapons in Europe. In some instances, however, differentiating which is which may prove difficult. The bad news for NATO is that it has got itself into a bit of a mess over the issue. The good news is that hardly anyone in terms of the general public has noticed yet, certainly as far as most of European opinion is concerned. Inasmuch as the issue has been aired recently, the controversy that has been provoked has been relatively muted and confined, and has not yet really resonated as an issue of public policy concern. But the Alliance cannot rely on that remaining to be the case.

Here is where one of the differentiation questions comes in straight away. From the outside looking in, many might argue that NATO needs to lift the veil of behind-closed-doors deliberations and be more transparent in its decisionmaking. Some in the Alliance might even say that the lack of public resonance is bad news, as it reflects a general lack of public awareness of or indeed interest in where things stand on NATO nuclear strategy. What is needed, so this strand of argument goes, is public debate, education, and engagement on the matter. However, as the saying goes, be careful what you wish for.

While the populace in most European NATO countries may have quietly forgotten about, or stopped worrying about, Alliance nuclear weapons strategy or forward-deployed nuclear bombs on European soil, once reminded of them they are likely to be as sensitive to these issues as they have ever been. The potential "fallout" from such a reminder may be highly unpredictable. In the current information environment, with short memories and attention spans, for populations and the news media suddenly to be reminded that there are some 150-200 elderly U.S. nuclear free-fall bombs scattered around Europe could have quite a shock effect. Part of the problem for the Alliance, including even those within it who might welcome a wider public debate, is that it might well not be at NATO's time of choosing, or on its own terms, that the issue suddenly grabs the public and media consciousness. That has not happened yet. Yes, debate has been revived on the future of NATO's nuclear posture, but so far only up to a point, and not really much beyond a relatively limited policy elite. Even so, the airing of disagreements has set off official alarm bells and encouraged NATO governments to try to put a lid on these discussions.

To understand how public flare-ups can occur, one only has to look back to the public anguish and rancor that accompanied the effort in the 1980s to deploy cruise and Pershing missiles in Europe as part of the intermediate nuclear force stand-off with the Soviet Union. The recent flurry of discussions has not yet come close to spilling over into public agitation in the same way. But it could have the potential to be at least as divisive.

In the circumstances of a renewed public engagement with the nuclear weapons issue, a NATO that has not reached a clear consensus on what these weapons are now for, whether and how they might be retained or even modernized, or why and in what manner they might be dispensed with — unilaterally or through negotiation — would be seriously disadvantaged, and could find events and opinion spinning rapidly out of its control. Certainly, in a situation in which consciousness of and attachment to the continued presence of nuclear weapons in Europe has been slight, reporting of any public debate will inevitably latch on to what remain, at this stage anyway, some awkward paradoxes and inconsistencies in the arguments surrounding these weapons.

A large part of the problem for NATO is that the status quo appears unsustainable for anything more than the very short to medium term because of the obsolescence of the weapons and the dual-capable aircraft (DCA) that are assigned to carry them. However, any initiative to try to change that status quo risks shining that oh-so-unpredictable public spotlight on the matter. Some within NATO who back retention of the nuclear capability argue that, with a bit of deft strategic communication to prepare the ground and opinion, it might be possible to finesse this problem. But this is probably a forlorn hope when it is not clear what the message will be, or even to whom it should chiefly be aimed.

The lessons of the debate over missile defense as it evolved in Europe illustrate the difficulties of framing a case for even a relatively modest future capability when there is instinctive popular suspicion and skepticism, no consensus or agreed perspective around Europe, and an opportunity for Russia to sow division through hostility and opposition — feigned or real. Admittedly, the George H. W. Bush administration approach to a missile defense shield in Europe, which involved cooking up bilateral arrangements with a couple of key allies while the rest of NATO observed somewhat peevishly from the sidelines, may have maximized the diplomatic hurdles. But even the Obama administration's "reset" campaign with the Phased Adaptive Approach, which was more easily digestible by NATO skeptics and Russia, may have bought only a certain amount of extra time and room for maneuver. The recent renewed rumblings from Russia suggest that the whole scheme may still be very much hostage to the fortunes of U.S.-Russo relations, and that in turn could still affect NATO perspectives.

There was a time when NATO's residual forward-deployed nuclear weapons formed part of a much larger arsenal of thousands of nuclear weapons in Europe that was a perfect recipe for the Cold War. They provided "glue" for the Alliance, ensuring the credibility of the notion of extended nuclear deterrence, while spreading out the risks, and at the same time answering the conundrum of how to make up for the massive Soviet conventional superiority when no one in the Alliance was ready to foot the bill for doing so by conventional means.

However, it is not a world now in which NATO can draw on any credit for the fact that it has already removed the vast bulk of that arsenal. Memories are short. What is past is past in that sense, and also in the sense that the origins of the remaining weapons stem from that bygone era. The 150-200 bombs, and their associated U.S. and allied aircraft and air crews, in Germany, Belgium, the Netherlands, Italy, and Turkey, resemble a hangover from the Cold War at a time when the world has, arguably, moved beyond the post-Cold War era to a post-post-Cold War age.

In an environment in which there is not the strategic imperative of the Cold War, populations are likely, if asked to think about it, to be at least as hostile to the continued hosting of such weapons as some were then. In this environment, an argument for their retention based chiefly on politics, to keep NATO together, is unlikely to prove durable, especially in the absence of a consensus that these weapons still have a credible and vital military role and rationale. Furthermore, it is a troubling paradox for NATO that touting tactical nuclear weapons (TNWs) as continuing symbols of Alliance cohesion and solidarity, when raising a debate on their future or even highlighting their continued presence, represents a potential risk to that cohesion.

Basing the retention of TNWs in Europe on the need to address a potential proliferation cascade in the rest of the world seems equally problematic from a public opinion perspective. It is doubtful whether this argument will really have much traction in most of Europe; that is, unless there is a sudden shocking turn of events in the long-running Iran stand-off, which is, of course, not beyond the realm of possibility. Unfortunately, absent such a development, the proliferation issue, the specter of more and more menacing nuclear weapons states or groups, could very well be perceived in the minds of much of European opinion as an argument *in favor* of NATO stepping up its disarmament agenda, and throwing the TNWs into that pot as a positive indication of the Alliance's disarmament commitment. In fact, such an outcome is just as likely as the Alliance's hope that public opinion will favor tactical nuke retention as a hedge against an uncertain world. In the current climate of public opinion in Europe on matters nuclear, the plausibility of forward-deployed U.S. nuclear weapons as a counter to nuclear threats emerging from the Middle East or South or East Asia must be open to serious doubt. For such a scenario, the U.S. strategic arsenal will continue to look like a much more obvious option.

As has been said elsewhere, the use of TNWs as arms control bargaining chips would also be a challenge, and not just because there is such an asymmetry in numbers now between NATO's stockpile and that of Russia. It is hardly a happy starting point for a negotiation when different NATO member states see different rationales for retaining these weapons, including some that have nothing to do with Russia, and others see no enduring military rationale for them at all.

And what kind of party in any potential negotiations would Russia be? Not one, perhaps, inclined to help NATO out of its own difficulties on the matter. From any arms control perspective, there may be significant challenges to pursuing isolated negotiations purely on TNWs. In fact, this could simply produce increased friction and acrimony within NATO, particularly among its European members. But, equally, a more comprehensive, multi-track approach—with tactical nuclear weapons merely part of a grander bargain—may also be unachievable given the current preoccupation of NATO members with other issues. These are among the many challenges for the Alliance on this issue, simply when viewed from the standpoint of presenting the subject for public consideration.

But for the fact that the actual weapons themselves, and the aircraft that would deliver them, are getting old and wearing out, the debate surrounding the Alliance's remaining forward-deployed nuclear weapons may in some ways be characterized as an accidental one. It could be said to have stemmed from a misreading of signals within the Alliance. The most misread of those signals within Europe may have been the speech on the future of nuclear weapons delivered by President Barack Obama in Prague, Czech Republic, on April 5, 2009. The speech was certainly noteworthy for the President's assertion of "America's commitment to seek the peace and security of a world without nuclear weapons." What seemed to be so quickly overlooked were the caveats that "this goal will not be reached quickly — perhaps not in my lifetime," and "make no mistake. As long as these weapons exist, the United States will maintain a safe, secure, and effective arsenal, to deter any adversary, and guarantee the defense of our allies."[2]

It was in the wake of this, plus other nonproliferation and disarmament developments and initiatives, as encouraged by a belief that elements within the Obama administration might favor the withdrawal of the Europe-based bombs that the renewed debate on their future got going. The German coalition government — spurred by the Free Democratic Party — stated that it would pursue the withdrawal of the remaining nuclear weapons from Germany. This received a qualified endorsement from others, and led to Germany, the Benelux countries, and Norway collectively calling for an open discussion of ways of further reducing the role of nuclear weapons in NATO. While many in the arms control community and among disarmament advocates applauded the opening this joint initiative presented, others were far from complimentary. Former NATO Secretary General Lord Robertson and former senior Pentagon official Franklin Miller accused Germany of lifting the lid of Pandora's box,[3] and essentially of wanting to throw off the burden of nuclear deterrence but still share in its benefits.

What it further highlighted is the simple fact that there is no unitary European perspective on this issue, but rather an assorted and antagonistic array of different views on the continuing utility of, and reasons for, these weapons. As is now widely acknowledged, the views range from:

- Southeast Europe (Turkey), where the proliferation concern is right on the doorstep,
- through Eastern and Central Europe and the northeast, where NATO and particularly U.S. guarantees—including the nuclear one—remain a very "live" concern in the face of what many perceive as a still-looming Russia, and where reassurance appears at a premium in the light of the missile defense wobble,
- to the northwest, where states do not share the same wariness of Russia or see another looming direct threat for which a link to an American nuclear riposte in readiness is the answer.

In the middle of all this is a rather agitated France, perhaps fretting about what complications a debate leading to the departure of U.S. weapons would add to its own continued status as a nuclear-weapons state. Then there is Britain, more ambivalent perhaps about what it all might mean for its own arsenal, but concerned primarily about Alliance, and especially transatlantic, cohesion. These twisted sinews of argument offer rich pickings for potential political, diplomatic, and journalistic dismemberment.

Since they nudged the door ajar on the issue of tactical nuclear weapons, NATO members have seemingly recoiled after glimpsing the potential confusion on the other side of the door. But they cannot, and maybe should not, close the door again completely.

NATO foreign ministers, led by U.S. Secretary of State Hillary Clinton, steadied matters for a while at their informal meeting in Tallinn, Estonia, in April 2010, affirming that there would no unilateral action by any member to alter the status quo. The Clinton/Tallinn formula served to clarify the Washington position. It also affirmed NATO's retention of nuclear status, in the context of shared responsibilities, while promising to work towards reducing the role of nuclear weapons. It was thus able to paper over what had clearly been revealed to be deep cracks in the European stance.

NATO's new *Strategic Concept*, adopted at the Lisbon, Portugal, Summit in November 2010, stated that the Alliance will "maintain an appropriate mix of nuclear and conventional forces," and will "ensure the broadest possible participation of Allies in collective defence planning on nuclear roles, in peacetime basing of nuclear forces, and in command, control, and consultation arrangements."[4] But the fact was that the *Strategic Concept* steered clear of any more specific refashioning of NATO's nuclear posture, and for good reason. That refashioning would instead be entrusted to a separate review. Again, it was a reflection of the concerns in Washington and certain other European capitals that this review was formulated as a Defense and Deterrence Posture Review (DDPR), to avoid isolating the nuclear issue. But the mood music from this review has developed into a steady beat of lowered ambitions and expectations. Reflective of the pitfalls across Europe and from Europe across the Atlantic, the chances that it will offer anything definitive on the future of forward-deployed nuclear weapons seem significantly diminished. Even talk of offering at least a path towards a reduced nuclear role in future NATO strategy via a reworking of the Alliance's declaratory stance on nuclear weapons use seems likely to hit the buffers of French misgivings.

In part, if there is renewed reluctance to press the issue, it stems from the fact that the world has moved on in the last couple of years since the debate was revived. It would hardly have been surprising to see the political appetite to take on this issue diminish as soon as the diplomatic pitfalls in doing so manifested themselves. Beyond that, the onset of economic crisis in Europe has sharply redirected political attention and priorities. If refashioning NATO's nuclear posture was not in the top 10 of most people's priorities before, it will have sunk even lower subsequently. Even within the circles of those for whom this remains a live issue, the picture has become more blurred. Quite apart from anything else, it is impossible to divorce the shape of NATO's future from the economic upheavals going on all around.

In addition, the nuclear issue — and the specific matter of those "tactical" bombs — can never be divorced from the broader question of NATO's future identity and orientation, which is still a work in progress. The new *Strategic Concept* may have been greeted with fanfare and applause in November 2010, but it may yet turn out to have been nothing more than a holding operation, embracing the more defensive preoccupations of some members, the more long-range, out-of-area perspective of others, and the more uncertain challenges of the future, such as cyber defense. The economic crisis and its potential security implications in and around Europe, Libya and the lessons of that intervention, the unfolding of the transition in Afghanistan, a newly unpredictable political atmosphere in Russia, the ongoing Arab Spring, the chronic Iranian headache, and a host of other questions may mean that the strategic landscape in the run-up to the Chicago, IL, summit has a very different topography from that anticipated even in the immediate aftermath of Lisbon.

Talking of topography, in a European context the main nodes in this debate have been Bonn, Germany, and the other host capitals, Paris, France, and the Baltic states. An overlooked, or at least relatively uncharted reference point, has been London, United Kingdom (UK). Partly, that is because it is to the UK government's liking. While it is one of three acknowledged nuclear weapons states in NATO, it has tended to pursue a pragmatic approach to the issue. As has been mentioned, the key driver in London is concern about Alliance cohesion, and especially the transatlantic bridge, with a particular wariness about the potential fallout in the U.S. Congress of any argumentative flare-up in Europe that could be portrayed as a further example of Europeans being reluctant to do their bit to shoulder the security burden. For all these reasons, London is likely to encourage — or at least not to find unwelcome — any trends that extend the status quo and keep the debate off the boil prior to Chicago.

There is, of course, an underlying concern in London about any momentum that might start to build towards Europe becoming a nuclear-free zone. There may be a worry in Paris, and even a certain paranoia and a little exasperation, that the British do not view these things with quite the required robustness. Maybe France does feel the pressure more acutely, as potentially the only continental European power in NATO with nuclear weapons and a continuing belief in nuclear deterrence. Paradoxically, a reduction to zero of the remaining U.S. nuclear weapons in the current European host countries could actually increase the potential value of British weapons in any extended deterrence linkage, as the British weapons are—in contrast to the French arsenal—declared to NATO. It could also increase the potential value of Britain to the United States as a strategic partner if the UK were to remain a willing host of U.S. weapons in certain contingencies. Many in Washington still remember when the British government of Margaret Thatcher, in 1986, allowed U.S. forces to use British bases and airspace to launch (albeit conventional) air strikes against Libya, when no other European ally would. In addition, nuclear weapons cooperation is one area where the much-vaunted (on the British side at least) "special relationship" really is special. But the dynamics of any move to denuclearize the other European NATO members could also have an impact on the nuclear weapons debate—such as it is—in Britain.

Britain has long since given up its own tactical nuclear weapons. The WE177 munition was taken out of service with the Royal Navy in 1992, and withdrawn from service with the Royal Air Force (RAF) in 1998. The country's only remaining nuclear weapon is the submarine-based Trident strategic system. Strictly speaking, the issues of the future of NATO's tactical weapons and that of the UK strategic force are entirely separate. Yet the fortunes of the former could have some ripple effect on the prospects for the latter. Britain's Trident force is currently based on four *Vanguard*-class ballistic missile submarines. While the British government is especially secretive about many aspects of its nuclear weapons capabilities, it (like the United States) has moved ahead of NATO in certain aspects of transparency and declaratory policy. In May 2010, the new Conservative-Liberal Democrat coalition government revealed that the UK's nuclear weapon holdings did not exceed 225 warheads in the overall stockpile, with up to 160 operationally available warheads. It also announced that it would reexamine the circumstances under which the UK might use its nuclear weapons.[5] Then, in October 2010, the *Strategic Defence and Security Review* (SDSR) announced the aim of a further reduction in declared holdings, to an overall stockpile of not more than 180 warheads, no more than 120 operationally available warheads, and with the number of warheads carried on each submarine on patrol reduced to just 40 on eight operational missiles.[6]

But Britain is also in the throes of early work to renew its nuclear force with a new generation of submarines. While the coalition government committed to replacing the current force, differences between the coalition partners have affected aspects of the process. While the Conservatives back a new submarine-based ballistic missile force, the Liberal Democrats have questioned the need for a like-for-like replacement. As a result, a final decision to go ahead with new submarines has been delayed until 2016, by which time there will have been a new general election in Britain. So the in-service date of the first new submarine, if indeed it is built, has also been delayed from 2024 to 2028. To accommodate Liberal Democrat policy, a new review of the options for replacement is under way, which should be completed by the end of 2012.

These various developments, plus more question marks over whether the UK Ministry of Defence (MoD) will be able to afford the expected £15-20 billion price tag, have led some to believe that a whole new debate could now take place on the decision to renew the Trident system, perhaps in the context of the next UK general election. Those who advocate it argue that there was no serious debate when the original decision to go ahead with a renewal of the Trident force was made by the previous Labour government under Prime Minister Tony Blair in 2006. Whether such a debate is a realistic possibility may be open to doubt, since it is questionable whether any of the mainstream UK parties would be willing to take it on. But were it to start simmering, the current British government may become a little nervous if there were to be an ongoing and potentially quite fractious debate under way within NATO about the future of nuclear weapons in the rest of Europe.

The underlying UK government rationale for pursuing a new generation of strategic nuclear weapons is as an insurance policy and a hedge against the uncertainty of what the threats will be in the decades ahead. In that sense, it remains wedded to the fundamentals of nuclear deterrence. But some even within the British military establishment have questioned whether the cost of what is being contemplated for the future is proportionate to the likely risk. That argument could find echoes in how NATO contemplates the cost of retaining forward-deployed nuclear weapons in Europe. Quite simply, do the potential risks justify the potential scale of future budgetary commitments?

At the same time it is keeping faith with the nuclear deterrence rationale, the British government has also been interested in exploring how to renew the broad application of deterrence to conventional capabilities in the modern world, in part to help sustain the rationale for continuing to invest in certain aspects of its conventional armed forces. How these two strands of future deterrence will be balanced has a bearing not only on the shape and character of the UK armed forces in the long run, but also possibly on London's attitude to how nuclear weapons will figure in overall NATO strategy, and indeed on how that strategy itself evolves.

More broadly, the tenor of debate over NATO as a whole has been shifting in ways that will affect the attitude in Europe towards the nuclear element of Alliance policy. First, there has been the reopening of the debate over burden-sharing more generally, not just nuclear, and especially the perception in Washington of European shirking. This was highlighted most publicly by the scolding parting shots of the then outgoing U.S. Defense Secretary Robert Gates.[7] Europe might respond positively to some of the criticism. But beyond renewed efforts to make "smart procurement" and the pooling of resources genuinely work better, there is no chance of Europe collectively — in the current circumstances — increasing the resources that it devotes to defense. Quite the reverse, in fact. Against that background of transatlantic frictions, added to even more pressure on European conventional capabilities, the arguments over the nuclear umbrella as an ultimate guarantor of security — and the place of forward-deployed TNWs as a part of that — could be significantly affected.

Then there is Libya. The outcome (inasmuch as it is yet possible to be definitive about it) has been portrayed as a success story for the Alliance, and more particularly for the leading European members of it. There were indeed significant and impressive military capabilities deployed that were ultimately applied successfully. The politics of it seemed to work as well, in the sense that the Alliance agreed collectively to take on command and control of the mission. But it was not, despite its code name Operation UNIFIED PROTECTOR, an entirely united effort in terms of the level of commitment among NATO member states. There was particular attention focused on the lack of German participation. There was also quite a high level of absenteeism from key aspects of the operation. So, while formally a NATO operation, it was in reality more a collection of 15 NATO members who took part. This only added ammunition to the locker of those wondering whether the "alliance" is not, in fact, devolving to a loose assemblage of pick-and-choose members.

Clearly, any new stirrings of concern on that front will play into the nuclear debate. So too the fact that, from the perspective of Washington, while Operation UNIFIED PROTECTOR was meant to be a Europe-led operation, the United States still ended up not only committing more resources than any other nation, but also providing capabilities which—while they may have been perceived in Europe as simply supportive and enabling—actually made the difference between sustaining the operation and not. In an atmosphere in which the renewed perception in Washington is of a Europe failing the burden-sharing tests, there is a danger for the European allies that nuclear burden-sharing will become the test of last resort.

As has been emphasized, the fact is that there is no collective "European perspective" on these questions. Perceptions of what amounts to security, and where the threats to security lie, remain in a state of continuing development. In addition to a legacy of historical perspective and geography, it is also being shaped by the different experiences of member states in the new age of austerity. The dynamic of the slow extraction from Afghanistan, and evolving judgments on the costs and benefits of that mission, will shape attitudes toward NATO and what it is for. The lessons of Afghanistan will also help to determine—along with the lessons from Libya—what appetite there will be for any kind of future entanglements, or "wars of choice," and therefore ultimately for what sort of requirements there might be for future nuclear weapons capabilities as a possible defense or deterrent. The trauma of economic upheaval will affect the appetite and ability to make defense provisions in Europe, and possibly what has been described as a "race to the bottom" among European defense budgets, especially with the spectacle of the U.S. Government also joining in the process.[8] It is also going to have an impact on perceptions of where the real threats to stability in Europe will lie in the medium term, and what role—if any—NATO should play in tackling them. Thus NATO, at Chicago or after, may have to adjust again if it wants to remain relevant to most Europeans. Having spent a decade trying to make NATO forces more deployable and better able to tackle the tasks of nation-building, the Alliance partners are likely to shift the focus again. In the context of evermore-squeezed budgets, the priority concerns may become more to do with internal stability and cohesion and less with military threats even from the near neighborhood, let alone further afield. That eventuality could also see a recalibration of the arguments over nuclear weapons, especially if austerity becomes increasingly prolonged and the question of the need to reinvest in the infrastructure to support the forward-based weapons starts to intrude more urgently. The fallout from austerity also impinges on the issue of reassuring NATO's eastern European members. Reduced European conventional capabilities, plus the specter of further U.S. conventional drawdowns in Europe, reduce Alliance willingness to address additional non-nuclear contingencies.

Of course, the evolving European position on the provision of missile defenses for the Alliance will have a bearing on how nuclear weapons fit into the portfolio of defense and deterrence options. The issue over the extent to which these options were alternative or complementary approaches was part of the discussion from early on in the debate. Positions on this issue are likely to evolve as the missile defense architecture in and around Europe starts to mature. Clearly, all the potential sensitivities surrounding this discussion are mixed up with lingering concerns about the Alliance's adaptability and continuing relevance more broadly, or else the NATO approach to the matter up to now would have been more categorical and confident.

Might NATO have avoided some of the potential pitfalls if it had been more transparent historically about the enduring role of nuclear weapons in its arsenal in Europe? Clearly it suited the Alliance to deemphasize that role over a long period, indeed not to talk about the weapons at all, and that is in part responsible for the low level of public awareness and understanding of the matter now. A greater continuity of debate might have made the dilemmas now less acute. The actual state of affairs is such that whatever arrangement NATO chooses for now is likely to provoke some degree of controversy, with or without a continuing role for the U.S. B-61 bombs.

The reality that Germany, a salient Alliance voice, appears to have retreated from its initial position is perhaps the most significant element in shaping how NATO will proceed. As well as second thoughts on the issue itself, it now has its hands full with a host of other more pressing problems. Bonn now seems to have settled on accepting NATO's identity as a nuclear alliance, but without requiring nuclear weapons on

German territory. On the other hand, Germany has accepted the principle that there will be no unilateral change. So Bonn probably hopes that nuclear weapons will not in the end be a dominating or defining issue in Chicago even as it continues to worry that it will remain hostage to that possibility.

Germany's troubled attitude may ultimately be shared by most of the European members of NATO as well. So what seems to be in the offing is continuing compromise, an elaboration perhaps, but no more, on the Clinton/Tallinn formula. The problem is that this compromise will not satisfy either side in the debate. For those attached to a "nuclear zero," it will be a missed opportunity. For those who see an enduring role for the weapons, it will presage continuing danger to NATO's cohesion and nuclear posture, and all the more so given that, with the current public mood, there is no realistic possibility of the Alliance's European members accepting the idea of stationing updated nuclear weapons on their territory.

In these circumstances, what is really a political issue may, by the choice of the political leaderships, spiral down to a technical matter and be dealt with by default. Again, the principal focus is on Germany and the lack of any dual-capable successor to its current *Tornado* strike aircraft. But there is also lingering uncertainty for those current B-61 hosts, the Netherlands, and Italy, whose future combat aircraft choice, the F-35 *Lightning*, may have been designed with dual capability in mind but which as a project may yet face an uncertain future.

However the tactical nuclear debate unfolds in the run-up to the Chicago summit and beyond, there is still a palpable sense that it has only just begun.

ENDNOTES - CHAPTER 13

1. The author's arguments do not necessarily represent the views of the BBC.

2. President Barack Obama, speech on nuclear weapons, Prague, Czech Republic, April 5, 2009.

3. Franklin Miller, George Robertson, and Kori Schake, *Germany Opens Pandora's Box*, London, UK: Centre for European Reform (CER) briefing note, February 8, 2010.

4. NATO *Strategic Concept, Active Engagement, Modern Defence*, Lisbon, Portugal, November 2010.

5. Statement by UK Foreign Secretary William Hague, House of Commons, May 2010.

6. *Strategic Defence and Security Review*, London, UK: HM Government, October 18, 2010.

7. U.S. Secretary of Defense Robert Gates, "Reflections on the Status and Future of the Transatlantic Alliance," speech to the Security and Defence Agenda group, Brussels, Belgium, June 10, 2011.

8. Tomas Valasek, "Race to the bottom," London, UK: Centre for European Reform, August 24, 2011.

PART IV

AMERICAN PERSPECTIVES

CHAPTER 14

AMERICAN PERSPECTIVES ON TACTICAL NUCLEAR WEAPONS

James A. Blackwell

In the 21st century, the United States is challenged by a growing need to extend deterrence beyond the scope of that which can be accomplished by strategic systems reserved for retaliation to a massive nuclear strike on the continental United States. Two distinguished analysts, Leo Michel and Jeffrey Larsen, provide perspective on how America views the contribution that U.S. nuclear weapons in Europe can make to U.S. security through extended deterrence in an increasingly complex global security environment. Then Guy Roberts, tapping his extensive arms control experience at the North Atlantic Treaty Organization (NATO), takes a prospective look at the upcoming North Atlantic Council review in Chicago, IL, of the Alliance's deterrent and defense posture (DDPR), with particular attention to the U.S. connection.

The challenges of extended deterrence begin with the question of the nature of security interests the United States has in Europe and how those interests are related to its interests in other regions as well as to its position in the international security system. The relationship with Russia may have been "re-set," but the nature and longevity of any resulting change are uncertain. Russia remains the only nuclear-armed state capable of destroying the United States and its European Allies, maintaining perhaps thousands of non-strategic nuclear weapons (NSNWs) (formerly known as tactical nuclear weapons) matched to missiles and aircraft that place all of NATO within their reach. New nuclear threats to the security of Europe loom on the horizon, some of which will require self-interested U.S. deterrence capabilities as well as those necessary for mutual security among Allies.

It is apparent that the United States has embarked on substantial reductions in resources allocated to national security—a cyclical feature of the American political culture that follows every major war with about a decade of decline in dollars spent on defense of roughly 30 percent from the wartime peak. A world characterized by continuing pressures for nuclear weapons proliferation is a world in which medium and smaller nuclear-armed states may see their nuclear roles change as well. Some long-time experts wonder if the United States were to remove its nuclear weapons from Europe, would France or the United Kingdom (UK) find itself with newfound influence, responsibility, and burden. The role of U.S. nuclear weapons in Europe will thus, inevitably, be reexamined.

While acknowledging the pressure on resources and despite the retirement of the U.S. Navy's nuclear-tipped, attack submarine-launched Tomahawk Land Attack Missile (TLAM-N), the authors point to expressed commitments by the United States to continue to maintain a Triad of nuclear weapon capabilities for central deterrence and to maintain and modernize both fighters and bombers capable of delivering nuclear weapons for extended deterrence. The *Nuclear Posture Review* (NPR) also expresses intent to conduct a full-scope life extension on the B-61 nuclear bomb explicitly to sustain its capacity for deployment in Europe. Neither author agrees with the notion that missile defenses could supplant the function performed by U.S. nuclear weapons in Europe. Larsen argues that missile defenses cannot do so until the arrival of a technology and weapons regime in which the defense is superior to offense—an eventuality not yet on the foreseeable horizon. Michel argues that missile defenses cannot provide sufficient confidence for Europeans confronted by so many Russian NSNWs and by strident Russian objections to missile defenses in Europe.

Despite the political and budgetary pressures for defense reductions, the authors articulated the continuity of the U.S. commitment to extended deterrence in Europe as expressed by the Barack Obama administration in various national security pronouncements. But Michel points out that the Schlesinger Task Force Report of 2008, apparently for the first time in so public a manner, revealed some of the internal disagreements within the U.S. military on whether the country should continue to bear the cost of this burden. Larsen notes that, while the 2010 NPR reinforces the American commitment to the classic burden-sharing deal of NATO nations hosting U.S. nuclear weapons, the NPR also announces U.S. plans to modernize its nuclear long-range strike capabilities and to work toward replacing the deterrence function of nuclear weapons with conventional and missile defense capabilities.

Some analysts wonder whether the United States might take the kind of approach to extended deterrence in Europe that it has already taken in Asia—removal of the nuclear weapons themselves but regularly exercising the capability to employ them in the region as a visible reminder to potential adversaries and assurance to existing allies. Both authors suggest that removal of U.S. nuclear weapons from Europe is not likely, at least not in the near future. The deployment of U.S. nuclear weapons in Europe will continue to serve as a deterrent against any Russian temptation to exploit the presence of its NSNWs to threaten, intimidate, or coerce NATO allies or others, especially in crisis. The continued presence of U.S. nuclear weapons in Europe will provide Allies with sufficient assurance to deter them from developing their own nuclear weapons capabilities. So far as the DDPR in Chicago is concerned, Roberts expresses the view that when the dust has settled, "the U.S. nuclear presence in Europe [will be] affirmed."

The circumstances under which nuclear weapons might be employed in a European crisis or conflict have changed dramatically with the end of the Cold War. Article V of the North Atlantic Treaty, invoked in response to the September 11, 2001, strike on the United States, remains very much in force. Russia has promulgated a new first-use doctrine for its non-strategic nuclear weapons as a means to "de-escalate" a conflict or crisis that it considers to be a threat to Russia and its people. It has practiced this doctrine in exercises; some speculate that it does so to compensate for its inferiority in conventional military capabilities. In stark contrast to the Cold War discussions of how "Flexible Response" might play out in the face of a Warsaw Pact attack, the kinds of contingencies under which NATO might employ its nuclear weapons today attract few discussants. Perhaps this reticence is the result of the underlying reality that NATO nuclear weapons are in fact "used" every day that they deter others from employing them against NATO members.

CHAPTER 15

THE ROLE OF NON-STRATEGIC NUCLEAR WEAPONS:
AN AMERICAN PERSPECTIVE

Jeffrey A. Larsen

INTRODUCTION

The ultimate purpose of U.S. nuclear weapons today remains the same as it has been since the late 1940s: to deter an armed attack against the U.S. homeland, its forces and interests abroad, and its friends and allies. For more than 60 years, this mission has been associated in the public mind with deterrence of an adversary's use of its own atomic weapons, and, more recently, of any weapon of mass destruction (WMD). Nuclear weapons have been thought of primarily as a tool — one of many available to a nation-state, including political, diplomatic, and economic efforts, conventional forces, and active and passive defenses — to prevent aggression of any kind against America's vital national interests.

This chapter argues that the denomination of certain U.S. nuclear weapons as "non-strategic" is not likely to continue much longer. The small number of weapons of this type will remain in the U.S. inventory, of course, but the name of the category itself will fall into disuse as a relic of the Cold War. Instead, today's non-strategic nuclear weapons (NSNWs) will be absorbed into the manned bomber leg of the Triad comprising what are now referred to as strategic weapons. This is due to the growing recognition that *any* nuclear use would have strategic consequences, and that these weapons still have a role to play in assuring allies through extended deterrence guarantees. In addition, the 2001 *Nuclear Posture Review* (NPR) created a "new Triad" that included all nuclear and non-nuclear strike capabilities in one category, so that in essence dual-capable aircraft (DCA)—fighter-bombers that can deliver either conventional or NSNWs—and B-61 tactical nuclear bombs have already been part of the larger matrix of nuclear forces for more than 10 years.[1] This implies that in the future, the entire U.S. nuclear arsenal will serve the needs of extended deterrence in Europe through off-shore guarantees, as it already does for America's allies in East Asia. The United States has global interests, and its military has global responsibilities. Nuclear weapons—*all* U.S. nuclear weapons—will continue to play a vital role as the ultimate guarantor of the nation's security for the foreseeable future.

Multiple studies have come to the conclusion that nuclear weapons are here to stay. Regardless of national objectives calling for a nuclear-free world, such weapons are likely to remain a part of the global security environment, and will continue to play a central role in U.S. security policy. Even if the United States were to take the lead in nuclear disarmament, some argue, it may nevertheless find itself one day facing an adversary that has nuclear weapons and believes they provide a measure of value to their national power. As a counterbalance, the United States needs to maintain a robust, safe, secure, and reliable nuclear force structure.[2]

America's attitude toward NSNWs historically has been that they are valuable political tools for reassuring allies, both in the North Atlantic Treaty Organization (NATO) and in other regions. This reassurance has rested upon their operational value as warfighting tools against the threat of invasion by a neighbor. But their current value appears to be diminishing, indeed, some analysts and politicians even see them as impediments on the road to Global Zero. Yet the United States is caught in the challenging position of having to continue guaranteeing security to other states, while facing uncertainty over the future of weapons that have traditionally served to show such a commitment to its friends and partners. In short, NSNWs may be obsolete, but at this point they still serve some modest purposes that argue against their elimination in the short term. In fact, as consensus builds for the proposition that *any* nuclear use would have strategic significance, thus rendering inappropriate such a term as "non-strategic" nuclear weapons, these weapons and their delivery systems may come to be seen in the future simply as one implement in the strategic forces toolbox available for a president's use in crises or conflicts.

BACKGROUND

The United States has adopted a defense-in-depth security concept since the dawn of the nuclear age. In simple terms, this means that when dealing with the possibility of nuclear attack by some nation-state or of nuclear terrorism by some nonstate actor, the United States will first attempt to prevent the spread of dangerous materials and know-how to other states via nonproliferation policies. If, despite our best nonproliferation efforts, a potential adversary succeeds in arming itself with nuclear weapons, the United States will attempt to persuade the other party that it has no chance of winning a war with the United States even with nuclear weapons, and that it would be foolhardy and cost-prohibitive to even contemplate such an effort. Should dissuasion fail, U.S. policymakers may consider taking preemptive military action to destroy the threat before it can materialize. Such efforts are categorized as a type of counterproliferation. Simultaneously, it has long been U.S. policy to deter that adversary from considering taking military action against the United States, its interests, or its allies through sowing fear, that is, through the threat of unacceptable retaliation in response to such an attack. This concept will surely remain a cornerstone of U.S. policy. Some anti-nuclear commentators go so far as to suggest that deterring nuclear use by an adversary may be the only legitimate purpose of such an arsenal. Should deterrence fail, however, the United States would rely on active defenses to intercept and blunt an attack, and on passive defenses to protect the homeland and the population from the effects of nuclear weaponry. Finally, should a strike reach the American homeland anyway, the concept of consequence management takes over, encompassing clean-up, response, attribution, and retribution for the attack.

Nuclear weapons, like all military force, can serve a number of purposes. In particular, they can be used for actual combat operations in their warfighting role, or they can be used to convince an adversary that he cannot achieve his objectives or will face devastating retaliation if he tries. If this latter purpose is pursued successfully, it would obviate the use of nuclear weapons in anger. This is what we call deterrence, the prime purpose of nuclear weapons in the arsenals of most nation states that possess them today.[3] Unfortunately, there are some states and nonstate actors in the world today that may decide to pursue nuclear weapons for their ostensible military value, hence the need to maintain U.S. forces to ensure deterrence.

President Barack Obama highlighted this continuing requirement for nuclear weapons in his April 2009 Prague, Czech Republic, speech in which he laid out a vision of a nuclear-free world at some future point. While highlighting the vision, he also emphasized the flip side: that while the United States would take "concrete steps towards a world without nuclear weapons," he recognized that the world was still a dangerous place. Accordingly, he said, "As long as these weapons exist, the United States will maintain a safe, secure, and effective arsenal to deter any adversary, and guarantee that defense to our allies."[4]

As a sovereign, independent nation-state, the primary U.S. national security goal must be the protection of its own people, territory, and interests. This is a core security requirement, and the deterrent value of America's nuclear arsenal is unquestioned in this realm. But as the President reminded us, the United States has also promised to protect many of its friends and allies around the world. It does this by extending its nuclear and conventional "umbrella" over more than 30 states. The concept of extended deterrence simply means that one state will provide security for another state through the threat of punishment against a third party that may wish to attack or coerce the second state. It is a logical extrapolation of deterrence theory, and is a promise not given lightly, nor to everyone. Extended deterrence commits the United States to the possibility of going to war with another great power if necessary in order to protect a more vulnerable allied state.[5] It is a policy that extends the protection of America's military, typically its nuclear umbrella, to friends and allies far from North America and the U.S.

homeland. The traditional U.S. rationale for extended deterrence has been to attempt to address the danger as far as possible from its shores, fighting, if necessary, an "away game." Of course, flexible extended deterrence does not have to be accomplished with nuclear weapons. During the Cold War, however, the two concepts were nearly always synonymous, and many of today's analyses still conflate the two ideas. In any case, when the United States chooses to give a security guarantee to another state, that commitment will include all measures of defense up to and including nuclear weapons as the ultimate deterrent. Cold War historian John Lewis Gaddis called this type of commitment "active deterrence" because it took a willful decision by the nuclear state to make such a guarantee.[6]

The purpose of extended deterrence during the Cold War was to provide security for America's allies. This required the United States to convince potential adversaries—meaning primarily the Soviet Union—that U.S. security commitments were genuine, and that they would be carried out if necessary. In addition, extended deterrence served a number of additional purposes. It induced caution among the nuclear players on the world stage; it discouraged adventurism, not only by the nuclear states but by those protected by the guarantee; and it may have helped to prevent nuclear proliferation among the allies. This latter point was part of the grand alliance bargain that the United States struck with its European allies (except France and England, of course): in return for a security guarantee, they agreed not to pursue their own nuclear capabilities.[7] This same bargain was in place in Northeast Asia for the purpose of keeping allies such as Japan, South Korea, and Taiwan nuclear-free.

In Asia, the United States has long-standing security commitments to Japan through the U.S.-Japan Security Pact.[8] Both sides have always assumed that this meant the possible use of U.S. nuclear weapons to protect Japanese territorial sovereignty against potential aggression, Japan's anti-nuclear stance in its constitution notwithstanding. In 2009, the U.S. Secretary of State during a visit to Japan publicly proclaimed that the solemn U.S. commitment to defend Japan was not only firm, but did include the ultimate weapon.[9] South Korea is also the recipient of a U.S. nuclear security guarantee though U.S. nuclear weapons stationed in South Korea until 1992, when they were removed and returned to storage in North America.[10]

The question at hand is whether those guarantees to other nations still reflect the vital national interests of the United States today, or, conversely, whether they actually decrease America's security by tying it to the defense of other countries. Even if the United States determines that continuing to provide a security guarantee to its allies is still a vital interest, it needs to ask whether extended deterrence requires forward-based nuclear systems. This was believed to be the case during the Cold War, but today there is another model that may prove instructive. Unlike the European situation, Northeast Asia and some states in the Middle East benefit from American security guarantees without having any U.S. weapons on their soil. Nor would such a guarantee necessarily require nuclear weapons — perhaps conventional forces, or, as some argue, robust multinational missile defenses could fill that requirement. Deterrence, after all, is essentially psychological, working on the perceptions of the potential adversary. Deployed weapons may not be required to assure allies or deter adversaries.

However, if the United States were to move toward an Asian model for Europe, it would certainly require greater emotional and psychological nurturing and more robust assurances to its allies that America was still there when and if needed.

THE *NUCLEAR POSTURE REVIEW*

The 2010 NPR may not have gone as far toward radical reductions or policy changes as some had hoped following President Obama's Prague speech, but it did serve as an important statement that laid out the administration's goals and made some modest moves in the direction of reduced reliance on nuclear weapons.[11] It emphasized the foundational concept that "the fundamental role of U.S. nuclear weapons, which will continue as long as nuclear weapons exist, is to deter nuclear attack on the United States, our allies, and partners."[12] It stated that the United States will continue to strengthen conventional capabilities and reduce the role of nuclear weapons in deterring non-nuclear attacks, with the objective of "making deterrence of nuclear attack on the United States or our allies and partners the sole purpose of U.S. nuclear weapons." In the new global security environment, the United States will consider the use of nuclear weapons only "in extreme circumstances to defend the vital interests of the United States or its allies and partners."[13]

The NPR focused on five key objectives of U.S. nuclear weapons policies and posture:

1. Preventing nuclear proliferation and nuclear terrorism;

2. Reducing the role of U.S. nuclear weapons in U.S. national security strategy;

3. Maintaining strategic deterrence and stability at reduced nuclear force levels;

4. Strengthening regional deterrence and reassuring U.S. allies and partners; and,

5. Sustaining a safe, secure, and effective nuclear arsenal.[14]

It is the fourth objective on this list that we normally think of when we consider the role of NSNWs. The NPR stated that the United States is "fully committed to strengthening bilateral and regional security ties and working with allies and partners to adapt these relationships to 21st century challenges. Such security relationships are critical in deterring potential threats, and can also serve our nonproliferation goals."[15] Nonproliferation is served by dissuasion—"demonstrating to neighboring states that their pursuit of nuclear weapons will only undermine their goal of achieving military or political advantages"—and by reassurance to America's non-nuclear allies and partners, assuring them "that their security interests can be protected without their own nuclear deterrent capabilities."[16]

For nearly 60 years, the United States has provided a nuclear umbrella over its allies through a combination of means—the strategic forces of the U.S. Triad, NSNWs deployed forward in key regions, and U.S.-based nuclear weapons that could be deployed forward quickly to meet regional contingencies. As the NPR makes clear, the mix of deterrent means has varied over time and from region to region.

This long-standing tangible commitment to U.S. allies in Europe, however, has been somewhat attenuated since the end of the Cold War by the reduction in the number, location, and visibility of forward-deployed U.S. nuclear weapons. Still, a small number (estimated, to be 150-200) of U.S. nuclear weapons remain in Europe. The NPR reiterates the standard Alliance claim that:

> although the risk of nuclear attack against NATO members is at an historic low, the presence of U.S. nuclear weapons—combined with NATO's unique nuclear-sharing arrangements under which non-nuclear members participate in nuclear planning and possess specially configured aircraft capable of delivering nuclear weapons—contribute to Alliance cohesion and provide reassurance to allies and partners who feel exposed to regional threats.[17]

In this sense the Obama administration is paying homage to the status quo in Europe, despite the President's visionary Prague speech.

The United States keeps a limited number of forward-deployed nuclear weapons in Europe, plus, as the NPR said, "a small number of nuclear weapons stored in the United States for possible overseas deployment in support of extended deterrence to allies and partners worldwide."[18] The NPR concluded that in the near term the United States will:

- "Retain the capability to forward-deploy U.S. nuclear weapons on tactical fighter-bombers and heavy bombers, and proceed with full scope life extension for the B-61 bomb including enhancing safety, security, and use control.
- Retire the nuclear-equipped submarine launched cruise missile (TLAM-N).
- Continue to maintain and develop long-range strike capabilities that supplement U.S. forward military presence and strengthen regional deterrence.

- Continue and, where appropriate, expand consultations with allies and partners to address how to ensure the credibility and effectiveness of the U.S. extended deterrent. No changes in U.S. extended deterrence capabilities will be made without close consultations with our allies and partners."[19]
- "Conduct a full scope B-61 (nuclear bomb) Life Extension Program to ensure its functionality with the F-35 and to include making surety—safety, security, and use control—enhancements to maintain confidence in the B-61. These decisions ensure that the United States will retain the capability to forward deploy non-strategic nuclear weapons in support of its Alliance commitments."[20]

In addition to its forward-deployed tactical nuclear forces, the United States has also relied on non-nuclear elements to strengthen regional security architectures, including a forward U.S. conventional presence and effective theater ballistic missile defenses. The role of those elements of extended deterrence, said the NPR, will increase:

> As the role of nuclear weapons is reduced in U.S. national security strategy, these non-nuclear elements will take on a greater share of the deterrence burden. Moreover, an indispensable ingredient of effective regional deterrence is not only non-nuclear but also non-military—strong, trusting political relationships between the United States and its allies and partners [as well as] enhancing regional security architectures.[21]

Strengthened regional security architectures include, according to the NPR, "effective missile defense, counter-WMD capabilities, conventional power-projection capabilities, and integrated command and control — all underwritten by strong political commitments."[22]

KEEPING U.S. OPTIONS OPEN

Specifically addressing the continuing importance of extended nuclear deterrence, the NPR made it clear that the United States will retain the capability to forward-deploy nuclear weapons on tactical fighter-bombers and heavy bombers. In addition, the Obama administration decided to proceed with a full-scope life-extension program for the remaining B-61 bombs, including safety, security, and surety enhancements. The B-61 will be deliverable by the F-35 Joint Strike Fighter and the B-2 bomber.[23]

Moving beyond Europe, the NPR stated that:

> in Asia and the Middle East — where there are no multilateral alliance structures analogous to NATO — the United States has maintained extended deterrence through bilateral alliances and security relationships and through its forward military presence and security guarantees.[24]

The United States withdrew its forward-deployed nuclear weapons from the Pacific region at the end of the Cold War. This included removing nuclear weapons from naval surface vessels and general purpose submarines, as well as from bases in South Korea. Since then, the United States has relied on "its central strategic forces and the capacity to redeploy non-strategic nuclear systems in East Asia, if needed, in times of crisis."[25] The Obama administration is:

pursuing strategic dialogues with its allies and partners in East Asia and the Middle East to determine how best to cooperatively strengthen regional security architectures to enhance peace and security, and reassure them that U.S. extended deterrence is credible and effective.[26]

Despite a 20-year declaration by the United States and NATO that U.S. NSNWs would be kept up to date as necessary and deployed in Europe, and that these weapons provided an essential military and political link between Europe and North America, the 2010 NPR dropped this critical phrasing.[27] So did NATO's new *Strategic Concept* that was approved in the Lisbon, Portugal Summit in November 2010.[28] These changes in phraseology, while not highlighted by U.S. or Alliance leaders, nevertheless represent a significant departure from the standard post-Cold War deterrence formula, and leave the door open for a future Alliance decision to remove the remaining U.S. warheads located in the European theater.

CURRENT U.S. NSNW FORCE STRUCTURE AND MODERNIZATION PLANS

The George W. Bush administration emphasized the possible role for nuclear weapons in regional contingencies in its 2001 NPR. At the same time, however, it pointed out that the United States had reduced its reliance on nuclear weapons by increasing the role of missile defenses and precision conventional weapons in the U.S. deterrent posture.[29] Similarly, the Obama administration, in its 2010 NPR, indicated that the United States would reduce the role of nuclear weapons in U.S. regional deterrence strategies by increasing its reliance on missile defenses and precision conventional weapons. Unlike the perception many held of the Bush administration's goals in the 2001 NPR, however, the Obama administration did not seek to acquire new nuclear weapons capabilities — in fact, the 2010 NPR was quite clear regarding which upgrades or improvements were allowed, and which were not, when dealing with modifications to the nuclear stockpile.[30] Nor did it automatically extend U.S. nuclear deterrence to threats from nations armed with chemical or biological weapons.[31] The administration pledged to retain and modernize the B-61 warheads. It moved away from the apparent strategy during the Bush administration of strengthening deterrence by making nuclear weapons appear more usable in a warfighting mode.[32]

According to open sources, the United States currently has the option of using the following weapons delivery systems for its remaining tactical bombs. The B-61 gravity bomb is the sole remaining tactical nuclear weapon for use by the F-15, F-16, and *Tornado* DCA in NATO burden-sharing arrangements. The B-61 Model 11 is an earth-penetrating version that can be carried by the B-2 and B-52 strategic bombers. First deployed in 1968, the B-61 is a family of weapons, with multiple variants (Models 3, 4, 7, and 11).[33] That the B-61 is the only remaining U.S. NSNW can be inferred from the NPR's call for the elimination of the TLAM-N.[34] A full-scope life extension program for the B-61 was approved in early 2010 and announced in the NPR. Plans are to have the renovated weapons ready about the same time as the DCA version of the F-35 becomes operational, in 2017 or 2018. According to open sources, the bomb will be based largely on the B-61 Model 4 design, but with upgraded safety, security, and surety features, and will be called the B-61-12.[35] According to open sources, there are currently some 500 B-61s in the U.S. inventory.[36]

The United States uses several manned aircraft to deliver the B-61 to its target. The F-16C/D *Falcon* is a single-seat fighter that entered the U.S. inventory in 1979 and is widely used, flown in the NATO Alliance by the Netherlands, Norway, Belgium, Turkey, and Poland. The F-15E *Eagle* is even older, having first entered the inventory in 1974, although the two-seat E model fighter-bomber entered service life more recently. It is flown by the United States, Japan, and Israel. The F-35 *Joint Strike Fighter* is beginning to enter the inventory, with a DCA nuclear variant expected to be operational by 2018. A fifth-generation fighter, it is the designated replacement for the F-16. The F-35 Block IV will be nuclear-capable. Other DCA states planning to buy some variant of the stealthy F-35 include Italy, the Netherlands, and Turkey. It is uncertain, however, if those versions will be of DCA design. Finally, the B-2 *Spirit* is a two-man strategic stealth bomber that can carry some models of the B-61, including the Model 11 earth penetrating version.

The Congressional Research Service (CRS), citing unclassified reports, has stated that during the past decade the United States reduced the number of nuclear weapons deployed in Europe and the number of facilities that house those weapons. Reports indicate that the weapons were withdrawn from Greece, Great Britain, and Ramstein Air Base, Germany, between 2001 and 2005.[37] According to the CRS Report, "the United States now deploys 150-200 bombs at six bases in Belgium, Germany, Italy, the Netherlands, and Turkey." This number is a significant reduction from the 125 bases where U.S. tactical nuclear weapons were stored in Europe in the early 1980s,[38] nor are there any U.S. NSNWs deployed or stored in any bases in the Pacific theater. This has been the case since the removal of U.S. nuclear weapons from South Korea in 1992, and was made permanent with the retirement of the TLAM-Ns beginning in 2010.[39] Finally, there are apparently no longer any reserve DCA forces based in the United States upon which the alliance can call.[40] In the future, the F-35 will presumably provide the United States with an expeditionary dual-capable vehicle in regional contingencies, but those plans are yet to be determined.

THE ROLE OF NSNWs IN NATO POLICY AND ALLIANCE STRATEGY

During the Cold War, America's extended deterrence commitments were commonly equated with nuclear weapons. Nuclear weapons alone do not ensure the credibility of deterrence, but they may be indispensable to achieving that goal. The level of commitment and credibility required for extended deterrence to work has very little to do with how the United States feels about that commitment. It is the mind of the protected partner that must be assured of America's commitment, and the mind of the potential adversary that must be similarly convinced of America's capabilities, and will.

Some analysts have questioned whether the United States needs to continue to deploy nuclear weapons in Europe. After all, they say, it has been 20 years since the collapse of the Warsaw Pact and demise of the Soviet Union; surely these weapons are no longer needed to ensure peace in a Europe whole and free. Yet official NATO policy still views NSNWs as a deterrent to any potential adversary, and they also serve as a link among the NATO nations, through shared responsibility for nuclear policy planning and decisionmaking. They also still serve as a visible reminder of the U.S. extended deterrent and assurance of its commitment to the defense of its allies. But as the CRS has written:

> If the United States and its allies agree that this assurance can be provided with either conventional capabilities or strategic nuclear weapons, the need for forward basing in Europe may diminish. Some argue that because these weapons play no military or political role in Europe, they no longer serve as a symbol of alliance solidarity and cooperation. Others, however, including some officials in newer NATO nations, have argued that U.S. non-strategic nuclear weapons in Europe not only remain relevant militarily, in some circumstances, but that they are an essential indicator of the U.S. commitment to NATO security and solidarity.[41]

Political trends in Europe may accelerate these changes to U.S. forward deployments of NSNWs. A number of factors appear to be driving the Alliance toward ending the nuclear mission—or at least removing the remaining U.S. warheads.[42] Russia has had a strategy for years of applying diplomatic and political pressure against the United States and its allies in Europe to remove the remaining U.S. warheads. The European allies are suffering from two generations of military and particularly nuclear malaise, with some seeming unwilling to continue this effort given the political and economic costs of buying a next generation of DCA. The technical expiration of the service life of both the warheads and their delivery systems dictates that a decision be made as to whether or not to continue the NATO nuclear deterrence mission. Organizational changes in recent years within the U.S. Office of the Secretary of Defense, as well as NATO's Nuclear Policy Directorate and Supreme Headquarters Allied Powers Europe (SHAPE) Nuclear Planning office, have already marginalized the nuclear mission to a considerable extent. The U.S. Air Force has never liked this mission, and has little in the way of U.S.-based DCA to back up mission requirements in Europe or Asia. For example, recognizing the changed international security environment, as well as these organizational and operational changes, several years ago NATO increased its minimum response time for alert aircraft from minutes, as it was during the Cold War, to weeks.[43]

Finally, there are various schools of thought within elite U.S. circles as to the value, role, and future of NSNWs in Europe. These range from traditional supporters, to believers in selective engagement, to proponents of arms control, to disarmament advocates. Professor David Yost has recently reviewed these distinctive views and abstracted some of the key questions under debate.[44]

Any of the factors urging the elimination of the remaining U.S. weapons in Europe could be accelerated by more dramatic and immediate events, such as a nuclear accident or incident in Europe involving U.S. weapons, a decision to arbitrarily end the U.S. mission (by either the United States/NATO or one or more of the host nation allies), or a decision to use the remaining NSNWs as bargaining chips in arms control negotiations with Russia. Any of these events would precipitate a much more drastic and publicly supported termination of the U.S. forward-deployed mission. To do little or nothing, kicking the can down the road, will allow the Alliance to maintain the status quo for a few more years, but with the ultimate long-term result of a slow withering-away of the mission. One analyst has called this possibility "disarmament by default."[45]

At their meeting in Tallinn, Estonia, in April 2010, NATO's foreign ministers sought to balance the views of those nations who sought the removal of the weapons with those who argued that these weapons were still relevant to their security and to NATO's solidarity. At the conclusion of the meeting, Secretary of State Hillary Clinton said that the United States was not opposed to reductions in the number of U.S. nuclear weapons in Europe, but that the removal of these weapons should be linked to a reduction in the number of Russian NSNWs. The foreign ministers also agreed that no nuclear weapons would be removed from Europe unless all 28 member states of NATO agreed.[46]

Others have raised the question whether the United States and NATO might benefit from the removal of these weapons from bases in Europe for reasons of safety and security, as well as cost-saving. Some analysts have suggested that, in response to these concerns, the United States might consolidate its nuclear weapons at a smaller number of bases in Europe. According to another study, officials at U.S. European Command have argued that weapons deployed outside of Europe could be just as credible as deterrents to attack on NATO as forward-deployed weapons are.[47] In fact, some observers now argue that reducing or eliminating U.S. nuclear weapons in Europe would not only address the Air Force's operational and security costs associated with their deployment, but also could serve as a signal to Russia of NATO's nonaggressive intentions.[48]

It is unrealistic to believe, as some analysts and certain NATO allies argue, that in the near-term missile defenses could supplant the function performed by U.S. nuclear weapons in Europe, either in terms of providing deterrence or in serving as a military or political substitute for the existing Alliance nuclear-sharing function. Missile defenses would be inadequate substitutes until the arrival of a technology and weapons regime in which the defense is superior to the offense. The transition to such a defense-dominant world, one in which, as President Ronald Reagan envisioned, nuclear weapons had become "impotent and obsolete," does not appear to be likely anytime soon, despite President Obama's call for a nuclear-free world.[49]

The NATO Alliance has several big questions that it needs to address during its ongoing Deterrence and Defense Posture Review (DDPR). These also have political implications for the United States and its force structure decisions. For example, does the Alliance believe that it still needs nuclear weapons stationed in Europe to survive as an alliance? How low can the number of U.S. forward-deployed weapons go and still provide assurance to the allies? Will the Alliance actually make a strategic decision regarding its nuclear future, or will it allow the capabilities to atrophy by default? And if the Alliance makes the decision to retain this mission, is there any structure as good for nuclear-sharing as the current DCA construct?

AMERICAN NATIONAL SECURITY INTERESTS

The United States has a number of national interests that may require the use, or threatened use, of nuclear weapons. First is homeland defense. The U.S.

Government must ensure the continued safety and security of its homeland and population against attack. The question is whether extended deterrence, and NSNW commitments to allies, can help achieve this goal. Some would argue that making commitments to overseas friends and allies against potential adversaries actually makes the United States *more* susceptible to threats, blackmail, or the risk of involvment in a conflict.

Second, the United States wants to continue assuring its allies of their security, maintain its alliances around the world, and provide a stabilizing presence where needed. But it must weigh those desiderata against the possibility that anti-nuclear or even anti-American attitudes could arise within allied societies if it were to choose to retain or modernize its forward-deployed nuclear forces in Europe. On the other side of the world, the United States faces the exact opposite dilemma: allied concerns in East Asia may be raised by a perceived diminution of U.S. guarantees, as evinced by a lack of will or lack of the visible wherewithal to provide extended deterrence. In either case, the Obama administration faces the possibility of frustrating key allied states in order to follow through on its Prague vision and the NPR's commitments. Moreover, convincing allies of U.S. resolve may not be possible in any case simply by pointing to existing capabilities.[50] Alliance cohesion is a fragile thing, and could be jeopardized by U.S. missteps even on the level of nuance.

Third, the U.S. Government also wants to manage change in the international system to avoid potential downsides. Downsides might include a loss of global influence, diminished security (particularly if rogue states or nonstate actors become more empowered as a result of diminished U.S. influence), or a loss of face in the event our commitment to President Obama's

Prague agenda with its goal of global nuclear zero should fall flat. Another potential downside could be that France takes on more of the nuclear leadership role in NATO. This may or may not be a bad thing, but it would certainly represent a stark change from the Alliance's comfortable security assumptions since the late 1960s.

Fourth, the West may decide to keep its remaining NSNWs as potential bargaining chips with Russia in future arms control negotiations. For example, U.S. nuclear warheads may be useful in obtaining a Russian commitment to reduce its numbers, to consolidate its weapons in more centralized facilities, to increase transparency, to de-mate the warheads from the delivery systems, to sharing security efforts, or simply to undertake no further increases.[51] Reductions may include on entire series of steps, such as setting discrete limits on the number of NSNWs warheads, establishing a single limit on all nuclear warheads (including non-strategic and nondeployed), limiting NSNWs to national boundaries, limiting declared storage facilities, or linking NSNW reductions and conventional limits or cuts. The challenge may be a lack of incentive for Russia to agree to any of these steps, given the huge disparity between its NSNW stockpile and that of the United States.

Fifth, given the U.S. nonproliferation agenda, it needs to weigh the possibility that if it removes its remaining forward-deployed weapons from Europe, one or two NATO allies may decide that they need to develop an indigenous nuclear weapons capability. They may choose this path if the United States were to remove its extended deterrence guarantee, or if they no longer felt assured that the United States would come to their aid when necessary, or if the United

348

States and the other nuclear powers actually began to make significant progress toward their avowed goal of a nuclear-free world. If this last eventuality came to pass, it could potentially diminish the nuclear aspects of the U.S. extended deterrence guarantee. Moreover, if any ally or other state feels threatened by another party that is not committed to the goal of Global Zero, it may decide that its vital national interests require it to violate its Nuclear Non-Proliferation Treaty (NPT) pledge and pursue nuclear weapons for reasons of national security. The ally most often linked to such potential behavior is Turkey.

Sixth, the United States does have real security interests in Europe, as well as in Asia and the Middle East. It maintains broad and deep cultural, historical, and economic ties to its European allies. Those interests might be threatened by a more aggressive or revanchist Russia, by a nuclear-armed Iran, or even by the rise of multiple nuclear states in the Middle East (perhaps in response to a nuclear Iran). There may also be well-founded military reasons for deploying a small number of U.S. nuclear weapons and their delivery vehicles in Europe for possible use in other regions. Obviously forward deployment of military forces does not apply merely to extended deterrence; it applies to many operational contingencies.

Seventh, it is important to keep in mind that the U.S. nuclear arsenal has a number of qualitative characteristics that give it a unique character and set of mission capabilities. This is an important variable to consider when determining future force size and structure in order to meet the multiple mission sets that nuclear weapons are asked to perform. The three most important and broadly-based categories of missions for nuclear weapons are to deter, to prevail in conflict, and to assure allies. Each of those missions has a different set of critical qualitative characteristics associated with it. As the U.S. stockpile gets smaller, both in terms of actual numbers as well as in the variety of warhead types remaining, it will behoove U.S. arms control negotiators and force planners to tread carefully when it comes to radical changes or reductions, as the adverse ripple effects on handling future threats or responsibilities may be severe.[52]

CONCLUSION

As President Obama observed in his strategic guidance to the U.S. military on January 5, 2012, "Our nation is at a moment of transition."[53] He was referring to the end of the Iraq War and budgetary issues, but his observation was equally true for the coming decisions the United States will have to make regarding its remaining non-strategic nuclear forces. The primary missions of the U.S. armed forces will continue to include deterring and defeating aggression, and must therefore be "capable of denying the objectives of — or imposing unacceptable costs on — an opportunistic aggressor."[54] While this mission can be conducted using various types of military force, the language of "unacceptable costs" has for three generations served as code for "nuclear weapons." Another of the military's continuing missions will thus be to maintain a safe, secure, and effective nuclear deterrent. As the 2010 NPR, 2011 *NATO Strategic Concept*, and 2012 *Strategic Guidance* have all declared:

> As long as nuclear weapons remain in existence, the United States will maintain a safe, secure, and effective arsenal . . . that can under any circumstances confront an adversary with the prospect of unacceptable damage, both to deter potential adversaries and to as-

sure U.S. allies and other security partners that they can count on America's security commitments.[55]

America has enduring national security interests, with nuclear weapons remaining a vital part of ensuring that security. As the U.S. security focus shifts from Europe to the Middle East and the Pacific Rim over the coming decades, the country may find that today's NSNWs will continue to play a similar role in assuring allies in those regions as they do and have done for generations of Europeans. They may no longer be called "non-strategic," and they may find themselves lumped together with other nuclear warheads, bombs, and strategic delivery systems that have deterrence and extended deterrence responsibilities. But even if no longer a discrete category of weapons, the political and military need for such weapons will continue to exist for the foreseeable future.

The United States today maintains the smallest arsenal of nuclear weapons since the 1950s, and the numbers continue to get lower. There is less concern over central nuclear war with a major global adversary. Yet as the President said in Prague and the NPR reiterated, "The threat of global nuclear war has become remote, but the risk of nuclear attack has increased."[56] Therefore we can expect the United States (as well as the other nuclear powers of the world) to maintain at least a small but robust inventory of nuclear weapons for years to come. They will continue to serve as they always have: as the ultimate guarantor of U.S. resolve, power, and national security.

ENDNOTES - CHAPTER 15

1. Assistant Secretary of Defense J. D. Crouch, "Special Briefing on the Nuclear Posture Review," January 9, 2002, available from *www.bits.de/NRANEU/docs/NPRSpecial.htm*.

2. For a good presentation of these perspectives, see *U.S. Nuclear Policy in the 21st Century: A Fresh Look at National Strategy and Requirements, Final Report*, Washington, DC: Center for Counterproliferation Research, National Defense University, with the Center for Global Security Research, Lawrence Livermore National Laboratory, July 1998. A newer, nonpartisan study is William J. Perry and Brent Scowcroft, chairs, *U.S. Nuclear Weapons Policy*, Independent Task Force Report No. 62, New York: Council on Foreign Relations, 2009.

3. An excellent overview of deterrence is Austin Long, *Deterrence From Cold War to Long War: Lessons from Six Decades of RAND Research*, Santa Monica, CA: The RAND Corporation, 2008. See also Amy F. Woolf, "Nuclear Weapons in U.S. National Security Policy: Past, Present, and Prospects," CRS Report for Congress, RL34226, Washington, DC: Congressional Research Service, December 30, 2008; *U.S. Nuclear Deterrence in the 21st Century: Getting it Right*, Washington, DC: The New Deterrent Working Group, July 2009; and Amy F. Woolf, "U.S. Nuclear Weapons: Changes in Policy and Force Structure," CRS Report for Congress, RL31623, Washington, DC: Congressional Research Service, January 27, 2006.

4. Barack Obama, "Remarks by President Barack Obama," Hradcany Square, Prague, Czech Republic, April 5, 2009, available from *www.whitehouse.gov/the_press_office/Remarks-By-President-Barack-Obama-In-Prague-As-Delivered/*.

5. For more reading on extended deterrence, see Long, *Deterrence from Cold War to Long War;* also Thomas Scheber, "Contemporary Challenges for Extended Deterrence," unpublished paper for National Institute of Public Policy, Washington, DC, 2009; Clark Murdock and Jessica Yeats, "Summary of Findings and Recommendations from June 3, 2009, Workshop on Extended Deterrence," unpublished PPT presentation, Washington, DC, Center for Strategic and International Studies, August 4, 2009;

and Steven Pifer *et al.*, "U.S. Nuclear and Extended Deterrence: Considerations and Challenges," Brookings Arms Control Series No. 3, Washington, DC: The Brookings Institution, May 2010.

6. John Lewis Gaddis, *The Long Peace: Inquiries into the History of the Cold War*, Oxford, UK: Oxford University Press, 1989.

7. With two notable exceptions, of course: Great Britain and France. For the rationale behind that decision, see Thomas Devine, "Extended Deterrence and Nuclear Nonproliferation: Lessons from European and East Asian Regimes Applied to the Middle East," Collection of Papers from the 2011 Nuclear Scholars Initiative, *Nuclear Scholars Initiative: Project on Nuclear Issues*, Washington, DC: Center for Strategic and International Studies, December 2011, pp. 33-43.

8. Officially the "Treaty of Mutual Cooperation and Security between Japan and the United States of America," signed January 1960, available from *www.mofa.go.jp/region/n-america/us/q&a/ref/1.html*.

9. According to news reports, the Secretary of State told the Japanese Foreign Minister that "Japan is a treaty ally of the United States, and . . . reaffirmed the U.S. commitment to the defense of Japan, including nuclear deterrents." Jim Garamone, "Secretary of State Clinton Meets Japanese Leaders on First Leg of Asian Tour," *Military News*, February 18, 2009.

10. "The Withdrawal of U.S. Nuclear Weapons from South Korea," The Nuclear Information Project, available from *www.nukestrat.com/korea/withdrawal.htm*.

11. For further examination of the development of the NPR, see David Hoffman, "Obama's Atomic Choices: Inside the Making of U.S. Nuclear Policy," *Foreign Policy* online, April 28, 2010.

12. Department of Defense, *Nuclear Posture Review Report* (NPR), April 2010, p. vii.

13. *Ibid.*, pp. viii-ix.

14. *Ibid.*, p. iii.

15. *Ibid.*, p. xii.

16. *Ibid.*

17. *Ibid.*, p. 32.

18. It is unclear if the wording in the NPR was referring to the soon to be retired Tomahawk Land Attack Miissle - Nuclear (TLAM-N) in storage in the United States, or more broadly to other NSNWs, including B-61 bombs.

19. NPR, p. xiii.

20. *Ibid.*, p. 27.

21. *Ibid.*, p. xiii.

22. *Ibid.*, pp.32-33.

23. The NPR made clear that "these decisions do not presume what NATO will decide about future deterrence requirements, but are intended to keep the Alliance's options open and provide capabilities to support other U.S. commitments." *Ibid.*, p. 35.

24. *Ibid.*, p. 32.

25. *Ibid.*

26. *Ibid.*

27. Examples of the previous phrasing, which has appeared in every NATO document since 1990 through 2010, including the 1991 and 1999 *Strategic Concepts*, include the following: "the presence of US nuclear forces based in Europe, committed to NATO, reinforces the political and military link between the European and North American members of the Alliance" (*NATO/OTAN Handbook*, Brussels, Belgium: NATO Office of Information and Press, 2001, p. 56); this exact wording was duplicated in the 2006 version of the *Handbook*. The 1999 *NATO Strategic Concept*, repeating the nuclear paragraphs from the 1991 version of that document, included this phrase: "The presence of United States conventional

and nuclear forces in Europe remains vital to the security of Europe, which is inseparably linked to that of North America." See "The Alliance's Strategic Concept," April 24, 1999, para. 42, available from *www.nato.int/cps/en/natolive/official_texts_27433.htm*.

28. "Active Engagement, Modern Defence: Strategic Concept for the Defence and Security of the Members of the North Atlantic Treaty Organisation," adopted by the Heads of State and Government in Lisbon, Portugal, November 19, 2010, available from *www.nato.int/lisbon2010/strategic-concept-2010-eng.pdf*.

29. Amy Woolf, "Non-strategic Nuclear Weapons," CRS Report for Congress No. RL32572, Washington, DC: Congressional Research Service, February 2011, p. 14 ; also see James J. Wirtz and Jeffrey A. Larsen, eds., *Nuclear Transformation: The New U.S. Nuclear Doctrine*, New York: Palgrave Macmillan, 2005. The New Triad has three legs: offensive military strike options, which included all three legs of the original Triad, but could also include non-nuclear strike systems; strategic defenses; and a responsive defense infrastructure.

30. See 2010 NPR, pp. 38-39.

31. While reducing the ambiguity in the U.S. negative security assurance offered to other nations, the Obama administration's 2010 NPR does state, however, that "in the case of countries not covered by this [negative security] assurance—states that possess nuclear weapons and states not in compliance with their nuclear non-proliferation obligations—there remains a narrow range of contingencies in which U.S. nuclear weapons may still play a role in deterring conventional or CBW [chemical and biological warfare] attack against the United States or its allies and partners." NPR, p. 16.

32. For more on the Bush administration's approach, see Roger Speed and Michael May, "Assessing the United States' Nuclear Posture," Chap. 7, in *U.S. Nuclear Weapons Policy: Confronting Today's Threats*, George Bunn and Christopher F. Chyba, eds., Washington, DC: Brookings Institution, 2006, pp. 248-296.

33. James N. Gibson, *Nuclear Weapons of the United States: An Illustrated History*, Atglen, PA: Schiffer, 1996; Robert S. Norris and

Hans M. Kristensen, "Nuclear Notebook: U.S. Nuclear Forces 2010," *Bulletin of the Atomic Scientists,* May 2010, available from *bos.sagepub.com/content/66/3/57.full.pdf;* and Robert S. Norris and Hans M. Kristensen, "U.S. Nuclear Warheads 1945-2009," *Bulletin of the Atomic Scientists,* July/August 2009, pp. 72-80.

34. NPR, p. 27; and Robert S. Norris and Hans M. Kristensen, "U.S. Tactical Nuclear Weapons in Europe, 2011," Nuclear Notebook, *Bulletin of the Atomic Scientists,* January 2011, available from *bos.sagepub.com/content/67/1/64.full.pdf.*

35. See, for example, "B-61 Mod 12 LEP," Arms Control Wonk, October 13, 2008, available from *lewis.armscontrolwonk.com/archive/2060/B-61-mod-12-lep;* also see "The National Nuclear Security Administration Strategic Plan: Making the World a Better Place," Washington, DC: U.S. Department of Energy, May 2011.

36. Steven Pifer, "The United States, NATO's Strategic Concept, and Nuclear Issues," Perspectives and Proposals on the NATO Policy Debate, Arms Control Association, and British-American Security Information Committee, May 2011.

37. Woolf, *NSNW,* pp. 15-16, from Norris and Kristensen, "U.S. Nuclear Forces in Europe 2011."

38. *Ibid.*

39. Woolf, *NSNW,* p. 15; NPR, p. 32; and Norris and Kristensen, *US Nuclear Weapons 1945-2009.*

40. During the Cold War, two U.S. air bases in the United States—Cannon, NM, and Seymour Johnson, NC—had responsibilities to train for and support the dual capable aircraft (DCA) role in Europe. That is no longer the case.

41. Woolf, *NSNW,* p. 24. Also see Simon Lunn, Chap. 1, "NATO Nuclear Policy—Reflections on Lisbon and Looking Ahead," *The NTI Study on Nuclear Weapons and NATO,* draft May 6, 2011, forthcoming; and Paul Shulte, "Is NATO's Nuclear Deterrence Policy a Relic of the Cold War?" Policy Outlook, Washington, DC: Carnegie Endowment for International Peace, November 17, 2010.

42. For representative arguments about the European social situation and NATO nuclear policy, see Jeffrey A. Larsen, "Future Options for NATO Nuclear Policy," Issue Brief, The Atlantic Council, August 2011, available from *www.acus.org/publication/future-options-nato-nuclear-policy*; Jeffrey A. Larsen, "The Future of U.S. Non-Strategic Nuclear Weapons and Implications for NATO: Drifting Toward the Foreseeable Future," Final Report from the 2005-06 Manfred Wörner Fellowship, Brussels, Belgium, NATO Headquarters, December 2006, available from *www.nato.int/acad/fellow/05-06/larsen.pdf*; Lunn, "NATO Nuclear Policy"; and Bruno Tertrais, "Extended Deterrence: Alive and Changing," *The Interpreter*, Lowy Institute for International Policy online, February 2, 2011, available from *www.lowyinterpreter.org/post/2011/02/02/Extended-Deterrence-Alive-and-changing.aspx*.

43. "NATO's Nuclear Forces in the New Security Environment," *NATO Issue Brief*, Brussels, Belgium: NATO Headquarters June 2004.

44. David S. Yost, "The U.S. Debate on NATO Nuclear Deterrence," *International Affairs*, Vol. 87, No. 6, 2011, pp. 1401-1438.

45. Steven Pifer, "NATO, Nuclear Weapons, and Arms Control," Arms Control Series No. 7, Washington, DC: The Brookings Institution, July 2011.

46. Woolf, *NSNW*, p. 25.

47. *Ibid.*, p. 26.

48. *Ibid.*

49. Reagan SDI speech.

50. See James Acton, "Extended Deterrence and Communicating Resolve," *Strategic Insights*, Vol. VIII, Issue 5, December 2009.

51. See Steven Pifer, "The Next Round: The United States and Nuclear Arms Reductions after New START," Brookings Foreign Policy Series, Paper 4, Washington, DC: The Brookings Institution, December 2010.

52. See Jeffrey A. Larsen and Justin V. Anderson *et al.*, *Qualitative Characteristics of Nuclear Weapons at Lower Numbers and Implications for Arms Control*, SAIC paper prepared for A5XP, Air Force Strategic Plans and Policy Division, November 2011.

53. "Sustaining U.S. Global Leadership: Priorities for 21st Century Defense," Washington, DC: The White House, January 2012, available from *www.defense.gov/news/Defense_Strategic_Guidance.pdf*.

54. *Ibid.*, p. 4.

55. *Ibid.*, p. 5. For more discussion on the international challenges facing the Obama administration, particularly with respect to nuclear policy and forces, see Christopher F. Chyba and J. D. Crouch, "Understanding the U.S. Nuclear Weapons Policy Debate," *The Washington Quarterly*, July 2009, pp. 21-36; also Keith B. Payne, "Maintaining Flexible and Resilient Capabilities for Nuclear Deterrence," *Strategic Studies Quarterly*, Summer 2011, pp. 13-29; and *National Security Strategy*, Washington, DC: The White House, May 2010.

56. 2010 NPR, p. iv; also see Obama Prague speech, April 5, 2009.

CHAPTER 16

NATO'S NUCLEAR DEBATE:
THE BROADER STRATEGIC CONTEXT

Leo Michel[1]

What purposes are served by U.S. non-strategic nuclear weapons (NSNWs) in Europe? If those weapons were reduced in number, consolidated in a smaller number of Allied basing countries, or eventually withdrawn altogether, what would be the effects on Alliance solidarity? Would the resources necessary to maintain U.S. NSNWs and dual-capable aircraft (DCA) in Europe, along with the capabilities of certain non-nuclear European Allies to carry out nuclear missions with their specially configured aircraft, be better spent on maintaining or upgrading other military capabilities?

As explained elsewhere in this book, such interrelated questions are at the core of the North Atlantic Treaty Organization's (NATO) debate over the future of NSNWs in Europe. But they also are linked to broader strategic preoccupations within NATO headquarters and most Allied governments. For despite concerted efforts by top officials and eminent wise men, the Alliance is still grappling with dilemmas that were not resolved by the new *Strategic Concept* and Lisbon Summit Declaration unveiled in November 2010. Put simply, these concern differing threat perceptions among the Allies, the demonstrated reluctance of some to accept the risks and burdens of certain operational roles, and the need for Allies to make hard choices on capabilities during what promises to be an extended period of defense budget austerity.

Hence, whatever course the Allies set regarding NSNWs in their Defense and Deterrence Posture Review (DDPR), which likely will be completed by NATO's Chicago, IL, Summit on May 20, 2012, they cannot afford to treat the subject in isolation. Solidarity on this sensitive topic will not guarantee solidarity on other challenges facing the Alliance. However, a perceived failure to achieve a substantial (versus superficial) consensus on the future of NSNWs could certainly deal a heavy blow to the Allies' ability to cooperate across the board.

DIFFERING THREAT PERCEPTIONS

NATO has been the primary guarantor of Europe's defense from armed attack since 1949. With the end of the Cold War, NATO assumed new roles: building defense and security partnerships with new democracies in Central and Eastern Europe that prepared many for Alliance membership; offering dialogue and cooperation on political-military issues to Russia, Ukraine, and other states of the former Soviet Union; and leading complex military operations in the Balkans, Afghanistan, and Libya. At the same time, NATO has performed the vital job of promoting intra-European as well as transatlantic collaboration on threat assessments, political-military strategy, defense planning, equipment standards and interoperability, and training and exercises. Still, as memories of the Cold War have faded and the Alliance has enlarged to 28 members, it is not surprising that the Allies have had a difficult time in developing common assessments and priorities regarding a range of 21st-century threats.

For many Americans, NATO's solidarity and effectiveness will be decided in the caldron of Afghanistan, where (as of early 2012) non-U.S. Allies and partners contribute approximately 37,000 of the 130,000 troops (including some 90,000 Americans) in the International Security Assistance Force (ISAF). European, Canadian, and American leaders broadly agree that, if Afghanistan were to become a failed state, terrorist networks would reestablish themselves there, posing an increased threat to European and American interests. But for some Allies, a desire to demonstrate solidarity with the United States (to ensure, among other things, that American commitments to European security remain strong) has motivated their participation in ISAF as much, if not more, than any perceived threat emanating from Afghanistan itself. Not surprisingly, public support for the ISAF mission is generally lower and eroding faster in Europe than in the United States, where memories of September 11, 2001 (9/11), remain sharp. Moreover, the precarious situation in Pakistan could heighten friction among the Allies, especially if some conclude that U.S. pressure against extremist sanctuaries is hindering more than helping chances for an orderly withdrawal from Afghanistan with or without a regional settlement.

Differing threat perceptions surrounded NATO's role in Libya, as well. Germany's abstention on United Nations (UN) Security Council Resolution 1973 (2011), which authorized member states to take "all necessary measures" to protect Libyan civilians, roiled its relations with many Allies—especially the United States, France, and the United Kingdom (UK).[2] While Germany subsequently joined the NATO consensus to launch military operations pursuant to Resolution 1973, the Merkel government's decision to withdraw German crews from NATO's Airborne Warning and Control System aircraft participating in Operation UNIFIED PROTECTOR signaled Berlin's desire to distance itself from the conflict. Of course, Germany was not the only Ally with reservations concerning the Libyan operation; several other Allies showed little enthusiasm for the operation in part because of their fatigue with the political, budgetary, and personnel demands of expeditionary efforts in Afghanistan and elsewhere.

Meanwhile, Russia's behavior has contributed to renewed attention to NATO's collective defense role. To be sure, Russia does not represent the type of immediate threat posed by the Soviet Union, and no Allied government advocates a return to Cold War models of territorial defense. Still, Russian actions in Georgia (especially during the August 2008 conflict) and elsewhere in the former Soviet space, combined with menacing statements — recall, for example, President Dmitry Medvedev's vow "to protect the life and dignity of [Russian] citizens, wherever they are"[3] — sparked particular concern among Central and Eastern Europe (CEE) Allies. Indeed, some divine a deliberate Russian strategy that extends from actions to discourage investments in southern energy pipelines to intimidating Ukraine and other neighbors in the "near abroad" with substantial populations of ethnic Russians. Such concerns recently were heightened by Medvedev's threat that Russia will take military countermeasures (to include deploying short-range Iskander missiles in Kaliningrad) to defeat NATO missile defenses if they are deployed without "legal guarantees" sought by Moscow.

Other Allies seem to assess Russian strategy and behavior in less threatening terms. Some are inclined to see Georgia as a one-of-a-kind action — an opportunistic show of force to destabilize a weak but impetuous neighbor and prevent further NATO enlargement. Similarly, noting examples of Russian cooperation with NATO (for example, Moscow's agreement in 2010 to expand use of the Northern Distribution Network for the transit of nonlethal NATO supplies to ISAF), some Allies tend to play down Russian leaders' criticism of NATO missile defense, attributing it to posturing for internal political reasons.

Differing Allied threat assessments extend beyond Afghanistan, Libya, and Russia. As the Group of Experts on NATO's *New Strategic Concept* noted in their May 2010 report,

> The global nuclear nonproliferation regime is under increasing stress; incidents of instability along Europe's periphery have revived historic tensions; innovative modes of gathering, sending, and storing information have brought with them new vulnerabilities; the security implications of piracy, energy supply risks, and environmental neglect have become more evident; and a worldwide economic crisis has spawned widespread budgetary concerns.[4]

Potential instability in the Western Balkans remains a leading worry for neighboring Allies. The United States and some Allies arguably are more worried than others about Iran's suspected nuclear weapons programs and ballistic missile capabilities or the possible spillover of Syria's internal unrest into Turkey. Still others give relatively high priority to resource, environmental, and maritime security issues in the Arctic region.

RESURGENT "BURDEN-SHARING" DEBATE

Contentious discussions among the Allies over how to share equitably the risks and burdens of Alliance membership are nothing new. However, such arguments by and large did not weaken the Alliance during its first 4 decades due to the Soviet Union's perceived existing threat to transatlantic security. With the end of the Cold War, NATO's enlargement to 28 members, and its progressively greater involvement in a range of operational activities, the burden-sharing debate arguably has gained in prominence and intensity.

The Bosnian and Kosovo interventions, beginning in 1995 and 1999, respectively, provided a taste of what was to follow. In the latter case, for example, U.S. pilots flew the overwhelming majority of missions throughout the 78-day campaign, although the participation of a small number of non-U.S. Allies increased toward the end of the operation. While these missions and subsequent post-conflict stabilization efforts by ground forces were not risk-free, no NATO military personnel were reported killed in combat.

In contrast, NATO's involvement in Afghanistan, especially since ISAF expanded into Taliban-controlled areas in 2006, has at times exposed serious tensions among the Allies related to burden-sharing. European Allies and Canada have suffered about one-third of the combat deaths among ISAF forces, with several suffering higher losses per capita than the United States. But NATO has had to cope with "caveats" — that is, restrictions imposed by some Allied governments or their parliaments on how and where their forces can be employed — and these have provoked both transatlantic and intra-European recriminations. For example, most of the nearly 4,700 German troops are effectively barred by the Bundestag from operating outside the northern region, and Turkey allows its 1,800 troops to operate only in or near Kabul. Some Allied troops are prohibited from conducting night-time or offensive missions. A top French military chief once called caveats a "poison for multinational operations," and his British counterpart at the time insisted publicly that other Allies take a larger role in combat.[5]

The prevalence and impact of caveats reportedly have diminished in recent years, but they have not disappeared altogether. Moreover, as ISAF gradually passes the lead for security operations in selected provinces and districts to Afghan forces, pressure will build within several troop-contributor nations now deployed in those areas (mostly in the north and west) to withdraw their forces entirely rather than allow their shift to training and mentoring functions, which are not risk-free tasks. The danger is that during the planned transition to an Afghan lead in 2014, the combat burdens and risks might fall even more disproportionately on those U.S. and other Allied forces now deployed in the more volatile southern and eastern regions.

NATO's experience in Libya confirmed that burden-sharing remains an issue in more limited operations, as well. While most Allies contributed militarily in some fashion, only eight (including the United States) participated in air strikes. On the positive side, the distribution of strike sorties among these countries was undoubtedly an improvement over the Kosovo air campaign. As Secretary of Defense Leon Panetta noted in October 2011:

> After the United States employed its unique assets in the first week of the conflict to destroy key regime military targets and air defense capabilities, Europeans took over the brunt of operations. France and the United Kingdom engaged on a large scale, flying one third of the overall sorties and attacking 40 percent of the targets. Their deployment of helicopters was criti-

cal to the later stages of this campaign. . . . Meanwhile Italy made valuable contributions to the air-ground mission and served as an indispensable base for Allied operations. Smaller countries also punched well above their weight. Denmark, Norway, and Belgium together destroyed as many targets as France . . . Canada, as always, contributed its fair share—and that was substantial.[6]

At the same time, NATO's Libya operation depended on the United States to provide key enabler capabilities. The latter included an estimated 80 percent of Intelligence, Surveillance, and Reconnaissance (ISR) assets; the lion's share of aerial refueling aircraft; hundreds of targeting specialists; and precision-guided munitions and other supplies for some of the striking nations whose relatively small stockpiles were rapidly depleted.

This mismatch of burden-sharing in operations results, in part, from underlying and growing disparities between U.S. and non-U.S. defense spending within the Alliance. As then-Secretary of Defense Robert Gates pointed out in June 2011, the U.S. share of all military spending by NATO Allies has gone from about 50 percent during the Cold War to more than 75 percent today. Put differently, while the United States spends over 4 percent of gross domestic product (GDP) for defense, the average for the rest of NATO is barely 1.4 percent. Even allowing for a bulge in U.S. spending associated with its 2003 invasion of Iraq, which several Allies opposed, these trends are unsustainable. As Secretary Gates put it:

> The blunt reality is that there will be dwindling appetite and patience in the U.S. Congress—and in the American body politic writ large—to expend increas-

ingly precious funds on behalf of nations that are apparently unwilling to devote the necessary resources or make the necessary changes to be serious and capable partners in their own defense. . . . Indeed, if current trends in the decline of European defense capabilities are not halted and reversed, future U.S. political leaders—those for whom the Cold War was *not* the formative experience that it was for me—may not consider the return on America's investment in NATO worth the cost.[7]

As Secretary Panetta warned the following October: "Many might assume that the U.S. defense budget is so large it can absorb and cover Alliance shortcomings—but make no mistake about it, we are facing dramatic cuts with real implications for Alliance capability."[8]

PRIORITIZING CAPABILITIES

Differences in Allies' threat assessments and their willingness to assume certain operational and budgetary responsibilities make it harder to agree on the priority of capabilities that need to be preserved, much less the new capabilities that must be developed. To date, NATO has been better at launching high-profile capabilities initiatives—recall, for example, the 1999 Defense Capabilities Initiative and 2002 Prague Capabilities Commitment—than delivering credible results. (As this chapter is written, the 2010 Lisbon Critical Capabilities package appears somewhat more productive than its predecessors.) Meanwhile, the overall financial and economic prospects for most Allies have degraded further since the NATO Secretary General outlined his "Smart Defense" concept in February 2011.

The fundamentals of Smart Defense are relatively straightforward. In an era of defense austerity, Allies should find more ways to cooperate multilaterally to make available the type, quantity, quality, and capabilities necessary for the Alliance as a whole to meet the level of ambition as set by its political leaders — that is, the set of contingencies ranging from major combat operations to smaller stabilization missions that NATO should be prepared for. Such multilateral cooperation could include, for example, "pooling and sharing" arrangements, joint procurement, and role specialization. Top NATO civilian and military officials are trying hard to implement the concept and have assigned a leading role to Allied Command Transformation to facilitate the process by which nations will identify new cooperative projects, select lead nations and partners, and (hopefully) implement their collective efforts.

Not surprisingly, however, Smart Defense will face the same challenges described hitherto as faced by NATO and other multinational efforts. For example, Allies that are more worried by proximate potential threats, whether to their territories or information systems, may be less inclined toward cooperative projects that seem directed to expeditionary and/or stabilization operations. Allies that share an expeditionary strategic culture, such as the UK and France, may favor bilateral cooperation over wider projects involving Allies believed to be excessively risk averse. Sovereignty issues remain an important consideration in many areas, even if they are given different weights depending on the size, capabilities, and political/ strategic culture of the individual Allies. In particular, those who seek to preserve some capability to act alone or in small coalitions of the willing outside NATO if their national interests so dictate, may be disinclined to invest in cooperative programs in the absence of assured access to those capabilities in the event of a crisis. In other words, they will be loath to join and/or fund cooperative projects on capabilities if one Ally or more can block consensus to permit their use.

Moreover, Smart Defense will not be a panacea for the capabilities shortfalls that likely will bedevil the Alliance for years to come. European pooling and sharing of its sparse ISR assets, for example, will not appreciably lessen Europe's overall dependence on U.S. systems, especially in the event of high-intensity conflicts. Yet European investment to develop major new ISR capabilities would be very costly, making it an unlikely (or, at best, highly selective) option in the predicted economic and financial environment.

IMPLICATIONS FOR THE NSNW DEBATE

With Alliance solidarity under strain from so many different directions, NATO and member government officials will need to tread carefully in framing any next steps on NSNWs. What might such caution mean in practice? Here are a few (admittedly modest) suggestions:

- Allies should avoid denigrating the threat perceptions of others. Those favoring a go-slow approach—for example, seeking agreement with Russia on meaningful transparency measures rather than proceeding directly to changes in NATO declaratory policy or negotiated reductions—are not necessarily paranoid vis-à-vis Moscow's (or perhaps Tehran's) longer-term intentions.[9] Conversely, those who question the specific contributions of NATO NSNWs to deterrence and defense are not necessarily anti-nuclear pacifists.

- In the wake of demanding operations that have exposed rifts among Allies over the equitable sharing of risks and burdens, approaches that shift responsibilities for maintaining NATO NSNWs to a smaller and smaller number of Allies are bound to chip away at a sense of solidarity. Hence, if reductions in overall NATO NSNW capabilities are contemplated, it might be preferable to fashion so-called horizontal or salami-slicing cutbacks (that is, spreading reductions over several basing countries) rather than vertical ones (whereby some Allies drop out of nuclear roles entirely, effectively shifting all their burden to others).

- Smart Defense will be hard enough to apply to conventional capabilities; applying it to nuclear burden-sharing may be too difficult to achieve in the present political climate. Given sovereignty and assured-access issues, the achievement of multinational cooperation appears more difficult the closer the project comes to affecting combat capabilities versus functions such as logistics, maintenance, training, and professional military education. Hence, while the concept of creating a multinational, dual-capable air unit to assume the role now played by European Allies with national dual-capable forces may seem attractive in theory, the political and practical obstacles to realizing such a project should not be underestimated.

- The hard realities of defense austerity will not disappear anytime soon. Thus, it is legitimate for Allies to ask themselves and each other whether the resources necessary to maintain and/or modernize NATO's NSNWs could be better used for conventional capabilities, such as the gaps in enablers highlighted by the Afghanistan and Libyan operations. The key here is to keep the debate honest. This means, for example, that the added cost of equipping future multirole aircraft (or extending the service life of a relatively small number of current aircraft inventories) with features necessary to maintain nuclear as well as conventional capabilities should not be exaggerated.[10] At a minimum, any cost savings from shedding dual-capable roles must be applied to other high-priority defense capabilities.

- Finally, in NATO's nuclear debate, respect for the unwritten consensus rule for decisionmaking will be vital. The consensus rule represents more than a mechanistic decisionmaking procedure. It reflects the NATO structure as an *alliance of independent and sovereign* countries, as opposed to a *supranational* body, and exemplifies for many the "one for all, all for one" ethos of the organization's collective defense commitment. NATO decisions are the expression of the collective will of its member governments, arrived at by common consent. Under the consensus rule, no Ally can be forced to approve a position or take an action against its will. This Alliance reality is especially important for decisions on the potential use of military force, which are among the most politically sensitive for any ally. But it is arguably as important for dealing with issues, such as NSNWs, which remain at the core of the Article V commitment.

ENDNOTES - CHAPTER 16

1. These are Mr. Michel's personal views and do not necessarily reflect official policy of the Department of Defense or any other agency of the United States Government.

2. United Nations S/RES/1973 (2011), Security Council Resolution 1973, Adopted by the Security Council at its 6498th meeting on March 17, 2011, available from *www.un.org/News/Press/docs/2011/sc10200.doc.htm*.

3. "Russia Marches into South Ossetia," Spiegel Online International, August 8, 2008, available from *www.spiegel.de/international/world/0,1518,570834,00.html*.

4. "NATO 2020: Assured Security; Dynamic Engagement. Analysis and Recommendations of the Group of Experts on a New Strategic Concept for NATO," May 17, 2010, available from *www.nato.int/strategic-concept/expertsreport.pdf*.

5. Interview of General Jean-Louis Georgelin, Chief of Defense, France, on Europe 1 Radio, September 22, 2008, available from *www.defense.gouv.fr/ema/le-chef-d-etat-major/interventions/interviews/22-09-08-interview-du-cema-sur-europe-1*.

6. Text of speech of Secretary of Defense Leon Panetta, Carnegie Europe, Brussels, Belgium, October 5, 2011, available from *carnegieeurope.eu/events/?fa=3392*.

7. Text of speech of Secretary of Defense Robert Gates, Security and Defense Agenda, Brussels, Belgium, June 10, 2011, available from *www.defense.gov/speeches/speech.aspx?speechid=1581*.

8. Panetta speech.

9. Three American experts have proposed that, as a foundation for future talks on nuclear forces, the United States and Russia should "disclose, on a reciprocal basis, the location, types, and numbers of tactical nuclear weapons that remain. This should pose few problems for the United States and its allies; well-informed

accounts of deployed American weapons have been around for years. But disclosing such data might prove difficult for Russia, given its penchant for secrecy and the political risks of confirming that it does indeed possess a far greater number of these weapons." See Frank Klotz, Susan Koch, and Franklin Miller, "Unfinished Business," *The New York Times,* December 13, 2011.

10. For the United States, this also implies continued implementation of the B-61 Life Extension Program.

CHAPTER 17

ROLE OF NUCLEAR WEAPONS IN NATO'S DETERRENCE AND DEFENSE POSTURE REVIEW: PROSPECTS FOR CHANGE

Guy B. Roberts[1]

I do think the principles of the NATO discussion [on NATO's nuclear posture] are already clear: first, that no Ally will take unilateral decisions; second, that as long as there are nuclear weapons in the world, NATO will need a nuclear deterrent.[2]

—NATO Secretary General
Anders Fogh Rasmussen

When the North Atlantic Treaty Organization (NATO) revealed it was going to issue a new *Strategic Concept* for the 21st century at the 2010 Lisbon, Portugal, Summit, there was much anticipation that is would announce deep cuts in the numbers of U.S. nuclear weapons based in Europe or at a minimum a major policy shift entailing a significantly reduced role for nuclear weapons in ensuring the common defense and security of the Alliance. Instead, the new *Strategic Concept* echoed the language of the 1991 and 1999 *Strategic Concepts* in stating that to protect and defend against the full range of today's security threats, the Alliance will "maintain a mix of conventional and nuclear forces."[3] Recognizing, however, the complex and changing security environment involving new threats (cyber-attacks for example) and new capabilities (missile defense), the heads of state tasked the North Atlantic Council (NAC) to undertake a review of NATO's deterrence and defense posture (hereinafter referred to as the DDPR) and provide a report at the next NATO summit scheduled for May 20, 2012.

While many disarmament advocates see this occasion as another opportunity to remove U.S. nuclear weapons from Europe for the reasons and factors discussed below, it is highly unlikely that there will be any substantive changes in either the posture or the policy. The DDPR process is deliberately designed in such a way as to ensure and reaffirm that NATO has the full range of capabilities necessary to deter and defend against any threat to the safety and security of the Alliance. However, while the DDPR will examine all capabilities, this chapter will limit its discussion to the nuclear dimension of that review, fully recognizing that the intent is to have an appropriate mix of conventional, nuclear, and missile defense forces as well as defenses against relatively new threats such as cyber-attacks.

THE ENVIRONMENT

Before discussing in detail the DDPR process and likely outcome, it is important to understand the environment in which this review is being undertaken. Several points are relevant.

An Increasingly Dangerous and Proliferating Security Environment.

According to NATO's most recent intelligence assessment, the security environment for the Alliance remains dangerous and uncertain, with the range and variety of potential risks and dangers facing the Alliance ever increasing and less predictable. These range from the continuing conflict in Afghanistan, unrest in the Balkans, the recent Libya operation, on-going efforts to stop piracy and terrorism, and the challenges of addressing new threats such as cyber-attacks.

Two of the greatest enduring threats to Alliance safety and security in the next 10 to 15 years are weapons of mass destruction (WMD) terrorism and WMD proliferation. As the U.S. WMD commission report states,[4] and as likewise reflected in NATO's Comprehensive Strategic Level Policy for Preventing the Proliferation of WMD, proliferation of such weapons is inevitable, presenting increased risks to Allied security and strategic interests. We can slow and impede WMD proliferation, but it will happen. This will in turn increase the likelihood of WMD terrorism. And of course we face the prospect of ballistic missile proliferation, as in Iran and North Korea.

In addition to the enduring challenges of such proliferation, uncertainties about the future relationship with Russia continue to worry eastern European members of the Alliance. While no nation is considered an adversary of the Alliance, the proliferation threat is real and growing, and future conventional attacks against NATO forces or territory cannot be ruled out.

While some NATO Allies continue to press for finding a path to "global nuclear zero" (more on that later), press reports in Russia state that it will triple its strategic missile production between the years 2011 and 2015. Russia is deploying new silo-based and mobile inter-continental ballistic missiles (ICBMs) and a new ballistic missile submarine with an advanced missile. By 2018, Russia plans to deploy a new "heavy" ICBM, which reportedly can carry 10-15 nuclear warheads. New advanced warheads are being deployed on other weapons, including those of low yield. Russia today enjoys more than a 10-1 advantage in tactical or non-strategic nuclear weapons (NSNWs) over the United States. While the United States pushed the "reset" button with Russia on cooperation and partnership, Russian military doctrine identifies NATO as a primary danger. Further, while Western countries are cutting military spending to deal with the global financial crisis, Russia plans to spend 20 trillion rubles ($611 billion) on defense through 2020. Ruslan Pukhov, director of the Moscow-based think tank, Center for Analysis of Strategies and Technologies (CAST), issued this glum assessment:

> The Russian authorities understand the country is doomed to be the kind of power that needs military might. 'Soft power' doesn't work for us. We need people to be afraid of us, and we seem to be unable to find a proper substitute for military power.[5]

The Chinese nuclear and conventional buildup is a distant but growing concern. China is deploying two types of new mobile ICBMs and developing multiple warhead ICBMs and submarines to carry new sea launched ballistic missiles (SLBMs). Recent reports indicate a massive tunnel system—possibly up to 5,000 kilometers (km) long—for building, deploying, and possibly launching nuclear-armed missiles. One is tempted to ask, "What are the potential long-term consequences for the West of watching as Russia and China modernize their nuclear arsenal while it sits back and simply maintains the status quo?" Worse, will the West continue to cut its nuclear forces out of a misguided notion that reducing the U.S. nuclear arsenal will motivate others to stop their modernization and building program?

Ballistic missile proliferation remains a continuing concern, with over 30 nations now possessing ballistic missiles. North Korea, Iran, and India are developing ICBMs. The Iranians are expected to test their Kavoshgar 5 rocket with a 628-pound capsule carrying a monkey to an altitude of 120 km (74 miles). A new International Atomic Energy Agency (IAEA) report is expected early in 2012 detailing Iran's continued determination to acquire nuclear weapons. Almost 3 years after President Barack Obama offered an "extended hand" to Iran, tensions rose further in 2011 as Washington accused Tehran of being behind an alleged plot to kill the Saudi Ambassador to the United States. Assuming this is true, one wonders whether Iran now believes that the relative decline and over-extension of American military power make it possible to commit such outrages against the United States and its allies with impunity.

State-sponsored and other terrorist groups continue to pursue acquiring WMDs. A video on Al Jazeera TV in February 2009, shown more than 100,000 times on various websites, featured a Kuwaiti professor openly talking about bringing four pounds of dry-powdered anthrax to Washington, and killing several hundred thousands of Americans. Anders Breivik, who killed over 70 campers on an island in Norway, spoke of his using anthrax weapons.[6]

A. Q. Khan, the "father" of the Pakistani nuclear weapons program, masterminded an international network of suppliers of materials, equipment, plans, and technical assistance to countries clandestinely seeking to develop their own nuclear weapons in violation of international treaties and legal norms. We have no idea of how many A. Q. Khan Networks may be operating today, but we do know there is a strong demand and those willing to meet it. Pakistan is continuing to build up its nuclear weapons program amid continued security concerns, and Prime Minister Singh has called for building up further India's nuclear arsenal due to concerns over other nuclear weapon states and the possibility of nuclear terrorism.[7]

Disarmament by Default?

While defense budgets have generally increased world-wide, that is definitely not the case in Europe. Partly in reaction to the deepening Eurozone financial crisis but also reflecting a trend that has been going on for some time, European Allies' defense budgets are in free fall. The average annual defense outlay is well below 1.5 percent of gross domestic product (GDP), and it will get worse. Potentially in 2012, nine nations will spend less than 1.0 percent of GDP on defense.

While the markets frequently express optimism that Euro leaders have "fixed" the Eurozone crisis, uncertainties persist. Many analysts believe that a financial catastrophe awaits the Eurozone. Greece with a government debt some 143 percent of the size of its economy may soon default. Italy, with a debt some 120 percent the size of its economy, now looks like it will follow Greece. Spain's credit rating was downgraded in October 2011, and Portugal and Ireland continue to teeter on the brink. The debt contagion long feared is now fact as the cost of borrowing continues to increase for governments that have resolutely refused to make the reforms necessary to balance the books. Indeed, Allied governments have routinely obscured their actual debt levels, and complicit western European leaders have for too long simply hoped for a miracle. In the face of these realities, one would be hard pressed to find anyone who will predict that defense spending will grow or even manage to hold the line. It is now projected that the high-performance aircraft that key NATO Allies intend to procure, the *Joint Strike Fighter*, including a "dual capable" (nuclear) variant, will cost more than $130 million a copy.[8] Based on current and projected defense budget figures, one wonders how Allies who have pledged to buy the craft, such as the United Kingdom (UK) and Italy, will be able to do so.

While the Barack Obama administration welcomed the willingness of our European allies to take the political and military initiative in Libya, allowing the United States to "lead from behind," it was the shrinkage of allied capabilities that caught most of the attention of the U.S. Congress and policymakers. Libya showed that while the United States. took a back seat—its aircraft were not involved in the air strikes— the allies that did participate in Operation UNIFIED PROTECTOR were forced to rely on U.S. planes for refueling and intelligence-gathering operations. During the Libya operation, the United States. made it abundantly clear that it expects its European allies to take the lead when crises erupt in their own backyard.

In a well-publicized speech in June 2011, then Secretary of Defense Robert Gates stated frankly that many countries were not taking part in the Libyan campaign because they could not; that those that were involved were running out of munitions; and that NATO had become a two-tiered Alliance in which only some members had combat capabilities, while others enjoyed the benefits of membership while refusing to pay the costs.

> The blunt reality is," he said, "that there will be dwindling appetite and patience in the US Congress . . . to expend increasingly precious funds on behalf of nations that are apparently unwilling to devote the necessary resources or make the necessary changes to be serious and capable partners in their own defense.

Gates also recognized, however, that the fall in Europe's defense spending "was highly unlikely to change."[9]

For the last 60 years Europe has assumed that the United States will rush to its aid in any crisis. Circumstances would suggest that such an assumption is a risky one to hold. Europe seems so far to have ignored U.S. warnings that it will not be business as usual. Ignoring Secretary Gates's warning, most European nations are continuing to slash defense spending. Many still have forces that are not deployable. Indeed, as the new UK Defense Minister warned,

> Too many countries are failing to meet their financial responsibilities to NATO, and so failing to maintain appropriate and proportionate capabilities. Too many are opting out of operations, or contributing but a fraction of what they should be capable of. This is a European problem, not an American one. And it is a political problem, not a military one.[10]

Despite NATO Secretary General Rasmussen's attempt to put a happy face on this gloomy picture by urging nations to pool resources — "smart defense" he called it — the fact is that defense spending will decline for some time to come. Allies have been unwilling to increase defense spending amid the economic crisis, so Rasmussen is now calling on NATO members to eliminate "redundancies" and sign agreements consolidating and integrating their capabilities, including arms purchases. As Rasmussen pointed out in a recent article in *Foreign Affairs*, the European allies continue to retreat on their political promise to spend 2 percent of GDP on defense. Far from that, their commitment to defense continues to shrink, much to the consternation of the United States:

By the end of the Cold War, in 1991, defense expenditures in European countries represented almost 34 percent of NATO's total, with the United States and Canada covering the remaining 66 percent. Since then, the share of NATO's security burden shouldered by European countries has fallen to 21 percent.[11]

In the U.S. Congress, the budget knives are out, and the failure of U.S. European allies to demonstrate a willingness to shoulder their fair share will in all likelihood make it even more challenging to keep U.S. weapons and forces in Europe.

Conventional Forces Continue to Shrink.

For those who argue that the nuclear deterrence posture of the Alliance as anchored by U.S. nuclear weapons in Europe can be replaced with an overwhelming deterrent posture anchored on a strong U.S. conventional force presence, the news from Europe is troubling. In May 2010, the United States withdrew the last Army division from Europe and announced that one and probably two infantry brigade combat teams (IBCT) will also be withdrawn. Under current defense cuts already proposed, another IBCT is likely to be withdrawn next year. U.S. forces in Europe remained well over 200,000 until the early 1990s. Under current plans, European-based troops will be reduced from 42,000 today to 37,000 by 2015, with the numbers likely to be reduced well below the current 2015 target figure.[12]

The United States Is the Only Major Nuclear Power That Is Not Modernizing Its Nuclear Weapons.

But it gets worse. As part of the proposed $450 billion cut in U.S. defense spending over the next 10 years, House and Senate subcommittees have proposed cuts of $400 to $500 million in the $7.1 billion request for maintaining U.S. nuclear infrastructure. This will put in jeopardy life-extension programs for the W-76, W-78, and B-61 bombs.

On October 11, 2011, Congressman Ed Markey (D-Mass.) sent a letter to the Joint Select Committee on Deficit Reduction, signed by 65 lawmakers, that was clear and to the point:

> The Berlin Wall fell. The Soviet Union crumbled. The Cold War ended. Yet 20 years later, we continue to spend over $50 billion a year on the U.S. nuclear arsenal. This makes no sense. These funds are a drain on our budget and a disservice to the next generation of Americans. We are robbing the future to pay for the unneeded weapons of the past.[13]

They recommended cutting $200 billion from the estimated $700 billion planned for nuclear weapons and related programs over the next 10 years.[14]

While the U.S. nuclear infrastructure decays and Congress dithers over whether to fund the much needed modernization programs necessary to maintain a safe, secure, and effective deterrent, Russia and China continue to modernize and upgrade their own nuclear weapons and infrastructure. While Russia has tested and is deploying new ICBM and SLBM systems, U.S. replacements for the aging Trident D-5 and ground-based Minuteman systems remain on the drawing board.[15]

U.S. Focus and Interest Shift to Asia.

Hillary Clinton, in an article in the November 2011 issue of *Foreign Policy* titled "America's Pacific Century," characterized the Asia-Pacific region as a "key driver of global politics" and called for a "substantially increased investment — diplomatic, economic, strategic, and otherwise — in the Asia-Pacific region."[16] A new survey shows that Americans view Asian countries, not European ones, as the most important partners for the United States. Moreover, a partisan divide has emerged in attitudes toward the relationship. A majority (57 percent) of Republicans now believe that the United States should take a more independent approach vis-à-vis Europe, a plurality of Democrats (42 percent) still supports closer ties with Europe, and independents are divided on the issue. As Americans turn away from Europe, they are turning toward Asia. A majority (51 percent) now see China, Japan, and South Korea as more important than the nations of Europe for U.S. national interests. Europeans should be particularly concerned that a strong majority of Americans under the age of 45 now see Asia as more important than Europe.[17] The Americans who most value Europe are rapidly disappearing from the stage.

The Global Nuclear Zero Movement.

Energized by President Obama's speech calling for a world free of nuclear weapons in Prague, Czech Republic in 2009, the movement has brought renewed pressures on one of the fundamental aspects of NATO's security posture and resulted in new initiatives for unilateral disarmament despite the threats discussed above. Indeed, the very concept of nuclear deterrence is now dismissed as a Cold War relic. Many in the disarmament movement reject the very notion of deterrence. They downplay or ignore the many other important and complex roles nuclear weapons play in ensuring the collective security of the Alliance. Former Secretary of State George Schultz at the Global Zero meeting in California asked, "How good of a deterrent is a nuclear weapon anyhow? What threat are they deterring? I don't see much usefulness myself."[18] Some "Global Zero" advocates have singled out the extended worldwide deterrence commitment of the United States, calling it, in the words of Barry Blechman, "a concept that served a vital purpose during the Cold War, but whose time has come — and gone. The first step towards nuclear abolition is eliminating reliance on nuclear deterrence."[19]

While the effectiveness of deterrence remains difficult to prove other than through anecdotal examples, Kenneth Waltz pointed out in his classic study, *Man, the State, and War* (1959), that:

> deterrence arises from a logical and a moral necessity. Because men are not angels, because states can be malevolent, and because the international system of states is itself a jungle, without an all-powerful world government to enforce order, something like deterrence is required. Deterrence is reason's attempt to check the perpetual temptation of evil.[20]

And, as Edmund Burke warned: "The only thing necessary for the triumph of evil is for good men to do nothing."[21] This evil includes the assumption that men will lie, cheat, and betray. Since the search for perfect security is a fool's errand in a world inherently beset by conflict, deterrence seeks to build security on the firmer foothold of a realistic view of human nature vice utopian. The realistic view is one seeing that the most reliable human motive is the preservation of things one holds most dear — particularly one's own life.

Those who argue for the abolition of nuclear weapons and indeed all weapons lose sight of the fact that war — not weapons — is the real villain. As the socialist Salvador de Madariaga, a key figure in the League of Nations disarmament efforts, presciently noted:

> The trouble with disarmament was (it still is) that the problem of war is tacked upside down and at the wrong end. . . . Nations don't distrust each other because they are armed; they are armed because they distrust each other. And therefore to want disarmament before a minimum of common agreement on fundamentals is as absurd as to want people to go undressed in winter. . . . Disarmers would avoid wars by reducing armaments. They run to the wrong end of the line. The only way . . . consists in dealing day by day with the business of the world . . . the true issue is the organization of the world on a cooperative basis.[22]

Our deterrence posture is such that we believe no regime, no matter how aggressive and risk-inclined, would be so foolish as to attack the Alliance, a move that would yield little advantage, and thereby incur an attack's clear consequence — utter destruction. Taken together, the empty commitments made towards a global nuclear zero and calls by the strategically-illiterate to remove the last U.S. nuclear forces from Europe, make the world's nuclear future more dangerous, not less so.

In 2010 certain officials from Belgium, Germany, Luxembourg, the Netherlands, and Norway proposed removing European-based U.S. nuclear warheads from Europe.[23] Other than being a feel-good gesture to burnish their disarmament credentials again, one wonders what end such a step would serve, particularly in view of the threatening international security environment discussed above. How would such a step enhance their security? These very same countries are also drastically cutting their respective defense budgets, and some are trying to neuter missile defense. This is strategic illiteracy of breath-taking proportions.

Those Europeans who want to get rid of U.S. nuclear weapons (and what about British and French systems?) should for a moment take a strategic view, realizing that in this anarchic, realpolitik world, empty unilateralism is as dangerous as uncontrolled proliferation. A world without nukes might be even more dangerous than a world with them. I am convinced that the advent of the nuclear age is the primary reason major powers have, since 1945, refrained from waging war with each other. It is very difficult to explain the absence of war among the major powers in the last 65 years without taking into account the consequences of nuclear weapons. If, by some miracle, we were able to eliminate nuclear weapons at some point, what we would have is a number of countries sitting around with breakout capabilities, or rumors of breakout capabilities—for intimidation purposes—and eventually a number of small clandestine nuclear stockpiles. This would make the United States and her Allies more, not less, vulnerable. The nuclear genie is now out of its aged and cracked bottle, and there is no way to put him back. "Are we actually going to see a world without nuclear weapons?" former Defense Secretary James Schlesinger rhetorically asked a Deterrence Symposium organized by the U.S. Strategic

Command in 2010. He continued: "This is the vision of many people, and I remind you that the dividing line between vision and hallucination is never very clear."[24]

THE DDPR PROCESS

> NATO's core business, its raison d'etre, is to protect our territory and our populations. . . . And in a world where nuclear weapons actually exist, NATO needs a credible, effective, and safely managed deterrent.[25]
>
> —Secretary General General Rasmussen,
> April 22, 2010

Undoubtedly these issues will have a significant impact on the DDPR process as it moves forward towards the May 20, 2012, Summit in Chicago, IL. Nevertheless, as confirmed by the new *Strategic Concept*, NATO remains a collective security alliance whose purpose, as embodied in Article V of the North Atlantic Treaty, is to defend the territorial integrity of all of its member states. To do so, NATO theoretically maintains military capabilities (1) to deter any attack, and, in the event deterrence fails, either (2) to defeat such an attack if it occurs, or (3) to convince the aggressor that it has miscalculated and that the costs of war far exceed any possible gains, thereby causing the aggressor to abort his attack.

In many respects the DDPR process reflects a continuation of a constantly transforming NATO which began, in my view, with the end of the Cold War and continues today. Consistent themes are evident from past *Strategic Concepts*, namely "security, consultation, deterrence and defence, crisis management, and partnership."[26]

At the November 2010 Lisbon summit, the Alliance declared that:

> NATO will maintain an appropriate mix of conventional, nuclear, and missile defense forces. Missile defense will become an integral part of our overall defense posture. Our goal is to bolster deterrence as a core element of our collective defense and contribute to the indivisible security of the Alliance.[27]

At the 60th anniversary summit in 2009, the Alliance reaffirmed that "deterrence, based on an appropriate mix of nuclear and conventional capabilities, remains a core element of our overall strategy."[28] NATO Allies affirmed the necessity of deterrence, so that is supposedly not an item for discussion in the DDPR. However, the "right mix" of NATO's strategic capabilities would be examined. More specifically,

> We have tasked the [North Atlantic] Council to continue to review NATO's overall posture in deterring and defending against the full range of threats to the Alliance, taking into account changes in the evolving international security environment. This comprehensive review should be undertaken by all Allies on the basis of deterrence and defense posture principles agreed in the Strategic Concept, taking into account WMD [weapons of mass destruction] and ballistic missile proliferation. Essential elements of the review would include the range of NATO's strategic capabilities required, including NATO's nuclear posture, and missile defense and other means of strategic deterrence and defense.[29]

This review will also include a new assessment on threats and the security environment. It will include a review of what contributions to security are provided by arms control and nonproliferation and disarmament initiatives. It will also assess emerging security challenges (cyber, energy security) as well as the enduring security challenges of terrorism and WMD. Ultimately, the report will recommend "the right balance" or "mix" between deterrence, defense, and missile defense, with the purpose of strengthening the Alliance posture.

The consultation and reflection phase of the DDPR was completed in July 2011. Four "scoping papers" were discussed and the North Atlantic Council held sessions with experts to discuss the costs and benefits of making changes to either declaratory policy or force posture. The NATO Deputies Committee will draft the report with the assistance of experts—the High Level Group or Nuclear Planning Group Staff Group on nuclear issues. During the DDPR process, a number of questions will need to be addressed. These include, but are not limited to the following:

- How can NATO best demonstrate Alliance solidarity and maintain a credible Alliance nuclear posture in its common commitment to war prevention?
- How can Allies ensure that the nuclear elements of their deterrence posture remain visible, credible, and effective?
- How should the political-military utility of the nuclear elements of the posture be assessed?
- Does such a requirement necessitate the current balanced mix of nuclear forces, or could it be satisfied solely with so-called strategic nuclear forces provided by the NATO Nuclear Weapon States (NWS)?
- Is the stationing of U.S. nuclear "substrategic" weapons in Europe still required, and is the maintenance of "dual capable aircraft (DCA)"

in their roles fulfilling high readiness requirements (i.e. training, exercises, certification etc.)?

- Do U.S. nuclear forces based in Europe and
committed to NATO provide an essential political and military link between the European
and the North American members of the Alliance?
- If not, what role do they play? What other factors should the Alliance stress to emphasize
and demonstrate the strength of the trans-At-
lantic link?
- Are the DCA nations committed to continue
their current role in Alliance nuclear strategy?
If not, what would they substitute for their contribution to deterrence?
- Can Alliance burden-sharing be visibly provided by other means?

NATO nuclear burden-sharing, including the presence of U.S. nuclear weapons in Europe, is perceived
by many allies as the most tangible manifestation of
the nuclear element of NATO's collective security
guarantee. Some have questioned the continued utility of that presence and have raised concerns about the
security of these weapons, the cost of modernization,
and the implications for disarmament and nonproliferation if they are retained.

Reflecting improvements in the security environment, NATO has reduced the number of U.S. nuclear
weapons stationed in Europe by over 95 percent.[30]
As part of the process of continually reviewing our
nuclear deterrence posture and following consultations within the Alliance, further steps in adjusting
the configuration of NATO's nuclear deterrence posture, including further reductions, should (1) take

into account the disparity between NATO and Russian stockpiles of short-range nuclear weapons; (2) be considered in the context of U.S.-Russian arms control negotiations; and (3) weigh the countervailing political effects within the Alliance and in the minds of potential adversaries. In that regard, the impact on the proliferation of WMD within and without the Alliance as a result of changes in the deterrence posture should also be considered.

Additionally, considering the importance of burden-sharing and consultation in the Alliance, Allied participation in the nuclear mission also lends credibility to their voice on the future of NATO's nuclear policy. Finding innovative ways to expand the sharing of risks and responsibilities among Allies will increase the credibility of the deterrent and manifest alliance solidarity, ultimately providing more leverage in negotiating reductions in U.S.-Russian non-strategic nuclear forces in Europe. The importance of sharing the risks and responsibilities of maintaining U.S. nuclear weapons in Europe and a robust consensus-based nuclear posture cannot be over-emphasized. In every discussion regarding the future of NATO's nuclear policy and potential changes to it, burden-sharing was considered the most important criterion by the Allies.

The Alliance continues to believe that a fundamental aspect of NATO's collective security posture is maintaining sufficient capability to meet the full spectrum of current and future threats and challenges from a position of strength. The Romans said it best: *Sic vis pacem, para bellum* (if one wants peace, prepare for war), and certainly the nature of mankind in that regard has changed little since Roman times. We entrust our security to our leaders, not to others. As former President Teddy Roosevelt said at the beginning of the last century; "There [can] be no greater calamity than for the free peoples, the enlightened, independent, and peace-loving peoples, to disarm while yet leaving it open to any barbarism or despotism to remain armed."[31] In that era (circa 1908), the Hague Peace conference had concluded, Andrew Carnegie was making plans to build the Peace Palace in The Hague, the Netherlands, many were writing that there would be no more wars. At the dedication of the Peace Palace in 1913, Carnegie predicted that the end of war was "as certain to come, and come soon, as day follows night."[32] Of course, less than a year later Europe was plunged into a catastrophic world war.

Who would have predicted what the next 40 years would bring? There is no case that I know of in history where a nation has been made secure by pursuing a policy of vulnerability. The tragic arc of history has demonstrated that such is a sure path to destruction and enslavement.

As stated in the *Strategic Concept*, "Deterrence, based on an appropriate mix of nuclear and conventional capabilities, remains a core element of our overall strategy."[33] I believe NATO will maintain its nuclear deterrent at the minimum level sufficient to preserve peace and stability consistent with and in response to the shifting and hopefully increasingly benign international security environment. The goal of the DDPR is to bolster or strengthen our security, not to maintain the status quo or diminish it. In this same context, the Alliance will continue to examine innovative ways to maintain and sustain a credible nuclear deterrent as one part in NATO's larger defense posture consistent with the principles of fair burden-sharing, the indivisibility of security, and maintaining a strong transatlantic link.

Furthermore, the United States and its NATO Allies will have to reconcile their DDPR conclusions with their interest in arms control and confidence-building measures intended to enhance transparency, particularly with regard to their relationship to Russia. Unfortunately, to date the Russians have demonstrated little interest in arms control or transparency with regard to non-strategic nuclear forces and have suspended their obligations for reporting and transparency under the Conventional Forces in Europe treaties. They continue to refuse to discuss transparency regarding their non-strategic nuclear weapons until all U.S. nuclear weapons are removed from European soil, and they have insisted that future discussions should include British and French nuclear weapons, a position rejected out of hand by both of these nations. Even those nations that are the strongest advocates of disarmament agree that any further reductions should be undertaken in the context of arms control negotiations with the Russians.

Finally, the most important and difficult task is to change the underlying security circumstances that lead nations to seek nuclear weapons. To that end, direct negotiations involving positive incentives (economic, political, and security arrangements) for states willing to abandon nuclear weapons aspirations, as well as cooperation with others to impose sanctions against recalcitrant actors, are essential. These are concrete actions, analogous to the Marshall Plan, to take a historical example, not mere gestures like the Kellogg-Briand Pact of 1929, which "outlawed war."[34]

Nuclear weapons are not empty symbols; they play an important deterrent role and cannot be eliminated. Foreign policy must be based on this reality. The DDPR will reflect the Alliance desire to remain strong with a posture that lowers the risks of the spread of nuclear weapons capability and the possibility of nuclear weapons use. What we need today is a new kind of surge—an intellectual, policy, and political countersurge to both the Global Zero movement and those who insist that defense budgets be cut irrespective of its impact on Alliance security. We need a new impetus to challenge the statements and assertions of groups like the Global Zero Movement.

In sum, I see the end result of the DDPR as one where the U.S. nuclear presence in Europe is affirmed. There are too many proven political and psychological benefits of the long-standing extended nuclear deterrence posture to justify change now and no real incentive to do so in light of the security environment. The weapons serve to deter aggression, persuade the nonpossessing Ally that there is no need to develop nuclear weapons himself, and are a visible and viable symbol of the transatlantic link between the United States and European Allies. There may be some minor adjustments in numbers, which should remain classified, but not many because of their potential for use as an arms control *quid pro quo* in U.S.-Russia negotiations. I do not see any changes in NATO's declaratory policy for a couple of reasons but most simply because the French will never go along with it. A NATO nuclear deterrent can play a significant and far-reaching role demonstrating Alliance solidarity in the face of aggression with WMD, and not just nuclear weapons. As I have often stated, the Alliance uses nuclear weapons every single day. They daily play an important political role in demonstrating solidarity, burden-sharing, and the incalculable consequences of aggression.

The weapons we have invented cannot be uninvented. We must live with them. They are an inevitable price human beings must pay to live in the age of technology. Living with destructive technologies is our lot, the debt we bear in behalf of progress. They are, after all, the ultimate guardian of our safety. Foreign policy must be based on this reality; and the United States should work with its Allies and strategic partners on those achievable objectives that lower the risks of the spread of nuclear weapons and the possibility of nuclear weapons use.

NATO is the world's most successful and longest-lived collective security organization. At the end of the day, I am optimistic that the Alliance will make the right and best choices in the difficult and challenging security and economic environment of today. As Bismarck allegedly observed, "If you like the law and sausage, you should see neither one of them being made."[35] So too with NATO's deterrence and defense posture.

ENDNOTES - CHAPTER 17

1. The views expressed here are my own.

2 Secretary General Anders Fogh Rasmussen, Monthly Press Conference, April 19, 2010.

3. See 1991 *Alliance Strategic Concept*, para. 39; 1999 *Alliance Strategic Concept*, para. 46; and the 2010 *Strategic Concept for the Defense and Security of the Members of NATO*, para. 19. See also the 2010 NATO Lisbon Summit Declaration, para. 30, available from *www.nato.int/cps/en/natolive/official_texts_68828.htm?mode=pressrelease*.

4. "World at Risk: Report of the Commission on the Prevention of WMD Proliferation and Terrorism," published December 3, 2008, available from *www.cfr.org/terrorism/world-risk-report-commission-prevention-wmd-proliferation-terrorism/p17910*.

5. Thomas Grove, "Analysis: Russia feeds arms addiction as soft power fails," October 11, 2011, available from *www.reuters.com/article/2011/10/11/us-russia-military-idUSTRE79A2CB20111011.*

6. See *en.wikipedia.org/wiki/anders_behring_breivik.*

7. Srinvas Laxman, "PM Singh Hints At Strengthening of India's Nuclear Weaponization Program," *Asian Scientist*, October 14, 2011, available from *www.asianscientist.com/topnews/indian-prime-minister-manmohan-singh-strengthen-nuclear-weaponization-program-102011/.*

8. U.S. Senate Committee on Armed Services, Hearing To Receive Testimony on the F-35 Joint Strike Fighter Program in Review of the Defense Authorization Request for Fiscal Year 2012 and Future Years Defense Program, May 19, 2011, Washington, DC, available from *armed-services.senate.gov/Transcripts/2011/05%20May/11-43%20-%205-19-11.pdf.*

9. Transcript of Defense Secretary Gates's Speech on NATO's Future, June 10, 2011, available from *blogs.wsj.com/washwire/2011/06/10/transcript-of-defense-secretary-gatess-speech-on-natos-future/.*

10. Viola Gienger, "Obama Returns to Bush Plan for Cutting Troops," *Bloomber.com*, January 5, 2012.

11. Anders Rasmussen, "The Atlantic Alliance in Austere Times" *Foreign Affairs*, July/August 2011.

12. David Rising and Desmond Butler, "US Military Forges Ahead with European Force Cuts," *San Francisco Examiner*, May 21, 2011.

13. A copy of the letter is available from *markey.house.gov/press-release/oct-11-2011-super-committee-freeze-nukes-fund-future.*

14. *Ibid.*

15. "Russia creates new mega-powerful ballistic missile," August 9, 2011, *Pravda*, available from *english.pravda.ru/russia/economics/09-08-2011/118691-ballistic_missile_russia-0/.*

16. See *www.tradereform.org/wp-content/uploads/2011/12/Foreign -Policy-Americas-Pacific-Century-by-Sec-Hillary-Clinton-November-2011.pdf.*

17. Judy Dempsey, "Survey Shows Americans Now Considering Asia More Important Than Europe," *New York Times,* September 15, 2011, available from *www.nytimes.com/2011/09/15/ world/survey-shows-americans-now-considering-asia-more-important-than-europe.html.*

18. George Schultz, "Let's Get Rid of Nuclear Weapons So We Can Win One More for the Gipper," October 12, 2011, available from *yubanet.com/usa/George-Schultz-Let-s-Get-Rid-of-Nuclear-Weapons-so-We-Can-Win-One-More-for-the-Gipper.php.*

19. Barry Blechman, "Extended Deterrence: Cutting Edge of the Debate on Nuclear Policy," August 13, 2009, available from *nautilus.org/napsnet/napsnet-policy-forum/extended-deterrence-cutting-edge-of-the-debate-on-nuclear-policy/.*

20. Kenneth Waltz, *Man, the State, and War,* New York: Columbia University Press, 1959.

21. Letter to William Smith, January 9, 1795, as quoted in John Bartlett, *Familiar Quotations,* 14th Ed., Boston: Little, Brown and Co., 1968, p. 454.

22. Salvador de Madariaga, *Morning without Noon,* Farnborough, UK: Westmead, Saxon House, 1973, pp. 48-49.

23. In actual fact, they simply proposed discussing the possibility as part of a Foreign Minister's meeting. See "Five Nations Ask Syg To Put 'NATO's Nuclear Policy' On Tallinn Agenda," available from *www.cablegatesearch.net/cable.php?id=10USNATO87.*

24. Global Security Newswire, August 17, 2010, available from *www.nti.org/gsn/.*

25. Speech, "On Alliance Solidarity in the 21st Century," Tallinn, Estonia, April 22, 2010.

26. See "NATO's Comprehensive Political Guidance endorsed by heads of state and government," para. 2, November 29, 2006,

available from *www.nato.int/cps/en/natolive/official_texts_56425. htm.*

27. See *www.nato.int/cps/en/natolive/official_texts_68828.htm? mode=pressrelease.*

28. Declaration on Alliance Security, 60th Anniversary Summit at Strasbourg/Kehl, Press Release 43, April 4, 2009, available from *www.nato.int/cps/en/natolive/news_52838.htm?mode=pressrelease.*

29. North Atlantic Council, Lisbon Summit Declaration, para. 30, November 20, 2010, available from *www.nato.int/cps/en/ natolive/official_texts_68828.htm?mode=pressrelease.*

30. The Report of the Secretary of Defense Task Force on DoD Nuclear Weapons Management, December 2008, states that deployed nuclear weapons in Europe "have been reduced by more than 97% since their peak in the 1970's," p. 59.

31. Theodore Roosevelt, State of the Union Address, December 5, 1905, available from *www.let.rug.nl/usa/P/tr26/speeches/ tr_1905.htm.*

32. Andrew Carnegie, "The Palace of Peace," Address delivered at the Hague, the Netherlands, August 29, 1913, available from *www.accesspadr.org/cdm4/document.php?CISOROOT=/ acamu-acarc&CISOPTR=1376&REC=6.*

33. *2010 Strategic Concept for the Defense and Security of the Members of NATO,* para. 19.

34. Kellogg-Briand Pact, or Pact of Paris, July 24, 1929. This pact renounced war as an instrument of national policy and was ratified by 63 nations.

35. While many sources attribute this quotation to Otto von Bismarck, recent research attributes it to lawyer-poet John Godfrey Saxe, who is quoted by the *Daily Cleveland Herald,* March 29, 1869, as stating that "laws, like sausages, cease to inspire respect in proportion as we know how they are made." Fred Shapiro, "Quote Misquote," *New York Times,* July 21, 2008, available from *www.nytimes.com/2008/07/21/magazine/27wwwl-guestsafire-t.html.*

PART V

ARMS CONTROL AS AN OPTION

CHAPTER 18

TACTICAL NUCLEAR WEAPONS AND NATO: ARMS CONTROL AS AN OPTION

James M. Smith

U.S. tactical nuclear weapons were introduced into Europe based primarily on their military utility but with the strong secondary purpose of ensuring alliance solidarity. They were introduced in the theater under the North Atlantic Treaty Organization (NATO) umbrella, with an equally strong burden-sharing role. Today, the military utility is legitimately questioned, their burden-sharing dimension is indeed a burden on economically challenged Alliance members, and only the political role remains strong and central. U.S. nuclear weapons remain in NATO for the political purposes of general assurance and NATO solidarity, and to give continued relevance to NATO nuclear policy as long as the members impute a nuclear dimension to the Alliance.

As these weapons have transitioned to primarily political roles, arms control has presented itself as a political answer to questions of how to manage further nuclear drawdowns and the possibility of eventual complete removal of the American weapons from the theater. Arms control is an established political process between Russia—with a substantial remaining strategic and tactical nuclear arsenal found particularly worrisome to the newer alliance members—and the United States, which has always undertaken its side of the bilateral negotiations with a keen eye to NATO positions and sensitivities. It is a process that, with thoughtful adaptation, offers significant promise as a vehicle for regulating and verifying nuclear weapon numbers, movement, and status as regarding the NATO area of operations.

This brief overview addresses arms control as an established process of arms regulation; summarizes major threads and issues raised in the chapters of this Part; and suggests an arms control agenda as a way ahead for addressing U.S. tactical nuclear weapons (TNWs) in NATO.

ARMS CONTROL AS A "WAY" OF ENHANCING NATIONAL SECURITY

Arms control developed as a practical offshoot from traditional approaches to disarmament, seeking regulation, reciprocity, and transparency in limiting numbers and capabilities of nuclear systems as opposed to near-term elimination of those systems. The international security environment of the Cold War dictated strategic reliance on nuclear weapons, and neither of the major nuclear powers and their associated alliances could guarantee their security without that set of nuclear capabilities. Arms control offered a systematic and verifiable process to lower the risks, costs, and consequences of potential conflict within a cooperative niche in the otherwise contentious East-West relationship.

Today the foundational situation has changed, resulting in an end to the intensely adversarial relationships prevalent during the Cold War, and a fundamental alteration of the alliance structure in Europe. Today NATO stands alone as the sole strategic security alliance on the continent, and Russia is not denominated as an enemy. In fact, cooperative mechanisms and efforts exist between NATO and Russia on several fronts. However, the sheer numbers of nuclear weapons remaining in the Russian inventory and the siting of many of those weapons in close proximity to NATO member states dictate that NATO seek options for systematized reduction and relocation of those weapons, and for a continuing deterrent posture while those reductions are still in process.

Thus, the November 2010 NATO *Strategic Concept* adopted at Lisbon states in part:

> Deterrence, based on an appropriate mix of nuclear and conventional capabilities, remains a core element of our overall strategy. The circumstances in which any use of nuclear weapons might have to be contemplated are extremely remote. As long as nuclear weapons exist, NATO will remain a nuclear alliance.[1]

However, it later records the following qualification:

> NATO seeks its security at the lowest possible level of forces. Arms control, disarmament, and nonproliferation contribute to peace, security, and stability, and should ensure undiminished security for all Alliance members. We will continue to play our part in reinforcing arms control and in promoting disarmament of both conventional weapons and weapons of mass destruction, as well as nonproliferation efforts.[2]

Arms control is embraced as a primary vehicle to enable the systematic and verifiable reduction of the residual Russian nuclear arsenals and other security factors related directly to the maintenance of that nuclear posture. Specifically, NATO embraces stability- and security-enhancing nuclear reductions both in general and in Europe—both Russian and NATO nuclear weapons in theater—as well as conventional arms control to address the perceived lack of stability that is prompting Russia both to retain its nuclear capabilities (particularly its large inventory of tactical nuclear weapons) and to elevate its doctrinal reliance on those weapons in the event of any major conflict scenario. Both Russia and NATO seek security and stability; the relationship between them has transitioned from adversarial and military to more broadly cooperative and political; and arms control offers a political process through which to address residual military dangers.

ARMS CONTROL THREADS AND THEMES

Thus, the 2010 NATO *Strategic Concept* as well as the authors in this Part have endorsed arms control as one primary vehicle by which to address both residual security challenges in Europe and the specific issues surrounding U.S. (and Russian) tactical nuclear weapons in theater. However, the authors also pointed out that this new arms control process must be broadened and adapted to best fit the new realities of the present environment. Issues, even objections, were raised concerning individual goals or forums for arms control, but consultative and cooperative approaches—here termed arms control writ large—were suggested for a wide range of regional security issues and concerns.

Interestingly, none of the authors chose U.S. tactical nuclear weapons as their singular focus in addressing the issues surrounding those systems. They instead addressed the issues from such departure points as conventional force issues; shifts in the global strategic environment and resulting regional implications; strategic force issues and control efforts; and common political, economic, and force modernization concerns of nations. The authors saw the multidimensional context as the important focus in framing tactical nuclear weapons issues for analysis.

Conventional force balances, the suspended Conventional Forces in Europe (CFE) framework, and overall military concerns were central to one author, and they were mentioned by the other authors as major factors for framing tactical nuclear weapons issues. Certainly Russia's concerns about its entire frontier, as well as regional balances, drive its tactical (and strategic) nuclear force posture and doctrine. Efforts to reinstate conventional forces transparency and cooperation in Europe were seen as fundamental to expanding the discussion toward addressing Russian nuclear weapons and positioning.

Shifts in the global strategic environment toward the Far East were suggested as altering national security resource decisions and affecting strategic forces considerations, particularly for Russia, but also for the United States and European states. In view of this altered environment, suggestions were made for changing the basis for strategic arms control discussions toward a comprehensive approach to nuclear weapons and toward consideration of European security issues based on the resulting enlargement of bargaining breathing room.

Aligned with some of those ideas, a comprehensive discussion of U.S.-Russia strategic engagement was presented as a framework for addressing tactical nuclear weapons issues. Several options were presented and assessed, along with bilateral conditions necessary to move forward on these fronts, with particular attention to composite limits on the full range of nuclear weapons, allowing each side flexibility in how it constitutes and postures its forces. U.S. nuclear weapons in Europe would be included in this composite discussion within the context of overall as well as regional stability.

Against this multifaceted backdrop, the discussion turned to the hard reality of national political and economic imperatives as these confront force modernization decisions associated with maintaining the nuclear status quo in NATO. The point was made that national and Alliance confidence and assurance are key within today's environment, and nonthreatening alternatives take on added salience. Thus such less bellicose factors as stability, emphasis on defense, and engagement itself may become more important than aggressive-seeming military capabilities in shaping this stability and assurance.

ARMS CONTROL TAKEAWAYS AND A WAY AHEAD

One primary takeaway from the Dickinson College workshop underpinning the present book is that an adapted arms control process can act as a central vehicle with which to address the core issues surrounding TNWs in Europe. Arms control and cooperative security present one avenue for addressing these issues, and it may be the preferred avenue given its vector toward transparency, cooperation, reciprocity, and stability. However, the traditional bilateral, security-focused, and formal arms control of the Cold War must be adapted to the new realities of Europe in order to be truly relevant.

Arms control must be balanced. It must move to a more consultative process that takes note of the range of national, regional, and sub-regional concerns. It must be aimed toward attaining assurance of regional stability within which nations do not have to place exaggerated emphasis on security in ordering their individual and collective agendas.

Arms control must be bundled. It cannot focus solely on TNWs, nor on strategic nuclear weapons, nor on conventional forces. Stability concerns address all of these as linked military implements. Today, missile defenses and conventional strategic systems are also linked into the equation, particularly by Russia. Consultative and cooperative approaches to each and all of these security issues must be incorporated into the broadened process for achieving regional stability.

Arms control must be backed. Nations cannot opt out. They cannot free ride. Whether the ultimate format selected is unilateral/reciprocal, bilateral, multilateral, or some mixture of these, the Alliance must be engaged, and the region must be engaged, if true stability is to be attained. In addition, those states with internal consultative mandates must engage those domestic processes so as to present a legitimately national position in the larger consultations. Participants must carry the long-term view into the process so that long-term stability can be the outcome.

Arms control, then, should be a primary vehicle by which NATO and its member states address the issues surrounding security assurance, stability, U.S. nuclear weapons in Europe, and NATO as a nuclear alliance.

ENDNOTES - CHAPTER 18

1. Active Engagement, Modern Defense: Strategic Concept for the Defense and Security of the Members of the North Atlantic Treaty Organization, adopted by Heads of State and Government at Lisbon, Portugal, November 19, 2010, p. 4.

2. *Ibid.*, p. 7.

CHAPTER 19

ARMS CONTROL OPTIONS FOR NON-STRATEGIC NUCLEAR WEAPONS

Steven Pifer

INTRODUCTION

Arms control agreements negotiated between Washington and Moscow over the past 50 years have focused on strategic offensive nuclear arms. Aside from the 1987 treaty banning intermediate-range nuclear force (INF) missiles and related unilateral steps, non-strategic nuclear weapons (NSNWs) have remained outside of arms limitation efforts. Following conclusion of the New Strategic Arms Reduction Treaty (New START) in April 2010, however, President Barack Obama called for including NSNWs in the next round of negotiations. This chapter provides background on NSNWs, reviews U.S. and Russian views on limiting such weapons, and outlines options for dealing with them in arms control arrangements. These options include confidence-building measures, unilateral steps, and negotiated legally binding limits.

The New START Treaty, which entered into force in February 2011, requires that the United States and Russia reduce their strategic offensive forces so that no later than February 2018, each has no more than 700 deployed strategic delivery vehicles—that is, intercontinental ballistic missiles (ICBMs), submarine-launched ballistic missiles (SLBMs), and nuclear-capable heavy bombers; no more than 800 deployed and nondeployed ICBM and SLBM launchers and nuclear-capable heavy bombers; and no more than 1,550 de-

411

ployed strategic warheads. The INF Treaty eliminated all ground-launched missiles and launchers for missiles with ranges between 500 and 5,500 kilometers.

The term "non-strategic nuclear weapon" is used here to include nuclear warheads for all delivery systems *not* limited by New START or banned by the INF Treaty. This category of nuclear warheads includes gravity bombs for aircraft other than nuclear-capable heavy bombers, nuclear warheads for naval cruise missiles and torpedoes, and nuclear warheads for anti-ballistic missile (ABM) and air defense systems. The NSNWs term would also capture any nuclear warheads for surface-to-surface missiles with ranges less than 500 kilometers and nuclear artillery shells, should such weapons remain in the arsenals.[1] NSNWs are also referred to as tactical or sub-strategic nuclear weapons.[2]

As a result of its 2010 *Nuclear Posture Review* (NPR), the U.S. Department of Defense announced that it would retire and place in the dismantlement queue the nuclear warheads for its sea-launched cruise missiles. This leaves the U.S. non-strategic nuclear arsenal consisting solely of B-61 gravity bombs. The Russians maintain a larger and more diverse non-strategic nuclear inventory, including gravity bombs plus nuclear warheads for torpedoes, sea-launched cruise missiles, ABM, and air defense systems, and possibly other kinds, totaling as many as 3,700-5,400 warheads. Many of those may be old and nearing retirement; the "nominal" load of Russian non-strategic nuclear delivery vehicles is believed to be around 2,100 warheads.[3]

U.S. AND RUSSIAN NON-STRATEGIC NUCLEAR WEAPONS

The United States plans to conduct a life-extension program for its B-61 bombs over the coming decade, which will take the three non-strategic variants and one strategic variant of the weapon and produce a single variant, the B-61-12.[4] (This will have the effect of blurring the distinction between strategic and non-strategic nuclear warheads.) Russian nuclear warheads generally have a shorter shelf life than their American counterparts, and the Russian practice is to retire old warheads and build new ones to replace them. While Moscow has not disclosed plans for its future non-strategic arsenal, some experts believe the Russians will replace their aging non-strategic nuclear warheads at a less than one-for-one rate, which would lead over time to a reduction in the overall size of their non-strategic nuclear stockpile. (See Table 19-1.)

Weapons	U.S.	Russia
Air- Delivered	500	800
ABM or Air Defense	0	700
Ground-Based	0	?[5]
Naval	0	600
Total	500	~2100

Table 19-1. U.S. and Russian Non-Strategic Nuclear Weapons.[6]

Of the 500 U.S. B-61 gravity bombs, some 200 are believed to be deployed forward at six air bases in Europe: one each in Belgium, Germany, the Netherlands, and Turkey and two in Italy. These weapons are designated for use by the U.S. Air Force and, under programs of cooperation, the Belgian, German, Dutch, and Italian air forces, which have dual-capable aircraft (DCA) that can deliver conventional or nuclear weapons.[7] There is no unclassified breakdown of the number of NSNWs in the European part of Russia, though Russia has national-level nuclear storage sites plus naval and air force nuclear storage sites on its European territory, including some sites situated close to North Atlantic Treaty Organization (NATO) allies such as the Baltic states and Norway.

Most, if not all, Russian non-strategic nuclear warheads are believed to be "demated" or separated from their delivery systems. U.S. non-strategic weapons are also demated in that no U.S. B-61 bombs are deployed on aircraft, though in Europe they are reportedly stored in warhead vaults in hangars that can house U.S. or allied delivery aircraft.

U.S. Views on Non-Strategic Nuclear Weapons.

President Obama in his April 5, 2009, speech in Prague called for reducing the number and role of nuclear weapons in U.S. national security strategy, a view echoed 1 year later in the *Nuclear Posture Review*. When signing the New START Treaty on April 8, 2010, the President noted, "As I said last year in Prague, this treaty will set the stage for further cuts. And going forward, we hope to pursue discussions with Russia on reducing both our strategic and tactical weapons, including nondeployed weapons."[8]

Were the Russians to agree, this would mean that, for the first time, the United States and Russia would be negotiating on all nuclear weapons in their arsenals with the exception of those retired and in the queue for dismantlement. The rationale for bringing NSNWs into the discussion is that it would be difficult in a new agreement to reduce deployed strategic nuclear warheads to a level below the New START limit of 1,550 without addressing the thousands of NSNWs (and nondeployed strategic warheads) in the sides' arsenals. Indeed, a primary critique of New START during the 2010 Senate ratification debate was that it failed to deal with non-strategic weapons; the treaty's ratification resolution required that the administration seek within 1 year of New START's entry into force to initiate negotiations to reduce the disparity between the United States and Russia in such arms.

Anticipating possible new negotiations with Russia, the administration in February 2011 set up inter-agency working groups to explore options for addressing NSNWs and to examine the kinds of verification measures that would be necessary to monitor limits on them. On March 29, 2011, U.S. National Security Advisor Tom Donilon said that reciprocal transparency on the "numbers, types, and locations of non-strategic forces in Europe" should be an initial step in getting ready for negotiations on such systems.[9] U.S. officials raised the subject of NSNWs in consultations with their Russian counterparts over the course of 2011, but there was no indication of an agreement to address these in a more formal negotiation.

NATO considerations will factor heavily in the U.S. arms control approach on NSNWs. The November 2010 NATO summit produced a new *Strategic Concept*, which reaffirmed the importance of nuclear deterrence for Alliance security. It also noted that NATO would "seek to create the conditions for further reductions [of nuclear weapons stationed in Europe] in the future," adding that the Alliance should "seek Russian agreement to increase transparency on its nuclear warheads in Europe and relocate these weapons away from the territory of NATO members. Any further steps must take into account the disparity with the greater Russian stockpiles of short-range nuclear weapons."[10]

NATO leaders also agreed to launch a Deterrence and Defense Posture Review (DDPR), which is to examine the "appropriate mix" of nuclear, conventional, and missile defense forces for the Alliance. The review is to be concluded by the May 20, 2012, NATO summit in Chicago, IL.

NATO allies hold a range of views on the need for American nuclear weapons deployed forward in Europe. Some allies, such as Germany, the Netherlands, and Belgium, see no territorial threat to the Alliance that requires U.S. nuclear weapons in Europe. The German air force is replacing its *Tornado* aircraft with *Eurofighters* — which will not be wired to carry nuclear weapons — and thus will lose its nuclear role when the *Tornadoes* are retired. The German decision could have a major, if not decisive, impact on Dutch and Belgian decisions about whether to retain a nuclear role for their air forces, which could in turn affect Italian and Turkish views on maintaining nuclear weapons on their territory. If decisions by individual NATO members lead to the abandonment of DCA, NATO could find itself disarming by default.

Other allies, including the Baltic states and countries in Central Europe, see a continued need for U.S. nuclear weapons in Europe as a means of underscoring the U.S. security commitment to NATO. Their view is shaped by concern that Russia might still pose a threat to their security. Russian statements on missile defense such as the one by President Dmitry Medvedev on November 23, 2011, threatening to target missiles on NATO countries hosting U.S. missile defense elements, fuel this concern.

It is doubtful that the DDPR will resolve the differences among Alliance members regarding threat perceptions and the need for U.S. nuclear weapons, and doubtful as well that it will go on to produce a final decision on whether or not U.S. nuclear weapons should remain deployed in Europe. It is more likely that the review will defer difficult questions — the DCA issue could be kicked down the road as the *Tornado* will remain in the German inventory until 2020-25 — and include language, building on that in the *Strategic Concept*, linking measures on U.S. NSNWs to steps by Russia regarding its non-strategic arsenal.

Such an outcome may be desirable for preserving flexibility for U.S. negotiators in a future negotiation with the Russians. If NATO were to decide at the Chicago summit to remove some or all U.S. NSNWs from Europe, that would reduce the bargaining chips in the U.S. negotiators' hands. If the Alliance were alternatively to decide that some U.S. nuclear weapons must remain in Europe for the foreseeable future, that would make it difficult for U.S. negotiators to explore what Russia might offer for removal of the B-61 bombs.

Russian Views on Non-Strategic Nuclear Weapons.

Although President Medvedev committed along with President Obama in April 2009 to a step-by-step process aimed at reducing, and ultimately eliminating, nuclear weapons, the Russians in 2011 showed little enthusiasm for engaging in early negotiations on further nuclear arms reductions of any kind. Instead, Moscow linked further reductions to concurrent or prior steps on a range of other questions. On March 1,

2011, Foreign Minister Sergey Lavrov declared at the United Nations (UN) Conference on Disarmament in Geneva:

> We insist that there is a clear need to take into account the factors that negatively affect strategic stability, such as plans to place weapons in outer space, to develop non-nuclear arms strategic offensive weapons, as well as unilateral deployment of a global BMD [ballistic missile defense] system. Nor could we ignore the considerable imbalances in conventional arms, especially against the backdrop of dangerous conflicts persisting in many regions of the world.[11]

Other Russian officials have reiterated this linkage but have not painted a clear path forward for untangling the bundle of questions. This may reflect uncertainty in Moscow as to where to go next on nuclear arms reductions. Russian officials have indicated privately that, before proceeding too far on a new negotiation, Moscow would want to know who will occupy the White House after the November 2012 U.S. election.[12]

The one specific position that the Russians have put forward on NSNWs is to call for their removal to national territory as a *precondition* for any negotiation on such weapons. Moscow likely understands that Washington will not accept that as a precondition.

Part of the Russian uncertainty about next steps on nuclear reductions undoubtedly stems from their concern about perceived disadvantages vis-à-vis NATO and Chinese conventional military forces. Russian conventional force capabilities declined dramatically after the collapse of the Soviet Union in 1991, and Russia lags the United States particularly in the area of high-tech, precision-guided weapons. Russian officials have announced a major 10-year rearmament program aimed at refitting the military with more advanced arms by 2020, along with an ongoing program of military reforms, but many analysts doubt that Moscow will fully achieve its ambitious goals.[13]

Given their conventional force weaknesses, the Russians may believe that they must rely more on nuclear forces—including NSNWs—than in the past (in much the same way that NATO during the Cold War depended on nuclear weapons to offset conventional force imbalances vis-à-vis the Soviet Union and Warsaw Pact). The 2010 Russian military doctrine stated:

> The Russian Federation reserves the right to utilize nuclear weapons in response to the utilization of nuclear and other types of weapons of mass destruction against it and (or) its allies, and also in the event of aggression against the Russian Federation involving the use of conventional weapons when the very existence of the state is under threat.[14]

It remains unclear, however, what rationale the Russians have for maintaining such a large number of NSNWs. NATO regards its non-strategic weapons as almost solely political in purpose; in a conflict, their use would aim primarily to signal the danger of escalation to a strategic nuclear exchange. Even if the Russian military regards its NSNWs more in military than in political terms—as it probably does—the number in their arsenal remains difficult to justify. In what plausible scenario would Russian military planners envisage the use of hundreds of non-strategic nuclear warheads?

General Arms Control Considerations.

If and when the United States and Russia discuss arms control for NSNWs—be it confidence-building measures, parallel unilateral steps, or legally binding negotiated limits—several considerations likely would apply. First, in contrast to New START, which constrains deployed strategic warheads and deployed strategic delivery vehicles such as ICBMs, the sides likely would focus on non-strategic nuclear warheads themselves and not seek to limit the delivery vehicles for such warheads. Neither the U.S. nor Russian militaries would want to reduce or constrain delivery systems that have primarily conventional missions and roles.

Second, the sides would have to decide whether to take a global or regional approach. While the NATO *Strategic Concept* might be read to imply a regional approach, the transportability of non-strategic nuclear warheads argues for global limitations. For example, an agreement limiting the number of non-strategic nuclear arms in Europe could be readily undercut by the ability of the United States to move warheads into Europe from bases in the United States and of Russia to move them from the Asian part of Russia.

Moreover, U.S. allies in Asia, particularly Japan, would object strongly to an agreement that had the effect of pushing Russian nuclear weapons out of Europe to Asian sites east of the Ural Mountains, which could increase the nuclear risk to them. During the INF negotiations in the 1980s, the Japanese government not only insisted that an agreement not increase the threat in Asia, it pressed for reductions of Soviet INF missiles in Asia proportional to the cuts being negotiated for Soviet INF missiles in Europe (in the end, the INF Treaty banned all INF missiles, regardless of location). Japanese diplomats have already raised this point with U.S. and NATO officials, and Washington likely will be sensitive to Tokyo's concern.

Third, any agreement limiting non-strategic nuclear arms would have to include *de jure* equality of limits for the United States and Russia. Any disparity in Russia's favor in a legally binding treaty would not be ratifiable in the U.S. Senate. For its part, Russia would likewise insist that it have equal rights with the United States.

Fourth, limits on NSNWs would require new verification provisions. The verification challenge posed by these weapons is that most or all are separated from delivery systems, which as noted above the sides would not wish to limit. Counting deployed strategic warheads under New START is made easier by their association with deployed strategic delivery vehicles, such as ICBMs and SLBMs, which can be located using national technical means of verification. But monitoring treaty limits on NSNWs would almost certainly require the negotiation of measures allowing the counting and inspection of nuclear warheads in storage facilities. This is not an insoluble problem — Washington and Moscow have accepted increasingly intrusive verification steps over the past 50 years — but it would mean breaking new verification ground.

Even with the design of new verification measures, there still may be a question regarding monitoring confidence. The U.S. military and intelligence community believe that the New START limit on deployed strategic warheads can be monitored with high confidence. This stems in large part from the association of deployed strategic warheads with deployed strategic delivery vehicles. Absent an "anytime, anywhere" inspection regime—which neither side likely could agree to at present—the sides would have less confidence in their ability to monitor limits on non-strategic nuclear warheads, which could be hidden much more easily than could ICBMs or SLBMs.

ARMS CONTROL OPTIONS

Confidence-Building Measures.

This chapter breaks down arms control options for NSNWs into three categories: confidence-building measures, unilateral steps (including parallel unilateral steps), and negotiated legally binding limits of a kind suitable for a treaty. Confidence-building measures include transparency steps, demating warheads, and relocating and consolidating warhead storage sites.

Transparency. Transparency would be one confidence-building measure. National Security Advisor Donilon proposed transparency regarding the "numbers, types, and locations" of NSNWs in Europe. An April 14, 2011, paper prepared by Poland, Norway, Germany, and the Netherlands, and endorsed by 10 NATO permanent representatives, called additionally for transparency regarding the command and control arrangements and operational status, concluding:

> Initial exchanges on conditions and requirements for gradual reductions of tactical nuclear weapons in Europe could be initiated as part of the process of enhancing transparency. In a first phase it would be useful to clarify the number of weapons that have already been eliminated and/or put into storage by the U.S. and the Russian Federation as a result of the PNIs [presidential nuclear initiatives] of 1991-1992.[15]

Others have also suggested that transparency regarding the implementation of the presidential nuclear initiatives (PNIs) could be a relatively simple initial step, since this would require the sharing solely of historical data.[16] Some Russian officials have suggested in private that transparency would be a logical first step on NSNWs.

Greater transparency regarding non-strategic weapons could be useful for several reasons. It would allow U.S. and Russian officials to shape better informed proposals for any formal negotiation and would provide, were a treaty to be concluded, the foundation for a data base that would likely be an essential element of the agreement. Greater transparency could also give the sides confidence that other confidence-building measures or unilateral steps were being implemented.

Demating. A second confidence-building measure would be for the sides to demate or separate non-strategic nuclear warheads from delivery systems. Removing the warheads would mean that it would take more time for them to be prepared for use. Since this may already be the operational practice on both sides, such a confidence-building measure would merely codify that practice. It could build confidence, though the military utility of such a measure would be less to the extent that nuclear warheads continued to be co-located on bases with their delivery systems.

Relocation/Consolidation. A third confidence-building measure would be to relocate and consolidate non-strategic nuclear warheads. In its *Strategic Concept*, NATO called for Russia to move its nuclear weapons away from the NATO-Russia border. This appears to be a particular concern for the Baltic states, and the

Poles remain wary of past suggestions by Russia that it might deploy nuclear weapons in Kaliningrad on the northern Polish border. If, as some analysts believe, Russia will be reducing the number of its NSNWs, relocation and consolidation might be possible on the Russian side. (As noted above, Japan would be concerned about measures that relocated nuclear weapons to sites east of the Urals, but Russia has nuclear storage sites in the European part of Russia that are well away from NATO member states.) Russia likely would not be willing to remove non-strategic (or strategic) warheads from the Kola Peninsula, but ending the storage of warheads close to the Baltic states could have a useful political impact.

Relocation and consolidation would be a more difficult proposition for the United States and NATO. Consolidation of warheads at fewer sites in Europe could end U.S. nuclear deployments in one or more countries. This could prove problematic for European governments: the basing of U.S. nuclear weapons in Germany and Belgium, for example, makes it easier for the Netherlands to host U.S. nuclear weapons, and vice versa. If the weapons were to be withdrawn from Germany, political pressure in the Netherlands and Belgium for a similar withdrawal would grow. U.S. and NATO officials worry that it would not be feasible to consolidate the weapons from locations in five countries to four because the reduction would not stop there — it could go instead from five to two, and perhaps to one or zero.

Unilateral Measures. A second set of arms control options is unilateral measures, perhaps conducted in parallel. Possible unilateral measures include a U.S./ NATO decision to unilaterally withdraw U.S. nuclear weapons from Europe, a unilateral no-increase commitment, and parallel unilateral reductions. As an example of the latter, in 1991 Presidents George H. W. Bush and Mikhail Gorbachev announced their presidential nuclear initiatives, a series of unilateral steps that eliminated thousands of nuclear weapons on both sides, including dramatic reductions in the two non-strategic nuclear arsenals.

U.S. Nuclear Withdrawal from Europe. One unilateral measure would be for the United States and NATO to agree unilaterally to withdraw some number of — but not all — B-61 bombs from Europe. Those weapons are seen as having virtually no military utility in the context of the full array of nuclear and conventional arms maintained by the U.S. military; their primary value is political, symbolizing the U.S. security commitment to Europe. If the primary rationale for the weapons is political, there may be nothing magic about the current number of 200. Indeed, even officials of NATO allies that wish a continued nuclear presence see the possibility for some reduction.

A more radical unilateral measure would be the removal of *all* U.S. nuclear weapons from Europe, in which case the U.S. extended nuclear deterrent would be based on the Asian model, i.e., extended deterrence for countries such as Japan and South Korea as provided by U.S. strategic nuclear forces and forward-deployable non-strategic nuclear weapon systems based in the United States. Such a move, however, would likely encounter opposition from a number of NATO allies who, under current circumstances, continue to value an American nuclear presence in Europe. It likely would also prove controversial in the U.S. Congress, which has expressed doubts about unilateral measures and would be sympathetic to views in the Baltic states and Central Europe. Moreover, it is unclear at this point whether such a unilateral U.S. move would elicit a *quid pro quo* from Russia other than an agreement to negotiate. While some U.S. officials believe the United States should size its overall nuclear arsenal strictly according to its calculation of deterrence needs, other U.S. officials would not support unilateral withdrawal even if deterrence was not degraded, believing that it would sacrifice a potential bargaining chip in any future negotiation with the Russians.

No Increase Commitment. A second unilateral measure which the sides might adopt in parallel would be a policy of avoiding an increase in the number of NSNWs. The United States has no plans for any such increase, and Russia presumably has no need to, given its large current arsenal. Such a measure might be relatively easy to adopt, but given its minimal practical impact, its political effect or contribution to confidence-building would be small.

A no-increase commitment might be matched with a commitment not to modernize non-strategic weapons, which would appear to be a more robust measure. Any commitments in this regard, however, could be difficult to square with the U.S. B-61 life-extension program and the Russian practice of building new warheads to replace old weapons. It is unclear, moreover, how the sides could be sure that a no-modernization commitment was being observed. Neither likely would be prepared to extend transparency to cover life-extension or production programs for nuclear weapons.

Parallel Unilateral Reductions. Another unilateral measure would be parallel unilateral reductions, under which the United States and Russia would each announce separate policy decisions to reduce its non-strategic nuclear arsenal, as was done by Presidents Bush and Gorbachev in 1991. One such possibility would be for Washington and Moscow each to state that it would reduce the number of its NSNWs by a certain percentage, say 50 percent. Given the large disparity in U.S. and Russian arsenals, the outcome would be unequal and thus not appropriate for incorporation in a formal treaty, but such a measure might be a positive interim step.

Negotiated Legally Binding Limits.

Negotiated legally binding limits in a treaty could take several forms. The limits might apply just to non-strategic nuclear warheads, or they might cover non-strategic warheads along with all nuclear warheads in a single group. Other possible limits could constrain non-strategic nuclear warheads to declared storage sites or to national territory. A more ambitious approach would be to fold U.S. and Russian non-strategic nuclear warheads into a negotiation that also involved conventional forces.

Separate Limit. One approach would be to negotiate a limit that applied only to U.S. and Russian non-strategic nuclear warheads, that is, all nuclear warheads except for those captured by the New START Treaty. Although this would be the most straight-forward way to limit non-strategic warheads, the huge numerical disparity between the U.S. and Russian arsenals — Russia holds an advantage ranging from four-to-one to ten-to-one, depending on how Russian weapons are counted — would make negotiation of a *de jure* equal limit very problematic, if not impossible.

Even were Washington and Moscow able to agree to an equal limit, the *de facto* outcome would likely generate criticism on one side or the other, if not both. For example, a limit of 1,000 non-strategic nuclear warheads could produce criticism in the U.S. Congress for its codification of a two-to-one Russian advan-

427

tage, since the United States has no plans to increase its non-strategic arsenal above 500 warheads. Critics in Moscow, on the other hand, would complain that the agreement forced only Russian reductions while allowing the United States the latitude to double its non-strategic arsenal.

Single Limit on All Nuclear Warheads. An alternative approach would be to negotiate a single limit covering all U.S. and Russian nuclear warheads: deployed strategic warheads, nondeployed strategic warheads, and non-strategic nuclear warheads, everything in the inventory except for those warheads that have been retired or are awaiting dismantlement (these might be limited under a separate regime). This single limit could be combined with a sublimit on the number of deployed strategic warheads. For example, the approach could constrain the United States and Russia each to no more than 2,500 total nuclear warheads, with a sublimit of no more than 1,000 deployed strategic warheads (the latter would amount to a reduction of about 35 percent from New START's level of 1,550 deployed strategic warheads).

The primary advantage of this approach is that it could create an important bargaining possibility. The United States under New START will have a significant advantage in nondeployed strategic warheads, and most, if not all, of its ICBMs and SLBMs will have been "downloaded," i.e., they will carry fewer warheads than their capacity. That allows the possibility to "upload" or put additional warheads back onto the missiles. The Minuteman III ICBM has a capacity of three warheads, but the U.S. Air Force plans to deploy each missile with only a single warhead. The Trident D-5 SLBM, which can carry as many as eight warheads, will have an average load of four-five warheads. Nondeployed strategic warheads will be stored and could, if New START broke down, be returned to missiles. The Russians appear to be implementing their New START reductions by eliminating missiles; the missiles remaining in the force will carry mostly full loads and thus could not be uploaded with additional warheads.

This gives the United States a numerical advantage in a category of strategic nuclear warheads to offset the Russian numerical advantage in non-strategic nuclear warheads. Assuming the United States and Russia each made full use of its permitted 1,000 deployed strategic warheads under the sublimit, the overall limit of 2,500 would allow each to choose its preferred mix of nondeployed strategic warheads and non-strategic nuclear warheads to make up the additional 1,500 warheads. The U.S. military might prefer to keep more nondeployed strategic warheads, while the Russian military chose to keep more non-strategic nuclear warheads. This approach would create a bargaining opportunity that would not be possible were strategic and non-strategic warheads addressed and limited separately. While letting each side keep more of its preferred warhead type, both would have to reduce their numbers to well below current levels.

Limit to Declared Centralized Storage Sites. Some nonofficial Russian experts believe that negotiating a numerical limit and associated verification measures to apply to non-strategic nuclear warheads would be too challenging and time-consuming. They therefore suggest that the sides instead negotiate a regime that would limit non-strategic nuclear warheads to declared centralized storage sites that would be located at some distance from non-strategic delivery systems.[17] Verification measures could be applied to confirm that warheads were not removed from these sites and perhaps to confirm the absence of nuclear warheads at emptied storage sites, but the measures would not seek to confirm the total number of warheads for purposes of a numerical limit in a treaty.

While the separation of non-strategic nuclear warheads from their delivery systems would be a positive step, the warheads would continue to exist and constitute a latent nuclear capacity that could augment deployed strategic warheads. As noted earlier, it may be difficult to reduce the New START limit of 1,550 deployed strategic warheads without negotiating numerical reductions in and limits on the large existing stockpiles of non-strategic nuclear warheads (and nondeployed strategic warheads).

Such an approach furthermore would be difficult for NATO to implement if the United States continued to maintain B-61 bombs in Europe. The locations where U.S. nuclear weapons are currently stored reportedly are all at military air bases, so an approach limiting nuclear warheads to declared centralized storage sites would require construction of a new site(s) for holding those weapons. That could prove costly and very difficult politically.

Limit to National Territory. Were the United States and Russia to get into serious negotiations on NSNWs, Moscow almost certainly would insist, as an element of any agreement, on a provision requiring that all nuclear warheads be based on national territory. That would require the removal of U.S. B-61 bombs from Europe. The United States should be prepared to consider this in the context of the right treaty. In private conversations, U.S. officials do not exclude this as a possible outcome, *depending on the other elements of the agreement.* NATO reactions would likely figure heavily in Washington's judgment, and those reactions—like the reactions of U.S. officials—would be shaped by what the Russians in the overall agreement were prepared to offer in return.

A variant of this approach would be to require that all nuclear warheads be based on national territory but allow for their temporary deployment overseas. New START offers a precedent: Article IV requires that all strategic delivery vehicles be based on national territory with the proviso that heavy bombers may deploy temporarily outside of national territory with notification to the other side. Assuming that the necessary infrastructure was maintained at some European air bases, such a provision in a new agreement would allow the theoretical possibility to return U.S. non-strategic nuclear warheads to Europe in a crisis, which might have some political value for assurance within NATO. The notification requirement presumably would pose no problem, since the principal point of returning the weapons would be to send a political signal regarding U.S. support and the risk of further escalation. However, such a scenario might prove implausible politically; most analysts doubt that in such a crisis NATO would be able to find consensus on a proposed response that would be seen by some allies as a risky and provocative move.

Negotiate in Broader Format. Finally, one further negotiated approach for dealing with U.S. and Russian non-strategic nuclear warheads would be to fold them into broader NATO-Russia or European negotiations along with conventional military forces. The logic here would be that, to the extent that Moscow believes its requirement for non-strategic nuclear warheads is driven by its conventional force disadvantages, such a negotiation could trade off nuclear reductions for conventional force cuts. In the Mutual and Balanced Force Reduction Talks that preceded the negotiation on the Conventional Armed Forces in Europe (CFE) Treaty, NATO at one point offered to withdraw 1,000 U.S. nuclear warheads from Europe in return for Soviet removal of a number of tank divisions from Central Europe.

While this approach has some logic, Moscow suspended its observance of the CFE Treaty in early 2008, and NATO and Russia have not succeeded in finding a way to restore the conventional forces arms control regime. The United States and United Kingdom announced in November 2011 that they were suspending certain CFE Treaty obligations with regard to Russia. Dealing with non-strategic nuclear warheads in a nuclear arms reduction agreement would be difficult enough even without bringing in the added complications raised by conventional force questions.

Negotiating Prospects.

The near-term prospects for addressing non-strategic nuclear warheads, either in a negotiated agreement or parallel unilateral measures, appear limited in 2012. Moscow is uncertain about next steps in nuclear force reductions and, in any event, likely will not take dramatic new steps until the Russians know the winner of the November 2012 U.S. presidential election. To the extent that the White House worries that arms control might become an issue in the U.S. presidential campaign, the administration probably will not offer major new ideas either.

Should President Obama be reelected, he has already indicated his desire to address non-strategic nuclear weapons. The specific view of a possible Republican president is less clear at this point. Many Republicans appear skeptical of the benefits of negotiated arms control, though one of the primary Republican criticisms of New START was that it did not address NSNWs.

On the Russian side, there may well be incentives in the medium term for negotiations on non-strategic nuclear arsenals. Under New START, the U.S. military will have little difficulty maintaining its full allotments of 700 deployed strategic delivery vehicles and 1,550 deployed strategic warheads. According to the September 2011 New START data exchange, Russia is already well below the 700 limit, with just 516 deployed strategic delivery vehicles. Some analysts have predicted that Russian deployed strategic delivery vehicles will fall to as low as 400, with only 1,250-1,350 deployed strategic warheads.[18] Alexei Arbatov believes the warheads could fall to as low as 1,000-1,100.[19] This situation could lead Moscow to decide to build back up to its New START limits. Alternatively, the Russians could seek to negotiate the limits down. Russian officials are also concerned about the U.S. advantage in nondeployed strategic warheads and upload capacity. These questions give U.S. negotiators leverage that — along with Moscow's desire to see U.S. NSNWs withdrawn from Europe — could be used to get Russia to reduce its overly large stock of non-strategic nuclear arms.

U.S. officials hope to hold increasingly substantive consultations with their Russian counterparts in 2012, which might prepare the ground for more serious engagement. But formal proposals and structured negotiations that might include non-strategic nuclear weapons likely will not get underway until sometime in 2013 at the earliest.

ENDNOTES - CHAPTER 19

1. The Russian presidential nuclear initiatives in 1991 included elimination of all ground-launched tactical warheads, but there have been questions as to whether some of these warheads may remain in the Russian inventory.

2. There is no agreed terminology between the United States and Russia on categorizing these weapons.

3. Hans M. Kristensen and Robert Norris, "Russian Nuclear Forces, 2011," *Bulletin of the Atomic Scientists*, Vol. 67, No. 3, May 2011, pp. 71-73.

4. Hans M. Kristensen, "B61 LEP: Increasing NATO Nuclear Capability and Precision Low-Yield Strikes," FAS Strategic Security Blog, June 15, 2011, available from *www.fas.org/blog/ssp/2011/06/b61-12.php*.

5. It is unclear whether the Russian Iskandr surface-to-surface missile has a nuclear warhead.

6. Kristensen and Norris, "Russian Nuclear Forces, 2011."

7. Hans M. Kristensen and Robert S. Norris, "U.S. Tactical Nuclear Weapons in Europe, 2011," *Bulletin of the Atomic Scientists*, Vol. 67, No. 1, January 2011, pp. 64-73.

8. Office of the Press Secretary, Remarks by President Obama and President Medvedev of Russia at New START Treaty Signing Ceremony and Press Conference, Prague," Washington, DC: The White House, April 8, 2010.

9. Remarks as Prepared for Delivery by Tom Donilon, National Security Advisor to the President, "The Prague Agenda: The Road Ahead," Washington, DC: The White House, Carnegie International Nuclear Policy Conference, March 29, 2011.

10. "Strategic Concept for the Defense and Security of the Members of the North Atlantic Treaty Organization," adopted by Heads of State and Government in Lisbon, Portugal, November 19, 2010.

11. Ministry of Foreign Affairs of the Russian Federation, Information and Press Department, "Statement by Mr. Sergey Lavrov, Minister of Foreign Affairs of the Russian Federation, at the Plenary meeting of the Conference on Disarmament, Geneva, Switzerland, March 1, 2011," available from *www.ln.mid.ru/ bdomp/brp_4.nsf/e78a48070f128a7b43256999005bcbb3/2de66a92e764 dbb8c3257846004dfd44!OpenDocument.*

12. Conversations with senior Russian officials in Moscow and Washington, May and August 2011.

13. For a more detailed discussion of how Russian conventional force weaknesses may shape their views on nuclear forces, see Roger N. McDermott, "Russia's Conventional Military Weakness and Substrategic Nuclear Policy," Fort Leavenworth, KS: The Foreign Military Studies Office.

14. "The Military Doctrine of the Russian Federation," approved by Russian Presidential Edict on February 5, 2010.

15. "Non-Paper submitted by Poland, Norway, Germany, and the Netherlands on Increasing Transparency and Confidence with Regard to Tactical Nuclear Weapons in Europe," April 14, 2011.

16. See Madeleine Albright and Igor Ivanov, "Moving Ahead on Reducing Nuclear Arms," *International Herald Tribune*, April 7, 2011.

17. See, for example, Alexei Arbatov, "Gambit or Endgame: The New State of Arms Control," The Carnegie Papers, Moscow, Russia: Carnegie Moscow Center, March 2011, pp. 31-33; and Anatoliy S. Diakov, "Verified Reductions in Non-strategic Nuclear Weapons," Moscow, Russia: Center for Arms Control, Energy and Environmental Studies, Moscow Institute for Physics and Technology, February 18, 2011, available from *www.armscontrol. ru/.*

18. See, for example, Pavel Podvig, Russian Strategic Nuclear Forces, "New START Treaty in Numbers," available from *www.russianforces.org/blog/2010/03/new_start_treaty_in_numbers.shtml.*

19. Alexei Arbatov, "Gambit or Endgame," pp. 13-14.

CHAPTER 20

TACTICAL NUCLEAR WEAPONS AND NATO: A CONVENTIONAL ARMS CONTROL PERSPECTIVE

Dorn Crawford

Discussion about nuclear weapons in the North Atlantic Treaty Organization (NATO) necessarily occurs on a European landscape. This puts the conversation in sharp contrast to the customary context of nuclear arms control: a dialogue between two global superpowers on how best to manage, and perhaps limit, their inventories of strategic weaponry, and thus reduce the risks of mutual destruction. Traditional frames of reference, terminologies, matters of scale, planning factors, and force structure issues do not make an easy transition to the theater environment.

The conventional arms control experience, on the other hand, arises primarily out of the European security dialogue. In contrast to the above, this body of work focuses on objectives and issues of a multilateral and regional character, and thus deserves consultation as a potential source of insights on how security concerns have been addressed in this context.

Tactical (or theater, or non-strategic) nuclear weapons (TNWs) have often been observed as constituting an essential rung in the escalation ladder between conventional and strategic nuclear forces. If that is the case, it is fair to contemplate the relative merits of treating their discussion either as a strategic nuclear topic stepped down, or as a theater conventional topic stepped up—with the truth, as usual, probably lying somewhere in between. The present effort offers a brief overview of current themes of conventional arms control, seeking threads that may inform our perspective.

OBJECTIVES

The most prominent products of the European conventional arms control effort—the Treaty on Conventional Armed Forces in Europe (CFE), the Vienna Document on Confidence- and Security-Building Measures (VDoc), and the Open Skies Treaty—all have as their fundamental premise the obligation to refrain from the threat or use of force in the mutual relations of the parties. Each has evolved in its own way to meet the changing needs of the post-Cold War security environment. The essential steps: build on maturing political relationships; apply new technology; and incorporate lessons learned and document best practices.

Perhaps because it represents the "hard arms control" end of the spectrum, with legally binding limits on holdings and robust verification measures—and, not coincidentally, is at the greatest present risk of unraveling—the CFE regime has probably undergone the most extensive conceptual retooling of the lot. The original objectives expressed in its mandate were of Cold War vintage:

- establish a stable and secure balance of conventional armed forces at lower levels;
- eliminate disparities prejudicial to stability and security; and,
- eliminate the capability for launching surprise attack and initiating large-scale offensive action.[1]

Most of the attempted adaptation and further elaboration of the CFE construct has represented a struggle to morph from its bloc-to-bloc origins to a truly multilateral character, in which imbalances and disparities are Sisyphean realities that can never be absolutely resolved but only continuously managed by collaborative effort.

The VDoc has emerged in some thinking as an azimuth for future conventional arms control efforts, with its principal orientation on military activities rather than military equipment holdings. Like CFE, the VDoc includes an extensive annual exchange of military information. But while CFE seeks to account for the entire military force structure (including higher headquarters, combat service support units, storage and maintenance depots, training establishments, airfields, and any other organization or facility holding, or likely to hold, equipment subject to the Treaty), VDoc focuses on field formations and combat units. By the same token, CFE verification provisions aim principally at intrusively inspecting military garrisons and their occupants; VDoc, while including limited opportunities to "evaluate" units in peacetime locations, has prominent components for inspection and observation of specified military activities in the field — and requirements to provide advance notification of such activities to other parties.

The Open Skies Treaty, while oriented on neither military facilities nor activities per se, still provides additional opportunities to observe such facilities and activities through the conduct of quota-based overflights of treaty parties' territories with sensor-equipped aircraft.

It seems fair to observe that whereas CFE's main aim is limitation, and verification of compliance with limits, VDoc and Open Skies instead emphasize transparency and predictability. The distinction is important—although similarities in the mechanics of the regimes, particularly between CFE and VDoc, have sometimes served to inhibit rather than promote the further development of one or the other. In the early days of their implementation, for example, the specter of "harmonization" was an all-too-convenient bogeyman for keeping a bright line between the two—not least by the couple of dozen participants in VDoc who are not party to CFE. In turn, after CFE adaptation became mired in unfulfilled Istanbul commitments, circa 2002, and particularly after Russia's 2007 "suspension" of its fulfillment of Treaty obligations, prospects for enhancing the VDoc regime were repeatedly derailed by fears of making it a substitute for CFE. Conversely, after the United States and most other Treaty parties took reciprocal CFE measures against Russia in late 2011, Russian officials prominently pronounced their satisfaction with relying on VDoc instead.

There may indeed be some fungibility at work here; but collateral efforts to revive CFE, on the one hand, and enhance VDoc and Open Skies, on the other, suggest that more fundamental environmental shifts may be in play as well. Some hypotheses derived from observing these processes:

- For a variety of reasons, standing force levels have declined so much that limits may be less important in enhancing security.
- Doctrine and force structure have changed enough that, even if legal limits remain useful, holdings of heavy equipment may not be the

right metric (and things are still enough in flux to leave uncertainty about what is).

- Economic and budgetary constraints are playing an increasingly prominent role in planning—not just in force sizing, but in development and implementation of arms control measures themselves as well (i.e., not just arms on the cheap, but arms control on the cheap).

In this environment, some general *objectives* can be discerned from contemporary efforts to update the conceptual model for conventional arms control:

1. Promote European and regional security *by building confidence and reducing uncertainty.*
   - In a post-bloc environment, building confidence is principally a function of knowing the character and limits of others' forces. There being no formal "balance" to be struck, actors acquire confidence from the stability and predictability resulting from an agreed system of limitations (of some sort), and seek what other security arrangements they find necessary beyond the arms control regime itself.
   - Uncertainty is reduced by obtaining detailed information on the disposition of others' forces, both static and dynamic, and conducting visits, evaluations, and inspections to verify the information supplied.

2. Maintain operational flexibility and operational security.
   - Given the continuing flux of force structure, doctrine, and technology, parties will tend to resist any obligations or constraints that may

turn out to be inconsistent with military requirements.

- States must sustain both unitary sovereign commitments to territorial defense, and, at least for NATO Allies, collective commitments.
- NATO members and aspirants must be prepared to field credible forces to meet out-of-area contingencies.

3. Reduce costs *in an environment of increasing fiscal austerity*.
- Parties are compelled economically to seek and sustain minimum levels of forces to meet legitimate defense needs.
- Resources will be difficult to find for new or more robust arms control implementation measures unless they can demonstrate a compelling security payoff.

Many readers may be surprised by the *absence* from the foregoing list of the following objective: "Establish a secure and stable balance of conventional armed forces." This was such a dominant theme of the original CFE negotiation that it is still heard from time to time, despite its manifestly Cold War formula for literally balanced opposing forces. But with the notion of such a "balance" amounting to a mathematical equation with no feasible contemporary solution, it seems clear that future successes in conventional arms control efforts will depend heavily on a final passage from the scene of the mindset behind this term.

KEY ISSUES

How might the three broad objectives inform discussion of the disposition of non-strategic nuclear weapons (NSNWs)? A look at the key issues that have helped shape these objectives may provide some insights.

Military Issues.

Modernization. Several components of this issue have helped define the course of the conventional arms control experience.
- New Systems. To the extent an arms control agreement enumerates the specific types and models of weapon systems it addresses, its viability depends heavily on the means it provides to incorporate changes over time. This has proven a major detriment to the operation of the CFE Treaty, which limits five major categories of equipment (battle tanks, armored combat vehicles, artillery pieces, attack helicopters, and combat aircraft), and lists what specific types and models are included in each category in a "Protocol on Existing Types." This Protocol was meant to be updated regularly and routinely as the parties declared the introduction of new types into their inventories — but quickly bogged down in disputes over types an inspecting party observed in the field and judged should be listed, while the owning party had elected not to declare it based on its own judgment of Treaty definitions. The Treaty provides no means to resolve such disputes other than by consultation; consequently, despite mammoth investments of time and effort by the interlocutors, the Protocol has been updated only once, provisionally, over the entire life of the Treaty. The VDoc contains no such enumeration, but is

widely understood to rely on CFE definitions and types for its inventory, and has thus been indirectly impacted as well. This is a pitfall to be avoided in future constructs if at all possible.

- New Categories. At the next level of generality, prospects of new systems entering service that do not fit comfortably into categories of equipment addressed by a conventional arms control regime are not easily anticipated. The CFE Treaty would require formal amendment, and the VDoc a corresponding change in its provisions, to accommodate developments like aerial drones, now commonly held by many of the parties, that would be awkward to classify in an existing category.

- Pace of Change. Obviously it is difficult to conclude an agreement on matters in flux, though on balance the CFE Treaty and VDoc were remarkably successful in doing so at the end of the Cold War. Still, with reducing uncertainty and enhancing predictability at the forefront of arms control goals, anticipation of and accommodations to change must feature prominently in the development of any NSNW agreement.

Arms control dialogue has seldom progressed far without entertaining questions of "quality vs. quantity" in determining the metrics of an agreement, including closely associated counting rules. Discussions underpinning conventional forces talks have touched on issues of force structure, doctrine, and equipment differences that can be striking among negotiating parties. Nevertheless, no weighting formula to score the potency of one model of weapons system over another, or of one category of equipment against another, has ever gained serious consideration in this dialogue, conventional or nuclear. In the end, a tank is a tank, and a warhead is a warhead, and counting rules for limitation and verification have had to proceed on that basis.

Are numerical limits meaningful? Is there an alternative? The persistence of questions like these testifies to the enduring concerns of participants that qualitative factors may increasingly outweigh quantitative ones in threatening stability and security. While NSNWs may not presently appear to be a hotbed of technological innovation, it would be wise to consider prospective developments in weighing the parameters of any agreement.

Mobilization. What roles do reserve forces and equipment stockpiles play in contemporary planning and operations, and how have they changed for the key players? Cold War scenarios for European conventional conflict relied heavily on assumptions about fleshing out, equipping, arming, and moving low-strength Soviet units, on the one hand, and redeployment of U.S.-based units, while drawing equipment from forward storage depots, on the other. By contrast, while scenarios like these have faded from the conventional scene, NSNW cases still rely on storage considerations, but on grounds of safety and security rather than mobilization. Can demating of NSNW systems perform a role similar to conventional storage in inhibiting potential for surprise attack? Conversely, to the extent that familiar themes of nuclear deterrence like survivability and retaliatory capacity still apply, deliberate storage measures, and especially transparency of the locations involved, may prove very difficult to achieve.

Mobility. Are modern forces sufficiently mobile as to render territorial constraints no longer appropriate? This is an increasingly compelling question in the case of modern conventional maneuver forces whose mobility is fundamental to contingency missions for which distance and duration may be hard to predict. For NSNWs that are air-delivered, mobility is primarily a function of the demating/storage provisions outlined above; once reconstituted, territorial constraints/locations of these highly mobile assets seem to have little practical consequence, though the signaling effect of basing schemes oriented on specific intent and concrete threat assessment may have political significance. Ground- and sea-launched systems similarly oriented on updated threats and deterrence calculations would share such import, of course, but also add practical utility to the retaliatory threat they would represent.

Political Issues.

Defense needs: What's the threat? As noted above, a central challenge to the adaptation and further elaboration of the CFE construct has been overcoming the bloc-to-bloc context in which it originated. A fundamental retooling was achieved in the adapted CFE Treaty, formulated in strict terms of individual national and territorial constraints and flexibilities. Still, concerns about "imbalances," usually between Russia and NATO, continue to be heard — most often, but by no means exclusively, from Russian representatives.

With no similar adaptive mechanism in play, discussions of NSNWs almost always take this cast, as if the only measure of merit is the numerical balance between NATO and Russia (with apologies to those who occasionally address other theaters that may be of interest to the United States). This perspective and its underlying threat assessment yield little room for forward thinking about current and projected military requirements.

Is there a credible case to be made for NSNWs that does not rely on a Cold War, East-West calculus? Certainly the efforts expended on Mideast scenarios to urge the fielding of a European theater missile defense system (and, for that matter, NATO out-of-area conventional operations) suggest that there should be such a case, provided only that a retaliatory component remains an essential element of a robust deterrence strategy. If so, we should be recasting our conversation about the continuing role of these weapons in these terms; if not, we should be seeking expedient means to reduce or eliminate them.

By the same token, we can and should reject Russian arguments that co-opt the onetime NATO posture of using NSNWs to compensate for conventional disadvantage. As amusing as such arguments are for their irony, they rely on the same fundamental premise of escalation from a massive NATO conventional attack that we have already dismissed in conventional arms control forums, as much for its laughability as for its quaintness.

Sovereignty.

What rules and limits should apply to the stationing of forces outside national territory? Inside? Complementary issues of what constraints are appropriate on where forces may be located have occupied much of the conventional arms control dialogue. On the one hand, the principle of inhibiting threatening concentrations of forces led to the original CFE Treaty's geographic structure of limitation, to the adapted Treaty's national and territorial construct, and to the VDoc's thresholds for notifying and observing, and its constraints on conducting military activities—including stationing and activities within national territory. On the other hand, basic principles of honoring national sovereignty were embedded in the CFE Treaty, and reinforced in its Adaptation Agreement, in the form of requiring formal host nation consent for the stationing of forces outside national territory.

In the first instance, the parties have accepted limits on their own sovereignty by adopting ceilings on the amounts of forces they may hold in the area of application, and, derivatively, where those forces may be located, by zone or territory. In a couple of cases of disproportionately large geography and force size (i.e., Russia and Ukraine), zonal and territorial boundaries cut across national boundaries to establish further sublimits on force concentration in sensitive areas. Enter the enduring "flank" debate, whereby Russia has perennially chafed at these sublimits as an infringement on its sovereignty—which of course it is, like all the other provisions of the Treaty (and treaties in general)—hence the need for its agreement, signature, and ratification. Nevertheless, the debate goes on, and has loomed large in Russia's "suspension" of its CFE obligations since December 2007.

Looming even larger, in the second instance, is the issue of host nation consent, hung up on the residual Russian presence in Georgia and Moldova, which combined with the flank issue essentially to derail the CFE Adaptation Agreement, resulting eventually in Russia "suspending" its participation, and in turn the reciprocal countermeasures recently undertaken by most of the other parties. Russia's 2008 incursion into Georgia, and subsequent stationing of forces in the breakaway provinces it has recognized as sovereign entities, have set very difficult roadblocks in the way of resolving this issue.

Analogous concerns could arise in discussing the disposition of NSNWs, with NATO members' present hosting of warhead storage sites a matter of both escalation guarantee and burden-sharing. In Russia, the principle of sovereign prerogative could again complicate efforts to arrange provisions for an unfocused withdrawal of forces within national territory. The notion of reorienting these forces on an updated threat, however, following the missile defense scenario, could give some shape and motive force to this prospect in both cases—and help guide not only location decisions, but revised (presumably reduced) requirements for holdings of NSNW assets as well.

Frozen Conflicts.

What can arms control regimes do to dampen, manage, or resolve persistent regional tensions? For most of the life of the CFE Treaty, interlocutors have struggled to find mechanisms to address the concerns of parties to these regional tensions, reinforcing principles of national sovereignty and the legitimacy of its monopoly of force, delegitimizing weaponry controlled by nongovernmental groups or outside parties, and exhorting governments to assert control of such assets, usually given the rubric "UTLE" (unaccounted, or uncontrolled, Treaty-limited equipment). There is little evidence to suggest that these efforts have borne much fruit in the Caucasus or Moldova, aside from continuing to draw attention to their problems.

By the same token, an NSNW regime is unlikely to play a significant role here, unless by the indirect route of stationing in these areas forces or facilities whose own security needs may increase the urgency of resolving regional tensions (e.g., the Gabala radar array in Azerbaijan as a potential component of a cooperative missile defense system).

Role of Alliances.

How do alliance relationships affect treaty participation? The CFE Treaty very carefully and purposefully reiterates the rights of the parties "to be or not to be" members of alliances. Obviously this has not kept NATO from being judged by its collective holdings as a source of security concerns (or reassurances) by those still determined to seek a "balance" of European forces. Indeed, the slowness of NATO to undertake major reductions in its collective CFE equipment ceilings was a prominent reason offered by the Russians as motivating their "suspension" of Treaty participation.

As noted earlier, this perspective seems even more prominent in the NSNW dialogue, which seldom escapes a NATO/Russia orientation. Refocusing threat assumptions to follow contemporary theater missile defense scenarios seems, once again, the appropriate and consistent course correction.

The "Reset."

How can arms control promote Russia dialogue and integration? Its troubles notwithstanding, CFE, not to mention VDoc and Open Skies, has provided a regular and intensive venue for dialogue and discussion of security concerns and prospects for cooperation. One step the Russians conspicuously did not take in the course of their CFE "suspension" was to discontinue participation in the Treaty's Joint Consultative Group, which meets weekly in Vienna to discuss Treaty-related concerns and seek solutions. Analogous bodies associated with VDoc and Open Skies provide similar consultative venues. The verification centers that conduct implementation activities for all three regimes foster extensive working-level contacts and dialogue as well.

These are all standard mechanisms associated with arms control agreements, so it is reasonable to assume than an NSNW accommodation would include similar provisions for implementation and consultation. Not drivers of the "reset," to be sure, but vehicles to exploit and facilitate it.

THREADS, SEAMS, AND GAPS

Overlaying a conventional arms control template on a dialogue about the role and disposition of NSNWs is an exercise in exploring potential threads of continuity and discontinuity, and considering lessons and leverages that might improve prospects for a successful outcome. From this perspective, a number of influences seem apparent. What happens with NSNWs has a:

- Substitution effect. The roots of NSNWs have commonly been traced to efforts to overcome deficits in conventional forces — initially by NATO, more recently by Russia. In an environment of mounting fiscal constraints and fragile economies, this logic may seem, if anything, to be growing in force. Certainly there is the risk of old arguments about "defense on the cheap" reasserting themselves in these conditions. But in the end, the existing question remains the same: what deficit needs to be compensated for? If the only measure of merit is to strike a "balance" between Russia and NATO, then perhaps (1) rumors of the demise of the Cold War were premature, and (2) our fiscal situation is not so dire after all. Even more importantly, given the resources already being applied to a revised threat assessment in the form of a European missile defense system, it certainly seems appropriate to apply forces already in the field to the same end.

- Collateral effect. Components of defense strategy seem to work best when consistent and complementary. U.S. conventional forces have long since been reoriented from a focus on a heavy central European campaign to flexible contingencies in the Mideast, Southwest or Northeast Asia, or elsewhere. A ballistic missile defense initiative at the center of present European collaborative defense efforts aims to counter prospective Mideast threats. If such core concepts as the continuity of the deterrence escalation ladder continue to apply, then a corresponding reorientation of NSNW assets to align with the strategy underpinning these conventional and missile-defense initiatives certainly seems an appropriate next (if not antecedent) step.

- Spillover effect. It is a well-worn diplomatic principle that arms control (and other diplomatic) successes can generate momentum in related deliberations. They may sometimes supply direct or indirect trade-offs to help balance objectives and outcomes — or simply improve the atmosphere for dialogue. Conversely, failures, or just a lack of successes, can weigh heavily on prospects elsewhere. This is little more than an application to social dynamics of Newton's first law (a body at rest tends to stay at rest, while a body in motion tends to stay in motion). In the most recent case, efforts to capitalize on the conclusion of the New Strategic Arms Reduction Treaty (New START) have been openly and undisguisedly applied to the CFE impasse — though without apparent effect to date. The Senate's conditions for ratification of New START instruct a similar derivative effort in controlling NSNWs — which, having arguably suffered more from inattention than disagreement, may be more fertile ground, at least for now. And, as the intermediate rung on the deterrence ladder, there may be some appeal in the logic of addressing it first, in the course of advancing more vigorously from the successful strategic nuclear case to the deadlocked conventional one. Obviously other political considerations (like election cycles) may affect specific timing, but a road map remains in order.

CONCLUSIONS

A conventional arms control perspective offers a number of implications for approaches to the issue of NSNWs in NATO. The most salient (and urgent) of these seems to be an updated threat assessment for NSNW planning, providing a logical model for both deployment and force-sizing. Such an assessment could:

- promote consistency and complementarity in defense strategies, assuming such an assessment would conform to those already in use for planning conventional forces and theater missile defenses;
- through a joint reorientation of NSNWs by NATO and Russia, even if undertaken as parallel unilateral measures, pave the way for improved collaboration on missile defense;
- reduce costs, not by substitution of NSNWs for conventional forces, but by a coherent reassessment to determine minimum needs; and,
- set the stage for generating renewed momentum in related areas of security concern like CFE and VDoc.

As timing and tactics permit, considerations like these may be of use in charting the way ahead in a complex and difficult post-Cold War setting.

ENDNOTES - CHAPTER 20

1. "Mandate for the Negotiation on Conventional Armed Forces in Europe," Agreement by the representatives of the 23 negotiating states, initialed in Vienna, Austria, January 10, 1989.

CHAPTER 21

ARMS CONTROL AFTER START

Malcolm Chalmers

Since the end of the Cold War, with little political controversy, the number of U.S. nuclear weapons in Europe has been reduced by 95 percent. This trend might have continued further. But political controversy has ensured that it has now been brought, at least temporarily, to a halt. The renewed focus on nuclear disarmament signaled in President Barack Obama's Prague speech on April 5, 2009, followed in October 2009 by the formation of a new German government committed to removal of nuclear weapons from its territory, provided encouragement for disarmament advocates throughout Europe, while raising alarms among supporters of the nuclear status quo. Old and familiar arguments seemingly forgotten after the end of the Cold War were dusted off. Countless conferences and seminars were initiated. After years of absence from the agenda, nuclear issues began to be debated once more at senior levels of the North Atlantic Treaty Organization (NATO) Alliance.

The basing of U.S. nuclear weapons in Europe does not excite the public passion of the 1980s, on either side of the debate. But echoes of that time remain apparent within the political elite of many NATO member states. They are particularly evident in those countries that were on NATO's front line facing the Warsaw Pact in the 1980s, but were also at the forefront of public protest against new NATO nuclear deployments. Opposition to nuclear deployments has remained an important element in their domestic politics, even as the previous rationale for deployment—the need to counter the Soviet Army deployed in the heart of Germany—has long since disappeared.

As in the 1980s, insistence on withdrawal of U.S. nuclear forces on European territory is not driven primarily by a belief in the likelihood of reciprocation, either by Russia or by non-nuclear nonaligned states. Rather, it is rooted in a belief that nuclear weapons are inherently distasteful and dangerous, and are, at best, a temporary necessity when faced by evident and immediate threats. The lack of any openly-argued operational role for these weapons is, from this point of view, a clear argument for their withdrawal. In contrast to those who point to the importance of U.S. nuclear weapons in Europe as symbols of transatlantic burden-sharing and reassurance, these critics put more emphasis on the symbolic importance of demonstrating NATO's commitment to disarmament.

In the absence of major new threats to European security, and in light of the opposition to continuing nuclear deployment in key hosting countries, it appears likely that these weapons will have to be withdrawn at some stage over the next decade or so. But this will not happen without a fight. Supporters of the existing arrangements have been vocal in expressing concern that nuclear withdrawal could undermine the credibility of NATO's commitment to nuclear deterrence more generally, and would be especially damaging if carried out without substantial reciprocation from Russia. They view anti-nuclear feelings in Germany, in particular, as part of a broader European reluctance to share security burdens that, in their view, are being borne disproportionately by the United States. They have powerful allies in NATO's new member states (especially in the Baltic republics) who view nuclear withdrawal as part of a wider disengagement trend that could undermine the credibility of NATO's collective defense commitments. Their concerns are also shared by France, which has been consistently sceptical of the Obama administration's commitment to global nuclear disarmament.

As this debate continues, the primary concern of most NATO member states has been to find a consensus on this contentious issue in order to be able to focus on other risks — the problems in Afghanistan, the uncertainties in the Arab world, the security implications of the financial crisis — that are of more pressing concern to the Alliance. The central theme that has emerged from these efforts at consensus-building — and was reflected in NATO's 2010 *Strategic Concept* — has been the desirability of finding ways in which the future of U.S. nuclear weapons in Europe can be addressed as part of a process of mutual reductions with Russia. Those governments that would prefer the removal of these weapons are, at least for now, willing to explore whether it is possible to get something from Russia in return. And those who support their continuing presence view the commitment to reciprocation as a way to head off the prospect of further unilateral reductions.

With key basing countries reluctant to commit to hosting U.S. weapons in the longer term, there are questions about how much can realistically be obtained from Russia in return for their removal. As long as confrontation with the United States and NATO is seen to be fulfilling a useful domestic political role, Russia's government may be unwilling to enter into any new agreement — whether on nuclear arms control or on missile defense cooperation — that would signal a reduction in this tension. As long as Russia sees it as in its interest for NATO to be divided on this question, moreover, it may be less inclined to agree to a process that would allow the Alliance to unite around a new approach.

Recent political unrest in Russia, however, suggests that it may be too soon for NATO to abandon the search for accommodation. A now reelected, but weakened, President Vladimir Putin might come to be convinced — perhaps in response to growing economic weakness — that it was in Russia's interests to resume and deepen the "reset" process. If he does so decide, a renewed attempt to achieve mutual reductions in non-strategic nuclear weapons (NSNWs) might not be a bad place to start.

It might be easier to achieve agreement on NSNW reciprocation than on missile defense, the primary focus of NATO/Russia efforts over the last year. NATO Secretary-General Anders Fogh Rasmussen is right to believe that agreement on missile defense cooperation would be a "game-changer," opening up the path to a fundamental restructuring of relations between Russia and the Alliance.[1] But, precisely because this is the case, such an agreement would also have to involve some fundamental changes in strategic approach by both Russia and the United States, the conditions for which may not yet exist. Russia is still very reluctant to agree on a cooperative approach that could give political legitimacy to the wider U.S. missile defense program, fearing that this would hasten the day in which its own strategic missile force came under threat. The United States, for its part, is unwilling to provide binding assurances that it will not develop missile defense capabilities that could threaten Russia's long-range missiles. Even if the current administration were to do so, Russia could not be confident (given its experience with the Anti-Ballistic Missile (ABM) Treaty) that future administrations would abide by such a commitment. It is precisely because missile defenses are believed—by many in both the United States and Russia—to have the long-term potential to change the future strategic balance that agreement to cooperate in their operation is so difficult.

In the case of NSNWs, by contrast, the technical characteristics of the systems in question are well-known and unlikely to change fundamentally. Support for Russian NSNW deployment is reported to be strong in the Russian Navy, which relies on TNWs to offset U.S. naval superiority and defend its strategic missile submarines. Like NATO in the Cold War, moreover, Russia believes that it may need a significant sub-strategic arsenal in order to offset the weakness of its conventional forces in the event of an invasion. But, as in NATO, Russian air and ground forces may be increasingly reluctant to devote substantial resources to maintaining an asset that cannot be used in more limited conflicts. Moreover, in contrast to NATO, the very size of Russia's arsenal—estimated at several thousand—should permit significant reductions to be made before reaching whatever minimum force levels its services now believe are needed. On the other hand, the heightening of the political saliency of these weapons within NATO may have made it harder for Russia to make unilateral reductions in its own forces without an expectation of getting something in return.

BROADENING START

Serious progress in efforts to make reciprocal NSNW reductions will depend on there being political circumstances, in both Russia and the United States, which favor such a process. If such conditions were to develop, however, the form in which reciprocal reduction was pursued would be critical in determining whether progress could be realized. There are, broadly speaking, two possible ways forward: inclusion of NSNWs in treaty-based arms reductions, or reciprocal reductions outside a treaty framework.

The main proposal currently being discussed under the first heading is for the next round of bilateral arms reductions to include limits on the total warhead stockpiles of both Russia and the United States. All nuclear weapons, it is now being argued, are "strategic" in their effects. NSNWs should therefore be included in any future agreement to reduce stockpiles.

One of the advantages of this approach is that it provides a way to address the problem of negotiating reductions in NSNWs when there is a large numerical disparity between U.S. and Russia forces in this category. Within an overall ceiling, the United States and Russia could separately decide the mix of weapon systems that they chose to maintain. Russia might decide, for example, to maintain more short-range NSNW warheads. The United States, by contrast, might prefer to keep a greater capability to "upload" its strategic missiles or bombers. Such an approach, since it would set global limits, would also avoid the adverse reaction from America's Asian allies that could be anticipated were an attempt made to limit the scope of any new treaty to U.S. and Russian NSNW arsenals in Europe. Both Russia and the United States would still retain the option of shifting nuclear forces from Europe to Asia. But they would not be given a treaty-based incentive to do so.

There are, however, some drawbacks to the all-inclusive treaty approach. First, it would mark an important dilution of the attention hitherto given to the strengthening of first-strike stability as an objective of strategic arms control. Like previous bilateral nuclear treaties, the main focus of the New START is the limitation of ballistic missiles and warheads deployed on these missiles. Because of this concern, the Treaty undercounts warheads deployed on strategic bombers, each of which is assumed (for treaty purposes) to be deployed with only a single warhead. This asymmetry in counting rules makes sense if one's objective is to focus restrictions on those systems — ballistic missiles — that are most suited to a disarming first strike. Were a successor treaty to focus on total warhead numbers, however, one stockpiled nuclear artillery shell would count as much as one warhead deployed on a long-range missile. This may make sense from a U.S. point of view. Given trends in Russian forces, together with the relative invulnerability of U.S. ballistic missile submarines, the United States can be relatively comfortable about its forces' ability to survive a first strike, even at much lower numbers. But Russian decisionmakers may be less sanguine, especially when account is also taken of growing U.S. conventional capabilities for long-range strike and ballistic missile defense.

Second, the assumption that NSNWs would be included in a legally binding treaty brings other problems. It is possible that the next few years could see some mutual reductions in the systems limited by the New START Treaty, with budgetary pressures providing an incentive for reductions in missile numbers in particular. In return for a further round of legally binding reductions in offensive forces, however, Russia seems certain to seek assurances on future U.S. deployments of strategic missile defense systems. Yet it is difficult to imagine the U.S. Senate being willing to

461

ratify a treaty that would place legally binding limitations on U.S. missile defenses. Nor does it currently appear likely that U.S. technology development will be at such a slow pace that Russia will no longer need to worry about where this might lead by the 2020s.

Third, even if the issue of missile defenses can be resolved, the proposal that New START's successor treaty should include limits on warhead stockpiles will involve formidable verification challenges. One of the main reasons why the current Treaty limits only numbers of missiles and deployed warheads is that it is possible to verify declared numbers of these systems with a high degree of assurance. But no techniques are available to provide a comparable degree of assurance for declarations of stockpiled warheads. A more limited level of confidence can be provided through mutual declarations on numbers of warheads stored (or at least based) at designated storage sites, with some attached inspection procedures. But it is likely to take significant effort to develop these procedures in ways that do not compromise warhead design information. And neither party to a treaty can be sure that the other does not have additional, undeclared, warheads in storage.

FALLING TOGETHER, BUT SEPARATELY

There is therefore a considerable potential for deadlock involved if NATO's leaders were to see New START's successor as the only possible means for limiting NSNWs in Europe. As a result, NATO's *Strategic Concept* was careful not to limit itself to this option:

> In any future reductions, our aim should be to seek Russian agreement to increase transparency on its nuclear weapons in Europe and relocate these weap-

ons away from the territory of NATO members. Any further steps must take into account the disparity with the greater Russian stockpiles of short-range nuclear weapons.[2]

The *Strategic Concept*'s focus on the location of Russian weapons should make a reciprocal process of reductions, and/or withdrawals, easier to achieve. As NATO has made clear, its greatest concern is with those NSNWs which are deployed in positions whose location strongly suggests that they have a specific role in relation to neighboring NATO member states. Russia, for its part, views U.S. nuclear weapons in Europe (for both historical and geographical reasons) as being deployed primarily to counter its own forces. The European location of both Russian and American weapons may not be very relevant in operational terms. Aircraft-launched weapons, in particular, could quickly be relocated to Europe in times of crisis. Despite this, however, significant political gains might still be achievable were the two countries to undertake reciprocal withdrawal from their forward locations, even if not all the warheads involved were dismantled. There would be concerns in Japan were Russia to move the weapons in question to its eastern borders, just as there might be Chinese complaints were the United States to redeploy its NSNW warheads to Guam or Australia. It would therefore be important for both countries to make clear that no such redeployment would take place.

Such a mutual withdrawal would be likely to work best, and be more sustainable, in the context of a broader set of confidence-building measures between NATO and Russia. These might include, for example, measures to demilitarize Kaliningrad, limit the size of exercises near each other's territory, and increase mutual transparency at military bases near the NATO/Russia frontier.

Whether or not specific confidence-building measures — nuclear or conventional — are undertaken, it seems certain that the U.S. conventional troop presence in Europe will be reduced in coming years as a result of the combined effect of budget cuts and the relative priority being given to preserving U.S. conventional capabilities in the Asia Pacific. Similar factors could also lead to further reductions in Russia's Europe-based forces, as it seeks to maintain adequate capabilities against potential threats to its south and east. NATO's European member states are also planning to reduce their conventional forces, whether or not there is any agreement with Russia to do so. In the absence of a new conventional forces agreement, American and Russian withdrawal from Europe could still be reversed over a period of months in the event of a new and protracted European security crisis. But the very fact that neither country feels that Europe is a priority for its conventional forces suggests that neither believes that such a crisis is likely. This broader context — mutual, but uncoordinated, reductions in conventional forces — may make it easier to achieve parallel progress in nuclear arms.

NUMBERS AND VISIBILITY

As in the case of conventional forces, therefore, reciprocal reductions in Europe-based nuclear forces may not take the form of a single all-encompassing process. They could, instead, involve some combination of gradual reductions and increased transparency. While both have an important role to play, however, it is the relationship between them that is critical. Thus, for example, all three NATO nuclear weapon states recently announced the total size of their nuclear weapon stockpiles (France in 2008, the United States and United Kingdom [UK] in 2010). In each case, these transparency announcements were accompanied by commitments to make further reductions (in the cases of France and the UK) or confirmation of large recent reductions (in the case of the United States).

This is a good model for future transparency announcements. NATO is therefore right to ask Russia to announce the total size of its arsenal, following the example of France, the United States, and the UK. But it would not be a confidence-building step were Russia to announce the size of its nuclear arsenal without any accompanying promises of reductions. If such an announcement were to confirm that Russia's arsenal was bigger than that of the United States, moreover, it could be seen as an act of defiance, reinforcing the perception that Russia is unwilling to enter into a serious process of trust-building.

While transparency on its own is therefore a mixed blessing, it does play a critical role in reinforcing the value of reductions that do take place. The decisions made by the UK and France to publicize the size of their arsenals, despite the lack of any accompanying verification, has enabled them to gain credit for the substantial post-Cold War reductions that both have made. By contrast, one of the reasons for the lack of follow-on to the 1991 U.S./Russia Presidential Nuclear Initiatives (authorizing large reductions in tactical nuclear arsenals in both countries) was Russia's failure to provide sufficient confirmation (such as relevant stockpile numbers) that it had fulfilled its own commitments.

This suggests that, if Russian leaders do decide that they want to pursue confidence-building steps in relation to their NSNWs in Europe, some combination of transparency and numerical reductions is likely to be needed. Were Russia to announce that it was removing a further 1,000 NSNWs from its stockpile over the next period, for example, and accompanied this with an offer to match the current levels of transparency of NATO's nuclear weapon states in relation to its total stockpile, it could make two important points. First, it would show that it was listening to concerns over the size of an NSNW arsenal that seems well in excess of the level that could plausibly be needed for self-defense, even allowing for Russia's conventional inferiority. Second, it could help revive the process of mutual information-sharing, begun by the establishment of arms control and confidence-building treaties signed in the 1980s, but now increasingly under threat.

A parallel argument can be made in relation to the much smaller stockpile of U.S. nuclear weapons in Europe. In unofficial analyses based on publicly-available U.S. government documents, the United States still deploys around 150-200 warheads in Europe, all of which are B-61 free-fall bombs,[3] but there has been no official statement confirming this fact. Nor has the United States (as of this writing) updated its announcement on the total size of its arsenal, first given at the Non-Proliferation Treaty (NPT) Review Conference in May 2010. A U.S. announcement that confirmed the total size of its deployments in Europe for the first time, if accompanied by a historical account of the reduction in this arsenal over time, could give added credibility to its claim to have a good record on disarmament since the end of the Cold War. As in the cases of France and the UK, such an announcement would have added credibility were it accompanied by further measures to reduce the size of its arsenal in Europe. The size and nature of such a reduction could be calibrated depending on whether it was taken in parallel with, or independent of, parallel measures by Russia.

There are several options for such a reduction. Even if all six warhead storage locations are kept, the United States could decide to reduce the average number of warheads per location from 30 to, for example, 10 or 20. It could also decide to reduce the number of facilities, for example, by closing one of the two Italian bases or one of the three north European facilities. Or, if it is judged that Russian reciprocal measures are sufficient to meet the criteria set out in the *Strategic Concept*, it could decide to withdraw all weapons from Europe, with or without a formal announcement to this effect.

A combination of parallel reduction and transparency measures, along the lines outlined above, could go some way towards building mutual confidence, while avoiding the complexities involved in subsuming these weapons within a global arms control regime. It might also include further detailed exchanges of information (for example, on locations of major storage sites) that could further build confidence in total arsenal declarations.[4] No regime currently exists that is able to verify warhead stockpiles with the degree of accuracy achieved in relation to deployed missiles, and it is hard to imagine that such a regime can easily be developed, given the ability of states to conceal warheads (and warhead components) in nondeclared locations. Given this, together with continuing transparency in relation to the most sensitive (START-counted) delivery systems, the steps outlined here may be as much as can be expected in the next phase of confidence-building. Were the security of either side after reductions dependent on a reliable accounting of the arsenal of the other, such unverified transparency would not be appropriate. For the purposes of confidence-building in relation to weapons whose primary purpose is symbolic, however, it offers the most feasible way forward. Neither side would have anything to gain from concealing weapons that would, in any case, be surplus to operational requirements. This calculus would change were the United States and Russia to seriously consider much deeper cuts in the sizes of their arsenals (for example to prevailing UK and French levels). Given current circumstances, however, it may make sense to accept a more limited level of transparency in return for making progress in down-sizing arsenals.

WIDENING START

If there is progress on reciprocal U.S./Russia NSNW reductions, it may be most likely to start with a package along the lines outlined here. But such a package should not be considered in isolation. It would affect, and be affected by, wider processes of arms reductions, both between the United States and Russia, and involving a wider group of countries.

Given the difficulties that were involved in getting the U.S. Senate to ratify the New START Treaty, the prospects for a follow-on treaty during the next U.S. presidential term are not high. Whether Senate objections were primarily motivated by strategic or party political considerations, the reality is that it is now very difficult to conceive of a new treaty that would be able to satisfy two-thirds of the U.S. Senate while still making a substantial contribution to wider security objectives.

That being said, it may still be possible to achieve significant further reductions in U.S. and Russian strategic arsenals within the framework of the existing treaty. Both countries are currently planning to spend significant amounts on modernizing their strategic forces (including new missiles and submarines) over the next 10-15 years. If some of this expenditure could be reduced or postponed as a result of cuts below New START ceilings (especially those for delivery vehicles), leaders in both countries may have an opportunity to make further mutual reductions, even without agreement on a new treaty. By the end of the decade, it is therefore possible that levels of both START-countable deployed delivery vehicles and warheads (currently 700 and 1,550 respectively) could be reduced substantially. The political plausibility and extent of such reductions are likely to be greater, however, if they take place in parallel with a process of mutual reductions and increased transparency in NSNWs.

Further significant reductions in American and Russian arsenals may also require some greater assurance that other nuclear weapon states continue to restrict their own arsenals at relatively low levels. The position of China is likely to be of particular importance. Given the concern that both the United States and Russia have about how China's growing power might affect their own security, both countries — and Russia in particular — will be nervous about removing one of the components where they still retain a significant edge.

As in the case of other nuclear weapon states, Chinese steps towards greater transparency would be more likely to contribute to confidence-building were they to be combined with commitments to restraint or reduction in capabilities. One recent estimate of China's nuclear arsenal, drawing primarily on U.S. Government sources, suggests that it has a total stockpile of around 240 warheads.[5] If this were to be confirmed officially, thereby placing China's arsenal at a level comparable to those of the UK and France, it should make it easier for the United States and Russia to reduce their own arsenals. The effect of such Chinese transparency would be significantly increased if it were also to announce that it had no plans to increase its arsenal above this level.

Such an announcement need not reveal any information on the location or readiness state of China's nuclear arsenal, any more than recent announcements by France, the United States, and the UK have done so. But it would still help reassure those who believe that China might be concealing a larger stockpile; and it would be a strong signal that China might be prepared to play a part in future mutual restraint regimes. Given uncertainties about the future missile defense capabilities of the United States, China seems unlikely to be willing to give an unconditional "no increase" commitment. Even so, greater Chinese transparency could be a useful contribution to confidence-building at a time when there is growing concern that U.S./China strategic competition may intensify dangerously over the next decade.

Were China to join the other recognized nuclear weapon states in making a stockpile declaration, together with offering some assurances on future plans, it would place pressure on India and Pakistan to consider confidence-building measures of their own. Even more than in the cases of Russia and China, however, it would be important to manage carefully the relationship between transparency and restraint for the two acknowledged non-NPT nuclear-armed states. Because of the difficult strategic situation in which it finds itself, Pakistan will be tempted to see increased transparency measures primarily as a means to further strengthen the deterrent value of its nuclear force. It might, for example, use a transparency announcement as an opportunity to overstate both the size of its arsenal (e.g., through the way it enumerates weapons) and its future plans for increasing it further. If this were to occur, there would be a danger that mutual transparency between Pakistan and India could fuel the risk of competitive nuclear buildups.

THE ALLIANCE AND ARMS CONTROL

A process of mutual reductions in U.S. and Russian nuclear arsenals could have a range of effects on current understandings of extended deterrence and burden-sharing within NATO, with potentially wider implications for alliance politics. For example, if the gap between the arsenals of the large and small nuclear-armed states does narrow, then alliances — including NATO — could become a more important element in shaping the structure of international nuclear stability. NATO, which refers to the strategic forces of the Alliance as providing the "supreme guarantee" of the Alliance's security, already acknowledges that the nuclear forces of the UK and France "contribute to the overall deterrence and security of the Allies."[6]

NATO and other U.S. alliances have another, probably more important, effect. The Nuclear NPT has been the central legal pillar in international efforts to prevent the spread of nuclear weapons. But it would not have been possible to persuade key U.S. allies in

Europe and East Asia to sign the Treaty as non-nuclear-weapon states without the willingness of the United States to extend nuclear deterrent guarantees to them. Given the inherent risks involved in such guarantees, however, allies still worry about whether U.S. promises would be bankable in times of war. Those European allies who believe that they are most at risk have therefore historically placed a high premium on evidence that the U.S. guarantee is credible, including the forward deployment of U.S. nuclear weapons.

Were the United States, along with Russia, to reduce the size of its nuclear arsenal to a level closer to those of the smaller nuclear weapon states, it would not necessarily require an end to forward deployment of U.S. nuclear forces in Europe. It would be hard to justify retaining the current level of such forces, which (at 150-200 warheads) is comparable to the total arsenal of the UK. If it were thought desirable to do so as a signal of extended deterrence credibility, however, the retention of a much smaller force (say 10 or 20 warheads) would be compatible in principle with a smaller overall U.S. arsenal.

If Russia were to make steep reductions in its own nuclear force, however, support for maintaining even a small U.S. nuclear force in Europe is likely to diminish, even among the more "exposed" alliance members such as Poland and the Baltic republics. It is possible to imagine a scenario in which deep cuts in U.S. and Russian global forces still left a few U.S. weapons in Europe. It is more likely that European NATO members will see such cuts as an opportunity to overcome their divisions on this difficult issue, and end this deployment entirely.

NATO WILL SURVIVE—WHATEVER HAPPENS TO NSNWS

The politics of U.S. nuclear weapons in Europe are now as much about reassuring the United States that its non-nuclear allies are not taking advantage of its generosity as about reassuring its allies that the United States will come to their aid if required. Indeed, these two requirements are closely interrelated. Were the United States to conclude that it was no longer worth offering protection to its allies because those allies are unwilling to do enough for their own defense, then the alliance would be damaged beyond repair. In this context, some in the United States argue, demands from European countries for the removal of nuclear weapons from their territory risk undermining support for NATO within the United States. Why should the United States risk its own cities in the event of a major war in Europe, they suggest, if European governments are not prepared to bear the political costs of basing U.S. nuclear forces on their territory? Nor is this seen as a uniquely nuclear phenomenon. European opposition to U.S. nuclear forces on their territory is often seen as part of a wider process of demilitarization, evident also in the lower levels of spending on conventional forces by European governments.

Yet NATO is stronger than some of its American critics believe. Its European members have been prepared to deploy significant numbers of their armed forces to Afghanistan, despite widespread public opposition to the war at home. They have done so, primarily, in order to show solidarity with the United States. In turn, the United States was prepared to make a vital contribution to NATO's recent campaign in Libya, where France and the UK played the leading role in pushing for United Nations (UN) and alliance action. Neither operation suggests an alliance in terminal crisis or decline.

The argument that the United States is about to abandon its interest in Europe in order to focus entirely on the Asia Pacific, is similarly overblown. After a decade in which the U.S. military has been focused on fighting difficult ground wars in Iraq and Afghanistan, some rebalancing is both inevitable and desirable. But it is far from clear that U.S. interest in Europe's restive neighborhood—the Mediterranean, the Middle East, and sub-Saharan Africa—is about to decline. Confrontation with Iran remains a central element in U.S. strategy, bringing with it an intensification of relationships with Iran's Arab rivals on the other side of the Gulf. U.S military involvements in Africa—for example, in Somalia, Kenya, and Uganda—are deepening, not declining. Irrespective of what its European allies do, the United States, for good or ill, seems to be committed to remaining a major military power in Europe's backyard.

Concerns over the impact of the NSNW debate on NATO's future are also at risk of being overblown. While there may be a temptation to draw comparisons with the 1980s Euro-missile debate, the current nuclear discussion within NATO is a pale echo of that period. Taking place in the shadow of worsening Soviet/U.S. relations, and with mass anti-nuclear demonstrations taking place across Europe, the Euro-missile crisis of the 1980s was rightly a central focus for intra-alliance concern. Today, in a Europe where major war is no longer the central security concern, and where the continuing presence of U.S. nuclear weapons on the continent had been almost forgotten until recently, apathy is a more common reaction than antagonism.

As in the past, the most likely causes for severe divisions within NATO are likely to come as a result of U.S. military adventures (such as Vietnam and Iraq) which most Europeans are not willing to support, but for which the United States will believe it needs allies. By contrast, and however the issue is resolved, the future of U.S. NSNWs in Europe is not likely to become an issue of comparable divisiveness.

ENDNOTES - CHAPTER 21

1. Speech by NATO Secretary General Anders Fogh Rasmussen to RUSI Missile Defence Conference, London, England, June 15, 2011, available from *www.rusi.org/events/*.

2. NATO *Strategic Concept*, para. 26, Brussels, Belgium.

3. See, for example, Robert S. Norris and Hans M. Kristensen, "US tactical nuclear weapons in Europe 2011," *Bulletin of Atomic Scientists*, January/February 2011, pp. 64-73.

4. Ten European NATO member states, led by Germany, the Netherlands, Norway, and Poland, submitted a "non-paper" to NATO in April 2011 with detailed proposals for mutual transparency in this area. See Federation of American Scientists, Strategic Security Blog, available from *www.fas.org/blog/ssp/2011/04/natoproposal.php*.

5. Hans M. Kristensen and Robert S. Norris, "Chinese nuclear forces, 2011," *Bulletin of Atomic Scientists*, November/ December 2011, pp. 81-87.

6. NATO *Strategic Concept*, para. 18, November 2010.

CHAPTER 22

THE CONVENTIONAL AND NUCLEAR NEXUS IN EUROPE

Jeffrey D. McCausland

In the aftermath of the Cold War, the United States was a party to a variety of nuclear and conventional arms control agreements, from the Treaty on Conventional Forces in Europe (CFE) to the "Moscow Treaty" on strategic nuclear weapons. Many of the agreements focused on Europe, which had been central to the East-West confrontation. Others were global. Some were bilateral with the Soviet Union and the Russian Federation as its successor state under international law. Several were multilateral and involved all of the states of Europe or had a more global focus. But with the disappearance of the Union of Soviet Socialist Republics (USSR), what little agreement there was among American policymakers about the central role and purpose of arms control in the post-Cold War period dissipated rapidly. As a result, arms control has not played an important role in policy discussions in the United States or Europe — except when it emerged from political disagreements over controversial systems like missile defenses or space weapons.

With the election of President Barack Obama, arms control appeared once again to be a viable policy option, but for a very different international security environment. By the middle of 2010, the Obama administration had published a revised *Nuclear Posture Review* (NPR), signed a follow-on agreement to the Strategic Arms Reduction Treaty (START) between the United States and the Russian Federation, and conducted a summit on the effective control of nuclear material. The administration also came to regard the Non-Proliferation Treaty (NPT) with renewed importance as a means to retard the proliferation of nuclear weapons. But this renewed commitment to arms control occurred in the absence of a grand strategy regarding the control of both nuclear and conventional weapons. It focused largely on the one area — strategic nuclear weapons and their delivery systems — which are arguably the "easiest" for the United States and Russia to find common ground. With this in mind, it is clear that a successful arms control strategy must better integrate and update existing agreements while seeking new accords that advance American national security interests broadly across the spectrum of nuclear and conventional weapons.

FROM STRATEGIC NUCLEAR WEAPONS TO NON-STRATEGIC NUCLEAR WEAPONS

Many in the United States believed that the need for improved relations between the United States and the Russian Federation had become increasingly important owing to the nature of the emerging security environment. Moscow and Washington had experienced serious disagreements over the previous decade, and at the onset of the Obama administration bilateral relations were perhaps in a worse state of repair than at any time since the end of the Cold War.[1] Consequently, early in the new administration, President Obama called for hitting the "reset button" in the relations between the two countries. Despite serious differences, the two sides were able to negotiate the so-called "New START" agreement by the spring of 2010, as previously mentioned. This measure was subsequently ratified by the United States Senate as well as the Russian Duma before the end of the year.

The Senate resolution ratifying New START also called on the administration to "seek to initiate, following consultations with NATO [North Atlantic Treaty Organization] allies," negotiations with Moscow "to address the disparity" in Russian and American non-strategic nuclear weapons (NSNWs), or what were formerly called tactical nuclear weapons (TNWs). The Senate further directed that this process be commenced within 1 year after New START's effective date early in 2012.[2] In March 2011 during a speech to the Carnegie International Nuclear Policy Conference, Tom Donilon, the President's National Security Adviser, underscored the desire of the administration to begin such negotiations. Donilon noted that Russian NSNWs would be a "priority" for any future discussions. He further observed that such discussions would occur in concert with negotiations with Washington's NATO allies on the role and number of American NSNWs forward-deployed on their territory.[3]

Washington's European allies showed clear support for these policies. NATO's *New Strategic Concept* adopted in November 2010 affirmed an Alliance goal to "seek Russian agreement to increase transparency on its nuclear weapons in Europe and relocate these weapons away from the territory of NATO members." It further requested that steps be taken to account for the disparity between NATO's and Russia's short-range or non-strategic nuclear stockpiles.[4] Efforts to enhance transparency and reduce the number of these weapons would seem a logical step from the perspective of both American and NATO interests. Since the end of the Cold War, the United States had dramatically reduced the number of NSNWs forward-deployed to Europe to approximately 200. These were scattered across NATO military bases in Belgium, Germany, Italy, the Netherlands, and Turkey. The Soviet Union (and subsequently the Russian Federation) had also unilaterally reduced its non-strategic nuclear stockpile as part of the so-called Presidential Nuclear Initiatives in the early 1990s, but it still retained a huge preponderance over the U.S. numbers.

Unfortunately, the Russian Federation displayed little to no interest in entering talks to reduce its NSNWs following the release of the *Alliance Strategic Concept* despite Alliance efforts to raise this issue in the NATO-Russia Council.[5] Moscow argued that these weapons could not be viewed as an isolated issue or a simple matter of U.S.-Russian arms control parity. Rather, they were part of a more complex security environment. Russian Foreign Minister Sergei Lavrov emphasized this point during New START confirmation hearings in the Duma in January 2011. Lavrov observed that it was impossible to divorce such weapons from a wider discussion of "strategic parity." He added that such discussion must include such issues as "conventionally armed long-range strategic weapon systems, the weaponization of outer space, ballistic missile defense, and the disparities in conventional forces."[6]

Many Russian experts have echoed Lavrov's last concern about Russian conventional inferiority with respect to NATO and a corresponding need to maintain NSNWs as a hedge.[7] It is widely believed that Moscow had as many as 20,000 non-strategic nuclear warheads in its stockpile at the end of the Cold War. The United States also deployed thousands of these weapons to Europe during the Cold War owing to NATO's perceived conventional inferiority in comparison to the Soviet Union and Warsaw Pact. They were seen as the escalatory link between forward-deployed conventional forces and American strategic nuclear forces. Consequently, policymakers considered them as an integral part of Washington's policy of extended deterrence.

While the number of these weapons has dropped significantly on both sides, it is still believed that Russia maintains between 2,000 and 4,000 NSNW warheads. The exact number is unknown, as is the distribution between naval, air, and air defense forces.[8] Correspondingly, the Russian military doctrine published in 2000 expanded the circumstances under which Moscow might use nuclear weapons. Russian military planners argued that such weapons could be used "in response to large-scale aggression utilizing conventional weapons in situations critical to the national security of the Russian Federation."[9] General Nikolai Makarov, Chief of the Russian General Staff, declared in late 2011 that "local and regional conflicts may develop into a full-scale war involving nuclear weapons." Makarov further commented that Moscow placed increased reliance on its nuclear deterrent due to the decline in its conventional forces.[10] Indeed, in the aftermath of a major exercise by the Russian Army in early 2011, NATO officials are reported to have concluded that in actual war Russia would depend on its NSNWs.[11] A further complication was Moscow's decision in 2007 to suspend theretofore required reporting and inspections measures in accordance with the Treaty on CFE. This suspension occurred less than 1 year prior to a conventional war with neighboring Georgia.

This disparity of views on reduction of NSNWs raises several important questions for American and

NATO policymakers. How can a broader policy approach for both NATO and the United States be crafted that addresses the linkage between NSNWs and conventional weapons? It is interesting to note in this regard that the Alliance's *New Strategic Concept* also seeks to "strengthen the conventional arms control regime in Europe."[12] Therefore, can progress in conventional arms control possibly be linked to proposed efforts to reduce NSNWs, all as part of a broader effort to stabilize the overall security situation among the United States, Europe, and Russia? And with this in mind, what is now the status of the CFE Treaty as the largest and most ambitious conventional agreement ever signed?

The linkage between nuclear and conventional forces had always been clear to Western and Russian strategists. Although nuclear weapons took pride of place in arms negotiations, talks on both strategic nuclear as well as conventional arms control negotiations have always sought to reduce the possibility of conflict at any level that might escalate to a major nuclear exchange. As a result, both sides made adjustments to their respective nuclear and conventional forces, either to account for changes by the other or to compensate for perceived inferiorities. Still, throughout the Cold War (and even in its aftermath) negotiations over nuclear and conventional weapons were conducted in separate forums. This approach was to some degree due to do the vast size of the respective conventional and nuclear stockpiles. Now in the aftermath of New START, with the changing security environment and the drawdown in conventional forces, neither side may enjoy the "luxury" of examining these issues separately. Thus, success in finding a way to negotiate with Moscow about NSNWs may depend on resolving the long dilemma over CFE and seeking other means to provide assurances about conventional as well as nuclear forces. At a minimum, progress in conventional arms discussions could improve the prospects for finding a resolution to the NSNW issue.

THE "ORIGINAL" CFE TREATY AND ITS ADAPTATION

In order to consider how conventional arms control might contribute to finding a solution to the problem posed by NSNWs, it is important to understand how the CFE Treaty came into being and many of the underlying issues that have been addressed over the past decade. The CFE Treaty was signed in Paris, France, on November 19, 1990, between members of NATO and the Warsaw Pact. It established limits on the aggregate total of conventional military hardware for the two blocs, required substantial reductions in each nation's conventional arsenal, and created an intrusive regime of inspections and verification. At its signing, many analysts hailed it as "the cornerstone of European security," and it is clearly the most ambitious and far-ranging conventional arms control treaty in history. It underscored a transformation of European security that is still in process and whose end state is unclear.[13]

The events that framed this transformation have been both largely peaceful and remarkable. Only a year before its signing, the Berlin Wall, which had served as perhaps the primary symbol of the Cold War for nearly 40 years, was breached. Six weeks prior to the Paris signing, Germany formally reunified into a single nation. The 22 nations that signed the CFE agreement have subsequently increased to 34.

One of the alliances, the Warsaw Pact, has dissolved and the other, NATO, has enlarged. A key signatory to this agreement, the Soviet Union, has disappeared and been replaced by a host of successor states. Finally, the nations that convened in Paris did so under the overall auspices of the Conference on Security Cooperation in Europe (CSCE). This organization has now grown to 56 members and become the Organization for Security Cooperation in Europe (OSCE), an entity now matured into an international organization. An adapted treaty that reflects many of these political changes was signed on November 19, 1999 at the OSCE Summit held in Istanbul, but has not yet been ratified by a majority of the states involved.

The initial treaty talks commenced in January 1988, with the following mandate agreed upon to guide these negotiations:

> The objectives of the negotiation shall be to strengthen stability and security in Europe through the establishment of a stable and secure balance of conventional armed forces, which include conventional armaments and equipment, at lower levels; the elimination of disparities prejudicial to stability and security; and the elimination, as a matter of priority, of the capability for launching surprise attack and for initiating large scale offensive action.[14]

The final agreement required alliance or "group" limitations on tanks, artillery, armored combat vehicles, combat aircraft, and attack helicopters—known collectively as Treaty Limited Equipment (TLE)—in an area stretching from the Atlantic Ocean to the Ural Mountains. Each bloc accepted the weapon limits shown in Table 22-1.

Treaty Limited Equipment	Group Limit
Tanks	20,000
Artillery	20,000
Armored Combat Vehicles (ACVs)	30,000
Attack Helicopters	2,000
Combat Aircraft	6,800

Table 22-1. TLE Limits.

Subsequent national limits for each treaty signatory were determined during negotiations among the members of the two respective alliances. Following the demise of the Soviet Union, the successor states (within the area of treaty application) determined their respective limits from the total allocated to the Soviet Union in May 1992. The three Balkan states (Lithuania, Latvia, and Estonia) did not participate in the negotiations to determine national limits for the "successor" states of the Soviet Union. They argued that their nations were not "successor states" but had been "occupied territory." Consequently, their territory was no longer part of the treaty's area of application. Still, following their entry into NATO, all have indicated a willingness to accede to the adapted CFE Treaty once it enters into force.

Bloc limitations for NATO and the former Warsaw Pact were further restrained by a series of five geographic nesting zones for land-based TLE with limits for each zone. These restraints were imposed to prevent destabilizing concentrations of conventional military armaments in critical localized areas. A four-zone area commences with a central region consisting of Germany, the Benelux, Poland, the Czech Republic,

Hungary, and Slovakia. The term "nesting" signifies that, beginning with this initial zone, each successive zone subsumes all the preceding zones, plus adjacent states and military districts. Cumulative limits are assigned on holdings of treaty-limited ground-based equipment in each zone. This construct has the effect of permitting free movement of equipment and units away from, but not towards, the central European region, which thus inhibits surprise attack in the area deemed, during the Cold War at least, to be the most vulnerable.

The Soviet Union (and subsequently the Russian Federation) further accepted a fifth zone, the so-called "flank zone." This portion of the agreement places limits on ground-based systems in the Leningrad and North Caucasus Military Districts in the Russian Federation. Norway is part of the northern portion of the flank zone, while the north Caucasus states (i.e., Turkey, Greece, Bulgaria, Romania, and Moldova) are in the southern portion. Limitations on helicopters and attack aircraft apply only to the entire area of application due to their ability to reposition rapidly.

One year after the signing of the initial agreement and as treaty implementation was commencing, Russian leaders began arguing for adjustments to their equipment limits. They began pressing concerns about Russia's equipment limitations, particularly in the flank region, and Moscow undertook a campaign to alter those limits. A final compromise was achieved at the first Review Conference in May 1996 that permitted Russia higher force levels in the flank zone, established a May 1999 deadline for Moscow to meet these adjusted levels, and reduced the overall size of the flank zone. Still, the problem of Russian force levels in this area has continued to be a major issue.

It was exacerbated by Russian military operations in Chechnya (which is in the flank region) and the conflict between Russia and Georgia in 2008. Concurrent with these events, treaty signatories had begun (as agreed at the 1996 CFE Review Conference) to embark on a "modernization" of the treaty, in order to adapt it more broadly to the changed European security architecture, one without a Soviet Union or a Warsaw Pact.

As previously mentioned, on November 19, 1999 (the ninth anniversary of the CFE Treaty), 30 national leaders signed an "adapted treaty" at an OSCE Summit held in Istanbul. The 19 NATO members accepted lower cumulative national limits. All signatories accepted the new structure of limitations based on national and territorial ceilings, consistent with the principle of host nation consent for the presence of foreign forces on any country's territory. The agreement also provided enhanced transparency through increased quotas for mandatory on-site inspections, operational flexibilities to exceed ceilings temporarily, and an accession clause that would allow additional states to join the treaty regime.

The parties also adopted the "CFE Final Act." This document contained a number of political commitments related to the Adapted Treaty. These included: (1) reaffirmation of Russia's commitment to fulfill existing obligations under the treaty to include equipment levels in the flank region; (2) a Russian commitment to exercise restraint in deployments in its territory adjacent to the Baltic; (3) the commitment by a number of Central European countries not to increase (and in some cases to reduce) their CFE territorial ceilings; and (4) Moscow's agreement with Georgia and Moldova on the withdrawals of Russian forces from their territories. President Bill Clinton noted in his statement at the conclusion of the Istanbul, Turkey, summit that he would not submit the agreement for review by the United States Senate until Russia had reduced weapons to the flank levels set forth in the Adapted Treaty to include removing its forces from Georgia and Moldova.

The most important agreed change in this Adapted Treaty was that the parties deleted the old treaty arrangements from the Cold War framework — eliminating the bloc construct and reflecting the new reality of a Europe no longer divided. The original treaty's group limits were replaced by national and territorial limits governing the TLE of every state. The treaty's flank limits were adjusted for Russia, providing Russia considerably more flexibility for deployment of armored combat vehicles (ACVs) in the Northern and Southern portions of the flank than it had under the original treaty. Corresponding transparency measures, which apply equally to Russia and all other parties, were a crucial part of this deal. Having taken the group structure out of the treaty to reflect that Europe was no longer divided, Allies and other states committed to lowering their ceilings in the Adapted Treaty. These ceilings became more explicit in the Adapted Treaty text and were then codified in Istanbul. Actual conventional force levels are currently well below those agreed ceilings and, in the case of NATO members, well below the original group limits.

Other provisions were adopted to reflect the new security environment. Russia's concerns about the three Baltic republics achieving NATO membership were addressed in two ways. First, the accession clause that was part of the Adapted Treaty was coupled with these states' readiness to enter the agreement once the Adapted Treaty took effect. Second, it was emphasized that the 1997 NATO-Russia Founding Act contained the following key sentence that addressed Russia's concerns about stationing Alliance forces on the territory of new member states:

> NATO reiterates that in the current and foreseeable security environment, the Alliance will carry out its collective defense and other missions by ensuring the necessary interoperability, integration, and capability for reinforcement rather than by additional permanent stationing of substantial combat forces.[15]

Throughout this period of the 1990s the treaty signatories also dealt with a raft of other implementation issues — the flank, destruction of Russian equipment — and reached, for the most part, a successful resolution of these concerns.

THE RUSSIAN "SUSPENSION"

On December 12, 2007, the Russian Federation officially announced that it would no longer be bound by the restrictions of the 1990 CFE Treaty, and suspended participation.[16] Moscow attributed this action to the fact that the 22 NATO members bound by the 1990 agreement had not ratified the 1999 Adapted Treaty. During a specially-called conference in June 2007, it provided a detailed list of "negative effects" of the conduct of NATO states that caused it to take this action.[17] These included overall NATO force levels, the flank limits, and other unspecified Alliance demands for additional transparency. In addition to these concerns, it was clear that Prime Minister Vladimir Putin and Russian leaders in general were angry over a series of issues, including NATO enlargement, the independence of Kosovo, and plans to install American anti-ballistic missiles on Polish territory. Nonetheless, Moscow reassured the other treaty signatories that it did not intend to dramatically increase its force levels in the territory adjacent to their borders. Russian President Medvedev underscored Russia's seriousness about its Treaty concerns when he described the existing agreement as both "unfair" and "non-viable." At the same time, Russian leaders have been quick to describe treaty contributions as valuable, and to reinforce the spirit of trust and cooperation it has engendered.

So far as ratification is concerned, NATO members have argued since the Istanbul Summit in 1999 that their ratification remained contingent upon Russia complying with the commitments it freely made when the Adapted CFE Treaty was signed. Clearly, the most contentious obligations were the full removal of all Russian military forces from the territory of the former Soviet republics Georgia and Moldova. Russia has adamantly denied this linkage, and Russian Prime Minister Putin publicly argued that "there is no legal link" between the Adapted CFE Treaty and these commitments.[18]

Still, it is interesting to note that despite these statements Russia has never formally "withdrawn" from the treaty but rather announced that it had "suspended" certain of its treaty commitments. Senior American officials have noted that Prime Minister Putin not only has an excellent understanding of the treaty's provisions but also rejected a proposal by the Russian Ministry of Defense to withdraw from the agreement. Even President Dmitri Medvedev seemed to indicate his preference for avoiding the treaty's "complete and final collapse" as he noted during a speech in 2007.

In response, NATO initially endorsed a "parallel actions package" in March 2008 in an attempt to avoid the treaty's demise. The package represented a serious shift in the NATO position, as it called for NATO countries to begin the ratification process (which is some countries such as the United States might take several months) while Russia commenced its force withdrawals. Once the forces had been removed from Georgia and Moldova, NATO countries would strive to complete ratification of the Adapted Treaty quickly. NATO members also pledged to address many Russian security concerns once the Adapted Treaty was in place. For example, all new NATO members that are not treaty signatories (Slovenia, Estonia, Latvia, and Lithuania) agreed to accede to it. NATO also announced that following final ratification it would be willing to discuss Russian concerns about future weapon ceilings and limitations placed on Moscow in the so-called "flank zones" that border Turkey, Norway, and the Baltic Republics.[19]

Unfortunately, the initiative made little to no progress. The effort was largely undermined by the deteriorating relations between NATO countries and the Russian Federation in the aftermath of the conflict in Georgia in the late summer of 2008. In fact, one expert observed that Russia's conduct in this conflict violated the principles contained in both OSCE documents as well as the preamble to the CFE Treaty. These documents call for parties to refrain from "the threat or use of force against the territorial integrity or political independence of any State," and commit the signatories to peaceful cooperation and the prevention of military conflict anywhere on the European continent.[20] The Georgia situation was further complicated by Moscow's subsequent decision to recognize South Ossetia and Abkhazia as independent nations.

Following the meeting of OSCE foreign ministers in June 2009, the so-called "Corfu Process" began to examine European security challenges. By early 2010, an effort was undertaken in the CFE Joint Consultative Group to develop a framework document that would simply contain principles of conventional arms control which all nations could agree upon. It was hoped that this would serve as a basis for new negotiations, and in the interim offer each state the option of complying either with the existing CFE Treaty or the list of specific requirements described in the framework document.

At the NATO Lisbon Summit in November 2010, the Alliance reaffirmed its continued commitment to the CFE Treaty regime and all associated elements. The Final Communiqué noted that although agreement had not yet been achieved, progress among the participating states was encouraging. The Allies further underscored the indivisibility of security for all parties and urged continued "efforts to conclude a principles-based framework to guide negotiations in 2011." They further stated that this process should build "on the CFE Treaty of 1990, the Agreement on Adaptation of 1999, and existing political commitments." While the ultimate goal remained, that is, to insure the continued viability of conventional arms control in Europe and strengthen common security, member states further recognized (as noted at the previous Summit) that "the current situation, where the NATO Allies implement the Treaty while Russia does not, cannot continue indefinitely."[21]

Despite these lofty goals, little progress was realized in achieving a framework document. This was largely due to Russian insistence on disallowing any language in the framework document recognizing "host nation consent" for stationing of foreign forces that included the phrase "within internationally recognized borders." Such insistence was obviously because of Russian recognition of the former Georgian provinces of Abkhazia and South Ossetia and the continued presence of Russian forces on their territory. By the summer of 2011 the Russian Deputy Foreign Minister Aleksandr Grushko declared that the negotiations had "ended up in an impasse" and blamed the West for this development.[22]

The failure to achieve agreement on the framework document prior to the September 2011 Review Conference, with the 4th anniversary of the Russian suspension of participation in the agreement now rapidly receding, has left Washington and its NATO allies with few choices. On November 22, 2011, the United States announced that "it would cease carrying out certain obligations" under the treaty with regard to the Russian Federation.[23] NATO allies quickly followed suit with similar announcements.[24] In addition, the United States and its allies argued that sharing of sensitive data by treaty signatories with the Russian Federation should be considered a compliance violation as the data is supposed to be provided only to "active" participants in the agreement.

It does, however, seem clear that American and NATO policymakers do not wish to terminate the treaty or argue that the Russian Federation is in "material breach." This is clear in a number of ways. First, the announcement reaffirmed the U.S. willingness to implement the treaty and carry out all obligations with the other signatories. Second, it offered to resume full implementation with Moscow should it decide to return to compliance. Finally, the United States declared that in the spirit of transparency it will "voluntarily inform Russia of any significant change" in American forces in Europe.[25] Thus the November 22, 2011, announcement appears simply to acknowledge that, after 4 years, the United States and its NATO partners could not continue to fulfill treaty obligations absent some reciprocity from Moscow. But this U.S. reaction may offer an opportunity to bypass the logjam that has occurred for the past 4 years. It could clear the agenda and allow negotiations to commence that consider other areas of mutual interest between Russia and NATO as well as other conventional arms proposals.

The failure to find a solution that would have allowed the Adapted CFE Treaty to enter into force was clearly a disappointment. Still American and European policymakers can take some solace from the fact that during the 4-plus years since the Russian Federation suspended its participation, the Alliance has been able to maintain internal unity on the issue. It seems clear in retrospect that the Russian Federation firmly believed that over time some NATO members would in fact "break ranks" and seek to ratify the Adapted CFE Treaty. At a minimum, the Federation hoped that the issue would cause increased friction among alliance members. Clearly this did not occur. Of course, it is important to realize that the Russian war with Georgia did serendipitously serve to enhance NATO unity.

It is also important to realize that the partial cessation of U.S. and its Allies' participation may complicate efforts to begin a new round of negotiations. A few states may need to terminate the existing CFE Treaty in order to begin discussions of a new agreement in order to comply with domestic legal requirements. Some legal experts believe that this could be accomplished by reopening the Adapted Treaty negotiations while maintaining the existing number of participating parties at 29 (absent the Russian Federation). This could also help to restrain an increase in forces in volatile subregions like the North Caucasus.

THE WAY AHEAD

In seeking a way ahead several cautions are in order. First, the historical record is clear that arms control can never be an "end" or objective of policy in itself. An arms control accord is neither good nor bad when examined in isolation. Each treaty or agreement has value only insofar as it provides a "way" to mitigate concerns over or threats to national security and thus reduce the possibility of conflict or limit its consequences. Consequently, a resurrection of the CFE Treaty or creation of a new agreement *de novo* must be consistent with both American and NATO security interests.

Second, at its very core any arms control agreement depends upon a harmony of interests among the signatories. This "harmony" is based on careful analysis by all potential parties that the benefits to be gained from entering the arms control regime outweigh the risks associated with the measures such a regime might require. These might include reducing military forces or accepting high levels of transparency that allow exchanges of sensitive data, verification, and inspections. One does not get something for nothing.

Third, it is often easy to dismiss the success of arms control since we lose sight of its focus. A successful agreement is one that contributes to the prevention of conflict and enhances stability. But measuring the efficacy of an arms control agreement is like trying to determine the success of a contingent condition like "deterrence." Arms control regimes, like deterrence, are difficult to correlate completely with causes and effects of policies, because their ultimate metrics are for events that we do not want to happen (wars, arms races, increased tensions, and so on). Thus apparently successful arms control, like apparently successful deterrence, can come crashing down in a heartbeat.

If the Alliance is to use conventional arms control to achieve it stated goals, what are some of the elements that might be contained in a future arms control strategy? First, every effort should be made to maintain firm ceilings on conventional forces, particularly in volatile areas such as the North Caucasus and Balkans. This must occur even if the CFE Treaty is discarded, and new negotiations to limit conventional weapons are commenced. Second, any negotiation must include the Baltic and Balkan states as potential signatories to a future agreement. Third, the inspection regime associated with any future agreement must be simplified. This would seem logical based on today's reduced possibility of a major conflict. Still there will be particular concerns over Russian concentrations of forces on the part of those states that share borders with the Russian Federation. Consequently, limitations could be negotiated on the movement and concentration of forces in geographically defined zones within such frontier areas (i.e., the Baltic States and Leningrad Military Districts). This would limit, but not prohibit, the deployment of any nation's forces on its own territory as well as the stationing of foreign forces even with a host nation's consent.

Fourth, every effort must be made to integrate efforts in conventional arms control with other arms control treaties and agreements in order to achieve the synergy of a comprehensive approach. This must include the Vienna Document (focused on confidence-

and security-building measures) and the Open Skies Treaty. These agreements provide an existing level of reassurance concerning conventional forces that should not be discounted. This is particularly true in the current security environment where the prospects of a major conflict in Europe seem remote. Still both can be strengthened and improved. The Vienna Document has not been changed or even tweaked since 1999, despite Russia's indication of interest in new proposals.[26] But it is still critical to remember that ultimately these agreements, while important, may not be a full substitute for an agreement that includes legally binding limits, information exchanges, and a verification regime.[27]

SHORT-TERM PROSPECTS

Arms control negotiations do not occur in a vacuum but rather are part of the ongoing political process within and between states. Consequently, prospects for success in conventional arms control and reductions in NSNWs may be limited in 2012 owing to both Russian and American national elections. In the meanwhile, it may still be possible to pursue cooperative security efforts between NATO and Russia concerning NSNWs.

This eventuality may, however, require a new paradigm for thinking about arms control when dealing with such weapons. Policymakers need to consider that the dramatic reduction in tensions has greatly reduced the possibility of a conflict between NATO and Russia. Consequently, NSNWs may actually pose a greater common threat to both sides based on the possibility that they could fall into the hands of a terrorist group and be used against either Russia or the

West. President Obama noted such a possibility in his remarks at the opening plenary session of the Nuclear Security Summit held in Washington, DC, in April 2010. He noted that "the single biggest threat to U.S. security, both short-term, medium-term, and long-term, would be the possibility of a terrorist organization obtaining a nuclear weapon."[28]

Nonofficial Russian experts have offered some ideas on this subject focusing primarily on enhanced transparency measures and consolidation of nuclear stockpiles. For example, Alexi Arbatov has argued that trying to limit the overall number of Russian and American NSNWs in Europe is clearly too hard at this moment. He has proposed that both sides consolidate their arsenals in their own centralized storage sites. These sites should be separate from air or naval bases to insure that the weapons could not be quickly combined with appropriate delivery systems. Both sides could then monitor any movement of the warheads without necessarily having specific information on how many warheads were stored at any site. Another expert, Anatoliy Diakov, has also urged Washington and Moscow to implement detailed transparency measures and data exchanges.[29]

Many of these ideas are consistent with suggestions made by the National Academy of Sciences in its report entitled *Global Security Engagement – A New Model for Cooperative Threat Reduction* (2009). This report recommends a renewed effort by American policymakers to create a new comprehensive threat reduction (CTR) program.[30] Such an approach would seem to be a logical extension of United Nations (UN) Security Council Resolution (UNSCR) 1540 – "Enforcement of Effective Measures Against Proliferation." This resolution was proposed/adopted because of the joint efforts of the

United States and Russian Federation. UNSCR 1540 is the first obligation binding on all UN member states under Chapter VII of the UN Charter to take and enforce effective measures against the proliferation of weapons of mass destruction (WMD). One of its requirements is that all states take and enforce effective measures to control nuclear weapons and materials in order to reduce the possibility of proliferation or their acquisition by terrorist organizations.[31] Hence it would seem to be a clear point of reference for Washington and Moscow in determining policy.

A FINAL WORD

During the course of the CFE negotiations, a Western arms control expert once remarked that he felt like he was watching 300 years of European hostilities unfold. Critics of this process frequently become so enmeshed in the technical details of definitions, counting rules, stabilizing measures, inspection regimes, etc., that they overlook the connection between these small points and the larger security issues. Still, while the devil may well lie in the details, the CFE accord is rooted in the collective attempt of over 30 sovereign states to improve their respective security. National fears and historical antagonisms may complicate the flow of negotiations, but they also contribute to the agreement's enduring value. It is thus important to keep such apparent untidiness in proper perspective as Europe gropes its way to reducing the possibility of conflict through a new architecture based on cooperative security.

The search for a new arms control strategy that addresses the question of non-strategic nuclear forces must seek to both extend and become a part of existing agreements. It must also combine our past experiences from both conventional and nuclear arms control. Finally, even as we profit from lessons of the past, we must also acknowledge the new realities that will govern the security environment of the future.

ENDNOTES - CHAPTER 22

1. Dmitri Trenin, "Thinking Strategically About Russia," speech at the Carnegie Endowment for International Peace, December 2008, p. 1.

2. Steven Pifer, "The United States, NATO's Strategic Concept, and Nuclear Issues," *Nuclear Policy Paper Number 6*, Washington, DC: Arms Control Association and British American Security Information Council, April 2011, p. 4.

3. Tom Donilon, "The Prague Agenda: The Road Ahead," speech at the Carnegie International Nuclear Policy Conference, Washington, DC, March 29, 2011.

4. North Atlantic Treaty Organization (NATO), *Strategic Concept for the Defense and Security of the Members of the North Atlantic Treaty Organization*, Lisbon, Portgual: NATO Press Office, November 2010, pp. 7-8.

5. Simon Lunn, "NATO Nuclear Policy—Reflections on Lisbon and Looking Ahead," in *The NTI Study on Nuclear Weapons and NATO*, Washington, DC: Nuclear Threat Initiative, 2011, p. 20.

6. Andrei Zagorski, "Russia's Tactical Nuclear Weapons: Posture, Politics, and Arms Control," Book 156, Hamburg, Germany: Institut für Friedensforschung und Sicherheitspolitik an der Universität Hamburg, February 2011, p. 34.

7. Ian Kearns and Simon Lunn, *NATO's Nuclear Policy after Lisbon – the Summit Documents and the Way Ahead*, Brussels, Belgium: European Leadership Network for Multilateral Nuclear Disarmament and Non-Proliferation, January 25, 2011, p. 15. For

a detailed discussion of the state of Russian conventional forces, see Margarete Klein, *Russia's Military Capabilities,* Berlin, Germany: Stiftung Wissenshaft und Politik, October 2009.

8. Dima Adamsky, *Russian Regional Nuclear Developments,* Washington, DC: Long Term Strategy Group, Department of Defense, September 2010, pp. 21-22. See also Amy F. Woolf, *Non-strategic Nuclear Weapons,* Washington, DC: Congressional Research Service, August 2009, pp. 17-18.

9. *Ibid.,* Woolf, pp. 14-15. See also Simon Saradzhyan, *Russia's Non-strategic Nuclear Weapons in Their Current Configuration and Posture: A Strategic Asset or Liability?* Cambridge, MA: Harvard University Press, Belfer Center, January 2010.

10. "Russian Military Chief: War Risks Have Grown," *Associated Press,* November 17, 2011.

11. "NATO: Major Exercise Shows Weakness of Russian Army," *Baltic News Service,* February 14, 2011.

12. NATO, *Strategic Concept,* p. 8.

13. Dorn Crawford, *Conventional Armed Forces in Europe (CFE) – A Review and Update of Key Treaty Elements,* Washington, DC: U.S. Department of State, March 2009, p. 2.

14. *Ibid.,* p. 5.

15. NATO, *The NATO-Russia Founding Act on Mutual Relations, Cooperation and Security Between NATO and the Russian Federation,* Paris, France: NATO Public Affairs Office, May 27, 1997.

16. Zdzislaw Lachowski, "The CFE Treaty One Year After Its Suspension: A Forlorn Treaty?" *SIPRI Policy Brief,* Stockholm, Sweden: January 2009, p. 1.

17. *Ibid.,* p. 4.

18. Wade Boese, "Russia Unflinching on CFE Treaty Suspension," *Arms Control Today,* May 2008.

19. *Ibid.*

20. Lachowski, p. 5.

21. NATO Public Diplomacy Division, "Press Release—Lisbon Summit Declaration," Brussels, Belgium: NATO Public Affairs, November 20, 2010, p. 9.

22. "Russia Says Consultation On Talks On Conventional Forces Treaty In Impasse," *Interfax*, July 4, 2011.

23. Victoria Nuland, "Implementation of the Treaty on Conventional Armed Forces in Europe," Washington, DC: Office of the Spokesperson, U.S. Department of State, November 22, 2011.

24. "UK Halts Military Data Sharing with Russia," *Ria Novosti*, London, UK, November 25, 2011, available from *en.rian.ru/world/20111125/169036481.html*.

25. Nuland.

26. "Talking Points by Mr. Mikhail Uliyanov, Director of the Department for Security Affairs and Disarmament of the Ministry of Foreign Affairs of Russia, at the Annual Security Review Conference," Vienna, Austria: Organization for Security Cooperation in Europe (OSCE), July 1, 2011.

27. Assistant Secretary of State Rose Gottemoeller, "Statement at the Annual Security Review Conference in Vienna, Austria," Washington, DC: U.S. Department of State, July 1, 2011.

28. Jeffrey Goldberg and Marc Ambinder, "The Ally From Hell," *The Atlantic,* December 2011, p. 50. See also President Obama, "Remarks by the President at the Opening Plenary Session of the Nuclear Security Summit," Washington, DC: Office of the Press Secretary, the White House, April 13, 2010.

29. Steven Pifer, "NATO, Nuclear Weapons, and Arms Control," *Arms Control Series, Paper 7,* Washington, DC: Brookings Institution, July 2011, p. 27.

30. Committee on International Security and Arms Control Policy, National Academy of Sciences, *Global Security Engagement – A New Model for Cooperative Threat Reduction,* Washington, DC: The National Academy of Sciences Press, 2009, pp. 1-4.

31. United Nations Security Council, *Resolution 1540 (2004),* New York: UN Secretariat, April 28, 2004.

PART VI

CONCLUSION

CHAPTER 23

SUMMING UP AND ISSUES FOR THE FUTURE

Tom Nichols
Douglas Stuart
Jeffrey D. McCausland

The authors and analysts who participated in this conference set themselves a difficult task: to consider the role and future of tactical or non-strategic nuclear weapons (NSNWs) in the North Atlantic alliance. Their answers cover a range of views, but at least two salient conclusions emerge from this volume. First, it should be evident that in the more than 2 decades since the end of the Cold War, the problem itself — that is, the question of what to do with weapons designed in a previous century for the possibility of a World War III — is understudied, both inside and outside of government. Tactical weapons, although less awesome than their strategic siblings, carry significant security and political risks, and they have not received the attention that is commensurate with their importance. Second, it is clear that whatever the future of these arms, the status quo is unacceptable. It is past the time for the North Atlantic Treaty Organization (NATO) to make more resolute decisions, a coherent strategy, and more definite plans about its nuclear status.

These decisions are fundamental to the identity of NATO. The United States and its closest allies must define what, exactly, the Alliance believes constitute its greatest threats in the future, and in doing so must clarify NATO's identity, purpose, and corresponding force requirements. So far, NATO remains a "nuclear alliance," but it is increasingly hard to define what that means. Today, this seems to be more a description of a situation rather than a strategic concept, denoting only that the United States maintains a small stock of tactical nuclear weapons in Europe and continues to declare a tie between European NATO's security and the U.S. strategic arsenal.

During the Cold War, this was enough. But does the continuation of a "nuclear alliance" now mean that America's extended deterrent in Europe is operative against threats from *any* source, and not just Russia? Indeed, does the presence of tactical nuclear weapons on the Continent represent an underlying belief that Russia is still NATO's chief adversary? If not, is NATO even an "alliance" anymore, or is it now a collective security arrangement meant to keep the peace in Europe and — as in the case of Libya — other theaters as well? If the Atlantic Alliance is going to find a new future as a collective security or peacekeeping organization, this in turn raises the question of whether it needs nuclear weapons at all.

What remains on the agenda in the wake of this report? Specifically, three issues need to be addressed in the near future.

1. *Do TNWs or NSNWs have a role in U.S. defense planning at all?* This is the logically prior question to determining NATO's future as a nuclear alliance. Since the advent of nuclear parity with the Soviet Union in the 1960s, American nuclear doctrine has continually, and sometimes intentionally, wavered on what the United States sees as the essential purpose of nuclear weapons. Specifically, Cold War deterrence conflated (again, sometimes intentionally, but also at times from confusion) two seemingly contradictory propositions, namely, that nuclear weapons exist only to deter the use of similar weapons against the United

States and its allies, and that nuclear weapons provide a military capability that makes them usable as actual instruments of war. The most recent U.S. overview of nuclear policy, the 2010 *Nuclear Posture Review* (NPR), recapitulated this ambivalence in its conclusions by noting that America's preference would be a world in which nuclear weapons serve only as a deterrent, but that the time had not yet arrived to declare deterrence to be the *sole* purpose of the U.S. arsenal. Without a determination on this overarching issue, the future of tactical weapons in Europe will remain unclear as well.

2. *Does NATO need to counter only Russia, or does it need to retain nuclear abilities for other uses?* The United States, Canada, and Europe need to decide what role NSNWs play in Atlantic security. It may well be pointless to try including the Russians in this conversation. Increasingly, Russia's thinking on nuclear weapons is driven by internal Russian beliefs and problems rather than actual threats from NATO or anyone else. The Alliance will have to decide how much Europe's security is threatened, if at all, by Russian foreign policy. In any case, the deployment of NSNWs in Europe should reflect potential threats to NATO's security rather than the haphazard distribution of forces left in the wake of the Warsaw Pact's collapse.

3. *Do TNWs need to remain in Europe itself?* Even if the United States and its European allies decide that NATO should maintain a capability to conduct sub-strategic nuclear strikes, it does not logically follow that NSNWs need physically to remain in Europe — especially if Russia is no longer the main security concern. The basing of TNWs presents significant security and maintenance challenges, as is the case with any installation where nuclear weapons are present. On a

more prosaic level, the presence of tactical arms scattered about Europe occasionally generates needless political problems, as evidenced by Germany's about-face on the issue, at first advocating for the removal of NSNWs, and then insisting they should remain for the foreseeable future. The Alliance, with the Americans leading on this issue, needs to make a clearer distinction between tactical *weapons* and the ability to engage in tactical *strikes*, whether in Europe or outside the NATO area. This is particularly important due to the costs not only to maintain the weapons but also to procure future aircraft and train crews that can employ theses weapons if directed to do so.

The role of nuclear weapons in Western security is an equation with multiple variables, each affecting the other. NSNWs are only a part of that equation. For nearly 5 decades, however, these weapons were a crucial link binding Europe's freedom to the American promise to wage nuclear war to defend that freedom as part of a common and allied endeavor. It will be difficult, but not impossible, to find greater clarity on this one issue. But it is imperative to do so, not only because of the importance of nuclear weapons themselves, but because the dilemmas raised by the presence of tactical nuclear weapons are central to the question of NATO's future.

ABOUT THE CONTRIBUTORS

JAMES A. BLACKWELL is a Special Advisor to the Assistant Chief of Staff, Strategic Deterrence and Nuclear Integration, Headquarters U.S. Air Force (USAF), Washington, DC. Dr. Blackwell is responsible for providing expertise and intellectual leadership on developing the organization while posturing the USAF during policy, strategy, planning, and budgeting reviews as well as engaging in arms control processes.

WILLIAM F. BURNS, Major General, U.S. Army (Retired), was the 9th Director of the U.S. Arms Control and Disarmament Agency. In 1992, he was President Bush's special envoy to Russia and other states of the former Soviet Union to negotiate the terms of U.S. assistance to dismantle former Soviet nuclear weapons. Later, Major General Burns served as chairman of the National Academy of Science's 1997 study on the future of U.S. nuclear weapons policy and co-chairman of the 2005 study on monitoring and verification of nuclear weapons reduction agreements.

EVGENY BUZHINSKI, Lieutenant General, Russian Army (Retired), served as an officer in both the Soviet and Russian Armies. His assignments abroad included the assistant military attaché to Cyprus and Turkey. Lieutenant General Buzhinski also served as Chief of the International Treaties Department.

MALCOLM CHALMERS is Director of Research and Professorial Fellow in British Security Policy at the Royal United Services Institute in London, United Kingdom (UK). He is also Visiting Professor of Defence and Foreign Policy in the Department of War Studies, Kings College, London. Professor Chalmers was a member of the UK Cabinet Office consultative group for the 2010 Strategic Defence and Security Review and was previously a Special Adviser to Foreign Secretaries Jack Straw and Margaret Beckett.

NICK CHILDS is a World Affairs Correspondent with BBC News, based in London. Before that, he was the Defence and Security Correspondent for BBC World Service. In 2002, Mr. Childs became the BBC's inaugural Pentagon correspondent, covering the aftermath of the September 11, 2001 (9/11) attacks, the conflict in Afghanistan, the buildup to the Iraq invasion, and the subsequent insurgency there and its aftermath.

ELBRIDGE COLBY is a research analyst at the Center for Naval Analyses, where he focuses on national security strategy, deterrence, proliferation, and related issues. From 2009 to 2010, he served as policy advisor to the Secretary of Defense's representative for the follow-on to the Strategic Arms Reduction Treaty, serving both on the delegation in Geneva and then as a Department of Defense point man for the Treaty ratification effort. Mr. Colby previously served as an expert advisor to the Congressional Strategic Posture Commission, as special assistant to the Chief of Staff in the Office of the Director of National Intelligence, as a staff member on the President's Weapons of Mass Destruction (WMD) Commission, and with the Coalition Provisional Authority in Iraq and the State Department.

DORN CRAWFORD, Lieutenant Colonel, U.S. Army (Retired), serves as a consultant in political-military affairs and policy analysis for the Bureau of Arms Control, Verification, and Compliance for the U.S. Department of State. Lieutenant Colonel Crawford's current efforts focus principally on implementation, review, and modernization of the Treaty on Conventional Armed Forces in Europe (CFE) and follow-on security frameworks, and on related components of the U.S. arms control program.

PAOLO FORADORI is an Assistant Professor in International Politics at the University of Trento (Italy). From 2009 to 2011, Dr. Foradori was Marie Curie Fellow at the James Martin Center for Nonproliferation Studies, Monterey, and at the Managing the Atom Project, Harvard Kennedy School. His research interests include: international relations theory, European security and defense policy, and nuclear proliferation.

GEORGE HUDSON is Professor of Political Science and Director of the Russian and Central Eurasian Studies Program at Wittenberg University. Dr. Hudson is editor of *Soviet National Security Policy under Perestroika* and co-editor (with Joseph Kruzel) of *American Defense Annual.*

JACOB W. KIPP currently is an Adjunct Professor at the University of Kansas and a weekly columnist on Eurasian Security of the Jamestown Foundations. Dr. Kipp served for many years at the Foreign Military Studies Office (FMSO) at Ft. Leavenworth, KS.

JEFFREY A. LARSEN is a Senior Scientist with Science Applications International Corporation and President of Larsen Consulting Group. He also serves as Adjunct Professor in the Josef Korbel School of International Studies, University of Denver; Adjunct Professor at Northwestern University; and as Adjunct Faculty at the George H.W. Bush School of Government and Public Service at Texas A&M University. A retired Air Force lieutenant colonel, Dr. Larson holds a Ph.D. in politics from Princeton University.

SIMON LUNN is an Associate Fellow RUSI London, Senior Fellow DCAF Geneva, Senior Fellow ELN London, and a consultant with NTI, Washington, DC. Mr. Lunn was Secretary General of the NATO Parliamentary Assembly from 1997 to 2007 following 8 years as the Deputy Secretary General.

JEFFREY D. MCCAUSLAND is a Distinguished Visiting Professor of Research and the Minerva Chairholder at the U.S. Army War College in Carlisle, PA. He also serves as a Visiting Professor of International Security at Dickinson College and a senior fellow at the Clarke Forum. He is a Senior Associate Fellow at the Abshire-Inamori Leadership Academy at the Center for Strategic and International Studies in Washington. He is also a Senior Fellow at the Stockdale Center for Ethical Leadership at the U.S. Naval Academy and the Carnegie Council for Ethics in International Affairs in New York. Dr. McCausland serves as a national security consultant for CBS Radio and Television.

LEO MICHEL is a Distinguished Research Fellow at the Institute for National Strategic Studies (INSS) (National Defense University), concentrating on transatlantic defense and security issues. Before joining INSS in July 2002, Mr. Michel served as Director, NATO Policy Office, within the Office of the Secretary of Defense.

GÖTZ NEUNECK is Deputy Director of the Institute for Peace Research and Security Policy at the University of Hamburg. Dr. Neuneck is also Head of the Interdisciplinary Research Group for Arms Control and Disarmament.

TOM NICHOLS is a Professor in the National Security Affairs Department at the U.S. Naval War College in Newport, Rhode Island, and an adjunct professor in the Extension and Summer Schools at Harvard University. Dr. Nichols is currently a Senior Associate of the Carnegie Council on Ethics and International Affairs in New York City and a Fellow of the International History Institute at Boston University.

STEVEN PIFER, Ambassador, U.S. Department of State (Retired), is a Senior Fellow at the Brookings Center on the United States and Europe and Director of the Brookings Arms Control Initiative. He focuses on arms control, Russia, and Ukraine. Ambassador Pifer has offered commentary regarding Russia, Ukraine, and arms control issues on CNN, Fox News, National Public Radio, and Voice of America.

LEONID POLYAKOV is the Chairman of the Expert Board, Center for Army Conversion and Disarmament Studies in Ukraine. Previously he served as an External Consultant to the Parliamentary National Security and Defense Committee. Mr. Polyakov also served as the Vice Minister of Defense for three years.

GUY B. ROBERTS was until recently NATO's Deputy Assistant Secretary General for Weapons of Mass Destruction Policy, and Director Nuclear Policy, NATO (2005-11). Mr. Roberts advised the Secretary General and the North Atlantic Council on nonproliferation, arms control, and disarmament issues.

PAUL SCHULTE is a Non-Resident Senior Associate of the Nuclear Policy Programme of the Carnegie Endowment for International Peace. Mr. Schulte also serves as a Senior Visiting Fellow at the Centre for Defence Studies at Kings College London, the School of African and Oriental Studies, and at the UK Defence Academy.

JAMES M. SMITH is Director of the U.S. Air Force Institute for National Security Studies (INSS) located at the U.S. Air Force Academy. Dr. Smith is also Professor of Military and Strategic Studies at the Air Force Academy.

NIKOLAI SOKOV is a Senior Fellow at the Vienna Center for Disarmament and Non-Proliferation. Dr. Sokov previously worked at the Ministry for Foreign Affairs of the Soviet Union and later Russia, and participated in START I and START II negotiations.

DOUGLAS STUART is holder of the J. William and Helen D. Stuart Chair in International Studies at Dickinson College. Dr. Stuart is also an Adjunct Research Professor at the U.S. Army War College.

RICHARD WEITZ is a Senior Fellow and Director of the Center for Political-Military Analysis at Hudson Institute. Dr. Weitz's current research includes regional security developments relating to Europe, Eurasia, and East Asia as well as U.S. foreign, defense, and homeland security policies.

Made in United States
North Haven, CT
26 March 2022

17582476R00293